FEMALE SERVANTS IN EARLY MODERN ENGLAND

A British Academy Monograph

The British Academy has a scheme for the selective publication of monographs arising from its British Academy Postdoctoral Fellowships, British Academy Newton International Fellowships, and British Academy / Wolfson Fellowships. Its purpose is to assist individual scholars by providing a prestigious publishing opportunity to showcase works of excellence.

Charmian Mansell is a historian of early modern England. She is a British Academy Postdoctoral Fellow at the University of Cambridge (2019–2024) and has previously held academic positions at the University of Exeter, Institute of Historical Research, University of Oxford, Queen Mary University of London, and University College London. She has published articles in *Continuity and Change, Gender & History*, and *The Historical Journal*.

FEMALE SERVANTS IN EARLY MODERN ENGLAND

Charmian Mansell

Published for THE BRITISH ACADEMY
by OXFORD UNIVERSITY PRESS

Oxford University Press, Great Clarendon Street, Oxford OX2 6DP

British Library Cataloguing in Publication Data
Data available

Library of Congress Cataloguing in Publication Data
Data available

Typeset by Newgen Publishing UK
Printed and bound by CPI Group (UK) Ltd, Croydon, CR0 4YY

ISBN 978-0-19-726758-5 (hardback)
ISBN 978-0-19-890865-4 (ebook)
ISBN 978-0-19-890866-1 (online)

Contents

List of Figures

List of Plates

(between p. 16 and p. 17)

List of Tables

Note on the Text

Data underlying all tables and figures is collected from depositions across the period c.1530–1649 and the five diocesan courts of Bath & Wells, Exeter, Gloucester, Hereford, and Winchester unless otherwise stated.

Plate 2 is reproduced with the kind permission of the Chapter of Gloucester Cathedral. All images in Chapter 2 are reproduced with the kind permission of Devon Heritage Centre, Gloucestershire Archives, Hampshire Record Office, Herefordshire Archive and Records Centre, and Somerset Heritage Centre.

Abbreviations

DHC	Devon Heritage Centre
EcHR	*Economic History Review*
GA	Gloucestershire Archives
HARC	Herefordshire Archive and Records Centre
HRO	Hampshire Record Office
JBS	*Journal of British Studies*
P&P	*Past & Present*
PCC	Prerogative Court of Canterbury
SHC	Somerset Heritage Centre
TNA	The National Archives
TRHS	*Transactions of the Royal Historical Society*

Place of publication is London unless otherwise stated.

Conventions

Original spelling and punctuation of quotations of primary material have been largely retained. The letters j, u, and v have been modernised, capitalisation standardised, and abbreviations and contractions used by the court clerks have been expanded. In a few places commas have been inserted to clarify obscure passages.

References to court cases are given as follows: Plaintiff v Defendant [with first names added where possible] (date). First names are standardised, but surnames retain their original spelling. *Ap*, used in Welsh surnames to mean 'the son of', has been retained.

Dates given are modern, with the year beginning on 1 January. Archaic monetary values are retained in quotations. In the pre-decimal system of 12 pence (*d.*) to a shilling (*s.*) and 20 shillings to a pound (*li.*), a mark was worth 13*s.* 4*d*. Metric units are given for distances and measurements.

Acknowledgements

In the final stages of writing this book, I look back and realise how incredibly lucky I am to have had the opportunity. This book would not have been possible without the Arts and Humanities Research Council, who funded the initial research carried out for my PhD at the University of Exeter. I received generous funding for collection and analysis of additional data and the redrafting of each chapter from the Economic History Society (who awarded me a one-year fellowship at the Institute of Historical Research in 2016–17), the University of Oxford's Women in Humanities programme (with whom I held a writing fellowship in 2018), and the British Academy (who awarded me a fellowship at the University of Cambridge). A bursary from the Women's Studies Group 1558–1837 also funded archival research in 2017. Having time and money to complete this project has meant so much.

Over the years, I have been back and forth to five county record offices on research trips. I am enormously grateful for the support and guidance of archivists and staff at Devon Heritage Centre, Gloucestershire Archives, Hampshire Record Office, Herefordshire Archive and Records Centre, and Somerset Heritage Centre. It is in these spaces that I've been at my happiest. Thank you to each of these county archives for their permission to reproduce images of church court depositions, as well as the Chapter of Gloucester Cathedral, who kindly allowed me to reproduce a photograph of the monument of alderman John Jones.

This is a book about community as much as it is about female servants. Writing a book can be a lonely pursuit and in my nomadic life over the last decade, finding community has sometimes been difficult. But there have been *many* more times when I have benefited from the generosity, kindness, intelligence, humour, and firm support of so many friends, colleagues, and family members. Thank you all so much.

Special thanks first go to Jane Whittle. This book wouldn't be the same without your guidance, brilliance, and steer. I have learnt so much from you and am grateful for your continued support. Thank you also to Laura Gowing and Nicola Whyte, who examined the original PhD thesis – I returned to your insightful feedback with more clarity when redrafting each chapter for this book. Enormous thanks also to Amy Erickson and Alexandra Walsham, who generously read chapters of this book and offered valuable feedback and encouragement. I'm so grateful to Alexandra Shepard, who read the entire manuscript with both the kindest and keenest critical eye, offering reassurance throughout the writing process. You really have been instrumental in getting the book over the finish line. I am grateful, too, to the anonymous readers of the book proposal and the full manuscript itself as well as the publishing team at the British Academy. The generosity of these readers in giving their time to comment on and engage with my work is so appreciated.

Other colleagues and friends have given their support along the way. Thanks to Matthew Fitzgerald for encouraging me to do the PhD in the first place. I'm grateful for the cohort of PhD students at Exeter who offered much companionship on the doctoral journey, both in the office and at the pub. Friendships I have made in various academic roles and institutions have been the life-blood of this book. I'm so grateful to Martin Andersson, Linda Briggs, Pippa Carter, Sarah Crook, Stef Eastoe, Jane Freeland, Mark Hailwood, Emily MacGregor, Angela Muir, Jonah Miller, Sofie Narbed, Naomi Pullin, Esther van Raamsdonk, Hillary Tayler, and Sonia Tycko for energising conversations over recent years.

Writing a book during a pandemic brought an unexpected source of support in the British Academy postdoctoral writing group. Without these writing sessions and the wonderful company, humour, fierce support, and comfortable silence of all its members over the last three years, this book would have taken even longer than it already has. Thank you so much for supporting me each Tuesday and Thursday – you'll all be so pleased to hear I'm no longer working on the book! Thank you also to the Women on the Move COST writing group and the Women's History Network writing group, where some of this writing has taken place. I am grateful to have been able to participate in the Opening Lines writing group at Cambridge and hugely appreciate the generous comments and encouragement from other members who read a draft chapter of this book.

To my brilliant friends – Helen Crutcher, Jessica Eglin, Natalie Fraser, and Daniel Jeffrey – who seem to have endless belief in me, even when I don't. Your unwavering support is so appreciated.

Finally, and most importantly, the unconditional love and support of my family over the years – Mum, Dad, Jemima, Sephron, Jordan, Lee, and Emmeline – means more to me than I can say. Thank you for believing that this book would eventually tumble over the finish line! I owe the biggest debt and gratitude to Josh Rhodes. We have been talking about servants for the best part of a decade. Thank you so much for your constancy, love, advice, and support. This book is so much better for the words you have added (and deleted!). Any mistakes or errors are entirely my own, but I couldn't have written this book without you.

This book is dedicated to my grandparents. For my Pap, whose tales of his life surreptitiously planted the seed from which my love of history and storytelling grew. I wish you could have read this. For my Nan Mansell, who *hated* being a servant but recalled such happy and vivid memories of her working life. I wish you could have read this too. And finally, for my Nan Pegler, who never seems to dwell on (or even remember!) her own history but continues to teach me everything about contentment. You are an inspiration.

Introduction

Matilda Bates was perched perilously in an apple tree in her master's orchard. As she shook the tree and gathered the fruit, loud voices rang out from the riverside. Peering between the tree's branches, she saw two of her neighbours washing clothes with their servants at the water's edge. She thought she heard one call the other a 'pockie whore', but she was busy collecting the apples and took no real notice of their squabble.[1]

*

Sybil Bevor straightened her hat and smoothed the front of her gown. Both were borrowed from a fellow servant and she felt strange in these clothes. As a 40-year-old widow with five children, the wages Sybil earned from service paid for food and rent on their small house, not for such things as fine clothing. But appearances were everything in court.[2]

*

For two nights Anna Elie watched over her sick neighbour, Thomas Crodie. When he died, she stood shoulder-to-shoulder with her master and mistress at his burial and dined and drank in honour of his life. Two weeks later, when Thomas's wife and children also fell sick and the death toll in the city soared, Anna realised the plague had come to Gloucester.[3]

*

[1] SHC, D/D/cd/18, Francis Abbott v Isabelle Light (1595).
[2] HARC, HD4/2/11, Thomas Hereford v Ann Vaughan (1599); Roger Prosser v Thomas Hereford (1600).
[3] GA, GDR/43, Thomas Weekes and Thomas Key v Richard Crodie, Eleanor Davys and Alice Dove (1579).

Isott Riches was in love with Frances Yarde. Her master and mistress disapproved of their courtship, but she didn't care. Frances was a gentleman, and she knew he would take care of her; he had offered her a position serving in his own home. Isott was fed up with being ill-treated. As she told her neighbour, she hadn't come to serve her mistress to be beaten, nor to be her drudge. She vowed not to tarry there long.[4]

* * *

What was it like to be a woman in service in early modern England? Who were these women? Where did they come from? In what kinds of households did they work and what were they hired to do? How did they fit within the local communities in which they lived? This book writes a new history of female service through close analysis of the day-to-day lives of over 1,000 women in service like Matilda, Sybil, Anna, and Isott, captured in witness testimony from English church courts between 1532 and 1649.

These women are important. Around 60 per cent of 15- to 24-year-olds worked in service in early modern England, hired by rural and urban households across the country.[5] Service played a key role in England's transition to a modern state: economic growth was apparently fuelled by the labour of single women, who married late.[6] But if this 'girl power' was at the root of economic growth, the labour that female servants carried out is nonetheless routinely relegated to the 'domestic'. Male servants 'in husbandry', whose work in the fields directly contributed to the economy, are set apart from female 'domestic' servants who worked within the home to meet the family's personal needs.[7] This book reconceptualises the work that female servants undertook. We find Matilda Bates high up in a tree, gathering apples for her master in 1595. Her work was defined by the rhythms of the agricultural year and took place *outside* the home. The apples she collected were sold to fill the household purse or were added to the household's food store. Matilda's fellow servants washed clothes at the nearby river, not inside the home. These women were not restricted to domestic spaces, nor was their work limited to domestic chores. They were at the economic and social centres of their communities.

English service is described as a life-cycle experience, bookended by childhood and marriage and offering men and women the skills, knowledge, and wealth needed to establish their own households. It was a contractual relationship: masters

---

[4] DHC, Chanter 858, John Roo v Frances Yarde (1568).
[5] Ann Kussmaul, *Servants in Husbandry in Early Modern England* (Cambridge, 1981), p. 3.
[6] Tine de Moor and Jan Luiten Van Zanden, 'Girl Power: The European Marriage Pattern and Labour Markets in the North Sea Region in the Late Medieval and Early Modern Period', *EcHR* 63 (2010), 1–33.
[7] Kussmaul, *Servants in Husbandry*, p. 4.

and mistresses hired men and women for their labour in exchange for wages, bed and board. But this wasn't Sybil Bevor's experience. The terms and conditions of her service as a 40-year-old widow with several children were different. She negotiated service by the day and lived in her own home. Her income kept her own household afloat; she wasn't saving for a future home. By reconstructing life stories of women like Sybil, this book reimagines service as finely graded, sometimes unbounded and flexible, experienced in a variety of ways by a variety of people.

We are used to thinking of service as structured, regulated, and operating within a rigid patriarchal framework that was codified in social, political, legal, and cultural practices. Household patriarchal order placed the male head in a position of privilege and power not only over his biological family but also over his servants and apprentices. The servant worked not to her own clock, but to her master's pace and rhythms and under his watchful gaze. Or so the story goes.[8] But this book extends the matrix of female servant social relations beyond the family and household. It looks outward to the key roles of servants like Anna Elie in their communities. Caring for her sick neighbour, attending his burial, and agreeing to testify in court to the oral will he made on his death bed, Anna actively engaged in the customs, routines, and practices of her neighbourhood. Women like her were not just household servants. They were integrated members of other groups and socio-economic units. They held multiple identities – as workers, neighbours, family members, friends, and even enemies – which simultaneously shaped their behaviours. They were deeply embedded in networks of sociability, charity, friendship and animosity, news and gossip, and credit and honour.

A central theme of this book is agency. In objecting to being beaten and treated like a drudge, what did Isott hope to achieve? How were her complaints received by society? Patriarchal labour relations relegated female servants to a position of disadvantage and deference, but these women could – and did – set their own agendas. Some directly breached the prescriptive codes and rules of behaviour demanded of them in legislation and literature. This book interrogates the structures of power that we imagine existed in early modern England and that set the boundaries of how we understand agency and freedom. What *were* the rules that servants like Isott were expected to live by, and how did they negotiate them? Rather than seeing refusal to accept ill treatment, poor pay, or lack of freedom as evidence of non-compliance or as a direct challenge to the patriarchal structures of service, this book reconsiders these structures altogether.

---

[8] See, for example, Tara Hamling and Catherine Richardson, *A Day at Home in Early Modern England: Material Culture and Domestic Life, 1500–1700* (New Haven, 2017), pp. 37, 69, 83.

Polemical tracts, legal statutes, and sermons act as the formal face of the 'institution' of service. These texts are routinely taken not only as prescriptive, evangelising rhetoric that sought to teach people *how to behave*. They are also assumed to reflect practice. Studies of criminal activity committed by and against servants take these texts as a benchmark of behaviour and misbehaviour, conformity and deviance. These texts routinely set the parameters of service as an institution.[9] The norms, values, strategies, and behaviours of institutions are of course laid bare at times of crisis or when problems arise.[10] But unless we cast our net wider to look at a broader range of experiences, we cannot easily disentangle practice and experience from expectations of society and state. To what extent *was* service an institution, with rules, regulations, and strict membership? Church court witness testimony – which only in a few cases directly set out to measure or regulate these women's behaviour – offers ample incidental evidence of everyday practices and behaviours of women in service. It allows us to recast the norms and values that underpinned this important form of labour.

This book stretches open the prescriptive codes of behaviour for women in service that were disseminated in legal treatises and didactic literature. By systematically analysing the characteristics of women in service, the patterns and conditions of their labour, and their place within the communities in which they lived and worked, a new picture of female service in sixteenth- and seventeenth-century England emerges. The stories of Matilda, Sybil, Anna, and Isott are emblematic of a history that is heterogeneous and diverse.

Service in early modern England

Service has never been static. The occupational descriptor 'servant' hides both the range of experiences of service at any point in the past, and its shifting meaning over time. In early modern western Europe, service grew as a sector from the late Middle Ages. The Black Death wreaked havoc on labour supply and demand, prompting new legislation to control labour shortages caused by depopulation. In the fourteenth century, statutes mandated longer contracts and restricted wages and mobility in a bid to strengthen serfdom.[11] But this labour that compulsorily bound the peasantry to a lord and his land was never to recover. Power to enforce new statutes now lay with central rather than local or manorial courts,

---

[9] Tim Wales, '"Living at Their Own Hands": Policing Poor Households and the Young in Early Modern Rural England', *Agricultural History Review* 61 (2013), 19–39.
[10] Anne Goldgar and Robert I. Frost, 'Introduction', in Anne Goldgar and Robert I. Frost (eds), *Institutional Culture in Early Modern Society* (Leiden, 2004), pp. xi–xxii at xx.
[11] 'The Ordinance of Labourers 1349' printed in Alexander Luders (ed.), *The Statutes of the Realm* (1810), pp. 307–9.

thereby reconfiguring lord–villein relationships and contributing, at least in part, to serfdom's decline.[12] The competitive labour market that emerged from the late medieval period brought with it at least one key freedom: the worker's right to leave their master. Master–servant relations were hierarchical but certainly less stratified than serfdom's labour relations, whereby each individual serf was bound to a wealthy landowner. Men and women across the social spectrum worked in service, and all but the very poorest in society could be masters.

In the eighteenth century, agricultural service declined as agrarian improvements reconfigured the labour force once more. Demand now was for day labourers, not live-in servants. Domestic servants became a marker of status, widening the socio-economic gap between employing families and their servants.[13] Preceding this long-run narrative of change, service between *c.*1530 and 1650 (the period this book covers) is considered relatively stable. Legally, the servant position was well defined. As with serfdom, legal interventions sought to regulate service, too. Wage rates were set locally for servants and other workers to control the labour market, and legal protection for both masters and servants was theoretically well established.[14] But this *was* a period of socio-economic change. Living standards rose for many, and middling sorts prospered. At the same time, society became more polarised and labouring people faced heightened exposure to poverty.[15] As this book argues, the stability of what service meant, how it operated, and how it was experienced was a legal fiction.

Female servants leave few traces in the archives. Their sex and social standing made them a largely illiterate group in the sixteenth and seventeenth centuries. While female literacy was higher in towns and cities, most women in this book lived in rural areas, where far fewer could read and write fluently.[16] Early

---

[12] On the transition from serfdom to service and the impact of the Black Death on labour regulation, see Mark Bailey, *The Decline of Serfdom in Late Medieval England: From Bondage to Freedom* (Woodbridge, 2014); Jane Whittle, 'Attitudes to Wage Labour in English Legislation, 1349–1601', in Jane Whittle and Thijs Lambrecht (eds), *Labour Laws in Preindustrial Europe: The Coercion and Regulation of Wage Labour, c.1350–1850* (Woodbridge, 2023), pp. 33–54; Chris Given-Wilson, 'Service, Serfdom and English Labour Legislation, 1350–1500', in Anne Curry and Elizabeth Matthew (eds), *Concepts and Patterns of Service in the Later Middle Ages* (Woodbridge, 2001), pp. 21–37.

[13] Kussmaul, *Servants in Husbandry,* pp. 10, 133–4.

[14] Servants who ran away could legally be forced to return to their masters, and masters who dismissed their servants before the end of the contract could be compelled to retain them. See Jane Whittle, *The Development of Agrarian Capitalism: Land and Labour in Norfolk, 1440–1580* (Oxford, 2000), pp. 280, 288–9.

[15] On the increasing numbers describing themselves as 'poor', see Alexandra Shepard, *Accounting for Oneself: Worth, Status, and the Social Order in Early Modern England* (Oxford, 2015), pp. 114–45. On the prosperity of the middling sorts, see, for example, Keith Wrightson, *English Society, 1580–1680* (1993), pp. 289–306.

[16] In London, female literacy stood at around 48 per cent by the 1690s (compared with *c.*21 per cent in rural East Anglia). David Cressy takes the ability to sign one's name as indicative of literacy. See David Cressy, *Literacy and Social Order: Reading and Writing in Tudor and Stuart England* (Cambridge, 1980), pp. 144–5.

scholarship on service relied on diary entries and correspondence of literate masters and mistresses.[17] But these commentaries on service told only a partial story that privileged the views of a literate class. The servant perspective (as well as the attitudes of less literate masters and mistresses) was absent.[18]

From the late 1960s, a new agenda was set. Ordinary people in early modern England whose 'voices' were hard to recover, including largely illiterate groups such as servants, were teased out of the archives. Administrative and legal records became the bread and butter of this new history from below: settlement examinations, parish listings, household accounts, court records, and a compendium of other sources that documented labouring people were unearthed. Ann Kussmaul's *Servants in Husbandry* applied statistical modes of investigation to some of these sources, focusing on agricultural servants between 1500 and 1800. Analysing service longitudinally through the lens of its eventual decline, Kussmaul tracked hiring patterns, lengths of contracts, and types of labour in these sources. Her pioneering work located rural servants within a broader history of agrarian change in England, but it was *male* experiences that were pivotal. Female servants, Kussmaul assumed, were hired not to contribute to the economic productivity of the household but to maintain the family's lifestyle. The hiring of live-in farm servants, she found, waned as day labourers became a cheaper source of labour on the larger, capitalist farms of the late seventeenth century.[19] As the argument goes, the decline of female live-in service came later with the advent of 'modernity'. Emerging job opportunities in the nineteenth century for women in shops, factories, and offices, alongside new time- and labour-saving technologies in the twentieth-century home, are among some of the reasons for the eventual decline of live-in service for women.[20] But female servants in early modern England were *not* solely hired for the personal care of the family. Entrenching their experiences within the domestic realm undervalues their economic role, overlooks the income-generating labour they carried out, and assumes the home was an economically unproductive space. We still know little about what female servants actually did in this period or the economic significance of their work.[21]

---

[17] Dorothy Marshall, 'The Domestic Servants of the Eighteenth Century', *Economica* 9 (1929), 15–40; J. Jean Hecht, *The Domestic Servant Class in Eighteenth-Century England* (1956).

[18] Alison Light's study of Virginia Woolf's servants is an exception. Though reliant on the letters and literature of the famous author, Light pushes beyond the employer-centred focus of her evidence, catching a glimpse of the servants' ambitions, hopes, and agendas, and is true to her aim of recovering the voices of the women who worked for Woolf. See Alison Light, *Mrs Woolf and the Servants* (2007).

[19] Kussmaul, *Servants in Husbandry*, pp. 133–4.

[20] For a summary of this historiography, see Lucy Delap, *Knowing Their Place: Domestic Service in Twentieth-Century Britain* (Oxford, 2011), pp. 1–15.

[21] For research in this area, see Jane Whittle, 'Servants in Rural England c.1450–1650: Hired Work as a Means of Accumulating Wealth and Skills Before Marriage', in Maria Ågren and Amy Louise Erickson (eds), *The Marital Economy in Scandinavia and Britain, 1400–1900* (Aldershot, 2005), pp. 89–107; Jane Whittle, 'Housewives and Servants in Rural England, 1440–1650: Evidence of Women's Work from Probate Documents', *TRHS* 15 (2005), 51–74.

The second half of the twentieth century also witnessed pioneering new work in historical demography and quantitative methodologies. Leading the way was the Cambridge Group for the History of Population and Social Structure, established in 1964. Important findings for service emerged as a by-product of other research agendas. Historical demographers found that men and women in early modern north-west Europe married and formed households late in life (in their late 20s). Explanation was found in the labour patterns of young people in life-cycle service.[22] Runs of census-like parish listings made it possible to reconstruct geographical mobility in early modern England. Parish population turnover was high, and servants were identified as among the most mobile in this itinerant society.[23] Their movements contributed to the urban population boom over the sixteenth and seventeenth centuries as droves of young migrant men and women flocked to London and other urban centres in search of service.[24] Historians sought to make sense of households that contained not just biological families but itinerant lodgers, servants, and apprentices.[25] Etymological studies found that when diarists talked of their 'family', they routinely included servants. The concept of the 'household-family' was born.[26] Servants, then, were important to both society and its local structures.

A history of service also emerged from scholarship of early modern crime, law, and order. History from below was accompanied by an interest in quantifying crimes committed by and against different social groups. High numbers of female servants involved in domestic homicide, theft, infanticide, and bastardy were identified. In asking *why*, researchers explored the intersection of social structures and patterns of crime.[27] Studies of community policing, punishment

[22] John Hajnal, 'European Marriage Patterns in Perspective', in D. V. Glass and D. E. C. Eversley (eds), *Population in History: Essays in Historical Demography* (1965), pp. 101–47.

[23] Migration in Cogenhoe (Northamptonshire), for example, between 1618 and 1628 was around 52 per cent. See Peter Laslett, *Family Life and Illicit Love in Earlier Generations: Essays in Historical Sociology* (Cambridge, 1977), pp. 65–86. See also Peter Clark, 'Migration in England during the Late Seventeenth and Early Eighteenth Centuries', *P&P* 83 (1979), 57–90; Peter Clark, 'The Migrant in Kentish Towns, 1580–1640', in Peter Clark and David Souden (eds), *Crisis and Order in English Towns, 1500–1700* (1972), pp. 117–63; David Cressy, 'Occupations, Migration and Literacy in East London, 1580–1640', *Local Population Studies* 5 (1970), 53–60.

[24] On urban servant migration, see Vivien Brodsky Elliot, 'Single Women in the London Marriage Market: Age, Status and Mobility, 1598–1619', in R. B. Outhwaite (ed.), *Marriage and Society: Studies in the Social History of Marriage* (London, 1981), pp. 81–100 at 90–7; Peter Earle, *A City Full of People: Men and Women of London 1650–1750* (1994), pp. 38–54.

[25] Laslett, *Family Life*, p. 13.

[26] See Naomi Tadmor, 'The Concept of the Household-Family in Eighteenth-Century England', *P&P* 151 (1996), 111–40. Alan Macfarlane's earlier study of the seventeenth-century clergyman diarist Ralph Josselin identified servants as family members. See Alan Macfarlane, *The Family Life of Ralph Josselin, a Seventeenth-Century Clergyman: An Essay in Historical Anthropology* (New York, 1977), p. 147.

[27] See James Sharpe, 'Domestic Homicide in Early Modern England', *The Historical Journal* 24 (1981), 29–48 at 39; Garthine Walker, *Crime, Gender and Social Order in Early Modern England* (Cambridge, 2003), p. 172; Peter Laslett, 'The Bastardy Prone Sub-Society', in Peter Laslett, Karla Oosterveen, and

of miscreants, and social tensions moved the history of crime beyond the study of individuals as faceless statistics.[28] Gender emerged as a crucial category of analysis as the patriarchal system of governance came under scrutiny.[29] Female servants were incorporated into a new research agenda in which order and disorder, power and vulnerability were intimately bound to gender. Here, servant–master sexual relations took centre stage. Martin Ingram showed that up to 70 per cent of bastardy cases heard in the church courts in the 1580s involved female servants, who 'were in a vulnerable position and were sometimes seduced only after considerable harassment and even the use of force'.[30] Bridget Hill argued that household sleeping and working arrangements made female servants susceptible to sexual advances.[31] More recently, Tim Reinke-Williams claimed that 'many masters believed they had the right to have sex with the women whose wages they paid, regardless of whether or not they consented'.[32] Troubling stories of sexual assault and rape have become a trope of female service. The distressing (often harrowing) stories of abuse experienced by some women at the hands of their masters are recalled throughout this book. But we shouldn't assume it was the norm. Illegitimate birth rates were low in this period.[33] As Tim Meldrum pointed out, 'acknowledging that some servants experienced the worst forms of sexual

---

Richard Smith (eds), *Bastardy and Its Comparative History: Studies in the History of Illegitimacy and Nonconformism in Britain, France, Germany, Sweden, North America, Jamaica, and Japan* (Cambridge, MA, 1980), pp. 217–46; Laslett, *Family Life*, p. 245 n.9; Keith Wrightson, 'Infanticide in Earlier Seventeenth-Century England', *Local Population Studies* 15 (1975), 10–22 at 11, 20–2; Laura Gowing, 'Secret Births and Infanticide in Seventeenth-Century England', *P&P* 156 (1997), 87–115.

[28] On the continuity of policing misbehaviour from the late medieval period, see Marjorie K. McIntosh, *Controlling Misbehavior in England, 1370–1600* (Cambridge, 1998). On Puritan reform and community policing, see Keith Wrightson and David Levine, *Poverty and Piety in an English Village: Terling, 1525–1700* (Oxford, 1979), chapters 5 and 7. On neighbourhood policing through shaming rituals such as charivaris and rough ridings, see Martin Ingram, 'Ridings, Rough Music and the "Reform of Popular Culture" in Early Modern England', *P&P* 105 (1984), 79–113.

[29] Prosecution of women for particular offences increased between 1560 and 1640 in what David Underdown termed a 'crisis of gender relations'. See David Underdown, 'The Taming of the Scold: The Enforcement of Patriarchal Authority in Early Modern England', in Anthony John Fletcher (ed.), *Order and Disorder in Early Modern England* (Cambridge, 1985), pp. 116–36. For rebuttals, see Martin Ingram, 'Scolding Women Cucked or Washed: A Crisis in Gender Relations in Early Modern England?', in Jennifer Kermode and Garthine Walker (eds), *Women, Crime and the Courts in Early Modern England* (Chapel Hill, NC, 1994), pp. 48–80; Lyndal Roper, *Oedipus and the Devil: Witchcraft, Religion and Sexuality in Early Modern Europe* (1994), pp. 37–53; Laura Gowing, *Domestic Dangers: Women, Words and Sex in Early Modern London* (Oxford, 1996), p. 28.

[30] Martin Ingram, *Church Courts, Sex and Marriage in England, 1570–1640* (Cambridge, 1988), pp. 264, 266

[31] Bridget Hill, *Servants: English Domestics in the Eighteenth Century* (Oxford, 1996), pp. 44–63, esp. pp. 44–5.

[32] Tim Reinke-Williams, *Women, Work and Sociability in Early Modern London* (Basingstoke, 2014), p. 77.

[33] In Romford (Havering manor), for example, only 1.8 per cent of births between 1562 and 1619 were described as illegitimate. See Marjorie K. McIntosh, *A Community Transformed: The Manor and Liberty of Havering, 1500–1620* (Cambridge, 1991), pp. 68–9.

violence and abuse is to recognise the outer limits of sexual interaction, not to elevate them to the norm'.[34]

Women in service are rarely studied outside the context of their masters' homes, binding them not only to patriarchy in its broad sense of male domination, but also more particularly to its narrower and literal meaning: 'rule of the father'.[35] While women's history has widened the search for evidence of female autonomy and self-governance, histories of service have lagged behind. The lives of female servants are both defined and limited by household patriarchy, with *prescription* often speaking for *practice*. Sixteenth- and seventeenth-century conduct literature on household order has come to bear heavily on how we understand service. These printed polemical texts were circulated as a means of social engineering. To their male (often Puritan) writers, a well-ordered household which instilled principles of deferential hierarchy and good conduct created an organised and disciplined Christian society.[36] The family represented a microcosm of the state and religion; 'the master is God's vice-regent in his family', proclaimed Thomas Carter in 1627.[37] In 1598, John Dod and Robert Cleaver advised servants to be 'as a dutifull childe is to his father; to bee reverent and lowly to them in all their words and gestures, to suffer and forbeare them, to obey'.[38] If bonded labour had all but disappeared by this period, vestiges of unfreedom remained. Writing in 1622, clergyman William Gouge argued that servants 'are not their own, neither ought the things which they doe, to be for themselves: both their persons and their actions are all their masters'.[39] These writers defined the role of each household member, including servants, and (deliberately) failed to entertain the idea that servants had lives outside their masters' homes.

Booksellers stocked these texts, and they appeared in inventories of the literate. There was, therefore, demand.[40] But we don't know whether these texts were actually read, nor whether male householders actively instilled the ideals of household patriarchy.[41] Realistically, the 'godly household' was an impossible ideal. Susan Amussen has observed that advice literature devoted more time to outlining how to govern than how to obey. 'Failed patriarchs' compromised household patriarchy

[34] Tim Meldrum, *Domestic Service and Gender, 1660–1750: Life and Work in the London Household* (Harlow, 2000), p. 104.
[35] Susan Amussen, *An Ordered Society: Gender and Class in Early Modern England* (New York, 1993), pp. 1–2.
[36] On the well-ordered household in advice literature, see Roger Richardson, *Household Servants in Early Modern England* (Manchester, 2010), pp. 124–40.
[37] Amussen, *An Ordered Society*, p. 37; Thomas Carter, *Christian Commonwealth* (1627), p. 246.
[38] John Dod and Robert Cleaver, *A Godlie Forme of Householde Government for the Ordering of Private Families* (1612), p. 381.
[39] William Gouge, *Of Domesticall Duties: Eight Treatises*, 3rd edition (1622), p. 604.
[40] Natasha Glaisyer, *The Culture of Commerce in England, 1660–1720* (Woodbridge, 2006), chapter 3; Natasha Glaisyer and Sara Pennell, 'Introduction', in Natasha Glaisyer and Sara Pennell (eds), *Didactic Literature in England 1500–1800: Expertise Constructed* (2016), pp. 1–18 at 4.
[41] Richardson, *Household Servants*, p. 140.

as much as 'unruly women'.[42] Many households had *no* patriarch: Laura Gowing pointed out that 'households headed by a husband and father were only one – if the most conventionally recognized – kind of social unit'.[43] Some servants in this book lived in households headed by widows, widowers, and never married men and women. They lived cheek-by-jowl with other non-family members: hired workers, lodgers, and the family's extended (sometimes distant) kin. The classic household structure – husband, wife, children, servants, and apprentices – nonetheless set the rules of conduct in this literature. These rules invariably form the social and micro-political backdrop against which recorded observations of female servant behaviours have been studied.

Even talking about unruly women and failed patriarchs fixes patriarchy as a rigid governing concept. Not all women who challenged patriarchal order were seen as unruly, and not all patriarchs who allowed some liberties were perceived as failing. But in all cases, the patriarchal *system* was in some way compromised. This book resists privileging the social structures described in prescriptive literature and avoids ascribing autonomy or agency according to the rules it set out. The experiences explored instead help *inform* our understanding of patriarchy and agency, of freedom and coercion. They guide us in delineating the boundaries of these concepts, in recognising where the edges were blurred, and in appreciating where gender was just one of several organising principles at play.

Though the study of female servants has expanded over the last fifty years, we still know relatively little about their lives. Historical demographers have integrated service into explanations of marriage patterns and household structure, while economic historians have studied male service through shifts in agrarian labour relations and industrialisation. Within social history, servants' criminal or illicit behaviour has loomed large. These strands of scholarship nonetheless fall short in reconstructing their quotidian experiences. As a holistic study of female service, this book intersects with scholarship on a range of topics – histories of the family, youth, space, community, law, labour, freedom, migration, and memory. Evidence of female servants' everyday experiences recorded in church court depositions opens a window onto almost every aspect of their lives.

Church courts

There were more than 250 ecclesiastical courts in sixteenth- and seventeenth-century England.[44] While secular law fell to criminal courts (local hundred, manorial, and borough courts; county-level petty and Quarter Sessions; and the

---

[42] Susan Amussen, *Gender, Culture and Politics in England, 1560–1640: Turning the World Upside Down* (2017), p. 52.
[43] Gowing, *Domestic Dangers*, p. 23.
[44] Christopher Hill, *Society and Puritanism in Pre-Revolutionary England* (1991), p. 289.

Assizes, Star Chamber, and King's Bench), ecclesiastical courts were underpinned by canon or spiritual law.[45] They issued marriage licences and administered wills and probate, and were effectively responsible for the moral and spiritual life of early modern society. Litigation demanded a significant proportion of the courts' time and personnel. Accusations of sex outside marriage, infrequent attendance at church, drunkenness, and other disorderly behaviour were among a litany of offences for which parishioners were presented. The church court investigated claims of clerical disorder and prosecuted negligent or even irreligious clerics. Aggrieved parishioners could litigate in this court against neighbours and strangers, friends and foes for transgressions including defamation, breached marriage contracts, tithe disputes, disagreements over administration of wills (testamentary disputes), and contested church seating arrangements. The church court sought to mediate and resolve antagonisms between parties.

Witness testimony forms the source base upon which this book primarily depends. Despite their orderly and often formulaic structure and appearance, church court depositions are unruly and unpredictable beasts. At times it is with tedium that I've trawled through repetitive narratives replicated from deposition to deposition and case to case. But in shaking out the contents of this archive, other emotions surfaced. Taunts, jests, and invective exchanged over garden hedges still bring amusement. At the other extreme, harrowing accounts of a husband's abuse of his wife were particularly difficult to read. I regularly unearthed more than can be understood, feeling frustration at a tantalising scrap of reported speech that has now lost its meaning, or a titbit of evidence from which the wider story can no longer be recovered.

It is easy to forget that these are not unmediated accounts of events. Despite swearing oaths, at least some witnesses gave false or prejudiced testimonies.[46] Simon Dansie deposed in the Hereford court that Watkin David Bever of Radnorshire had confessed to him that he had falsely testified under oath in a 1599 matrimonial dispute. Despite being reminded of the dangers of committing perjury, Watkin had told an untruth in court to 'keepe a man and his wife together'.[47] What we read therefore shouldn't be taken at face value; the 'fictions of the archives', as Natalie Zemon Davis described court documents, reflect the

---

[45] In practice, the remits of what was punishable in the ecclesiastical courts and the temporal courts sometimes overlapped. For a detailed account of this in relation to sexual (mis)behaviour, see Martin Ingram, *Carnal Knowledge: Regulating Sex in England, 1470–1600* (Cambridge, 2017), pp. 13–16.

[46] Barbara Shapiro, 'Credibility and the Legal Process in Early Modern England: Part One', *Law and Humanities* 6 (2012), 145–78; Barbara Shapiro, 'Credibility and the Legal Process in Early Modern England: Part Two', *Law and Humanities* 7 (2013), 19–54; Hillary Taylor, 'The Price of the Poor's Words: Social Relations and the Economics of Deposing for One's "Betters" in Early Modern England', *EcHR* 72 (2019), 828–47.

[47] HARC, HD4/2/11, Thomas Hereford v Ann Vaughan (1599); Roger Prosser v Thomas Hereford (1599).

legal, social, and cultural worlds in which they were produced.[48] Frances Dolan has reminded us that 'many who read depositions most carefully seem to locate evidence of an elusive speaking subject when a deposition appears to *depart from convention, to exceed legal formulae*'; instead, she argued, the conventional might actually be more plausible.[49] Aspects of testimony might function as plot devices. The volume of church court suits in which witnesses recall peering through holes or chinks in walls, doors, and windows to unmask incriminating behaviour marks these descriptions out as legal motifs, suggesting three-way collusion in story-telling between the litigant, their legal counsel, and the witness.[50]

Nor are depositions verbatim transcripts of the words witnesses spoke, diligently copied out by court clerks. Testimony was moulded to fit legal conventions and the story arc of the case. This archive was in part constructed by the court notaries, who filtered witnesses' words and redrafted them into the third-person narratives we read today (see Figure 0.1, for example). Malcolm Gaskill's tripartite model of early modern records – of conduct literature reflecting how society *should* behave, literary sources (such as ballads and pamphlets) intonating how people *seemed* to behave to contemporary commentators, and legal documents representing people's *actual* behaviours – overlooks the administrative and legal role of the court in constructing its records.[51]

The challenges of analysing court material are well known. We should be especially wary of thinking that women's depositions are direct evidence of their rarely heard voices. Witnesses were coached by male counsel and their words were placed in the hands of male scribes. The thousands of men and women who filed into the Exeter, Gloucester, Hereford, Wells, and Winchester courts to testify between 1532 and 1649 all encountered and interacted with these scribes. Teasing out where a witness's story ends and a notary's editing begins is virtually impossible. Each deposition was read back to the witness, though whether the signatures, initials, and marks inscribed at the foot of each testimony are indicative of consent, compliance, or even coercion is lost to us. The witness's accomplished signature, short lettering, or shaky subscription next to the notary's long, flowing script remind us that this was a physical interaction between court officials and witnesses over four hundred years ago. Testimonies were made collaboratively.

---

[48] Natalie Zemon Davis, *Fiction in the Archives: Pardon Tales and Their Tellers in Sixteenth-Century France* (Cambridge, 1987), pp. 4–5.
[49] Frances E. Dolan, *True Relations: Reading, Literature, and Evidence in Seventeenth-Century England* (Philadelphia, 2013), pp. 144–5.
[50] Ingram, *Church Courts*, p. 244; Lena Cowen Orlin, *Locating Privacy in Tudor London* (Oxford, 2007), pp. 189–92.
[51] Malcolm Gaskill, *Crime and Mentalities in Early Modern England* (Cambridge, 2000), p. 21. On the problems of this model, see Dolan, *True Relations*, pp. 122–3.

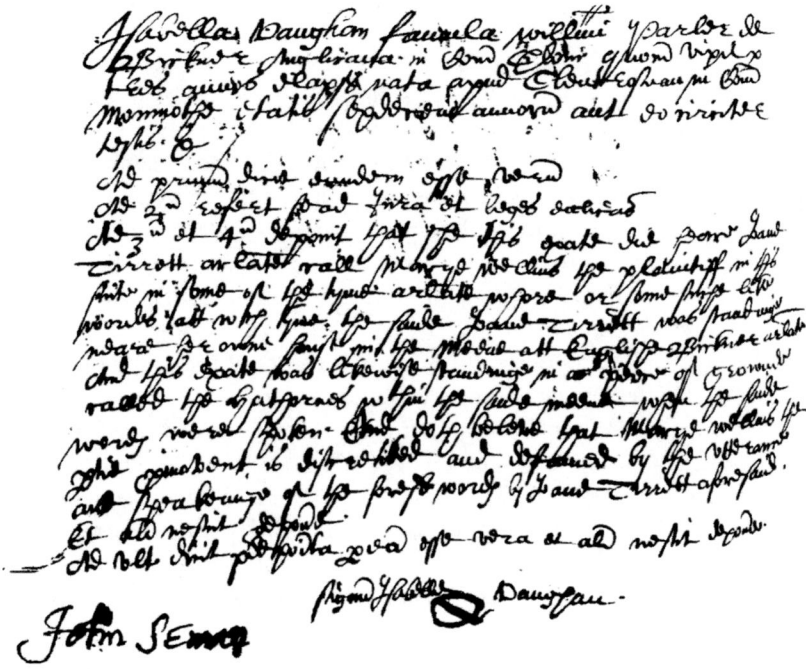

Figure 0.1 Deposition of Isabella Vaughan, *famula* (servant) of William Parler of English Bicknor (Gloucestershire, 1605)

Source: GA, GDR/95, Mary Wellins v Jane Tirrett (1605)

Though imperfect, depositions are nonetheless a guide to the *plausible*. An account of a witness reaping in a field at noon and hearing defamatory words pass between her neighbours tells us something about plausible working patterns, even if the event is entirely fictitious or subject to the imperfections of memory. Truth lies on a spectrum. The testimony may or may not have been precisely her own words or even an account of what happened *at that time on that day*. But to pass as a truthful account in court, the tale she told reflected her own experiences in some way. Day-to-day life was folded into the fabric of the credible story she related. The snippets of everyday practices, interactions, and behaviours recorded in the testimonies of many witnesses were also often incidental to the cases themselves. Systematic study of depositions offers the possibility of writing a history of female service from a compendium of scraps of evidence of servants' lives. This does not make it an incomplete history, but rather one that captures the enormous variation of service and catches a glimpse of women like Matilda, Sybil, Anna, and Isott at various points in their lives.

Methodology

Like any detailed study of one type of source, the conclusions of this book are bound to the context in which the source was produced. In other words, the litigation heard in these ecclesiastical courts shapes the evidence recorded. Chapter 1 outlines in detail the ways in which the institution of the church court comes to bear on the female servants in this book. But, I argue, the depositions from which evidence is drawn broadly reflect the behaviours, practices, and experiences that were familiar to this disparate group of women who self-identified or were identified by others as servants.

In this book, all cases heard in the church courts of the dioceses of Bath & Wells, Exeter, Gloucester, Hereford, and Winchester in the period 1532–1649 that generated witness testimony serve as a 'meta-source'. This meta-source amounts to a database containing details of almost 9,000 cases, over 15,000 litigants, and more than 27,000 witnesses. Full quantification of this archive 'makes it possible to study the wider social and institutional context' in which the 1,093 female servants identified within the records lived.[52] Placing their experiences within the entirety of the archives from which they are drawn connects servants to and contextualises them within the broader practices, behaviours, and attitudes of wider society.

As narrative sources, depositions are typically analysed qualitatively. Their structure and arrangement make quantitative or systematic analysis a less obvious approach, though it is not without precedent.[53] This book synthesises quantitative and qualitative approaches to recover servant experiences, employing the 'micro-exemplary' methodology set out by A. W. Carus and Sheilagh Ogilvie.[54] Depositions are carefully interpreted to determine *how* evidence should be counted, and the linguistic challenges of the source in making these decisions are discussed throughout the book. Each case that contains evidence of one or more female servants has been transcribed and coded, allowing systematic *qualitative* analysis. These approaches are interdependent and 'mutually indispensable' to the book.[55] Quantification allows for the typicality of experiences to be

---

[52] A. W. Carus and Sheilagh Ogilvie, 'Turning Qualitative into Quantitative Evidence: A Well-Used Method Made Explicit', *EcHR* 62 (2009), 893–925 at 919.

[53] See, for example, Sheilagh C. Ogilvie, *A Bitter Living: Women, Markets, and Social Capital in Early Modern Germany* (Oxford, 2003). Alexandra Shepard's work on worth and credit showcased the rewards to be reaped from quantitative analysis of statements of worth in church court testimonies. See Shepard, *Accounting for Oneself*. Maria Ågren et al., Jane Whittle, and Mark Hailwood have followed Ogilvie's approach by quantifying work activities noted in court records. See Maria Ågren (ed.), *Making a Living, Making a Difference: Gender and Work in Early Modern European Society* (Oxford, 2017); Jane Whittle and Mark Hailwood, 'The Gender Division of Labour in Early Modern England', *EcHR* 73 (2020), 3–32. Peter Clark also quantitatively analysed migration histories given by over 7,000 witnesses to understand mobility patterns. See Clark, 'Migration in England', 57–90.

[54] Carus and Ogilvie, 'Turning Qualitative into Quantitative Evidence', 894.

[55] Ibid.

assessed – did female servants routinely milk cows, for example? (The answer is yes, and is explored in detail in Chapter 6). Where numbers are small, the limitations of quantification are acknowledged. Qualitative analysis is simultaneously undertaken at every level in interpreting the statistics compiled from depositions. Patterns and commonalities in practices, labour, and behaviours are identified, as is the significant variation of servant experiences captured in this vast archive.

It is a conscious decision to focus on *female* servants. Male servants have received attention elsewhere, notably in agrarian histories. As Michael Roberts pointed out,

> [i]n writing about women's history there is a strong temptation to contrast their experience with that of men. Since our knowledge of social, as of political, history still largely concerns men, there is a danger that the study will degenerate into a search for the ways in which women 'participated' in social processes which are still defined in terms of male experience.[56]

Roberts himself feared he had fallen into this trap, but he noted that 'only when we have worked out ways of identifying the "female" characteristics of social processes can we then begin to re-write history from the *human* point of view'.[57] This book is a history of gender. I write about distinctly female experiences but interrogate the enduring structures of patriarchy and agency that are male-centred and continue to shape the histories of women that we write. I, too, seek the '*human* point of view' by pulling apart this archive.

Landscapes, economies, and people

London has been fertile ground for studying female service.[58] The metropolitan population pulled in droves of young migrant women (and men) from the countryside and other smaller urban centres with the promise of work. This migration contributed to the city tripling in size between 1580 and 1640 to as many as 380,000.[59] London was a unique setting for service. The intensely urban spatial and social dynamics of work and life were different here to those in small towns and rural parishes. The built environment placed households in closer proximity to one another and each house contained more people. Often two or more households,

---

[56] Michael Roberts, 'Sickles and Scythes: Women's Work and Men's Work at Harvest Time', *History Workshop Journal* 7 (1979), 3–28 at 21.
[57] Ibid. 21.
[58] See Meldrum, *Domestic Service and Gender*; Eleanor Hubbard, *City Women: Money, Sex, and the Social Order in Early Modern London* (Oxford, 2012), esp. chapter 3; Reinke-Williams, *Women, Work and Sociability*, pp. 84–92; Gowing, *Domestic Dangers*.
[59] Roger Finlay, *Population and Metropolis: The Demography of London, 1580–1650* (Cambridge, 1981), p. 60; Hubbard, *City Women*, chapter 1.

including lodgers, apprentices, and servants, lived under one roof.[60] But even by 1660, only a quarter of England's population lived in urban centres.[61] Most female servants in this period lived and worked in the countryside. Though similarities existed, their experiences were likely very different. In the increasingly commercialised metropolis, more masters and mistresses ran shops, practised trades, and carried out mercantile business. The work their servants carried out was not the same as a husbandman's servant or the servant of a country gentleman. Female migrants who came to London in search of service might experience anonymity and freedoms that were not possible elsewhere. As Gowing put it, London servants were 'probably both freer than their rural counterparts, and more vulnerable'.[62] Female servants outside the capital have received far less attention and so we know very little about rural servants' lives, despite a wealth of information in court records.[63]

This book examines female service in southern and western parts of England. The dioceses of Bath & Wells, Exeter, Gloucester, Hereford, and Winchester covered six counties: Somerset, Cornwall, Devon, Gloucestershire, Herefordshire, and Hampshire. Their jurisdictions also spilled beyond modern-day county borders. The diocese of Hereford covered parts of Shropshire, Montgomeryshire, and Radnorshire, and the church court of the diocese of Bath & Wells governed parts of Dorset. The Winchester court also held jurisdiction over the Isle of Wight. The geographical reach of this study is illustrated in Plate 1.

The five dioceses were unequal in size and population. Bath & Wells, Gloucester, and Winchester represented medium-sized jurisdictions. In 1600, the population of Somerset stood at 169,984, Gloucestershire at 101,256, and Hampshire at 104,197. Exeter diocese was much larger, extending across Devon and Cornwall and containing a total diocesan population of 361,479. Herefordshire contained a smaller proportion of the country's population, housing just 62,054 people in 1600.[64] Much of this southern and western landscape was rural but contained several urban centres. The largest included Bristol and Exeter, which by 1660 contained 16,000 and 11,500 inhabitants respectively, while Gloucester, Plymouth, and Winchester were significantly smaller, housing between 3,000 and

---

[60] Mark Merry and Philip Baker, '"For the House Her Self and One Servant": Family and Household in Late Seventeenth-Century London', *The London Journal* 34 (2009), 205–32 at 206, 213.
[61] Jonathan Barry, 'South-West', in Peter Clark (ed.), *The Cambridge Urban History of Britain* (Cambridge, 2008), pp. 67–92 at 67.
[62] Gowing, *Domestic Dangers*, p. 15.
[63] Jane Whittle's work is a notable exception. See Whittle, *Development of Agrarian Capitalism*, chapter 5; Whittle, 'Servants in Rural England'; Whittle, 'Housewives and Servants'. There has been limited work on servants in other urban centres. See, for example, Amy M. Froide, *Never Married: Singlewomen in Early Modern England* (Oxford, 2005), esp. chapter 4; Paul Griffiths, *Youth and Authority: Formative Experiences in England, 1560–1640* (Oxford, 1996), esp. chapter 7; Wales, '"Living at Their Own Hands"', 19–39.
[64] S. N. Broadberry, B. M. S. Campbell, Alexander Klein, Mark Overton, and Bas van Leeuwen, *British Economic Growth, 1270–1870* (Cambridge, 2015), p. 25.

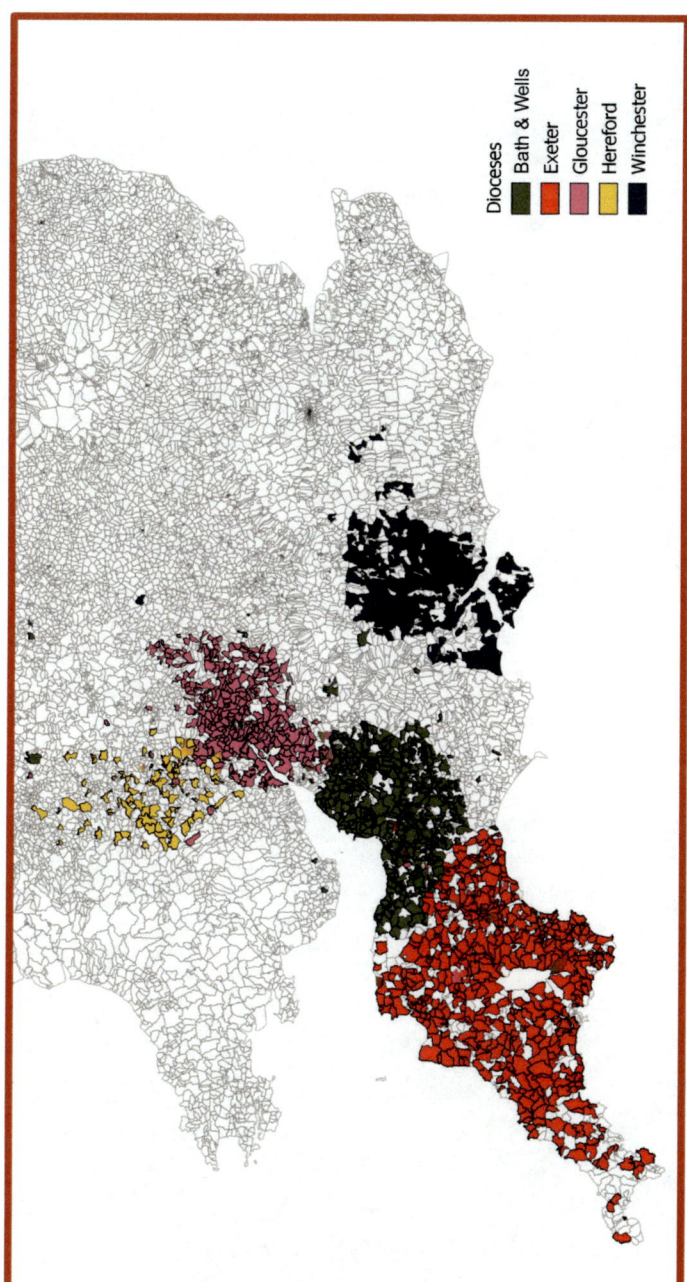

Plate 1 Map of parishes generating witness testimony across the dioceses of Bath & Wells, Exeter, Gloucester, Hereford, and Winchester, c.1532–1649

Note: Occasionally deponents were drawn from outside the dioceses.

Dioceses

- Bath & Wells
- Exeter
- Gloucester
- Hereford
- Winchester

Plate 2 The Monument of John Jones, Alderman of Gloucester (Gloucester Cathedral, *c*.1631)

5,000 people in the period 1600–60.[65] Many smaller but economically significant towns were also littered across these regions, including Bath, Cheltenham, Crediton, Hereford, Southampton, Taunton, and Wells.

These dioceses contained a web of topographies, landscapes, and economies. Agriculture was primarily pastoral, as accounts of farming recalled in the courts' tithe disputes reveal. Sheep were to be found pasturing upon the chalk lands of Hampshire. The diocese of Exeter was primarily an area of pastoral farmland and livestock production, containing less productive upland regions in the north and fertile land for corn production in the south.[66] Herefordshire was a 'mixed agriculture' county, or according to antiquary and sixteenth-century traveller John Leland, a landscape of 'corn, grass and wood'.[67] The parts of Shropshire that the Hereford diocesan court covered encompassed a variety of landscapes, including large areas of wood-pasture and open pasture, in which livestock farming flourished.[68] Gloucestershire contained woodland areas and regions of pastoral farming, with an internationally recognised wool-producing economy in the Cotswolds and the Vale of the Severn.[69] Its landscape supported a fluctuating rural cloth-working trade in the southeast of the county. Similarly, Devon's pastoral farming maintained a strong textile industry, with cloth production central to the economies of Exeter and large towns such as Cullompton and Tiverton.[70] Tin mining was important to the Cornish economy, while coal mining was a significant industry in west Gloucestershire.[71]

Coastal settlements across Devon, Cornwall, Somerset, and Hampshire connected England to the continent and beyond. Plymouth was a growing port with a burgeoning fishing industry in this period.[72] Cornish villages such as

---

[65] The populations of Gloucester and Plymouth were *c*.4,750 and *c*.5,400 respectively in 1660, while Winchester's population was *c*.3,120 in 1604. See Barry, 'South-West', p. 71; C. W. Chalklin, 'South-East', in Peter Clark (ed.), *The Cambridge Urban History of Britain* (Cambridge, 2008), pp. 49–66 at 53.

[66] M. A. Havinden and R. Stanes, 'Agriculture and Rural Settlement, 1500–1800', in Roger Kain, William Ravenhill, and Helen Jones (eds), *Historical Atlas of South-West England* (Exeter, 1999), pp. 281–93 at 281.

[67] Ann Kussmaul, *A General View of the Rural Economy of England, 1538–1840* (Cambridge, 1990), pp. 182–94; John Chandler (ed.), *John Leland's Itinerary: Travels in Tudor England* (Stroud, 1998), pp. 222, 226.

[68] James Bowen, 'A "countrie" consisting wholly of woodland, "bredd of Oxen and Dairies"? Agricultural regions and rural communities in lowland pastoral Shropshire during the early modern period', in Christopher Dyer and Richard Jones (eds), *Farmers, Consumers, Innovators: The World of Joan Thirsk* (Hatfield, 2016), pp. 49–62.

[69] David Rollison, *The Local Origins of Modern Society: Gloucestershire 1500–1800* (1992), p. 25.

[70] M. A. Havinden, 'The Woollen, Lime, Tanning and Leather-Working and Paper-Making Industries *c*.1500–1800', in Roger Kain, William Ravenhill, and Helen Jones (eds), *Historical Atlas of South-West England* (Exeter, 1999), pp. 338–44 at 338.

[71] S. Gerrard, 'The Tin Industry in Sixteenth-and Seventeenth-Century Cornwall', in Roger Kain, William Ravenhill, and Helen Jones (eds), *Historical Atlas of South-West England* (Exeter, 1999), pp. 330–7; Rollison, *Local Origins*, p. 39.

[72] David Harris Sacks and Michael Lynch, 'Ports, 1540–1700', in Peter Clark (ed.), *The Cambridge Urban History of Britain* (Cambridge, 2008), pp. 377–424 at 401.

Mevagissey and St Ives became important fishing centres.[73] Exeter enjoyed strong trade connections with France, exporting Devonshire broadcloth.[74] Bristol and Gloucester were important as organising and trading centres.[75] Bristol traded wares from Somerset, Gloucestershire, and Wiltshire including cloth, lead, coal, iron, and calfskin.[76] Southampton remained a principal trading post in Hampshire but by 1600, trade had made its shift to London.[77]

Some of these settlements were also important posts in the movement and migration of people. These were not closed communities.[78] This book offers important rural and urban counterpoints to the London-centric studies of female service to date, but many witnesses had migrated from across the country. Welsh-born witnesses were recorded and Welsh surnames ('Jones', 'Williams', and 'Griffen') and forenames ('Evan', 'Morgan', and 'Rice', for example) appear across all five courts, but particularly in the Hereford and Gloucester courts. Depositions capture migration between Wales and Minehead in Somerset, as well as continental trade and sea travel from Cornwall to Newfoundland and Spain.[79] Just a little evidence of black lives emerges from this archive, though race is almost never explicitly mentioned. This book compares the experiences of female servants across these regions of England to understand the impact of economic, topographical, and social difference on their lives. This wasn't a homogeneous country, and experiences were shaped by place.

How to use this book

This book has three parts. Part I sets out the book's parameters, exploring exactly *who* female servants were and *how* they were recorded in the church courts. Chapter 1 identifies patterns and trends in the courts, outlining the geographical distribution of cases as well as building profiles of typical litigants and witnesses who filed into the courts. It establishes the scope of the courts' business and explores how patterns of litigation influenced female servants' interaction with church courts in this period. Chapter 2 looks more closely at the profiles of the 1,093 female servants identified in the records. The breadth and variation

---

[73] Mark Overton, Jane Whittle, Darron Dean, and Andrew Hann, *Production and Consumption in English Households, 1600–1750* (Abingdon, 2004), p. 55.
[74] Harris Sacks and Lynch, 'Ports, 1540–1700', p. 400.
[75] Rollison, *Local Origins*, p. 25.
[76] Harris Sacks and Lynch, 'Ports, 1540–1700', p. 400.
[77] Ibid., p. 399.
[78] Scholarship on news networks makes this clear. See, for example, Richard Cust, 'News and Politics in Early Seventeenth-Century England', *P&P* 112 (1986), 60–90; Lloyd Bowen, 'News Networks in Early Modern Wales', *History* 102 (2017), 24–44.
[79] See, for example, SHC, D/D/cd/56, Office v William Amerie (1623); DHC, Chanter 859, Joanna Johns v Jacob Escourt (1577); Chanter 855, Cuthbert Marshall v Juliana Roughan (1559).

of experiences of service that spanned the social spectrum are laid out in this chapter, as is the idea of servant 'identity'. Chapter 3 sets out the demographic structure of service for women, challenging the idea that English service was uniformly coincident with only the premarital stage of life. Part I therefore offers a more detailed reconstruction of female servant lives for this period than has been attempted before, showing service to be contingent, fluid, and flexible.

Part II reconstructs patterns of labour. Chapter 4 outlines female servant mobility in comparison with that of other social groups. It examines the length of time they remained with the same masters and mistresses and explores how mobility shaped their experiences of integration and belonging. Chapter 5 presents new evidence on the conditions under which women were hired, young women's 'choices' in finding work, and the contracts they negotiated. Here, I interrogate the extent to which women entered freely into a contract of service. In Chapter 6, the types of work these women were hired to do are analysed in detail for the first time, demonstrating the varied nature of female service and the inaccuracy of characterising it as domestic labour.

Part III traces the footsteps of service in three ways: spatially, socially, and temporally. Chapters 7 and 8 present social and geographical studies of service, considering how itinerant women established themselves in the communities in which they served. Chapter 7 reorientates our understanding of female service by locating the working and social experiences of these women beyond the domestic realm through quantitative analysis of the spaces in which their own testimonies and the depositions of others recorded them. Moving beyond a narrative of service that locates women almost exclusively within the home, Chapter 8 explores their interactions with members of the communities in which they worked and lived. The connections they developed and maintained over distance and time demonstrate their embeddedness within local communities. In Chapter 9, the role of geographical distance as well as memory in the formation and retention of communities for female servants is brought to the fore. While service was largely a life-cycle experiences, memories of service years later connected women to this work, the households in which they had served, and the land on which they had toiled. In this book, almost every aspect of this key institution is dissected: its demographic profile, mobility and migration patterns, literacy rates, work practices, and the nature of contracts. Early modern service was not the static or stable institution we thought it was. It was finely graded, fluid, and often contingent.

Part I

Chapter 1

Church Courts and Their People

George Withie was no stranger in Thomas Rowe's house. His visits were frequent, as were his promises of marriage to Thomas's servant, Marie Brimpton. Calling at the house in Walton in Somerset one winter's day, he told Marie of a dream he'd had the night before. She had been standing at the foot of his bed and he had pulled her to him, lying with her all night. But Marie wasn't fooled. She warned him 'you shall not lye with me till we be married, for you see howe manye doe falsifie theire promises, and for my parte, I am but a servant, and if your frends should not consent to our marriage we weare undon. Nowe the world is com to passe that people must deale warilye and have witnes'.[1]

* * *

Fears of single motherhood brought women like Marie to court in pursuit of would-be husbands who had allegedly reneged on promises of marriage. Marie's warning to George against indulging in erotic flights of fancy may never have happened. Most likely, it was a retrospective fiction churned out by her trusted allies, whose testimonies sought to defend both the supposed betrothal and her chastity. Either way, they told a story of a servant's legal competence and her understanding of the dangers of illicit actions. She knew that a bride-to-be could become an unmarried mother and, in turn, a plaintiff in a court suit. In a world of increasing litigiousness and shifting meanings of proof that necessitated eyewitnesses and dealing 'warilye', she saw those around her as potential witnesses.[2]

It was well known that church courts were stages upon which litigation was performed. When Elizabeth Smith of Leominster (Herefordshire) called Eleanor *ap* Thomas 'a hoore and an arrand hoore' in 1600, she was fully aware of the legal

---

[1] SHC, D/D/cd/41, Marie Brimpton v George Withie (1609).
[2] On eyewitnesses, see Andrea Frisch, *The Invention of the Eyewitness: Witnessing and Testimony in Early Modern France* (Chapel Hill, NC, 2004), pp. 12–13.

path her words might take her down, adding 'I will saie it and stand to it'.[3] Others recited the law to avoid attending court: Somerset husbandman Philip Creese initially refused to testify against his neighbour in 1629, insisting that only court citation could legally compel him.[4] Once compelled, deponents took to the stage, with scribes and notaries occupying front-row seats in the thousands of lawsuits they documented. These men were often long-standing personnel: Winchester notary Alexander Dearing had been in post for at least fifteen years while John Atwell, Jacob Huish, Edward Huish, and Marcus Tabor had each amassed more than twenty years' experience in the Bath & Wells court.[5] Thousands of witnesses likely stood before them, but the formulaic depositions these men documented betray few signs of the opinions they must have formed. Audible, visual, and material cues such as eloquence of speech and ability to sign one's name were all nonetheless telltale signs of status. Encrypted within the various marks, symbols, initials, and signatures that concluded each witness's deposition are stories of upbringing, training, and status. Physical appearance and clothing laid bare one's position in society, though visual depictions of witnesses are rare. The description of 40-year-old widow Lucy Spiring of Wellington (Somerset) offers a rare but happy moment for the historian. In 1630, her credibility as a witness came under attack when the opposing party pointed out the incongruity of her dress and social status. She admitted

> that the hatt she weareth and the cloake band are Ellinor Coleborne's, wief of the partie producent, & her upper petticoate is her owne mothers & the rest of the cloathes are her owne.[6]

Lucy stitched together her own identity with two she borrowed on the day of her court appearance. How she dressed mattered, her clothes operating as 'technology of identification'.[7] The physical appearance of witnesses resists systematic study (though I return to servants' clothes in Chapter 2). But depositions nonetheless routinely bear hallmarks of a society fond of categorising, ranking, and ordering by gender, age, marital status, and occupation. Each strand of an individual's identity was appraised to determine his or her social standing. These markers of rank featured, too, in schemas of social order outlined by contemporary commentators.[8] Hierarchies were complex and changeable: status could be acquired through marriage, economic prosperity, and other means of betterment. These hierarchies directly correlated with who participated in court and who did not.

[3] HARC, HD4/2/11, Eleanor *ap* Thomas v Elizabeth Smith (1600).
[4] SHC, D/D/cd/65, William Creese v John Reade (1629).
[5] For cases in which these men testified as public notaries, see HRO, 21M65/C3/4–5, and 9; SHC, D/D/cd/28, 32, 34, 44, 49, 51, 54–6, 58, 60–1, 65–6, 72, and 130–1.
[6] SHC, D/D/cd/65, Priscilla Carpenter v John Coleborne (1630).
[7] Steve Hindle, 'Technologies of Identification Under the Old Poor Law', *The Local Historian* 36 (2006), 220–36.
[8] For example, see Thomas Smith, *De Republica Anglorum*, ed. Mary Dewar (Cambridge, 1982), pp. 64–77; Edward Chamberlayne, *Angliae Notitia: Or, the Present State of England* (1669); Gouge, *Of Domesticall Duties*.

Managing disputes (both in and out of court) was a communal affair, involving what Julie Hardwick has termed 'litigation communities'.[9] Participation in court was common. But courts were not socially inclusive spaces. While Steve Hindle identified grassroots state formation through the accessibility of the courts to those of lower status, legal agency wasn't equally apportioned.[10] Alexandra Shepard has shown that for women in particular, participation was 'highly contingent on their marital status and between places and over time and was shaped by the matters in dispute as well as the gender of the litigants for whom they testified'.[11] Different groups participated in legal processes to different degrees. Understanding the social diversity of *each* legal forum is essential to grasp which groups had legal agency within it and in what contexts or situations.

This chapter firstly describes and interrogates the institutional frame that colours the legal proceedings in this book. It identifies trends in litigation and witness production across the corpus of depositions, drawing a blueprint of the five diocesan courts studied here, which serves as a meta-source for this book.[12] The chapter then explores how female servants appear in court depositions, and sets out the challenges of identifying them. The court's proclivity for certain types of witnesses intersected with social norms around agency, dependency, and obligation. Early modern England was a service society in which virtually every relationship was one of master and servant. As Urvashi Chakravarty observed, the idea that one's master was 'the locus of both obligation and freedom' was not unfamiliar to early modern people.[13] The female servants of this study participated in court litigation alongside thousands of men and women. But they were few in number. The act of a servant testifying encapsulates an apparent paradox: that she should willingly serve her master and fulfil *any and all* obligations to him (including testifying on his behalf), while at the same time her deposition should be given freely upon oath. Thirdly, then, the chapter brings the underlying legal conventions of the church court into conversation with issues of consent, obedience, and obligation that further complicate the servant's place within it. The bonds of labour could constrain servants' legal agency. But female servants could – and did – come to court to pursue legal justice of their own, and their testimonies speak to more than just their positions as household servants.

---

[9] Julie Hardwick, *Family Business: Litigation and the Political Economies of Daily Life in Early Modern France* (Oxford, 2009), pp. 89–92.

[10] Steve Hindle, *The State and Social Change in Early Modern England, c.1550–1640* (2000), p. 89.

[11] Alexandra Shepard, 'Worthless Witnesses? Marginal Voices and Women's Legal Agency in Early Modern England', *Journal of British Studies* 58 (2019), 717–34 at 717.

[12] Carus and Ogilvie, 'Turning Qualitative into Quantitative Evidence', 894.

[13] Urvashi Chakravarty, *Fictions of Consent: Slavery, Servitude, and Free Service in Early Modern England* (Philadelphia, 2022), p. 72.

Charting litigation

Ecclesiastical courts were central to early modern England's complex legal system. The country's twenty-one dioceses contained over 250 church courts, which had four important functions: to correct, adjudicate, verify and record, and license.[14] The first two of these functions were fulfilled through litigation they heard and pursued. Not all cases generated witness testimony, but depositions capture an extensive picture of church court litigation.[15] Depositions were introduced part way through the court process. Beforehand, the aggrieved plaintiff had appointed a proctor, who (as their legal agent) lodged the complaint (libel) on their behalf. The defendant was then summoned (cited) to appear in court. He or she could lodge their own complaint and both plaintiff and defendant were then asked to respond to accusations under oath. If no resolution was reached, witnesses were summoned.

Types of litigation

Table 1.1 summarises the main disputes and offences recorded in depositions. Suits fell into two categories: office (*ex officio*) cases and instance cases. *Ex officio* suits were pursued by churchwardens and officials against delinquent parishioners. The bishop or his deputies also made intermittent circuits (known as visitations) of small clusters of parishes to root out undetected wrongdoers. By this approach, the court regulated clergy, enforced religious uniformity, and controlled sexual misbehaviour. But most witnesses testified in instance suits: only around 15 per cent of cases that summoned witnesses were *ex officio* and most of these were heard after 1600.[16] Illicit sex or sex outside marriage (labelled variably as 'incontinency', 'adultery', and 'fornication', and occasionally including accusations of incest) was the most likely *ex officio* suit to summon witnesses. Correction of sexual 'misbehaviour' intensified over the period (as Figure 1.1 shows), with more witnesses testifying in these cases from around 1600, mirroring heightened prosecution found elsewhere.[17]

---

[14] On the number of church courts, see Hill, *Society and Puritanism*, p. 289. On the functions of the church court, see R. B. Outhwaite, *The Rise and Fall of the English Ecclesiastical Courts, 1500–1860* (Cambridge, 2006), p. 5.

[15] The full complement of court records (including act books which documented the court's day-to-day business) provide a more complete account but full reconstruction of court business is outside the scope of this book.

[16] In 1561, for instance, 282 office cases were recorded in the Gloucester court book but only sixteen generated depositions (see GA, GDR/18–19). Ralph Houlbrooke identified similar patterns in the Winchester court. See Ralph A. Houlbrooke, *Church Courts and the People during the English Reformation, 1520–1570* (Oxford, 1979), p. 274.

[17] McIntosh, *Controlling Misbehavior*, p. 73, graph 3.5; Wrightson and Levine, *Poverty and Piety*, chapters 5 and 7; Ingram, *Carnal Knowledge*, esp. chapter 12.

Classification	Nature of dispute or offence
Clerical	Absence from benefice; abuse of the curate; simony.
Matrimonial	Annulment; bigamy; divorce; marriage formation; separation.
Personal	Assault; debt; defamation; swearing; testamentary; usury.
Religious	Church seating; discord; heresy; non-attendance at church; rejection of communion; witchcraft.
Sexual	Adultery; bridal pregnancy; harbouring a person liable for punishment; incest; incontinence; rape.
Taxation	Church rates; tithes.

Table 1.1 Taxonomy of disputes and offences recorded in church court depositions

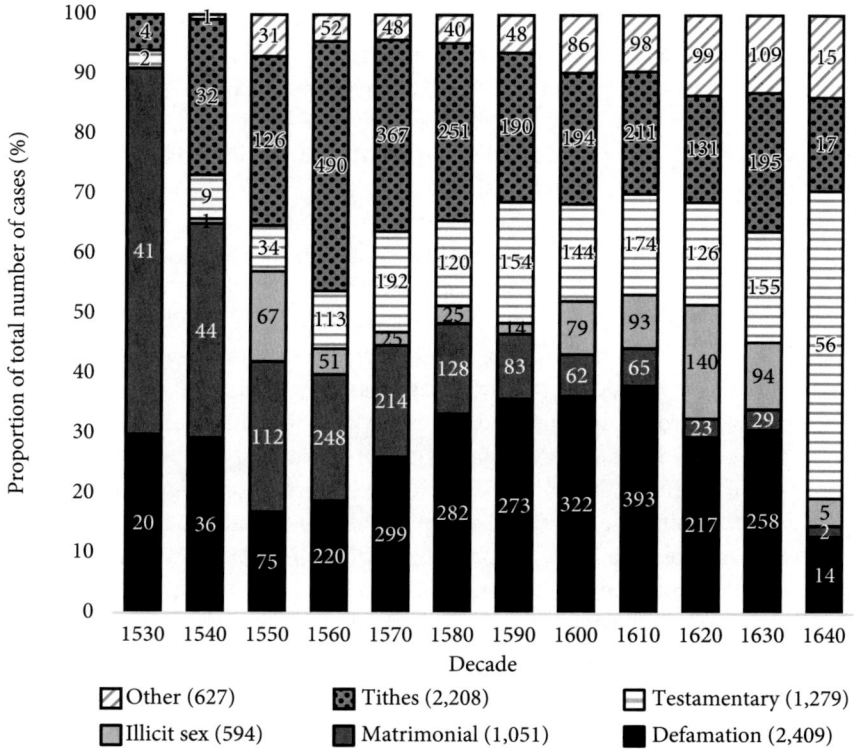

Figure 1.1 Deposition-generating cases (where type of case known)

Instance suits were complaints made by lay people against each other (inter-party disputes). As an arbitrator in these suits, the court sought to nurture parochial harmony and promote neighbourly love. For early modern people, these disputes were not trivial. Legal action was necessary to protect their reputations and local standing. Instance suits typically concerned probate (disputed wills), tithes, defamation, and marriage formation, with a smattering of other key cases including disputes over seating in church. Defamation and tithe cases brought the highest number of witnesses to court. Defamation generally arose from heat-of-the-moment altercations: the plaintiff's social standing had been compromised when the defendant had used actionable words (i.e. words that met the legal requirement for a defamation suit such as 'whore' or 'rogue') against them. Countersuits were common and defamation litigation increased over the period.[18] Quarrels could occur anywhere – in houses, streets, and fields – and defamation was both a rural and a metropolitan phenomenon. Tithe disputes, meanwhile, were rooted in the fields. Tithes were a tax: a tenth of the value of crops growing or livestock grazing on the land was payable to tithe owners. Payment of great tithes (cereals and pulses, such as wheat, barley, beans, and oats) and small tithes (cheese, wool, milk, and other produce) was made in cash or kind on 'reckoning days'. The 1549 Great Tithes Act fixed liability for tithe payment to parochial custom, provoking local disputes over what the custom *was*.[19] Suits against parishioners who refused to pay reached a peak in the 1560s, representing over 40 per cent of all litigation. Bad harvests, rising prices, and the dissolution of monasteries (which shifted tithe ownership from clerical to lay hands) also contributed to heightened tensions.[20]

Matrimonial disputes primarily concerned marriage formation. While banns were supposed to be read and solemnised in church, other traditions of union (such as betrothals) were legal. Establishing whether a binding union had taken place was sometimes difficult, and as we saw in the case of Marie Brimpton, responsibility to secure marriage for jilted brides and grooms fell to the church courts.[21] Over the period, increasing clarification and rigidity of marital law made successful prosecution more difficult.[22] Matrimonial disputes waned: they comprised 21 per cent of all cases in the 1560s but only 7 per cent by the first decade of the seventeenth century. Preference for profitable, lengthier disputes (such as tithe and probate litigation) also probably contributed to the decline.[23]

The court's role in proving and administering probate made it an obvious forum for testamentary suits. Authenticity of a will was typically the source of conflict, with litigants quibbling over what the testator's final deathbed instructions

---

[18] Similar patterns are found in Wiltshire, Chester, and especially London by the seventeenth century. See Ingram, *Church Courts*, pp. 68, 296–7; Christopher Haigh, 'Slander and the Church Courts in the Sixteenth Century', *Transactions of the Lancashire and Cheshire Antiquarian Society* 78 (1975), 1–13; Gowing, *Domestic Dangers*, p. 33, table 1.

[19] Houlbrooke, *Church Courts and the People*, pp. 149–50.

[20] Ibid., pp. 148–50; Christopher Hill, *Economic Problems of the Church from Archbishop Whitgift to the Long Parliament* (New York, 1956), pp. 90–1, 96; Outhwaite, *The Rise and Fall*, p. 96; Anne Tarver, 'The Due Tenth: Problems of the Leicestershire Tithing Process 1560–1640', *Transactions of the Leicestershire Archaeological and Historical Society* 78 (2004), 97–107.

[21] Ingram, *Church Courts*, pp. 191–2.

[22] Ingram, *Carnal Knowledge*, pp. 325, 419.

[23] Houlbrooke, *Church Courts and the People*, p. 65; Ingram, *Church Courts*, pp. 50, 192.

had been. But executors and overseers were also regularly challenged in court for mismanagement of wills and legacies. These lengthy suits consistently represented between 14 and 20 per cent of cases in the period from the 1570s to the 1630s. In the 1640s, on the eve of civil war and a hiatus of the courts, 51 per cent of the small number of disputes heard concerned probate. For litigants, this was undoubtedly essential business and no clear alternative legal forum existed for their disputes. For the church courts, these were lucrative suits at a time when court business was officially suspended.

Record survival

Church court depositions are links of a broken chain. Few verdicts were issued because most cases were resolved out of court. Other strategies were sometimes at play beyond seeking a favourable ruling. As Tim Stretton noted, litigation might be pursued to 'delay, derail, or facilitate a different suit, or to cost opponents money'.[24] Individual cases, therefore, can seldom be reconstructed from start to end. Chance also determines the corpus of depositions found in the archive. An unknown proportion have not survived and no *completely* unbroken run for this period exists. But surviving material is substantial. Depositions survive for 8,740 cases heard across the Bath & Wells, Exeter, Gloucester, Hereford, and Winchester courts between 1532 and 1649. A more complete set of depositions survive for the Bath & Wells, Exeter, and Gloucester courts (as Table 1.2 shows).[25]

Levels of litigation aren't easily compared because the dioceses differed in size. The diocese of Exeter, for example, sprawled across the two large counties of Devon and Cornwall. In the 1560s, its business exploded, towering above the other courts: the 719 cases it heard represented 57 per cent of *all* cases heard that decade. Across the five courts, the 1560s, 1570s, and 1610s were the most adversarial decades, in which 41 per cent of all suits were heard. Just 3 per cent of cases were heard before 1550 and few depositions exist for the 1640s. When orders came in 1641 for the suspension of the courts upon civil war, not all came grinding to a halt. The Exeter, Hereford, and Winchester notaries took down depositions from only four cases between them in the 1640s.[26] But testamentary suits continued to be heard in the Bath & Wells and Gloucester courts until the late 1640s.[27] Table 1.2 gives the impression of a rise and fall of the church courts between 1532

---

[24] Tim Stretton, 'Women, Legal Records, and the Problem of the Lawyer's Hand', *JBS* 58 (2019), 684–700 at 690.
[25] Exeter church court records were damaged while housed in a chamber over the cathedral's north porch in the nineteenth century. See J. A. Vage, 'The Records of the Bishop of Exeter's Consistory Court, *c.*1500–1660', *Transactions of the Devon Association* 114 (1982), 79–98 at 81–2.
[26] No deposition-generating cases were recorded in the Winchester court after 1637.
[27] Probate business also continued elsewhere. See Outhwaite, *The Rise and Fall*, p. 78.

	Bath & Wells	Exeter	Gloucester	Hereford	Winchester	All courts	
	N	N	N	N	N	N	%
1530s	11	—	—	—	73	84	1
1540s	52	—	20	—	73	145	2
1550s	115	281	100	—	—	496	6
1560s	131	719	104	—	314	1,268	15
1570s	236	344	336	1	327	1,244	14
1580s	78	399	235	—	181	893	10
1590s	156	189	235	70	159	809	9
1600s	459	16	348	65	38	926	11
1610s	500	297	286	—	—	1,083	12
1620s	565	2	188	29	1	785	9
1630s	594	135	94	19	49	891	10
1640s	62	1	50	3	—	116	1
Total	**2,959**	**2,383**	**1,996**	**187**	**1,215**	**8,740**	

Table 1.2 Deposition-generating cases by decade

and 1649, though it is important to remember that this is a truncated history and the courts returned two decades later (although they were never quite the same).[28]

In many respects, little had changed by the early 1640s. The courts continued to hear almost every type of case. But the period witnessed gradual shifts. Defamation and testamentary litigation grew and the preoccupation with sex outside marriage heightened, which gradually redefined the church court. By the outbreak of civil war, people seldom sought its arbitration in matrimonial suits. These shifting patterns of litigation shaped not only the role of the church court, but also who participated as plaintiffs, defendants, and witnesses.

Coming to court

On court days, the cathedrals and their host cities of Exeter, Gloucester, Hereford, Wells, and Winchester were hives of activity. Testimonies were usually taken down in the homes of clergymen or lawyers surrounding the cathedral, but occasionally

---

[28] For debate on the decline of the church courts, see Christopher Haigh, 'Anticlericalism and the English Reformation', in Christopher Haigh (ed.), *The English Reformation Revised* (Cambridge, 1987), pp. 56–74 at 67; Outhwaite, *The Rise and Fall*, esp. chapters 9, 10, and 15; Hill, *Society and Puritanism*, p. 296.

elsewhere.[29] Witnesses responded to a series of questions (articles). From 1600, opposing parties increasingly posed interrogatory questions (functioning as a cross-examination). Depositions recorded only *responses* to articles and interrogatories, with the *questions* recorded separately (though replies are suggestive of questions asked). Each deposition contains a short biographical introduction to the witness. The 1413 Statute of Additions established legal conventions for women's and men's testimony: marital status (singlewoman, wife, or widow) was recorded to express the social standing of a female witness, while occupation or rank (husbandman or gentleman, for example) denoted the status of male witnesses.[30] Age and how long the witness had known each litigant was routinely recorded, as well as the witness's place of residence and birth (sometimes accompanied by a more complete migration history).

Witnesses were required to come to court unless they were too aged, unwell, poor, or distant to travel.[31] Yeoman John Whitehed of Wheathill (Somerset) came voluntarily to depose in October 1601:

> finding himself agreed with the grosse and uncivill behavioure of the said Hill [the defendant], hee came to testifye in this cause a truth according to his knowledge.[32]

Others were coerced by litigants or compelled by the court. No-shows could be excommunicated, a considerable punishment in small parishes where participation in church and in community practices were virtually one and the same.[33] But many *were* reluctant witnesses, testifying only when forced. Not everyone wanted to be involved in other people's disputes.

Surviving depositions cover almost every parish, though geographical distribution of litigation was uneven. Complexities of the legal system go some way to explain disparities. Some parishes fell outside the jurisdiction of the diocese, lying in districts known as peculiars which held separate courts.[34] Uncertainty about

---

[29] William Husband (ed.), *Depositions in the Consistory Court of the Bishop of Bath and Wells, Vol. 1: Office Depositions 1601 to 1605* (Croydon, 2019), p. xvii.

[30] See 'Henry V: May 1413', in Chris Given-Wilson, Paul Brand, Seymour Phillips, Mark Ormrod, Geoffrey Martin, Anne Curry, and Rosemary Horrox (eds), *Parliament Rolls of Medieval England* (Woodbridge, 2005), *British History Online* www.british-history.ac.uk/no-series/parliament-rolls-medieval/may-1413 [accessed 3 May 2023].

[31] Taking evidence locally was unusual and was scrutinised in a 1629 case. The Bath & Wells court appointed a commission to examine Jane Androwes of Shipham in the local church due to her illness, but as Jane was too ill to travel even to the church, evidence was taken in her house. In defence of this irregular process, depositions were taken from the registrar, notary, and local vicar. See SHC, D/D/cd/65, Margaret Jervis v William Androwes and Jane Androwes (1629). For other examples, see F. S. Hockaday, 'The Consistory Court of the Diocese of Gloucester', *Transactions of the Bristol and Gloucestershire Archaeological Society* 46 (1924), 195–287 at 264.

[32] SHC, D/D/cd/32, Thomas Maicock v Edward Hill (1600–1).

[33] Ingram, *Church Courts*, pp. 342–4.

[34] Peculiars were monastic, royal, episcopal, or cathedral properties lying inside a diocese but exempt from the bishop's or archbishop's oversight. See Houlbrooke, *Church Courts and the People*, pp. 34–5; Outhwaite, *The Rise and Fall*, pp. 1–2.

the court's remit meant that some suits were heard in secular courts instead.[35] Although fewer *ex officio* cases generated depositions, local differences in the intensity of policing also contributed to uneven geographical distribution of cases. Churchwardens were required to submit a list of issues demanding the authority's attention; some were diligent, others overzealous, and many more probably turned a blind eye to their neighbours' transgressions.

Rural suits dominated the courts. Large urban centres produced no more than 9 per cent of all litigation, although cities such as Gloucester and Exeter generated a disproportionately high volume of cases in relation to their populations.[36] Cases concentrated around cathedral cities, where the courts were held. In the Gloucester diocese, the highest volume of litigation stemmed from parishes falling within a 24-kilometre radius of Gloucester, stretching from Berkeley in the south to Bishop's Cleeve in the north.[37] Travelling to court could be impractical and costly for parishioners at the peripheries of the diocese: Cornish people account for just 16 per cent of Exeter diocesan depositions.[38] This is not to overlook early modern mobility: markets, fairs, work, and leisure regularly drew rural society into towns. But life was very different across the patchwork of settlements – large towns, small towns, rural villages, and isolated hamlets – that made up early modern England. Exeter, Gloucester, and Winchester stand out as distinctly urban, boasting inns, taverns, hospitals, shops, large markets, and county-level courts that would have been familiar amenities to their large populations. But smaller towns could hold as many as 2,000 inhabitants or as few as 300 souls.[39] Some rural-dwellers had next-door neighbours, while others lived in solitary homes away from other people.

Cataloguing and classifying descriptions of over 27,000 witnesses and 16,000 litigants creates imagined communities. Populations recorded in the pages of depositions appear united by gender, occupation, place of residence, and so on. But these shared features tell us little about the *relationships* or *experiences* of litigants and witnesses – in short, they aren't much to stake claims of community on. They do, however, matter at the macro level in understanding legal agency. Certain types of litigation encouraged the participation of litigants and witnesses with certain attributes. These attributes mattered in court.

---

[35] Sexual offences were frequently heard in secular courts, especially in urban centres. See Ingram, *Carnal Knowledge*, p. 391.

[36] Exeter accounted for 6.2 per cent, Gloucester for 8.4 per cent, Leominster (curiously, not Hereford) for 5.6 per cent, Wells for 7.6 per cent, and Winchester for 5.9 per cent. Based on estimated county populations of 1600 and populations of the two cities around 1660, *c.*3 per cent of the diocese of Exeter lived in Exeter, and 5 per cent of the population of Gloucestershire lived in Gloucester. See Broadberry et al., *British Economic Growth*, p. 25; Barry, 'South-West', p. 71.

[37] Shepard also noted that less litigation arose from parishioners living distant from cathedral cities. See Shepard, *Accounting for Oneself*, p. 17.

[38] On Cornish remoteness, see Mark Stoyle, 'The Dissidence of Despair: Rebellion and Identity in Early Modern Cornwall', *JBS* 38 (1999), 423–44 at 424.

[39] Peter Clark and Jean Hosking, *Population Estimates of English Small Towns, 1550–1851* (Leicester, 1993).

Gendered litigation

Richard Wunderli described the London consistory as becoming 'a women's court' by the late fifteenth century.[40] Proportions of female litigants and witnesses exploded in the metropolis, but as Table 1.3 shows, the rural church court was a man's world.[41] Over two-thirds of plaintiffs, almost three-quarters of defendants, and around 85 per cent of witnesses were men. Urban women, meanwhile, were more inclined to litigate and testify than rural women. As Table 1.4 shows, over a third of female participants in the church courts lived in towns or cities. Gloucester and Exeter women were equally or more likely to litigate than their male counterparts. Astonishingly, over 40 per cent of Exeter witnesses were women, compared with just 14 per cent in the diocese of Exeter (Devon and Cornwall) as a whole. Only in the Hereford court were urban and small-town dwellers less prominent, probably because the data set is smaller and there were fewer towns in Herefordshire. From 1600, women's involvement in almost all types of disputes increased. Women in the Bath & Wells court accounted for 17 per cent of witnesses on average across the period; by 1640 the proportion had risen to almost 22 per cent. Change came, but it was gradual and legal participation for women was highly contingent on many different factors.[42]

Women and men pursued different types of suits in court. Reputation was at the heart of matrimonial and defamation suits. A woman's reputation was regularly founded upon her sexual chastity while men's management of money was more often scrutinised.[43] Differences reflected explicitly gendered legal cultures, though motivations for litigating could overlap. In fact, men and women came to court in relatively equal numbers as plaintiffs in matrimonial suits (see Table 1.3).[44] They litigated to secure a match, avoid scandal, and restore their social standing. In these cases, an unsuccessful marriage stained both male and female reputations (though women might carry the additional burden of a child conceived out of wedlock). Defamation cases produced similar gendered patterns. The London court was unique in its exceptionally high proportion of female defamation

---

[40] Richard Wunderli, *London Church Courts and Society on the Eve of the Reformation* (Cambridge, MA, 1981), p. 76.

[41] On London courts, see ibid., p. 75; Gowing, *Domestic Dangers*, pp. 13–14, 33; Robert Shoemaker, *Prosecution and Punishment: Petty Crime and the Law in London and Rural Middlesex, c.1660–1725* (Cambridge, 1991), p. 215.

[42] Shepard, *Accounting for Oneself*, p. 19; Shepard, 'Worthless Witnesses?', 717–34.

[43] See Gowing, *Domestic Dangers*, p. 110. Other scholarship demonstrates that women's honour was also based on their diligence as housewives and that male and female anxieties about reputation often overlapped. See Garthine Walker, 'Expanding the Boundaries of Female Honour in Early Modern England', *TRHS* 6 (1996), 235–46; Alexandra Shepard, *Meanings of Manhood in Early Modern England* (Oxford, 2003), chapter 7.

[44] Patterns varied regionally. Female participation as plaintiffs in these suits ranged from 40 per cent in the Hereford court to 51 per cent in the Gloucester court. In Wiltshire, Ingram found that female plaintiffs outnumbered males 'in a ratio of about 3:2'. See Ingram, *Church Courts*, p. 194.

	Plaintiff					Defendant					Witness				
	M		F		Total	M		F		Total	M		F		Total
	N	%	N	%		N	%	N	%		N	%	N	%	
Bath & Wells	1,719	69	781	31	2,500	2,251	73	830	27	3,081	8,031	83	1,669	17	9,700
Exeter	1,309	69	597	31	1,906	1,655	73	604	27	2,259	5,535	86	890	14	6,425
Gloucester	1,265	66	651	34	1,916	1,433	71	576	29	2,009	5,627	83	1,174	17	6,801
Hereford	138	70	58	30	196	138	73	52	27	190	720	84	141	16	861
Winchester	623	63	372	37	995	843	71	352	30	1,195	3,390	89	407	11	3,797
All courts	**5,054**	**67**	**2,459**	**33**	**7,513**	**6,320**	**72**	**2,414**	**28**	**8,734**	**23,303**	**85**	**4,281**	**16**	**27,584**

	Plaintiff					Defendant					Witness				
	M		F		Total	M		F		Total	M		F		Total
	N	%	N	%		N	%	N	%		N	%	N	%	
Defamation	1,011	42	1,390	58	2,401	1,368	56	1,065	44	2,433	5,281	73	1,973	27	7,254
Illicit Sex	134	92	11	8	145	502	80	125	20	627	1,442	93	104	7	1,546
Matrimonial	511	54	428	46	939	509	51	491	49	1,000	2,201	84	436	17	2,637
Testamentary	718	64	398	36	1,116	773	66	394	34	1,167	3,539	82	803	19	4,342
Tithes	1,973	97	68	3	2,041	2,122	95	102	5	2,224	7,630	96	332	4	7,962
Other	389	88	55	12	444	575	87	89	13	664	2,205	90	245	10	2,450
All cases	**4,736**		**2,350**			**5,849**		**2,266**			**22,298**		**3,893**		

Table 1.3 Gender distribution of litigants and witnesses (by court and type of case)

		Plaintiff		Defendant		Witness	
		M	F	M	F	M	F
Urban centre	N	237	154	158	164	1,866	698
	%	12	19	7	19	9	18
Small town	N	318	184	391	162	3,191	712
	%	15	23	17	19	16	18
Rural parish	N	1,501	479	1,738	547	15,204	2,560
	%	73	59	76	63	75	64

Table 1.4 Place of residence of litigants and witnesses

litigants: by 1633 around 85 per cent were instigated by women, while the damaging consequences of an insult concerned both men *and* women in the rural courts.[45] Women litigated against defamatory accusations only slightly more than men, comprising 58 per cent of all plaintiffs (and 44 per cent of those accused). In these cases, women's participation does not appear constrained.

But female involvement was significantly lower in disputes over financial recompense or gain (tithe and testamentary cases). Just 3 per cent of plaintiffs and 5 per cent of defendants in tithe suits were women. Tithe ownership was generally restricted to men and tithe payment officially fell to household heads; so only in widowhood could women litigate. They appeared more regularly as litigants in testamentary disputes, comprising around a third of plaintiffs and defendants, but it is surprising that this proportion is not higher given that wives were routinely selected by their dying husbands as executrixes.[46] However, in addition to the predominantly widowed women who litigated in testamentary suits, married women adopted other roles in pursuit of bequests. Court testimony shows that probate administration was far from beyond their concern. In 1638, Eustace Peeke of Tavistock (Devon) took William Carew to court for failing to deliver a feather bed that was bequeathed to his wife, Jane Peeke, by her former mistress. Under coverture laws, Eustace had legal ownership of the bed upon marriage, but his wife nonetheless actively pursued the legacy, testifying as a key witness in the case.[47] Inheritance rights were also hotly fought on behalf of orphaned young women (and men) when, during their minority, their legal guardians had squandered their deceased parents' estates. In 1606, Richard Yarneton of Bishop's Cleeve

[45] Laura Gowing, 'Language, Power and the Law: Women's Slander Litigation in Early Modern London', in Jennifer Kermode and Garthine Walker (eds), *Women, Crime and the Courts in Early Modern England* (London, 1994), pp. 26–47 at 27.
[46] Amy Louise Erickson, *Women and Property in Early Modern England* (London, 1993), pp. 156–8.
[47] DHC, Chanter 866, Eustace Peeke v William Carewe (1638).

(Gloucestershire) charged Thomas Smith with the improper administration of Alice Smith's goods, including her daughters' marriage portions.[48] Litigating on behalf of these women was materially important to their futures. Women's legal agency in these suits was contingent, but not absent.

Different types of litigation demanded different forms of proof, which in turn determined who litigated. A surprising pattern emerges in cases concerning illicit sex. Despite the state's apparent concern with policing female sexual conduct, over 80 per cent of those accused of sex outside marriage were men.[49] Pausing to think about how the court arrived not only at a verdict but also apprehension of the accused explains this pattern. Differences lay in proof of culpability. Female 'guilt' was often founded on the material evidence of pregnancy, whereas it could only be established by witness testimony for men. Women's names are not absent from depositions in these cases; typically, the male defendant's alleged sexual partner *was* named. Act books surely pick up more female defendants who were presented to court, but testimony was routinely not required. The woman's pregnancy was probably both the alert the court had acted upon and the evidence upon which the truth was established.

Establishing the facts in each case also required different types of evidence. Capacity to bear witness was shaped by these requirements. Three broad types of witness testimony can be identified:

1. the witness confirmed long-established parochial traditions, customs, and practices (tithe and church seating disputes);

2. the witness confirmed the occurrence of a formal act, procedure, or event to which they had been specifically invited (tithe, testamentary, and matrimonial suits);

3. the witness reported an incident to which they had incidentally or by chance been an eye or ear witness (defamation suits).

In the first type of witnessing, authority was measured by longevity of knowledge as well as the gender of its custodian. Older men with long memories of their parish and its customs were routinely summoned: in 1618, for example, 72-year-old gentleman Edward Walrond of Seaton (Devon) could recall who had sat in a contested church pew over the last forty years, deposing that it 'was in tymes past the formost seate in the south syde of the said church'.[50] This same culture of witnessing is found in other courts where parish customs needed to be established.[51] Tithe cases also called on older, male parishioners who could set out

---

[48] GA, GDR/100, Richard Yarneton v Thomas Smith (1606).
[49] On state control and sex, see Griffiths, *Youth and Authority*, esp. chapter 1.
[50] DHC, Chanter 867, John Manson and Robert Starre v William Redwood (1618).
[51] Andy Wood, *The Politics of Social Conflict: The Peak Country, 1520–1770* (Cambridge, 1999), pp. 169–88; Tim Stretton, 'Women, Custom and Equity in the Court of Requests', in Garthine Walker and

the historical practices of paying tithes. But tithing was also a ritualistic event, a regular procedure which required formal witnesses to observe the moment when a tenth of a crop was set apart for the tithe owner. Women comprised just 4 per cent of witnesses in tithe disputes. They weren't excluded altogether but this second form of witnessing heavily privileged men's words over women's. Testamentary and matrimonial suits hinged on similar forms of evidence. Though wills were (for the most part) written legal documents, their production relied on an oral culture of witnessing. Those on their deathbeds more regularly called for men to witness their wills, and the scribe (often a deponent) was also a man.[52] Witnessing deathbed instructions was a patriarchal duty, while women usually appear as 'accidental' bystanders.[53] In 1631, 50-year-old widow Elizabeth Carie of Middlezoy (Somerset) heard Margery Pennie's will when she was hired 'to attend her in her sicknes'.[54] The labour of care disproportionately fell to women, and it was often in this capacity that they testified. How many women like Elizabeth were there, slipping silently in and out of the sick chamber, but whose testimonies *weren't* requested? Local institutional dynamics mattered, too. In the south and south-west, there are no signs that women regularly participated in the formal culture of witnessing of deathbed instructions *in court* in the way that Alexandra Shepard identified for the south-east, London, and the north. She found almost half of all female witnesses testifying in these cases, whereas the figure is much lower here (just 21 per cent, and this is consistent across all five courts).[55]

Similarly, proof of a legal marital union relied on the testimonies of invited witnesses to the couple's betrothal, who again tended to be men (as Table 1.3 shows). Even when betrothal audiences were mixed, male testimony was preferred. Minister John Honiborne deposed in 1594 that Thomas Hurford and Christian Escott of Siston (Gloucestershire) were betrothed in the

> presence, sight and hearing of Mr Edward Poynts Esquier, Walter Welshe Esquier, Thomas Collins, William Bagley, John Taylor, Richard Honiborne, Mrs Margaret Barklye, Joane Kent, Johane Dappens, Margaret Lantroe and Dorothie Hathewaye.[56]

Unfortunately, the presence, sight, and hearing of the five female witnesses was not sufficient for them to be called to court in this case. Only men testified. Women were routinely overlooked as witnesses in this capacity, but we do find them more regularly commenting on other aspects of a couple's courtship

---

Jennifer Kermode (eds), *Women, Crime and the Courts in Early Modern England* (1994), pp. 170–90; Nicola Whyte, 'Custodians of Memory: Women and Custom in Rural England *c*.1550–1700', *Cultural and Social History* 8 (2011), 153–73.

[52] Gowing, *Domestic Dangers*, p. 51; Cressy, *Literacy and Social Order*, p. 15.

[53] Craig Muldrew, 'The Culture of Reconciliation: Community and the Settlement of Economic Disputes in Early Modern England', *The Historical Journal* 39 (1996), 915–42 at 932.

[54] SHC, D/D/cd/71, Richard Clarck v John Woodmill and Joanna Pennie (1631).

[55] Shepard, 'Worthless Witnesses?', 730–1.

[56] SHC, D/D/cd/18, Thomas Hurford v John Chilcott, Peter Arnold and Thomas Arnold (1594).

such as the exchange of gifts: Francis Oliff, a married gentlewoman of Shipton Oliffe (Gloucestershire), deposed that she bought cloth in 1612 to be made into a wedding band for Mary Belcher's husband-to-be.[57] *What* men and women were asked to depose was gendered, and legal freedom or agency was constrained by the more limited role women played as deponents in this litigation.

Fewer women were disregarded as witnesses in cases where the words of chance bystanders were required. Defamation witnesses particularly gave evidence of this sort, as defamatory exchanges were usually unplanned. Consequently, a higher proportion of female witnesses testified in these suits (27 per cent), which has been well documented elsewhere.[58] What is less frequently observed is that women testifying in this capacity acted as gatekeepers of sexual reputation and community belonging. Although older, married women were called upon to inspect the bodies of women suspected to be pregnant outside wedlock, men more routinely policed extramarital sex in both official and unofficial capacities.[59] But in defamation suits, women were often required to comment on more than just the words spoken. They reported the extent of reputational damage caused when insults such as 'whore' were used, thereby policing the reputations and social standing of the defamed and influencing the boundaries of social inclusion. Legal agency for women was limited but they weren't prohibited from litigating or testifying in any type of suit. Where legal conventions circumscribed participation, they found other ways to be heard.

Witnessing across the life cycle

Some women (and men) were more likely to be heard than others. Youth made a compelling case for testimony to be discredited.[60] In 1637, John Pearse of Bradninch (Devon) reminded the court that witness Clement Salter 'is now very young in yeeres', while John Smith described him as 'a very poore youth'.[61] Female witnesses were on average 39 years old, while men were typically six years older. The youngest and very oldest members of society were seldom witnesses. At the age of 10, John Gotan of Newton Abbott (Devon) was the youngest witness recorded and far from typical.[62] Centenarian witnesses were also rare. Nicholas Cornworthie of Halberton (Devon) far exceeded life expectancy, testifying in 1570 at the ripe age of 103.[63] While litigants' ages were not recorded, each deponent's approximate age was set down by the court notary, often as a multiple of five or ten years. Almost half of

---

[57] GA, GDR/114, William Clifford v Mary Belcher (1612).
[58] Haigh, 'Slander and the Church Courts', 1–13; Gowing, *Domestic Dangers*, chapter 2; Ingram, *Church Courts*, chapter 10; Shepard, 'Worthless Witnesses?', 732.
[59] On policing pregnant unmarried women's bodies, see Laura Gowing, *Common Bodies: Women, Sex, and Reproduction in Seventeenth Century England* (New Haven, 2003), p. 71.
[60] Gowing, *Domestic Dangers*, p. 50; Shepard, *Accounting for Oneself*, p. 133.
[61] DHC, Chanter 866, Alice Stephens v Caleb Saunders (1637).
[62] DHC, Chanter 855a, Alice Tremyll v Richard Bolle (1564).
[63] DHC, Chanter 857, John Pyle and Thomas Sweteland v Robert Whytefylld (1570).

recorded ages ended in zero.[64] Decadal thresholds (20, 30, 40 and so on) were most common among those over 40.[65] Those in their 20s were much more evenly dispersed across the range 20–29. Notaries frequently captured an impression of age for older witnesses, while ages of the young were recorded more precisely.

As Table 1.5 shows, the youngest and oldest witnesses testified in small numbers, except in tithe cases where those over 60 appeared regularly. In these cases, they were recorded in almost equal numbers to those in the 25–44 age bracket (containing the largest proportion of witnesses). Long residence in a parish signalled authority but this was explicitly gendered. Men acquired status and authority as they aged; older women could be perceived as 'a source of trouble'.[66] Women comprised 16 per cent of witnesses overall, but just 9 per cent of those aged 60 and over. At the same time, women represented almost a third of all witnesses under 25.[67] Gender discrimination was clearly at play, but it was less pronounced for the youngest witnesses (who themselves were heavily subtracted from the witness pool). Shepard attributed this pattern elsewhere to female servants' participation in matrimonial, defamation, and sexual incontinence cases.[68] As I show later in this chapter, female servants *were* primarily involved in these disputes. But gender difference was less marked for the under 25s in *every* type of suit brought to court. Given that youth and femininity are usually pronounced factors in discrimination, possessing both characteristics limited the exercise of authority as a witness less than we might think.

Unsurprisingly, younger witnesses also tended to be unmarried. While single life wasn't a bar to accruing social capital, marriage was nonetheless an important milestone that bestowed status.[69] It turned men into householders and patriarchs who ruled over the household-family, and it opened doors to local standing as officeholders.[70] While a married woman forfeited ownership of her assets under coverture laws, marriage nevertheless came with the management of her own household and elevated social capital within the neighbourhood.[71] In church courts, marital status was only systematically recorded for female witnesses. Labels included 'wife' and 'widow', with a broader lexicon used to describe never married

---

[64] Percentages in each court: Bath & Wells (43); Exeter (48); Gloucester (45); Hereford (50); Winchester (51).

[65] See also L. R. Poos, *A Rural Society after the Black Death, Essex 1350–1525* (Cambridge, 1991), p. 193; Keith Thomas, 'Numeracy in Early Modern England', *TRHS* 37 (1987), 103–32 at 126; Alexandra Shepard and Judith Spicksley, 'Worth, Age, and Social Status in Early Modern England', *EcHR* 64 (2010), 493–530 at 498.

[66] Gowing, *Domestic Dangers*, p. 50.

[67] Similar patterns are found in London, where more than half of church court witnesses under 25 were women. See ibid., p. 50. For elsewhere, see Shepard, *Accounting for Oneself*, p. 22.

[68] Shepard, *Accounting for Oneself*, p. 22.

[69] On single women and social capital, see Froide, *Never Married*, esp. chapter 5.

[70] On office-holding, see Henry R. French, *The Middle Sort of People in Provincial England, 1600–1750* (Oxford, 2008), p. 108.

[71] Bernard Capp, *When Gossips Meet: Women, Family, and Neighbourhood in Early Modern England* (Oxford, 2003), p. 25.

	Under 25						25–44						45–59						60+					
	M		F		All		M		F		All		M		F		All		M		F		All	
	N	%	N	%	N	%	N	%	N	%	N	%	N	%	N	%	N	%	N	%	N	%	N	%
Bath & Wells	661	67	328	33	989	11	3,276	82	710	18	3,986	45	1,858	86	298	14	2,156	24	1,542	89	182	11	1,724	19
Exeter	445	70	192	30	637	10	2,442	86	412	14	2,854	46	1,435	90	158	10	1,593	25	1,085	91	103	8	1,188	19
Gloucester	438	66	229	34	667	10	2,261	81	518	19	2,779	42	1,375	87	210	13	1,585	24	1,372	89	171	11	1,543	23
Hereford	48	66	25	34	73	9	260	79	69	21	329	40	156	88	21	12	177	22	219	91	22	9	241	29
Winchester	191	71	80	30	271	8	1,516	90	177	11	1,693	47	838	92	73	8	911	25	652	93	46	7	698	20
Defamation	697	61	441	39	1,138	16	2,756	74	970	26	3,726	53	1,052	77	319	23	1,371	20	589	80	152	21	741	11
Illicit sex	140	67	70	33	210	13	651	81	154	19	805	50	327	83	66	17	393	24	185	89	23	11	208	13
Matrimonial	217	66	112	34	329	12	1,192	85	212	15	1,404	52	545	87	79	13	624	23	298	84	59	17	357	13
Testamentary	203	60	133	40	336	8	1,486	82	337	19	1,823	44	1,008	87	149	13	1,157	28	667	83	137	17	804	20
Tithes	384	88	54	12	438	6	2,602	96	107	4	2,709	35	2,030	96	76	4	2,106	28	2,339	97	79	3	2,418	32
Other	92	73	34	27	126	5	810	90	91	10	901	37	588	91	61	9	649	27	671	91	64	9	735	31
Total	1,733	67	844	33	2,577		9,497	84	1,871	16	11,368		5,550	88	750	12	6,300		4,749	90	514	10	5,263	

Table 1.5 Age distribution of male and female witnesses

women: 'singlewoman', 'spinster', 'maiden', and the Latin *ancilla, puella,* and *virgo.* Unmarried women were sometimes described in relation to their fathers: in 1572, 20-year-old Joan Fremantell of Romsey (Hampshire) was labelled 'the daughter of John Fremantell'.[72] Terminology shifted and this descriptor disappeared from depositions after 1611, marking a subtle change in how the legal position of a never married female witness was framed. Being 'the daughter of' aligned an unmarried woman's status with her father's, whereas 'singlewoman' (and equivalents) denoted a self-supporting unmarried woman (being a 'wife' or 'widow', meanwhile, aligned her status with her (late) husband's).

Recording of marital status was patchy. It accompanied less than a third of female names in the Exeter court, while scribes in the Bath & Wells and Hereford courts were more diligent: marital status was recorded for 90 per cent of female witnesses. Overall, around 50 per cent of female witnesses were married (Table 1.6). Proportions of never married women varied considerably, though this group was probably most affected by under-recording. Where marital status was particularly under-recorded, proportions of never married women were especially low. In other words, marital status was more routinely recorded in these courts when the woman was married or widowed. Less than 1 per cent of female witnesses in the Exeter court were recorded as singlewomen compared with 28 per cent of women in the Hereford court (where marital status was systematically recorded). Accounting for under-reporting, between 25 and 30 per cent of all female witnesses were likely never married.[73] Shepard suggested that it was their household connections that explain singlewomen's frequent appearance in court (i.e. servants testifying for their masters and mistresses). She found up to 70 per cent of all singlewomen were servants. But as Table 1.6 shows, *much* lower

	Bath & Wells		Exeter		Gloucester		Hereford		Winchester		All courts	
	N	%	N	%	N	%	N	%	N	%	N	%
Married	871	52	213	24	609	52	67	48	225	55	1,985	46
Never married	413	25	3	<0	172	15	40	28	21	5	649	15
(of whom servants)	(163)	(40)	—	—	(51)	(30)	(11)	(28)	(8)	(38)	—	—
Widow	216	13	51	6	172	15	21	15	56	14	516	12
Unspecified	169	10	624	70	221	19	13	9	105	26	1,132	26
Total	1,669		891		1,174		141		407		4,282	

Table 1.6 Marital status of female witnesses

[72] HRO, 21M65/C3/5, George Barton v Margaret Jenvye (1571–2).
[73] Some of the sample jurisdictions studied by Shepard (Chichester and Lewes, and York) recorded similar proportions to the courts here. See Shepard, 'Worthless Witnesses?', 724.

proportions of singlewomen were servants in the five courts of this study. The testimonies of singlewomen were therefore *not* primarily generated through the (coercive) bonds of the servant–master relationship. I return to the capacity in which servants testified in the second half of this chapter.

Means to testify

If occupational descriptors are to be believed, old age was no bar to labour, women rarely worked, and men never juggled multiple jobs. Elderly men are routinely listed in depositions with occupations: we find the testimonies of William Sevye, a 78-year-old mariner in Devon, Richard Wall, a 97-year-old husbandman in Gloucestershire, and Richard Averall, a 90-year-old labourer in Herefordshire.[74] Of 4,282 female witnesses, only two were listed with an occupational descriptor: bonelace maker Grace King of Yeovil and seamster Melisia Beale of Kingsdon (Somerset).[75] And John Boye of Selworthy (Somerset) was one of only a handful of witnesses to proffer two occupations: as a weaver 'and using husbandrie also'.[76]

This picture doesn't chime with the realities of working life. Ninety-year-old men were rarely *active* husbandmen and labourers. Rather, their stated occupations harked back to a past life, serving as a reminder of their social status.[77] Grace and Melisia *weren't* the only working women in early modern England. In a reversal of the trend we saw earlier in which only *female* marital status was recorded in court depositions, occupational descriptors were reserved almost exclusively for men. Women's work was extensive and varied but descriptors rarely invite its study. John Boye's multitasking *wasn't* unusual. William Mark of St Issey (Cornwall), for example, was recorded as a tailor in 1599, and only when pressed about his working life by opposing witnesses did he add that 'sometymes when he lackethe worke he gothe to husbandrie'.[78] The temporary, sometimes volatile and often shifting conditions of labour are not captured by occupational descriptors. Nor can they tell us everything about the nature of work. It is difficult, for example, to know whether a mercer (textile dealer) produced the cloth he sold, or whether an apothecary made the drugs that were available in his store.

---

[74] DHC, Chanter 856, Thomas Yonge v William Fox (1569); GA, GDR/57, Nicholas Lewes and George Turner v Humfrey Roberts (1584); HARC, HD4/2/13, John Richardson v William Mare (1628).

[75] SHC, D/D/cd/65, Marie Bashiler v Joanna Hilson (1629); D/D/cd/55, Lucy Seymor v Florence Hilborne (1620).

[76] SHC, D/D/cd/5, Griffen v William Tuppe (1599).

[77] For example, see Margaret Pelling, 'Old Age, Poverty, and Disability in Early Modern Norwich: Work, Remarriage, and Other Expedients', in Margaret Pelling and Richard Smith (eds), *Life, Death and the Elderly: Historical Perspectives* (1991), pp. 74–101 at 82.

[78] DHC, Chanter 855, Lucas Betty v Elena Payne (1559); Lucas Betty v Richard Bennett (1559). Shepard notes that occupational descriptors do not always match work tasks. See Shepard, *Accounting for Oneself*, pp. 149–50.

Despite these inherent challenges, occupational descriptors do allow systematic study of 'the social reach of the overall data set' (at least with reference to men).[79] They tell us something about how male witnesses made a living and self-fashioned occupational identity. Occupations are collected here for over 17,000 male witnesses (see Table 1.7). Labourers, butchers, smiths, clothiers, husbandmen, and gentlemen all testified. Husbandmen were abundant, comprising around 42 per cent of all male witnesses. Almost half the men who testified worked in agriculture (husbandmen, yeomen, and farmers), reflecting the countryside setting of most disputes. The regional importance of the cloth trade is also evident: between 60 and 70 per cent of men engaged in crafts, trades, and retail carried out work connected with cloth and leather. Weavers alone comprised 31 per cent of all occupations listed in this category. This wasn't a court of gentlemen, nor of the poor, but men from both walks of life testified. These were the men that female servants worked for and alongside.

Different archives capture traces of different 'types' of working lives. Though occupational descriptors are a blunt measure of occupational structure, comparison with two other data sets – wills made and proven in the Prerogative Court of Canterbury (PCC) between 1653 and 1660, and a 1608 muster roll from Gloucester – suggests that church courts summoned a broad cross-section of society as witnesses (see Table A.1). The wealthy were slightly more prominent as will-makers than as deponents, while labourers and servants (who seldom lodged wills in the PCC) more routinely appear in the muster roll than as witnesses. It is true that those with the lowest earning potential infrequently testified: just 245 male witnesses (a little over 1 per cent) self-identified as labourers. But as I've shown, the church court was a site in which social status was performed, scrutinised, and then contested, and early modern occupations were not rigidly defined. The labourer might masquerade as a husbandman (a particularly sticky occupational descriptor), hoping the opposing party wouldn't challenge it.[80] The adversarial nature of disputes encouraged exaggeration, after all.[81] Interrogatory questions about wealth raised by defendants against opposing witnesses also indicate that the poor – an imprecise group comprising labourers and those on parish relief – *did* testify. Their relative poverty was 'not a bar to inclusion', even if their authority came under attack.[82]

---

[79] Shepard, *Accounting for Oneself*, p. 19.
[80] On labourers as husbandmen in court, see Shepard, *Accounting for Oneself*, p. 247.
[81] Stretton, 'Women, Legal Records', 688.
[82] Shepard, *Accounting for Oneself*, p. 118.

	Bath & Wells		Exeter		Gloucester		Hereford		Winchester		All courts	
	N	%	N	%	N	%	N	%	N	%	N	%
Agriculture	4,552	62	774	48	2,644	54	401	62	1,709	60	10,080	58
Husbandmen	3,408		658		1,720		180		1,362		7,328	
Labourers	27		44		130		20		24		245	
Yeomen and farmers	1,097		72		771		200		300		2,440	
Other	20		—		23		1		23		67	
Clergy	305	4	106	7	225	5	40	6	108	4	784	5
Crafts/trades/retail	1,768	24	337	21	1,328	27	84	13	744	26	4,261	25
Building and construction	107		25		45		3		23		203	
Cloth and leather	1,091		236		880		48		454		2,709	
Food and drink	238		30		152		10		99		529	
Smiths and makers	332		46		251		23		169		821	
Gentlemen	352	5	181	11	333	7	110	17	138	5	1,114	6
Mariners and fishermen	24	<1	29	2	39	1	—	—	23	1	115	1
Merchants, professions and officials	100	1	35	2	38	1	8	1	52	2	233	1
Mining and quarrying	57	1	19	1	19	<1	—	—	5	<1	100	1
Miscellaneous and unidentified occupations	2	<1	2	<1	2	<1	1	<1	3	<1	10	<1
Servants and apprentices	87	1	119	7	200	4	4	1	26	1	436	3
Service sector	74	1	12	1	40	1	—	—	39	1	165	1
Total	7,321		1,614		4,868		648		2,847		17,298	
No occupation given	711		3,921		759		195		884		6,470	

Table 1.7 Occupations of male witnesses

Note: Percentages given are the total number of male witnesses listed with an occupation.

Depositions tell us how authority and credibility mapped onto demographic attributes. Much less ink was spilled transcribing the words of the labouring poor, the young, the unmarried, or women in these courts. The perceived suitability of a witness was age-related, gendered, and linked to marital status. Men acquired influence as they aged, while less stock was placed in the words of older women. Being married was a hallmark of authority within a community. But young unmarried men and women *were* selected as church court witnesses. Some were simply in the right place at the right time to hear defamatory words or a will being made. They witnessed by chance. But like their older, married counterparts, single young people offered others forms of testimony that marked them as authorities on custom, social practice, and the transgressions of their neighbours. Depositions richly document the lives of those whose attributes placed them in categories that weren't quantitatively significant. Legal agency *was* limited, but socially marginal groups testified in numbers large enough to study and their presence reminds us of their social and economic significance. It is to female servants – ubiquitous but apparently unimportant in court if their gender, status, age, and marital status is anything to go on – that we now turn.

Female servants in the church courts

Identification

Scattered through the thousands of pages of court depositions are 1,093 female servants – the largest group studied to date. This includes women who were in service at the time of testifying, those who had formerly served, and some who were probably still in service but whose depositions reflected on past experiences. They appear as plaintiffs, defendants, and witnesses and are also mentioned in passing by other deponents (see Table 1.8). They account for less than 4 per cent of female litigants (186 of 4,873) and 13 per cent of female witnesses (540 of 4,281). A separate, relatively large group of 367 female servants had no formal legal role but were referred to by other witnesses.

Meticulously combing through these records is the only way to systematically pull these women from the archive. Time-consuming and laborious, identifying them is no easy feat. They are hidden in plain sight because 'servant' was used with caution in legal documents. Writing in 1604, legal scholar William West set out the occupations and titles that were appropriate for inclusion in court indictments: 'Duke, marques, earle, vi[s]co[u]nt, archbishop, bishop, knight, servant at the law … baron, esquier, gentleman' were all good inclusions, as were 'alderman, doctor, archdeacon, deane, parson, parish clarke, widow, singlewoman' and 'marchant, grocer, tailer, shoomaker, tanner, currier, broker, husbandman,

	Bath & Wells		Exeter		Gloucester		Hereford		Winchester		All courts	
	N	*%*	*N*	*%*	*N*	*%*	*N*	*%*	*N*	*%*	*N*	*%*
Plaintiff	37	*14*	25	*18*	33	*16*	1	*7*	23	*23*	119	*16*
Defendant	19	*7*	18	*13*	16	*8*	—	—	14	*14*	67	*9*
Witness	207	*79*	98	*70*	159	*76*	14	*93*	62	*63*	540	*74*
(Famula)	*(4)*		*(9)*		*(50)*		—		*(2)*		*(65)*	
(Ancilla)	*(30)*		—		—		—		—		*(30)*	
(Serva)	—		—		—		—		*(19)*		*(19)*	
(Serviens)	*(3)*		*(6)*		*(8)*		—		*(1)*		*(18)*	
Total	**263**		**141**		**208**		**15**		**99**		**726**	
Referred to	*140*		*73*		*106*		*12*		*36*		*367*	

Table 1.8 Female servants in church court depositions (by court and role in case)

ostler, habberdasher, miller, draper, goldsmith, butcher, chapman, labourer, spinster, and every other addition of any lawful occupations'. But, he argued, '[s]ervant, butler, etc. are *not*, for that they are common to gentlemen, yeomen etc. and *so incertein*'.[83]

The perennial problem of 'incertein' terminology looms large. Close affinity to the plaintiff or defendant made witnesses objectionable in court and complaints were routinely raised against litigants who called on their biological kin, servants, or apprentices as witnesses.[84] In common law proceedings, servants were often not called servants. To be 'the servant of' invoked legal dependency on a master; the phrase could thereby implicate masters in their servants' transgressions. 'Labourer', 'groom', or 'husbandman' for male servants, and 'spinster' for their female counterparts, were preferred alternatives in both secular and ecclesiastical courts.[85]

Just a quarter of female servant witnesses in this study were identifiable because 'servant' (typically expressed in Latin as *famula, serviens, serva*, and *ancilla*) was recorded in the biographical introduction to their deposition. Practices and terminology varied regionally, but *famula* was favoured by church court scribes, as Table 1.8 shows. It appeared consistently between 1549 and 1618 but began to slide out of usage in the seventeenth century.[86] The Bath & Wells and Exeter court

[83] William West, *The Second Part of Symboleography* (1604), p. 94v. Italics my own.
[84] Henry Conset, *The Practice of the Spiritual or Ecclesiastical Courts to which is added a brief discourse of the structure and manner of forming the libel or declaration* (1685), p. 115.
[85] Whittle, *Development of Agrarian Capitalism*, p. 261.
[86] *Ancilla* was used as early as 1569 in the Bath & Wells court, but predominantly between 1606 and 1616, appearing once again in 1648. *Serviens* was almost exclusively a sixteenth-century term. *Serva* was restricted to the Winchester court where few post-1600 depositions survive.

scribes applied these descriptors less readily and there is no evidence of their use in the Hereford court.[87] The etymology of these Latin descriptors underscores uncertainties around the servant–master labour contract and what a servant *was* in early modern England. *Famula, serviens, serva,* and *ancilla* are all generally translated to 'servant' in this period, though classically they were part of the Roman language of enslavement.[88] Vestiges of unfreedom are embedded in the language of service, and though early modern service was not slavery, I argue in this book that unfreedom nonetheless continued to underpin some experiences. *Ancilla* experienced an interesting linguistic shift that makes it particularly difficult to define with certainty.[89] Three overlapping definitions existed in late medieval England: a general female servant; a woman hired to attend a woman of rank; and simply a young maiden.[90] *Ancilla* was only used in the Somerset court, describing fifty-nine women. Thirty were identifiable as general servants but it was also assigned to women living with kin: in 1606, *ancilla* Agnes Prickett of Pensford lived with her mother, and in 1616 *ancilla* Katherine Grimstead of Burnham-on-Sea lived with her grandfather.[91] Women *were* hired to serve their families, but only *ancillas* whose servant status is clear in the depositions are counted among the servant population here.

For three-quarters of female servant depositions, it is *not* the biographical preamble that tells us they were servants. Most were simply listed as 'singlewomen'. And for litigants and women mentioned contextually (with no biographical introduction), all we have is a name. Instead, we find clues in the text of the depositions themselves: those who referred to a master or mistress or described themselves (or were identified by others) as servants can be labelled 'servant' with confidence. Only those who meet these criteria have found their way into this book, meaning some female servants necessarily fall through the cracks. Not all single women were servants and sometimes labour relationships are unclear. A young woman living outside her parents' home is indicative *but not proof of* her servant status. In 1638, 19-year-old Elizabeth Comb of Exeter (Devon) deposed that 'she liveth in howse with Jane Comb ... but is no kynne unto her', despite the shared surname.[92] Elizabeth may have been Jane's servant, but she equally could have been a lodger, paying for bed and board with the profits of work carried out at her own hands.

---

[87] This is unsurprising in the Exeter court where occupational descriptors were sporadically recorded.
[88] Chakravarty, *Fictions of Consent*, p. 9.
[89] Ibid., p. 54.
[90] P. J. P. Goldberg, 'What Was a Servant?', in Anne Curry and Elizabeth Matthew (eds), *Concepts and Patterns of Service in the Later Middle Ages* (Woodbridge, 2000), pp. 1–20 at 3–6. Cordelia Beattie found *ancilla* used as an occupational descriptor in medieval poll tax returns. See Cordelia Beattie, *Medieval Single Women: The Politics of Social Classification in Late Medieval England* (Oxford, 2007), p. 81.
[91] SHC, D/D/cd/30, John Lighte and Phyllis Lighte v Margaret Poole (1606); D/D/cd/48, Richard Jones v Jane Browne (1616).
[92] DHC, Chanter 866, Jane Comb v Anne Lichfield (1638).

Excluding women like Elizabeth means that no assumptions are made about service; the women of this book were all described as female servants.

Participation

The servant witness

To take the largest group first, almost three-quarters of female servants participating in the courts were witnesses. An unsettling legal tension skirts the edges of their appearance. On the one hand, they weren't ideal witnesses. On the other, the ties that underpinned their dependency on masters and mistresses could be mobilised in court. Unequal power relations could be exploited, raising the question of how far servant testimonies were extracted through coercion or bribery. This tension, too, mirrors the social problem of service represented in contemporary literature: that the servant was simultaneously part of the home and family as well as an outsider, an alien, who could easily compromise and challenge the family structure.[93] I have shown that testifying was not always a free choice. Some came to court voluntarily, but an unknown number were compelled to give evidence by court citation or the provocation of a litigant party. Was to demand testimony from one's servant to automatically receive it?

Ability to testify freely was challenged frequently in court, and witnesses were regularly asked about their labour relationship to those for whom they testified. Elizabeth Snarlinge of Coberley (Gloucestershire) was emphatic in 1639 that despite serving the plaintiff, she would 'not forswear herselfe (god assisting her) but will speake ye truthe'.[94] Jane Hewes of Norton (Gloucestershire) hinted at the hierarchy of bad witnesses in 1629: she admitted that she was servant to the plaintiff but added that she 'is not of in any degree of kindred to him'.[95] The household-family contained bonds of different strengths; as an enemy within, a servant could more freely discredit, expose, and spoil the reputation of her master or mistress than biological kin might.[96]

In practice, servants regularly testified for their masters and mistresses: Joanna Iago of Poundstock (Cornwall) testified in 1580 that she had heard Elizabeth Markes call Mrs Sidwell Callerd, her mistress, an 'arrant whore and curtayle whore'. She added that her mistress's 'good name must needs be the worse for speaking of the words ... because the sayd Mris Callerd was ever ... taken for an honest gentlewoman'.[97] Table 1.9 indicates the capacity in which

---

[93] Chakravarty, *Fictions of Consent*, p. 92.
[94] GA, GDR/204, Eleanor Mills v Anna Smith (1639).
[95] GA, GDR/168, John Greaves jun v Charles Cartwright (1629).
[96] As Carolyn Steedman notes, servants were part of the family-unit, not the family itself. See Carolyn Steedman, *Labours Lost: Domestic Service and the Making of Modern England* (Cambridge, 2009), p. 19.
[97] DHC, Chanter 860, Sidwell Callerd v Elizabeth Markes (1580).

	Bath & Wells		Exeter		Gloucester		Hereford		Winchester		All courts	
	N	%	N	%	N	%	N	%	N	%	N	%
Current master/mistress is litigant	33	17	25	27	41	27	2	17	15	25	116	23
Testifying for	24		17		34		1		11		87	
Testifying against	4		3		1		—		1		9	
Unknown	5		5		6		1		3		20	
Former master/mistress is litigant	44	22	21	22	37	25	3	25	17	28	122	24
Testifying for	24		12		20		2		12		70	
Testifying against	18		3		7		1		2		31	
Unknown	2		6		10		—		3		21	
Master/mistress is not litigant	120	61	48	51	72	48	7	58	29	48	276	54
Total	197		94		150		12		61		514	

Table 1.9 Capacity in which female servant witnesses testified (by court)

Note: Only includes data where the relationship between servant and litigant can be established.

female servants testified. In just under 50 per cent of instances, they had served one of the litigant parties and most frequently testified *for* rather than *against* them (on 91 per cent of occasions). Discussing slavery, Saidiya Hartman suggested that liberty was not absolute upon being manumitted; instead, a form of 'indebted servitude' played out between master and former slave that relied on obligation and indebtedness.[98] That 69 per cent of former servants testified *on behalf of* those they had once served indicates that obligation did not simply disappear upon departure. The statistics bind servants to those who hired them, though coercion is harder to substantiate.

In cases of marital breakdown, servants' impetus to testify on behalf of former mistresses is apparent. Although these cases were infrequently heard in the courts, mistresses almost always procured testimony from their former female servants, indicating the unique position a servant held in observing the dynamics of her host family. In 1611, four women testified against their former master, Thomas Mathewe of Cheltenham (Gloucestershire), whom they charged with spousal abuse. No other witnesses testified, and these depositions do not appear to have been extracted coercively, as all four servants had already left the couple's service. It is likely that the servants testified out of compassion and care for their former mistress.[99]

But the chance of testifying *against* a master or mistress clearly increased after service had ended: 31 per cent of former servant witnesses testified against their past employers while virtually nobody testified against their masters or mistresses while they were still in service. In 1592, Joanne Powell of Broad Marston (Gloucestershire) claimed her mistress, Alice Richmond, had made her tell a lie about one of her neighbours. As the tale unravelled, Joanne 'did exclayme & crye out against her [Alice], saying she had undone her & had procured her to affirme an untruth'.[100] Capacity for coercion in a mistress–servant relationship was acknowledged here, but the neighbour acquitted Joanne of culpability by bringing her to court to testify *against* her mistress. The plaintiff snapped the cord that tethered this servant's reputation to her mistress's (but also, presumably, eliminated Joanne's prospects of being retained in Alice's service). Departure from service appears to have given women greater freedom and power to object to injustices experienced during service. Notably, servant witnesses often testified to sexual abuse they had suffered at the hands of their former masters.

Testimony was therefore constrained by labour relations.[101] All sorts of social and economic ties and obligations underlie court depositions but they are

---

[98] Saidiya Hartman, *Scenes of Subjection: Terror, Slavery, and Self-Making in Nineteenth-Century America* (New York, 1997), pp. 131–2. See also Chakravarty, *Fictions of Consent*, p. 196.
[99] GA, GDR/114, Elizabeth Mathewe v Thomas Mathewe (1611).
[100] GA, GDR/65, John Yate v Alice Richmond (1592).
[101] See Taylor, 'Price of the Poor's Words', pp. 828–47.

only sometimes visible. Even when a servant testified for someone outside the household, her testimony was not always freely given. Mary Maylard of Yarpole (Herefordshire) testified in a defamation suit in 1629. She had served neither litigant, but one opposing witness objected to her deposition on the grounds that her master, George Wall, 'is a mortall enemie unto Thomas Dirry [the plaintiff's husband]' and 'did cause the said Mary Maylard his servant to come to depose in this cause against the said Jane Dirry'.[102] Expectations to support masters and mistresses didn't even dissolve upon their deaths. Testamentary suits brought testimony from women who had served the testator. In many of these cases, they testified on the behalf of the children or relatives of their deceased masters or mistresses. In return, servants could be beneficiaries in the wills of those they had served: Emmeline Sturt of Burnham-on-Sea (Somerset) was bequeathed a smock and a kerchief by her dying mistress in 1616 and came to testify in court a year after her death.[103] Sometimes, mutual obligation was more obvious between servants and surviving relatives, who as I show in Chapter 5, might take these servants into their own homes. Benefits to testifying complicate the question of coercion. Rather than being compelled to testify, servants might seek reward or gain in deposing in their master's or mistress's suit. Financial gain has been the focus of work on perjury, but indirect or less tangible benefits could also secure a servant's testimony. In defamation cases, for instance, where household reputation was at stake, a servant's voice was a natural contribution to the team of witnesses assembled in its defence; after all, as quasi family members, the repute of the household was also their own.

Freedom to testify was provisional and deeply contingent on the extent to which the female servant was yoked to her master and his household. For some, freedoms could be negotiated. In many cases, too, female servants came to testify outside the immediate orbit of the household. In defamation cases, they routinely testified to cross words exchanged in streets and houses by their neighbours (as Figure 1.2 shows). They testified in matrimonial suits, supporting male and female friends and kin whose marriage plans had gone awry. The networks in which they rooted themselves were not just networks of coercion. Table 1.9 shows that in 54 per cent of cases female servants testified on behalf of litigants who were *not* their masters or mistresses. It was not the master–servant bond that compelled many to testify in court. Like other women, female servants were go-betweens in a couple's relationship, delivering messages and gifts. They were embedded in social and economic communities across places in which they had lived and worked. They participated in cultures of reciprocity, mutual support, and exchange like other members of early modern society. I return to their networks in Chapter 8.

---

[102] HARC, HD4/2/13, Jane Dirry v Sybil Francke (1629).
[103] SHC, D/D/cd/50, William Sim and Joanna Sim v William Sim (1617).

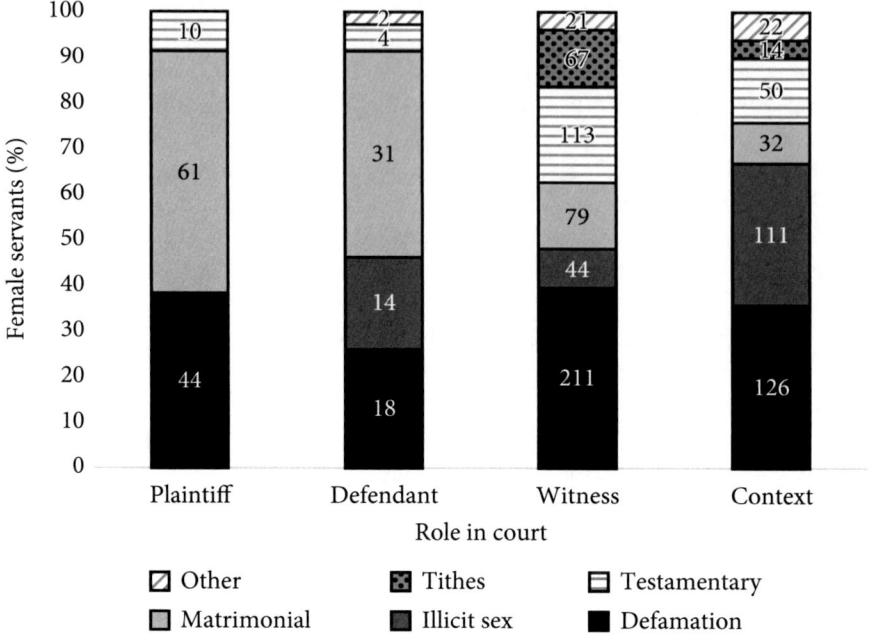

Figure 1.2 Distribution of female servants across litigation

The litigating servant

While almost 50 per cent of women recorded in church court depositions were plaintiffs and defendants, only a quarter of female servants appeared as litigants (see Table 1.8). The cost of litigation perhaps prohibited female servants from pursuing court suits, but some poor servants *did* litigate and we should be wary of assuming all female servants were poor.[104] Rather, the low number of female servant litigants is partly a fiction of the records. A plaintiff's or defendant's gender is easier to identify than her occupation, and some female litigants are likely to be unidentified servants.

When female servants litigated, their suits overwhelmingly concerned marriage and defamation. As plaintiffs, they sought legal action to recover their social standing when insults such as 'whore' or accusations of extramarital sex were bandied around. They rallied the testimonies of their neighbours, families,

---

[104] Gowing found that London litigation cost between £1 and £10. See Gowing, *Domestic Dangers*, p. 48. Those worth less than £5 could be exempt from fees but it's unclear how common *in forma pauperis* prosecutions were in the church courts. See F. D. Price, 'The Administration of the Diocese of Gloucester, 1547–1579' (Unpublished thesis, University of Oxford, 1939), p. 37.

masters, mistresses, and friends as they faced the loss of an imagined post-service married life and sometimes the additional concern of a child born out of wedlock. Their appearance as litigants represented a crisis point in their lives but this does not make them atypical servants (nor atypical litigants). The concerns that servants expressed through litigating were shared with other women in service who *didn't* litigate in the courts.

Although some men and women never married, marriage was seen as a gateway to full adult life.[105] Depositions capture some servants on this threshold. Like Marie Brimpton, whom we met at the beginning of this chapter, over half of female servant plaintiffs were in pursuit of men they claimed had reneged on a promise of marriage. These were high-stakes suits with mixed results. Verdicts scarcely survive, and out-of-court settlements were common, making outcomes difficult to trace. Almost twice as many female servants were plaintiffs as defendants, although this disparity likely reflects the challenges of female servant identification. Masters and mistresses frequently testified for their female servants in these suits, often outlining their working relationship: in 1556, Richard Yeat of Woodbury (Devon) recalled John Wyllys asking for permission 'that he might marye with *his mayde*'.[106] By contrast, not all defendants brought witnesses of their own, reducing opportunities for their servant status to be revealed. The testimonies of masters and mistresses on behalf of their servants in this capacity highlight the other side of the servant–master relationship. Cynically, their testimonies were simply a strategy to protect the household's reputation, which might be stained by a failed match. More generously, the affective bonds of a much-loved household member and the responsibility to secure them an appropriate marriage brought them to court.

Female servants were typically single women, and damage to their reputations was costly. Defamation cases unsurprisingly accounted for the highest number of women in service recorded across the depositions (35 per cent). Due to the same recording inconsistencies, they were recorded more frequently as plaintiffs than as defendants. Almost all forty-four of the female servant plaintiffs sought restitution against false accusations of sex outside marriage, founded either on slanderous speech or hearsay of an illicit liaison. Most defamation cases involving female servant plaintiffs are similar in form and content to the thousands brought by other women. But occasionally, accusations specific to servants surfaced. In 1610, Anne Norris of Wells (Somerset) litigated against her neighbour Elizabeth Clutterbuck. Anne had once been the servant of innkeeper Thomas Norris and his wife and

---

[105] Between 1575 and 1700, an estimated 20 per cent of men and women never married. See Froide, *Never Married*, p. 6; E. A. Wrigley and R. S. Schofield, *The Population History of England 1541–1871: A Reconstruction* (1981), pp. 255–65; David R. Weir, 'Rather Never than Late: Celibacy and Age at Marriage in English Cohort Fertility', *Journal of Family History* 9 (1984), 340–54 at 346.
[106] DHC, Chanter 855, Margerie Awstyn v John Wyllys (1556).

('upon good liking', according to one witness) she had married her master when her mistress died. Together, they now ran the Sign of the Hart in Wells. When Elizabeth allegedly called Anne a 'scandall' and directed her to 'goe fall to thye old occupation', it emerged that Anne's successful marriage and departure from service was not taken with 'good liking' by all.[107] Transition to married life could be difficult, and not just for those whose flimsy betrothals fell apart before banns could be read or ceremonies held. The relationship between master and servant could prompt social discontent, in this case when a servant moved up in the household's hierarchy from 'servant' to 'wife'.

Preservation of sexual reputation invariably lay behind the defamation suits that female servants pursued. But only in a handful of depositions do we find them accused by the court of illicit sex. As I showed earlier in this chapter, pregnancy constituted clear proof of premarital sex for women, making witness testimony immaterial in their prosecution. Close examination of the fourteen illicit sex cases with female servants named as defendants confirms the limited circumstances that led to their prosecution and infrequent appearance as defendants in the deposition books. In nine cases, no witnesses were produced; only the defendant's response to the allegation (which invariably amounted to a confession of guilt) was required. The remaining five cases all have peculiarities. A 1605 suit against servant Agnes Wood of Sampford Brett (Somerset) prompted the testimonies of seven witnesses. But extramarital sex was but one of a litany of her alleged offences. Thomas Blinman claimed she 'did piss in a glasse and gave it to men to drinke'. Others disparaged her for living apart from her husband and claimed that while he was 'a plaine countrie man', she dressed like a gentlewoman. The extent of Agnes's 'misbehaviour' likely explains the production of witnesses in this case.[108] Two cases centred on pregnant servants who had evaded detection by crossing county boundaries. Three of the seven witnesses who testified against widowed servant Mary Wyeman (alias Carpenter) of Newent (Gloucestershire) in 1616 lived outside the county and deposed that Mary had 'come into Monmouth sheere greate with child' over a year earlier to be delivered. Slipping away from Gloucestershire, Mary had concealed her pregnancy and the baby later had died. The court was therefore reliant on witness testimony to prove the offence.[109] In a 1610 Somerset case, just one witness from the parish of Chard testified to the illegitimate pregnancy of servant Edith Godwyn, but the offence was historic and Edith's whereabouts were unknown to the witness.[110]

As in defamation suits, a grudge occasionally prompted a female servant to be questioned over sexual deviance. In 1615, Elizabeth Gawen of Turkdean

---

[107] SHC, D/D/cd/43, Anne Norris v Elizabeth Clutterbuck (1610).
[108] SHC, D/D/cd/34, John Atwell v Agnes Wood (1605).
[109] GA, GDR/122, William Heywood v Mary Wyeman (1616).
[110] SHC, D/D/cd/130, Office v Edith Godwyn (1610).

(Gloucestershire) was accused of sex outside marriage with Robert Harris. The suit was pursued by her former mistress, Mrs Bannister, to (according to one witness) 'drive her [Elizabeth] out of the countrey because shee would not dwell with her any longer'.[111] A final case cited both a female servant, Joan Williams of Wanstrow (Somerset), and her alleged partner, Robert Comb, for living suspiciously together in 1632. It produced five witnesses who confirmed their affair. Significantly, no illegitimate child was recorded in this case; witnesses were called precisely *because* no offspring resulted from their union.[112] These cases were therefore relatively unusual in generating witness testimony. Proof typically lay in the servant's pregnancy, and those whose illicit relations *did not* result in the birth of an illegitimate child likely evaded prosecution.

Tarnished reputation was not the only impediment to a servant's future. Setting up a household also relied on economic means. A small number of women in service were litigants in testamentary suits. Former servants who had since married sought to claim or defend their right to promised bequests. Service also had a bearing on inheritance upon coming of age. In 1584, a dispute arose in the Bath & Wells court concerning the payment of legacies to Juliana Knorle (alias Hardinge). Juliana was a minor when her father died. Witnesses claimed Juliana had already received her entitlement from her father's will: she had been lodged, fed, and clothed in John Croydon's house, and several payments of money and goods were made at various points, including on her wedding day. But Juliana argued she had worked in John's service before marriage. She had received no wages and contended that the economic value of her labour sufficiently covered 'her meate and drinke and apparell'. Put simply, Juliana hadn't been an economic burden to him; her labour had benefited his household purse and had paid for her keep. She should, therefore, not be required to offer John part of her father's legacy in recompense.[113] The suit was a matter of both finance and principle.

We're used to thinking of service as constraining women's choices and that their poverty prevented them from acting on their own behalf. But those who litigated in church courts expressed concerns unconnected to their working lives. Their suits reveal anxieties about their futures, such as how to manage their economic and social position within communities. Often on the precipice of adulthood, these futures were perhaps more uncertain than those of their married counterparts, but no less important to protect. They sought legal action in court and found support from neighbours and friends who testified on their behalf. Many women who were litigated *against* lived not at the margins of society, but at its centre.

---

[111] GA, GDR/122, Robert Payne v Elizabeth Gawen (1615).
[112] SHC, D/D/cd/66, Office v Joan Williams and Robert Comb (1632).
[113] SHC, D/D/cd/17, John Croydon and William Hobbes v Juliana Knorle (alias Hardinge) (1584).

Shadowy servants

A third of the 1,093 female servants identified were neither litigants nor witnesses. Instead, they were referred to contextually by other witnesses, without having any formal legal role in the suit. In 1571, for example, Agnes Lovell of Alvington (Devon) was mentioned in her father's deposition. He told the court she had received 20 shillings from her former master, Roger Byrdwode, upon his death.[114] Elsewhere, these servant shadows appear in cases where men were accused of sexual deviance. They were named sexual partners and account for just under a third (111 of 367) of the 'referred to' female servants (see Figure 1.2). Occasionally, named and unnamed female servants were implicated in allegations of defamation. In 1567 in Fordingbridge (Hampshire), Ralph Winge made the following claim:

> Agnes Hindes, sarvannte to Gawen Barrow, was with childe the last sumer or ells my wiff was never with childe ... he ys a bawdy knave & hath lien with her xx [20] times.

Gawen Barrow unsurprisingly brought charges against him in the Winchester court.[115] But most women in service noted in passing by other witnesses were in no way integral to the legal dispute. They were referred to simply because they just *happened to be there*, appearing like extras in a TV show. Their incidental presence reminds us just how ubiquitous these women were in early modern society. When servant Sybil Castle (alias Salter) described washing clothes in a brook in Bromsberrow (Gloucestershire) in 1587, she located her fellow servant Alice Kirton (alias Milwarde) not only at the scene of an altercation but also at her site of work.[116] By including these women in their depositions, witnesses turned a fleeting lens onto their lives.

Conclusion

It seems remarkable that patterns of cases, litigants, and witnesses are so consistently replicated across the church courts of early modern England. Tithe, testamentary, defamation, and matrimonial suits dominated the courts. Before 1600, matrimonial suits comprised a major source of business, but they dwindled in the first decades of the seventeenth century and gave rise to an increased number of testamentary suits. A typical witness was male, around the age of 45, and of middling social status. Female witnesses were usually married, and a higher proportion of them were recorded in defamation suits. Across the courts, proportionally more female than male litigants and witnesses came from urban areas,

---

[114] DHC, Chanter 857, Testament of Roger Byrdwode (1571).
[115] HRO, 21M65/C3/4, Gawen Barrow v Ralph Winge (1567).
[116] GA, GDR/65, Sybil Stone v Anne Webb (1587).

but most were drawn from the villages and hamlets of the south and west. The near unanimity of these patterns tells us not only about litigating in this period and who brought certain suits to the courts. It also tells us about the underlying values, norms, and concerns of society. Social and marital status, gender, and age brought authority. But particular offences, cases, and charges anticipated witness testimony that was predicated on different forms of knowledge. Witnessing a prearranged event was a form of social and economic currency as well as a patriarchal duty. Sometimes providing evidence required the authority of a long-term resident of a parish who could testify to a particularly parochial custom. In other cases, witnesses were simply those present at the time. From this perspective, no one of legal age was barred from testifying.

As a corollary of this, the testimonies of unusual or atypical witnesses shouldn't be overlooked, nor taken as unrepresentative. 'Unlikely' witnesses – the 10-year-old boy in a defamation suit or the 18-year-old female servant in a tithe case – seem remarkable only at a distance when analysing this material quantitatively, without digging deeper into the historical record. The underlying context of a witness's invitation to court surfaces when examining individual testimonies but is obscured when analysing depositions at a macro level. Such contexts have enormous explanatory power, especially when considered alongside the social, economic, and geographical patterns of litigation heard in the church courts and the profiles of the people who flocked to them.

Taking female servants as a discrete group of plaintiffs, defendants, and witnesses in the courts illustrates the importance of combining macro- and granular-level study: the micro-politics of their appearance can be set alongside the broad patterns and trends observed across the five courts. While women in service infrequently engaged with the courts, they shared many of the same concerns other men and women expressed as litigants – namely reputation. Their anxieties as litigants were also interlaced with those of their age group: their involvement as plaintiffs and defendants in matrimonial and testamentary suits indicates apprehensions – over marriage and the material assets required to set up a household. At times, their position as labourers in their masters' and mistresses' homes necessitated their appearance in court (particularly as witnesses). In defamation suits, they defended the honour and reputations of those they worked for. In tithe disputes, they upheld their masters' rights and the legitimacy of their working practices in the fields. And they continued to serve even once they had left, testifying in testamentary suits to the contents of their former masters' and mistresses' wills. At the same time, female servant testimonies were not only a product of their labour relations, nor did they entirely lack agency or free will in testifying. Closer analysis indicates the range of circumstances that led to a female servant's name being inscribed within the pages of these deposition books. As the next two chapters show, this range reflects the fact that this was no homogeneous group of women.

Chapter 2

Tracing Lives

An hour before daybreak on 19 January 1607, Thomas Nashe led a small group to the church of Brockworth in Gloucestershire. Clutching candles and holding lanterns in outstretched arms to light their way in the dark, the group passed by husbandman George Long, who was watering his horse. George glanced at the group but said nothing. They continued to the church, where Mary Mayo was waiting for Thomas. At the break of day, the pair were married in front of the handful of witnesses Thomas had brought with him and the couple slipped Edward Browning, the parish vicar, 3s 4d in payment. Two months after the wedding, the baby came. They named her Anne.[1]

Twenty-four years later, alderman John Jones of Gloucester died. A memorial stands in Gloucester Cathedral: 'Thrice mayor of this city', it proclaims and also, 'Principal Registrar of the Diocese of Gloucester'. The effigy projecting from the wall depicts a bearded man with brown-greyish hair, a younger version of the 72-year-old buried within the cathedral. He wears a ruff and a mayoral gown, edged with fur. The memorial records a life dedicated to clerical work: John holds a deed in one hand and a book in the other. On both sides stand pots of writing implements, flanked by stacks of folded deeds. The memorial is mounted at the west end of the cathedral's south aisle, in the spot where the consistory court was held.[2] *Months before he died, John made a will. He promised to 'give Anne Nashe my servant if shee be dwelling with me at my decease fortie shillings. And likewise to everie maid servaunt thirteene shillings fower pence a peece.'*[3]

* * *

---

[1] GA, GDR/105, Office v Edward Browneinge (1607); GDR/168, Margaret Hill v Thomas Whittingham (1630).

[2] Irvine Gray, 'The Iconography of Archives, IV: The Monument of John Jones at Gloucester', *Journal of the Society of Archivists* 3 (1969), 488–9 at 489.

[3] TNA, PROB 11/159/495, Will of John Jones (1631).

Anne Nashe was the baby conceived out of wedlock by Thomas Nashe and Mary Mayo. Following their clandestine marriage, she was baptised on 20 March 1607 and a succession of sons followed: first John (*b*. 1609), then Richard (*b*. 1611), followed by Gyles (*b*. 1615), Thomas (*b*. 1619), and finally William (*b*. 1622).[4] The family lived in Brockworth, just outside the city of Gloucester. How the couple made a living is unknown but we find Anne's brothers listed as labourers and husbandmen in scattered records years later. This was not a wealthy household and with six children to support, Thomas and Mary's resources must have been stretched. In 1618, as the eldest child (but still only 10 or 11 years old), Anne was sent to work. She was found a place in the family home of John Jones and his second wife, Elizabeth, in Longsmith Street in the city. She stayed with them for at least twelve years.

I first encountered Anne in a matrimonial suit heard in the Gloucester court in early 1630, testifying on behalf of her fellow servant Margaret Hill, who claimed Thomas Whittingham had promised to marry her. Anne's testimony was taken just six weeks after John Jones made his will and one year before he died in 1631. Bestowed upon her in name, the 40 shillings she was bequeathed was a higher sum than any other servant in his house was to receive, reflecting her long service. She may have still lived with John when he died, though what happened to her is lost. She doesn't subsequently appear in Gloucester or Brockworth parish registers, so we don't know whether she married or when she died. Nonetheless, alongside a constellation of other records, Anne's 1630 deposition is key in reconstructing at least a partial history of her life *before* 1630. The events recorded in church court depositions are not just moments frozen in time. We might not see what happened *later* that day, or the *next* day, or the following week, month, or year. And only rarely do we see what happened the previous evening, or the week, month, or year *before*. But testimony offers more than just a passing glimpse.

Anne's listed place of birth leads me to the Brockworth parish register, which records her baptism and introduces me to her father, Thomas. Just four entries earlier in the register, I find Thomas's marriage to her mother, Mary. A quick search finds her parents' names indexed in my database of court depositions and I catch them in George Long's testimony, standing before the vicar in Brockworth church, who was later accused of solemnising their clandestine marriage. I reconstruct the couple's family from baptism records of their five other children, uncovering the probable pinch point that led to Anne's early entry into service. Turning back to Anne's deposition, I learn that John Jones was her master in 1630. Prominent among Gloucester's elite, records of his life are not scarce. Probate documents and material culture tell a story of his work, life, and family in the early seventeenth century. I even read that he commissioned the monument (Plate 2) himself,

---

[4] GA, P62/IN/1/1, Register of baptisms, marriages and burials for the parish of Brockworth (1559–1780).

Figure 2.1 Mark of Anne Nashe of Gloucester (1630)
Source: GA, GDR/168, Margaret Hill v Thomas Whittingham (1630)

visiting it upon its completion and complaining that his face was painted a little too red! While he took a stroll around the cathedral, the story goes, it was altered, and satisfied with the changes, he gave the workmen some money for a drink. Two days later, he died.[5] Beginning with just one servant deposition, the entwined stories of Anne Nashe and John Jones can be pieced together.

Pulling together the fragmentary archive of Anne's life, we find a young girl from a poor home who entered the household of a prominent member of the civic elite. She rubbed shoulders with people from very different backgrounds to her own. Merchants, other city governors, and public servants would have regularly visited this house. The household labour force was comprised of both pencil pushers and labourers. Some were both: 18-year-old George Francombe served in the house, too, but his deposition also described him as a clerk. He was fully literate, signing his name at the foot of his deposition in neat secretary hand. The household's literate culture was likely a far cry from Anne's family home. But it was one to which she became accustomed. Her signature was much less clear than George's but bore resemblance to her initials (see Figure 2.1). On St Clements Day 1629, her deposition tells us, she sat drinking with George and seven others. All bar one showed signs of literacy in their depositions: they signed or marked their initials.

Even Anne's fellow servant, Margaret Hill, could probably read.[6] Anne told the court that Margaret's intended husband

> did give unto & bestowe upon the said Margarett a braser lock with the inscription of many letteres upon the same, which letters being turned that it made a word then the said lock might be opened or els not.

---

[5] Rev. Beaver H. Blacker, 'Alderman John Jones, of Gloucester', *Gloucestershire Notes and Queries: Part XVI* (1882), pp. 143–5 at 145.
[6] Margaret was probably from a family of city governors like John Jones. The Hills are prominent in records of the civic elite. Mercer William Hill was an alderman at the same time as John Jones (between

Appreciation of this combination lock as a token of courtship required Margaret to be literate. Anne's literacy, by contrast, appears more limited as she was unable to identify the word that the letters spelled out. Both Anne and Margaret were servants, hired to work in the same household. But their backgrounds and social standing were not analogous, reminding us of the question posed in Chapter 1: what did 'servant' mean?

One way to answer this question is to ask another: who served in early modern England and why? As Chapter 1 demonstrated, service meant legal dependence, which is why court clerks were reticent to use the term in court documents. This same dependence professes poverty of the servant and yokes them to a low rung of the social ladder. Service had once simultaneously offered a labour solution to the children of the medieval poor *and* a means of socialisation for the children of well-to-do merchants and gentry. But by the fifteenth century, Jeremy Goldberg argued, this 'social inclusivity' was diminishing, especially for women, as the labour became increasingly menial and inappropriate for the daughters of respectable society.[7] By the sixteenth century, Alan Macfarlane argued, 'the institution of servanthood might be regarded as a disguised means whereby wealth and labour flowed from the poorer to the richer'.[8]

This chapter takes each deposition as a starting point, stretching it open and outwards as far as possible to gather traces of the social structure of service and the identities of women who served. The chapter takes two approaches. First, I collect material signs of identity. Self-evaluations of servants' worth and wealth, as well as how others evaluated their socio-economic place, offer one perspective.[9] Objects and goods that these women noted in their possession are also emblematic of identity. Even the physical mark a servant left on the page of her deposition – her signature, initials, or sign – invites a closer look. Second, I collect helpful markers – names, places, dates, ages, and occupations – littered throughout these narratives. I cross-reference them with other sources – baptism, marriage, and burial registers – that record administratively important life events, as well as wills and other documents. From these markers, I can reconstruct something of the wider lives of women in service. These women were not just servants. They were daughters, sisters, friends, and (later) wives and mothers.

Service for early modern women, I argue, is not a straightforward story of labour flowing from poor to rich. What was meant by 'servant' is opaque but servants were not a homogeneous group: a gentleman's servant wasn't socially

---

1614 and 1635). A Thomas Hill, goldsmith, was also sheriff in 1626, alderman in 1628, and mayor in 1640. Information from a box of notes on Gloucester compiled by Peter Clark, held at the University of Exeter and consulted in 2017 with the permission of its custodian, Jonathan Barry.

[7] Goldberg, 'What Was a Servant?', p. 20.

[8] Macfarlane, *Family Life*, pp. 209–10.

[9] Statements of worth are analysed extensively in Shepard, *Accounting for Oneself*.

equal to a menial servant.[10] Servants came from a range of backgrounds and were hired by households across the socio-economic spectrum. Gentlewomen, teenage girls from labouring and middling backgrounds, as well as daughters of penniless widows, and young children from the bursting homes of overstretched labourers, all served. But rarely are distinctions and differences explored. In this chapter, I tease out the fine gradations of status within service. Most women in service came from labouring homes, but the 'poor' were highly stratified. The social function of service was therefore different for different types of women. For the poorest, service could be a lifeline, offering shelter, food, drink, and clothing. For others, it was an opportunity for advancement (though advancement was far from guaranteed, nor was it equitable). By tracing histories of these women in depositions and other archives, the chapter uncovers the myriad reasons they entered service: to seek training in practical and social skills, to escape poverty, and by compulsion.

Servants and status

As I showed in Chapter 1, occupational descriptors in church court depositions both reflected and refracted social status. But as the descriptor 'servant' tells us little about a woman's socio-economic identity, we must look for other clues to who she was. Her beginning is an obvious place to start: what did her family's household look like? What can we say about her upbringing? Female servants seldom gave the names or occupations of their parents in their depositions. Cross-referencing servants' surviving baptism records (containing at least one named parent) with other sources yields only a few positive matches. Occupations of just eleven fathers of servants in the data set could be identified – five husbandmen, three yeomen, a dyer, a vicar, and a tailor. Fortunately, female servants fashioned identity in their depositions in other ways.

Signs and marks

We begin at the end. The final splash of ink at the foot of the deposition was also the final performance of status: the deponent's signature or mark. At a material level, this mark symbolised consent or agreement that the words on the page reflected their oral testimony and had been spoken freely, however notional that freedom may have been. The ability of a witness to sign their name in full has also been interpreted as a benchmark of literacy and, in turn, social status. Those who

---

[10] J. S. Cockburn, 'Early-Modern Assize Records as Historical Evidence', *Journal of the Society of Archivists* 5 (1975), 215–31 at 223.

scrawled a circle or a cross on the page or scribbled a seemingly random series of pen strokes are assumed to have had no literacy at all.[11] Systematic quantitative analysis of signatures yields low female literacy rates, reinforced by the observation that 'most women did not need to be able to write. The domestic routine of cooking and sewing and child-rearing had little need for reading, and it scarcely afforded the time.'[12]

But the various assortments of signatures and marks left on court records can show *degrees* of literacy. Initialling has been redefined as the basic ability to *read*, with signing in full signifying the ability to *write*. In London, ability to read was 'far more broadly socially diffused than the ability to write'.[13] Alternative categories of literacy have been proposed: 'letteracy' – the ability to recognise and reproduce letters – further expands society's engagement with text.[14] Revisiting traditional readings of signatures and marks on legal documents moves us beyond binary distinctions of 'literate' and 'illiterate', and towards literate cultures.

In the century between England's break with Rome and its civil war, literacy was still a nascent currency. English Protestantism encouraged communicants to read the Bible, thereby embedding literacy in religious discourse. By the end of the seventeenth century, theologian Richard Baxter was advocating for masters to teach their servants to read (though he is silent on writing) 'if they be of any capacity and willingness'.[15] Servants *were* interacting with text in a variety of ways. Earlier, I introduced Gloucester servant Margaret Hill, who received a combination lock from her suitor, which required literacy to operate its mechanism. Elsewhere, depositions capture other female servants encountering written words. In 1603, gentleman William Hodges of Ilchester (Somerset) continually sent letters to his former servant Rose Perrie, who had married and moved to London. One witness deposed that

> Mr hodges in the subscription of his name in his saide letters did sett downe for his owne name a W & an h. and R underneath betwxt the W & h which did serve, in the construction of diverse of creditt that have seen the same, for William hodges and Rose hodges.

These love letters, inscribed with initials symbolising their relationship, were intended for Rose to read herself, indicating her literacy.[16] As Eleanor Hubbard imagined, most people would have wanted to read and write their own love

[11] Cressy, *Literacy and Social Order*, pp. 53–4.
[12] Ibid., p. 128.
[13] Eleanor Hubbard, 'Reading, Writing, and Initialing: Female Literacy in Early Modern London', *JBS* 54 (2015), 553–77 at 573.
[14] Mark Hailwood, 'Rethinking Literacy in Rural England, 1550–1700', *P&P* 260 (2023), 38–70 at 45.
[15] Richard Baxter, *A Christian directory, or, A summ of practical theologie and cases of conscience directing Christians how to use their knowledge and faith* (1673), p. 582.
[16] SHC, D/D/cd/34, John Atwell v William Hodges (1603). On courtship and literacy, see Diana O'Hara, 'The Language of Tokens and the Making of Marriage', *Rural History* 3 (1992), 1–40 at 16.

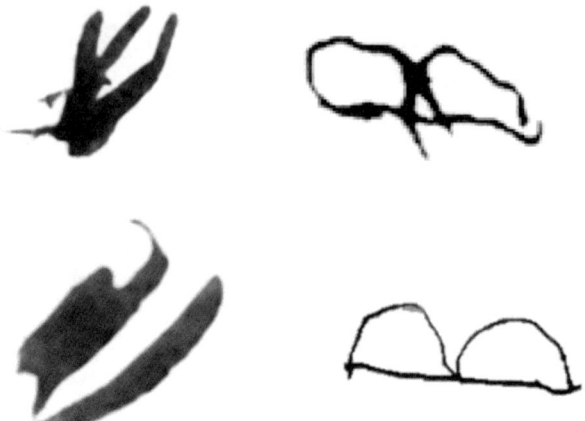

Figure 2.2 Marks of Agnes Cardnoll and Agnes Barons
Left: Agnes Cardnoll of West Buckland (Somerset, 1604); Right: Agnes Barons of Ilsington (Devon, 1636)

Source: SHC, D/D/cd/34, John Atwell v John Dumett (1604); DHC, Chanter 866, William Harries v Audrey Rowell (1636)

letters without requiring literate intermediaries.[17] As I will show, others, too, sought literacy to make better sense of the world in which they lived.

Elsewhere, intermediaries guided servants with low literacy through textual documents. In 1604, Agnes Cardnoll of West Buckland (Somerset) was shown by her master a

> noate in writtinge, and told her that he had receaved the same from one Wilmott an apparitor of this court, and that the contents [were] thereof that she this respondent must bee at Wells uppon Monday then following to depose.

The text had to be decoded for Agnes as she likely could not read; the mark at the foot of her deposition casts only the vaguest impression of an attempted letter 'c' (see Figure 2.2). Her master showed her the document, its physicality bearing an authority that supplemented his oral summary of the text.[18] Others showed some signs of literacy but not enough to read with full comprehension. Agnes Barons of Ilsington (Devon) signed her deposition twice with a 'B' in 1636 (see also Figure 2.2). But when approached to testify by 'one Ford', he 'shewed her a paper & said it was a process [court citation]'.[19] These textual encounters remind us that in this overwhelmingly oral society where full literacy was the exception, the written text as physical 'proof' was still embryonic. The *combination* of seeing written words on a page, the physical identifiability of a document by its physical markers (seals,

[17] Hubbard, 'Reading, Writing, and Initialling', 575.
[18] SHC, D/D/cd/34, John Atwell v John Dumett (1604).
[19] DHC, Chanter 866, William Harries v Audrey Rowell (1636).

symbols, etc.), and some reliance on the literate to accurately read it aloud was the basis of *most* people's consent or acceptance of a document as 'proof'. Low literacy of course heightened susceptibility to deceit and coercion. But to suppose that the inability to read or sign one's name routinely barred his or her agency when presented with a text is to overlook the extent of this fundamentally oral culture.[20]

For many female servants, signing their deposition wasn't the first time they had put pen and ink to paper. Some had signed wills and other legal documents. Servant Christian Stock of Huntspill (Somerset) and three other witnesses recalled being asked 'to subscribe theire hands and marks' to John Lush's will in the 1630s.[21] Servant Anna Ingram of Stow-on-the-Wold (Gloucestershire) deposed in 1605 that she had witnessed the sealing and delivery of a tithe lease one year earlier. She had inscribed her mark on its reverse and identified the lease exhibited in court as the very same: she 'doth verie well remember that the marke whereto her name is sett on the backside of the deed now exhibited is the selfe same marke'.[22] Anna's mark was neither a full signature nor letters of the alphabet, but it was carefully crafted and identifiable to *her*.

Signatures and marks were subscribed to 454 of the 542 female servant depositions (84 per cent), as Table 2.1 shows.[23] Only four signed with their full names: Joan Lewes (1603), Elizabeth Howard (1612), Mary Davis (1637), and Elizabeth Adkinson (1644). Forty-eight marked their initials, twenty-four produced alternative letter shapes, and the rest left an assortment of marks and signs deserving closer attention.

Signature literacy (depicted in Figure 2.3) unsurprisingly mapped onto higher social status. Elizabeth Howard was the servant of Sir Thomas and Lady Anne Seymore of Frampton Cotterell (Gloucestershire) and was described as 'Mrs Howard'. Probably a lady-in-waiting, Elizabeth's title 'Mrs' reflected her elevated status.[24] The Howard duchesses of Norfolk (where Elizabeth was born) 'gained prestige for educating young women in their households' and this was presumably a reciprocal arrangement in which Elizabeth was educated in another noble home.[25] But not all signing servants were of high rank. At the turn of the seventeenth century, Joan Lewes also signed her full name. She served yeoman James and his wife Sara Charmbury in Bathampton (Somerset), and similarities between Joan's signature and her master's (especially the letter 'J' in both their names) suggest her literacy may have been acquired or honed during service.[26] Opposing witnesses in the

---

[20] On consent, illiteracy, and service, see Chakravarty, *Fictions of Consent*, pp. 145–7.
[21] SHC, D/D/cd/80, John Lush v John Long (1638).
[22] GA, GDR/95, Edmund Chamberlen v Richard Perkes and Edward Broughton (1605).
[23] By 1590, signatures or marks were standard; just seven of the eighty-seven unsigned female servant depositions were taken after this date.
[24] GA, GDR/114, Anne Seymore v Thomas Seymore (1612). On 'Mrs', see Amy Louise Erickson, 'Mistresses and Marriage: Or, a Short History of the Mrs', *History Workshop Journal* 78 (2014), 39–57 at 44.
[25] Sharon D. Michalove, 'Equal in Opportunity? The Education of Aristocratic Women 1450–1540', in Barbara Whitehead (ed.), *Women's Education in Early Modern Europe: A History, 1500–1800* (New York, 1999), pp. 47–74 at 56.
[26] SHC, D/D/cd/34, Marcus Tabor v Thomas Powle (1603).

	Female servant witnesses	With mark/signature		Signatures and letters						Other marks			
				Full name		1 initial	2 initials	Alternative letters	All		Cross	Circle	Straight line	Other
	N	Nª	%	N	%	N	N	N	N	%	N	N	N	N
Bath & Wells	210	197	94	2	1	18	4	13	37	19	43	25	2	90
Exeter	98	72	73	—	—	10	1	3	14	19	12	10	2	34
Gloucester	158	120	76	2	1	6	2	8	18	15	20	13	2	71
Hereford	14	11	79	—	—	—	—	—	—	—	2	5	—	5
Winchester	62	54	87	—	—	7	—	—	7	13	12	6	3	26
All Courts	*542*	*454*	*84*	*4*	*1*	*41*	*7*	*24*	*76*	*18*	*89*	*59*	*9*	*227*

Table 2.1 Signatures and marks of female servant witnesses (by court)

Note (a): Servant marks were sometimes a composite of different types (e.g., a cross and a circle) so the figures in this column add up to less than the sum of all mark types.

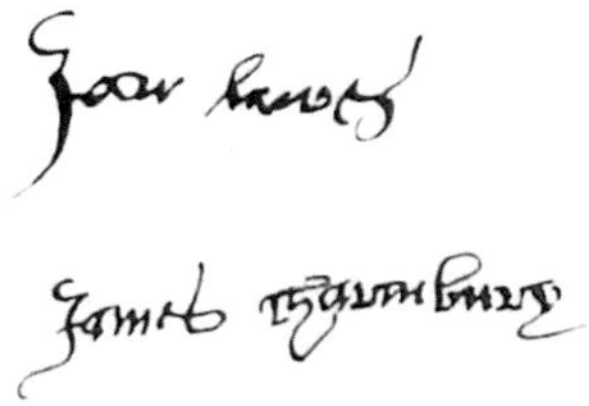

Joan Lewes (top) and her master, James
Charmbury, yeoman (bottom),
Bathampton, Somerset
*SHC, D/D/cd/34, Marcus Taber v
Thomas Powle (1603)*

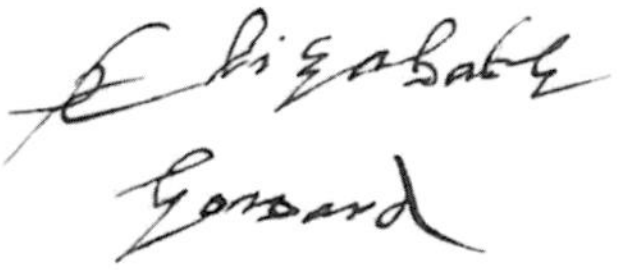

Elizabeth Howard,
*Frampton Cotterell, Gloucestershire
GA, GDR/114, Anne Seymore v
Thomas Seymore (1612)*

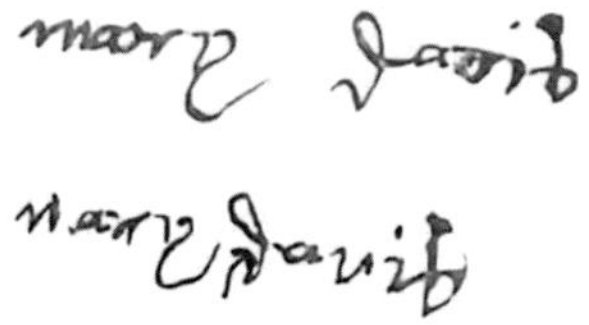

Mary Davis,
*Midsomer Norton, Somerset
SHC, D/D/cd/80, Edith Salmon v
Moore (1637)*

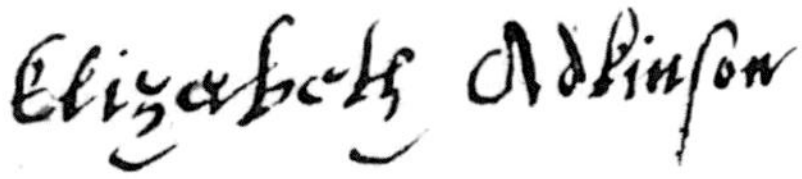

Elizabeth Adkinson,
*Slimbridge, Gloucestershire
GA, GDR/205, Elizabeth Parke v
Margaret White (1644)*

Figure 2.3 Female servant signatures

adultery case that prompted Joan's testimony attempted to discredit deponents. They levelled accusations of poverty and youth at other servants. But Joan was spared, perhaps regarded as a young woman of standing (though not the same standing as Mrs Howard). Mary Davis of Midsomer Norton (Somerset) served her aunt and uncle, Eleanor and Thomas Frye. Thomas was, like James Charmbury, a yeoman. Both Mary and her aunt Eleanor were deponents in a testamentary dispute concerning the will of an elderly neighbour, Edith Pruett (whom Mary had sometimes served). Mary inscribed her full name neatly on the page twice, as was customary (first after her deposition and then after her interrogatory responses). Meanwhile, Eleanor's two marks on the page did not precisely resemble each other, nor were they discernible letters. Mary had lived with the couple for just one year, and had probably learned to write elsewhere. That a servant was more literate than her mistress (especially within the same kin network) raises an important question: what kind of education or training did Mary expect to receive serving in her aunt and uncle's house? Fifty years old, Eleanor was twice Mary's age. The difference in literacy might reflect a generational gap as ability to read and write increased over the seventeenth century.[27] Though Eleanor managed her own household, her servant Mary possessed skills that she did not.

---

[27] SHC, D/D/cd/80, Edith Salmon v Moore (1637).

Figure 2.4 Mark of Eleanor Weeks of Exeter (Devon, 1615)
Source: DHC, Chanter 867, Henry Cockram v Bartholomew Jaquinto (1615)

This period of rising literacy complicates any attempt to take ability to read and write as a straightforward marker of status. Certainly, the poorest servants rarely had full literacy. But nor did all servants of high rank sign their names. As Figure 2.4 shows, the mark servant Eleanor Weeks of Exeter (Devon) left on her 1615 deposition was an unidentifiable impression made with a single, continuous pen stroke (at best, a dubious letter 'W'). But, she told the court, she was 'a gentlewoman borne'.[28] Joan and Mary, meanwhile, served prosperous but not aristocratic or even gentle families. Though rural schooling was piecemeal, and children were probably taught individually, their signatures show that female servants *could* learn to read and write. A case heard in the Gloucester court in 1601 concerning the mismanagement of Elizabeth Hallowes's father's will shows that service and learning to read were not incompatible experiences for young women. According to witnesses, Elizabeth had been placed in the service of William Harding around the age of 17 or 18 before 68-year-old widow Alice Norrys of Gloucester had taken her in 'to borde and to be taught to read and sewe' (interestingly, no mention of writing is made).[29]

Initials, Hubbard argued, signify the ability to read.[30] Of the forty-eight initialled female servant depositions, most (85 per cent) signed with one single letter (usually their first name initial). Just seven signed with both initials. Again, social status partly explains initialling literacy. Elizabeth Backer of Newent (Gloucestershire) was the servant of Thomas Williams (alias Baker), possibly a relative. She signed her 1594 deposition with both initials (Figure 2.5) and claimed to be worth £3, considerably higher than most servant self-appraisals, as I show later in this chapter.[31]

Witnesses living and serving in two inns in Wells (Somerset) in 1623–4 varied significantly in their ability to write their initials, as Figure 2.6 shows. Katherine Dossett (alias Davies) was 29 years old and the wife of a shoemaker named Richard when she testified in 1624. She had served the innkeeper Richard Robbins (alias Perriman)

[28] DHC, Chanter 867, Henry Cockram v Bartholomew Jaquinto (1615).
[29] GA, GDR/89, Elizabeth Hallowes v Edward Trotman (1601).
[30] Hubbard, 'Reading, Writing, and Initialling', 555.
[31] GA, GDR/79, Anne Williams v Francis Donne (1594).

Figure 2.5 Marks of Elizabeth Backer of Newent (Gloucestershire, 1594)

Source: GA, GDR/79, Anne Williams v Francis Donne (1594)

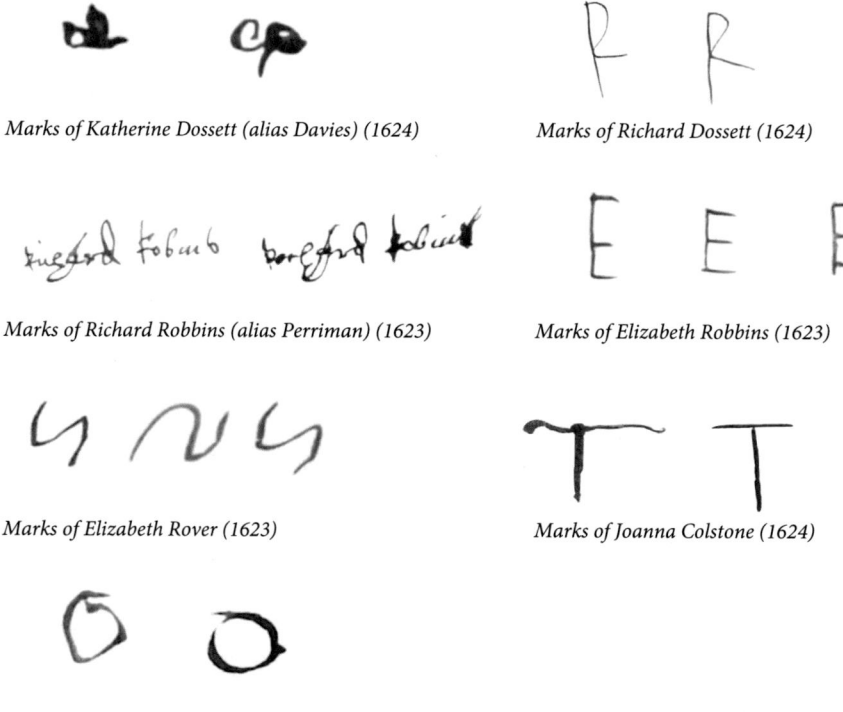

Marks of Katherine Dossett (alias Davies) (1624)   *Marks of Richard Dossett (1624)*

Marks of Richard Robbins (alias Perriman) (1623)   *Marks of Elizabeth Robbins (1623)*

Marks of Elizabeth Rover (1623)   *Marks of Joanna Colstone (1624)*

Marks of Margery Sheppard (1623)

Figure 2.6 Marks from the Red Lion and The Crown inns in Wells (Somerset, 1623–4)

Source: SHC, D/D/cd/57, William Bellamie v John Bradford and Margaret Jett (1623); D/D/cd/59, Thomasina Vernon v Anna Denby (1624)

and his wife Elizabeth in the Red Lion before her marriage that year. Katherine's two marks on her deposition are small, cautious, and similar, bearing some resemblance to letters (possibly a 'c' for Catherine and an upside-down 'd'). Her husband Richard was a deponent in the same case and also made letter shapes: he signed his testimony with a clear capital 'R'. Katherine's master and mistress did not testify in this case, but they had deposed in a different suit one year earlier. Richard signed his full name while Elizabeth signed with a clear 'E'. Their former servant, 40-year-old singlewoman Elizabeth Rover, also testified. The mark she made was a curved line (possibly a letter 'S'), which she reproduced three times. The literacy of female servants in this inn was limited, especially given their master's and mistress's capabilities, but indicates some recognition of letter shapes. In the nearby inn of The Crown, run by widow Anne Glover, similar patterns are found. Servant Joanna Colstone did not mark her deposition with her own initials but left a bold letter 'T' twice at the foot of her deposition in the same year as Katherine. Margery Sheppard served alongside Joanna. Despite Joanna's two perfect executions of the letter 'T', Margery's deposition was completed with a simple circle – or perhaps the letter 'o'.[32] These servants were actively engaged in running these urban inns. Their work likely exposed them to simple literacy in the keeping of accounts.

At a time when reading and writing wasn't universal even among elites and the middling sorts, what did literacy mean to a woman in service? What tangible benefit might be gained? Was literacy expected from servants by some masters, or expected to be taught *in* service by some women? Some female servants *may* have learned to write at home. In February 1639, Elizabeth Snarlinge of Coberley (Gloucestershire) witnessed her master, Francis Smith, make his will. Comparison of her marks on the surviving copy of the will and her court deposition three months later shows consistency (see Figure 2.7). All marks were identical, deliberate, and executed with intention: to produce the letter 'S'. Perhaps Elizabeth inherited this mark from her family – the letter 'S' for 'Snarling' (or it might refer to 'Smith', her master's surname).[33] The capital 'P' that Joan Prince of Cliddesden (Hampshire) inscribed at the foot of her deposition in 1580 leaves a similar impression (see also Figure 2.7).[34] Elizabeth and Joan weren't just servants. They were also daughters, and their marks articulated familial identities that were more constant than their service. Aligning themselves with their biological family wasn't a subversive move. But they nonetheless subverted the identity of 'servant' that scribes otherwise assigned them in court. Marks like these stress alternative identities that expand the servant's world beyond her master's home.

Recalling Anne Nashe and her fellow servant Margaret Hill at the beginning of this chapter, women from different walks of life literally served in the same

---

[32] SHC, D/D/cd/57, William Bellamie v John Bradford and Margaret Jett (1623); D/D/cd/59, Thomasina Vernon v Anna Denby (1624).
[33] GA, GDR/204, Eleanor Mills v Anna Smith (1639); GDR/R8/1638/53, Will of Francis Smith of Coberley, yeoman (1638/9).
[34] HRO, 21M65/C3/8, William Anteren v Joan Prince (1580).

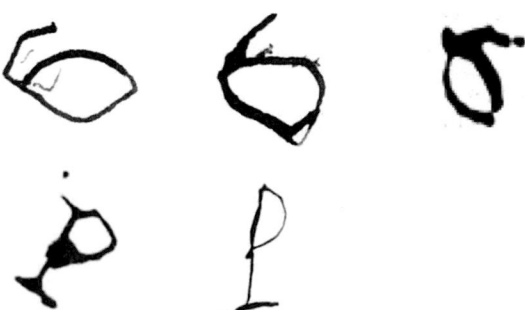

Figure 2.7 Familial marks of Elizabeth Snarlinge of Coberley (Gloucestershire, 1639) and Joan Prince of Cliddesden (Hampshire, 1580)
Top: Elizabeth Snarlinge of Coberley (Gloucestershire, 1639)
Bottom: Joan Prince of Cliddesden (Hampshire, 1580)

Source: GA, GDR/204, Eleanor Mills v Anna Smith (1639); GDR/R8/1638/53, Will of Francis Smith of Coberley, yeoman (1638/9); HRO, 21M65/C3/8, William Anteren v Joan Prince (1580)

households. As Anne's mark reminds us, she probably learned to write her initials in John Jones's literate household, a skill she may have valued and seen as socially advancing. But in many cases, the social distance between masters and servants wasn't so great. Most female servants had no expectations of gaining literacy from service, nor was it likely as several masters and mistresses didn't sign with names, initials, or letters at all. Husbandman John Daye of Stogursey (Somerset) signed with a one-line mark in 1575, and his servant Jocosa Standefaste made a similar sign.[35] In 1605, 22-year-old Garthred Weight of Pensford (Somerset) signed her deposition twice with two circles joined by a short line (possibly the letter 'g'), as shown in Figure 2.8. Garthred's master, glover Sampson Silke, was just two years older and a witness in the same case. His mark (also made twice) resembled Garthred's, raising the question of whether it might be a trade mark which Garthred duplicated (and not a letter 'g' after all). But Sampson was a witness on two other occasions: in 1603 (two years earlier) and again in 1619. His marks are not consistent, and neither resembles his 1605 mark. In fact, Garthred's mark demonstrates greater pen control than her master's.[36] If literacy is a marker of education and status, servants did not uniformly hover on a lower rung of the socio-economic ladder than those who hired them in this period. In some cases, servants may have possessed skills that their masters and mistresses did not. In other cases, neither servant nor master or mistress demonstrated great literacy.

Where a female servant learned letter shapes is only one important question here. Most servants did not produce letters when signing. What can we say about them? Across the corpus of marks, there are patterns and commonalities,

[35] SHC, D/D/cd/15, John Standefaste v Elizabeth Stephens (1575).
[36] SHC, D/D/cd/34, Marcus Taber v John Bailie (1603); D/D/cd/36, Joanna Raymond v Joanna Allin (1605); D/D/cd/54, Office v Joanne Allen (1619).

Figure 2.8 Marks of Garthred Weight and her master Sampson Silke of Pensford (Somerset, various years)
Top: Garthred Weight (1605)
Bottom (left to right): Sampson Silke (1605); Sampson Silke (1605); Sampson Silke (1603); Sampson Silke (1619)

Source: SHC, D/D/cd/34, Marcus Taber v John Bailie (1603); D/D/cd/36, Joanna Raymond v Joanna Allin (1605); D/D/cd/54, Office v Joanne Allen (1619)

discernible levels of skill, and a range of highly individualistic impressions left on the page. Crosses and circles were the most frequently made mark, accounting for over 40 per cent of all subscriptions. A cross did not necessarily indicate religious leaning.[37] It appeared at the beginning of the alphabet in children's writing manuals known as horn books and therefore might have been the first mark learners made.[38] David Cressy has argued that people reproduced the cross (as well as other marks) when they 'did not know how to write their names; it was a question of capacity, not of choice'.[39] The cross is therefore symbolic of illiteracy and has been described as representing 'the ruse of mutual contract', a symbol of assent that 'undermines its own authorizing capacity'.[40] Many servants could not read but depended on the court clerk to read back their deposition before they signed. But as I've argued, this reliance was part of early modern England's oral culture, and servants were far from alone in their lower levels of literacy. We should be cautious in assuming the cross represents 'an absence of specific assent' among servants.[41] A cross or a circle was also variable. As Figure 2.9 shows, some crosses and circles were rudimentary. But others demonstrate controlled penmanship. Pentecost Leonard of Wellington (Somerset) drew an almost perfect circle in 1609, and Susan Haukes of Cheltenham (Gloucestershire) drew a cross encased in

---

[37] Cressy, *Literacy and Social Order*, pp. 57–8.
[38] Hailwood, 'Rethinking Literacy', 61.
[39] Cressy, *Literacy and Social Order*, p. 58.
[40] Chakravarty, *Fictions of Consent*, p. 145.
[41] Ibid.

Figure 2.9 Circles and crosses
Circles (top, left to right): Anne Bache of Castle Morton (Worcestershire, 1597); Agnes
Munke of Twyford (Hampshire, 1581); Anna Squire of Exeter (Devon, 1635)
Crosses (bottom, left to right): Joanna Manshipp of Mark (Somerset, 1611); Margery Walton
of Croft (Herefordshire, 1601)

Source: HARC, HD4/2/11, Richard Burnell v Margery Bache (1597); HRO, 21M65/C3/8, John Weke
v Alexander Oldfelde (1581); DHC, Chanter 866, Mary Blight v Suzan Richardson (1635); SHC,
D/D/cd/28, Richard Hobbes v Cicilia Whiting (1611); HARC, HD4/2/11, Juliana Walton v Dorothy
Whetstone (1601)

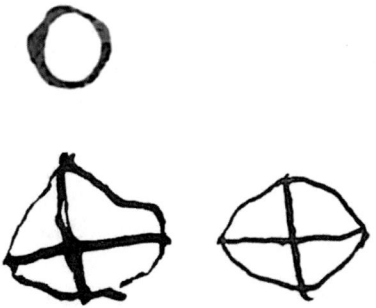

Figure 2.10 Marks of Pentecost Leonard and Susan Haukes
Top: Pentecost Leonard of Wellington (Somerset, 1609)
Bottom (left and right): Susan Haukes of Cheltenham (Gloucestershire, 1622)

Source: SHC, D/D/cd/43, Susan Filburie v Agnes Androwes (1609); GA, GDR/148, Eleanor
Lane v Thomas Horwood (1622)

a circle twice in 1622 (see Figure 2.10). These women did not lack skill with a pen.
They produced neat and individuated shapes, reminding us that this was probably
not the first time they had made these marks.

Outside court and in the fields, sheep were marked with initials and designs
for identification by their owners.[42] The rural economies in which most female
servants lived and worked depended on precise marks being recognised, described,

---

[42] This evidence is abundant in Quarter Sessions sheep theft examinations.

Figure 2.11 Elaborate marks
Top: Sara Reynolds of Sandford Orcas (Dorset, 1601); Bottom: Joanna Lucks of Curry Rivel (Somerset, 1613)

Source: SHC, D/D/cd/32, Leonard Leister v Thomas Downe (1601); D/D/cd/45, Joanna Piper v John Gardner (1613)

and reproduced. Replication of a mark signifies practice. To return to Table 2.1, 120 female servants made more than one mark when deposing and almost half of the second and occasional third marks were irrefutably identical to the first. Another third were recognisable attempts at duplication. Some duplicated marks were crosses or circles, but others were more elaborate. Take the depositions of Sara Reynolds of Sandford Orcas (Dorset) in 1601 and Joanna Lucks of Curry Rivel (Somerset) in 1613 (both Figure 2.11). Both repeated intricate, unique symbols in the two parts of their depositions. Many left inky marks like these that evade easy classification but precise duplication attests to a culture in which symbols and shapes were repeatedly drawn and held meaning. Female servants were embedded in this culture.

Like a working man's coat of arms, some marks made by male witnesses represented their trades.[43] Tailors drew little pairs of scissors. Husbandmen drew the instruments of their work: sickles and scythes appear periodically. But women, too, made trade marks. A sickle appears at the bottom of Maria Perrie's 1607 deposition (Figure 2.12). Maria had served gentleman Francis Buckland of West Harptree (Somerset) half a year earlier. In this rural economy, his household likely relied at least in part on husbandry, but Maria made no mention of carrying out husbandry (rather, she recalled washing clothes in his service). Perhaps her mark was an echo of a working life in the fields or her own family's agrarian household economy.[44] Several other female servants attempted this recognisable shape, while in 1617, Joanna Warman of West Monkton (Somerset) signed twice with a mark resembling an arrow (also Figure 2.12), mirroring a

---

[43] Andrew Favine, *The Theater of Honour and Knighthood* (1623, translated from the French of 1620), p. 16.

[44] SHC, D/D/cd/40, Peter Scriven and Barbara Scriven v Agnes Naish (1607).

Figure 2.12 Occupational symbols
Top (left to right): Maria Perrie of Wells (Somerset, 1607); Margery Addams of Westbury-on-Severn (Gloucestershire, 1606); Catherine Pepet of Ludlow (Shropshire, 1599)
Bottom (left and right): Joanna Warman of West Monkton (Somerset, 1617)

Source: SHC, D/D/cd/40, Peter Scriven and Barbara Scriven v Agnes Naish (1607); GA, GDR/100, Mary Syer v Margaret Wodcocke (1606); HARC, HD4/2/11, Fox v Mary Hereford (1599); SHC, D/D/cd/50, Elizabeth Musgrove v Simon Courte (1617)

Norfolk fletcher's mark identified by Cressy.[45] Other patterns united deponents across the country: a carefully drawn swirl left on the page by servant Elizabeth Forte (alias Williams) of Berrow (Somerset) in 1612 matched a mark made by a Norwich tailor. The same precision Elizabeth accomplished is also notable in the perfect star drawn in 1625 by Elizabeth Prior of Trowbridge (Wiltshire), who told the court she was worth nothing but her clothes (see Figure 2.13).[46] These symbols were not meaningless. The huge variety encompassed within the category 'other' (scarcely possible to capture here) reflects the many identities that female servants assumed. They were not *mimicking* the shapes and forms made by others. Rather, their marks were steeped in meaning that both reflected their sense of self and demonstrated their belonging within a range of finely graded social groupings among labouring people.

The meanings of most of these symbols are lost to us, but that doesn't mean they had no meaning. Binary thinking of society as literate or illiterate abandons the vibrant range of marks men and women left on the page in favour of an overly simplistic reading of each witness's socio-economic status. The assumption that a servant's rudimentary mark indicates inability to consent is to misunderstand this

---

[45] SHC, D/D/cd/45, Richard Moore v Agnes Dawkes (1612); D/D/cd/50, Elizabeth Musgrove v Simon Courte (1617).
[46] SHC, D/D/cd/59, Marie Collins v Juliana Blackwell (1625); Cressy, *Literacy and Social Order*, p. 60.

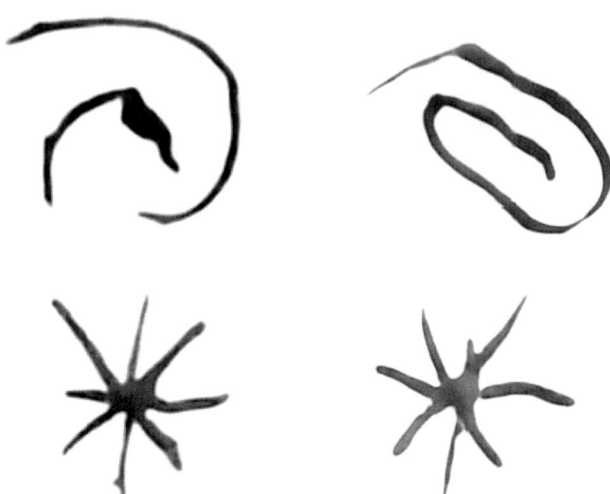

Figure 2.13 Marks of Elizabeth Forte (alias Williams) of Berrow and Elizabeth Prior of Trowbridge
Top: Elizabeth Forte (alias Williams) of Berrow (Somerset, 1612)
Bottom: Elizabeth Prior of Trowbridge (Wiltshire, 1625)
Source: SHC, D/D/cd/45, Richard Moore v Agnes Dawkes (1612); D/D/cd/59, Marie Collins v Juliana Blackwell (1625)

period before written documents weighed more heavily as legal proof. Men and women across society read the world around them and participated in oral and mixed cultures of literacy. Studying the variety of signatures and marks of female servants tells us not only about their literacy or social status, but also about their identities. Their repetition of marks and recognition of the importance of accurate duplication reflects their participation in an increasingly literate world.

Expressing wealth

The variety of marks left on depositions by female servants reflect a world at a crossroads between the written and spoken word. Their signatures and marks are articulations of identity as much as signifiers of status and education. Literacy was fluid at this time and although concentrated in wealthier households, it was attainable to anyone with some free time and the right tutor (both *theoretically* available to those of modest status). Material wealth (money, goods, and property), meanwhile, was less attainable. Those who had it sat atop the pyramid of respectability, while others scrambled to earn a living and maintain credit. Female servants, it is generally assumed, were poor and, by extension, among the scrambling.

As I showed in Chapter 1, while status mattered in court, plenty of witnesses testified who were *not* high-status married men of middle age. Litigants selected those with familial and labour ties to them. They opted (or perhaps settled) for witnesses with illegitimate children, a criminal past, or other stains on their character. Unravelling the cloaks of respectability in which witnesses attempted to shroud themselves became the task of the opposing side. The interrogatory questions they asked sought to undermine the witness's character and place their social position under scrutiny. The 'worth question' – in which witnesses were asked to estimate how much they were worth – was designed to force witnesses of limited means to admit their poverty, thereby casting their depositions as unreliable. Other witnesses were also asked to appraise the wealth of fellow deponents. Given the importance of reputation and credibility in early modern England (and therefore in court), evaluations of worth were highly subjective on both sides.[47] While a witness might inflate their own socio-economic standing, opposing witnesses might correspondingly puncture it. But, as Alexandra Shepard found, these statements of worth were nonetheless 'reasonably reliable reflections of the extent of their moveable property'.[48]

How female servants articulated their worth in court varied: their statements captured the material wealth and capital they could possess, their personal reflections upon their work, and the economic strategies, intentions, and aspirations they held. As Table 2.2 shows, just under a quarter of 540 female servant witnesses were questioned about their worth. Of these, around a third placed a monetary value on their assets, while two-thirds offered alternative assessments. These proportions remained stable over time and were remarkably similar to the

	Bath & Wells		Exeter		Gloucester		Hereford		Winchester		All courts		Spicksley/ Shepard data	
	N	*%*	*N*	*%*	*N*	*%*	*N*	*%*	*N*	*%*	*N*	*%*	*N*	*%*
Monetary estimate	22	35	5	26	12	44	2	18	—	—	41	32	80	30
Non-monetary estimate	40	65	15	74	15	56	9	82	10	100	89	68	187	70
Total	**62**		**20**		**27**		**11**		**10**		**130**		**267**	

Table 2.2 Responses to the 'worth question' by female servant witnesses (by court)

Note: Judith Spicksley and Alexandra Shepard's data covers the dioceses of Cambridge and Ely, Canterbury, Chester, Chichester, Salisbury, and London.

Source: J. Spicksley and A. Shepard, *Worth of Witnesses in the English Church Courts, 1550–1728* [data collection] (2020), UK Data Service. SN: 5652, http://doi.org/10.5255/UKDA-SN-5652-1

---

[47] Craig Muldrew, *The Economy of Obligation: The Culture of Credit and Social Relations in Early Modern England* (Basingstoke, 1998), pp. 148–72.
[48] Shepard, *Accounting for Oneself*, p. 82.

proportions found by Judith Spicksley and Shepard elsewhere in the country. Compared with other women, female servants were more likely to give a cash estimate of their wealth. Shepard found that around 16 per cent of all women, and just over a quarter of single women, reported monetary values in court.[49] The lower figure is unsurprising because married women comprised a large proportion of female witnesses. As *femmes couvertes*, they relinquished their individual rights to property or goods, and were defined instead by their husband's worth. When testifying in 1628, husbandman's wife Margaret Lovett of Twigworth (Gloucestershire) did not (like male witnesses) give a monetary total of her worth. Like so many other married women, she didn't even respond to the question.[50] That female servants gave cash estimates more often than other single women highlights their different experience of youth. The category 'singlewomen' comprised servants, casual workers living outside their parents' homes, and those who lived with parents. Those living at home with parents could – and did – respond with statements of dependency, thereby reducing the proportion of single women reporting cash values: single woman Anna Masie from Wrington (Somerset) responded in 1631 that 'she is a single wooman and a maide not married, and she liveth with her parents from whome she hath her mainetenance'.[51] Servants depended instead (or at least, to a greater degree) on their labour and earnings. They were self-sufficient, proudly holding up their savings in court to attest to their worth when questioned.

Monetary values of worth ranged from as little as the 13s 4d claimed by Margaret Allen of Eastington (Gloucestershire) in 1568 to the princely sum of £60 stated by Eleanor Weeks of Exeter (Devon) in 1615. Margaret's 13s 4d (two-thirds of £1) was a common wage amount.[52] Eleanor's exceptionally high monetary worth, meanwhile, is explained by her status as a gentleman's daughter.[53] In between these two opposites lies a broad cross-section of society from which female servants came. Their expressions of worth were subjective, the same values expressed both positively and negatively. Richarda Cock of Churston Ferrers (Devon) optimistically deposed that 'she is a poore woeman and liveth under her mother and *hopeth* she is worth xls [40 shillings] her debtes paied'. Deposing in February 1635, Richarda had left service at Christmas when her master 'refused to geve her such wages as she demannded'.[54] Despite her optimism, 40 shillings was considered little by others. One woman's wealth was another's pocket change: Jocosa Standefaste of

---

[49] Ibid., pp. 40, 53.
[50] GA, GDR/168, John Turley and Elizabeth Turley v William Harris (1628). Occasionally married women gave alternative responses, recording themselves as labouring women even though the law declared them worth nothing. See Shepard, *Accounting for Oneself*, pp. 214–18.
[51] SHC, D/D/cd/71, Edmund Lawrence v Edward Badman (1631).
[52] Whittle, *The Development of Agrarian Capitalism*, p. 271.
[53] GA, GDR/24, Margery Cloterbooke v John Batte (1568); DHC, Chanter 867, Henry Cockram v Bartholomew Jaquinto (1615).
[54] DHC, Chanter 866, Joanne Penny v Joanne Taylor (1635). Italics my own.

Stogursey (Somerset) put it nicely in 1575, testifying 'that she is woorthe to the vallewe of twenty nobles [more than three times as much as Richarda] and neither poorer nor ritcher'.[55] Jane Wheeler of Gloucester described herself in 1622 as 'litle worth besides her wearing apparell', but when commenting on the worth of her fellow servant Jane Tustian, she deposed that

> the said Jane Tustian is a poore maide servant … & this deponent is verily perswaded that the said Jane Tustian is very litle or nothing wirth besides her apparrell & is not worth as she taketh it forty shillinges.

Her hypocrisy is apparent; Jane Tustian was 'poore' despite being potentially worth 40 shillings *more* than Jane Wheeler herself.[56] The framing of wealth reflected both hyperbole in court (to which we must pay attention) and personal perceptions of wealth.

Most frequently, female servants esteemed themselves to be worth 40 shillings, the figure representing 35 per cent of all monetary values. Shepard also noted the importance of this sum; in her data set, it accounted for between a fifth and around a quarter of cash values given between 1550 and 1625.[57] Forty shillings was stated even more regularly by women in service, for whom it was a standard annual wage.[58] What did these sums of money mean to the women that held them? For most, service was a means of income generation between childhood and marriage. More than that, it is supposed to have *facilitated* marriage, with wages saved to set up future marital homes. Jane Whittle, for example, calculated that in late sixteenth-century Norfolk, a servant couple with no prospect of inheritance would serve for between three and four years to save enough to buy and stock a small cottage upon marriage.[59] Plenty of female servants pointed to their earnings through service: Anna Smith of Southampton (Hampshire) in 1594 deposed that 'she is a pore servant & liveth by her labor'.[60] Agnes Filmore of Rockbeare (Devon) also lived 'by her labour & service' in 1617, and Marie Lovell of Stoke Gifford (Somerset) in 1633 'eweth [owes] nothing & hath nothing but her service to maintaine her'.[61] But none of these women mentioned marriage, nor of course did all female servants marry.

Median worth across all female servants was £5 13s. Given that servant backgrounds were so varied, age had little bearing on their self-estimates of wealth. Thirty-year-old Elizabeth Beard of Bishop's Tawton (Devon) was worth

---

[55] SHC, D/D/cd/15, John Standefaste v Elizabeth Stephens (1575).
[56] GA, GDR/148, Rebecca Lane v Elizabeth Bick (1622).
[57] Shepard, *Accounting for Oneself*, p. 94.
[58] Whittle, 'Servants in Rural England', p. 92.
[59] Ibid., pp. 101–3.
[60] HRO, 21M65/C3/10, Joan Morrell v Thomasine Stoner (1594).
[61] DHC, Chanter 867, John Matthewe v Agnes Wills (1617); SHC, D/D/cd/77, Isabella Willis v Maria Spiring (1633).

£10 in 1615 while Mary Malin of Gloucester, just two years older only two years earlier, was worth just £2.[62] The very youngest servants *did* tend to give lower estimates: 16-year-old Isabella Vaughan of English Bicknor (Gloucestershire) and 17-year-old Salame Freynes, also of Bishop's Tawton, stated their worth as 40s and 20s in 1605 and 1615 respectively.[63] But age and wealth correlate weakly because servants didn't start on a level playing field. Wealth wasn't only earned by female servants, it was also inherited. Eleanor Weeks of Exeter (Devon) – the 20-year- old gentlewoman servant we've already encountered – had 'beene servant in howse unto Mrs Hull about 3 yeeres & she had £60 given her by her father'. Her three years in service wasn't the primary basis of her wealth.[64] Eleanor was affluent compared with most servants, but others similarly reported economic reliance on family. Salame Freynes, worth just 20 shillings, added that 'her father is yet liveinge', reminding us that her future worth was tacked to her inheritance. If this anticipation of her father's death seems morbid, the reality was that most people lost at least one parent in their youth.[65] Servant Alice Inwood of Portishead (Somerset) deposed in 1596 that 'shee hath v*li* [£5] given her in her fathers will', a bequest that may have been particularly welcome in the economic crisis of the 1590s.[66] In 1622, Susan Haukes of Cheltenham (Gloucestershire) – whose circle and cross mark is reproduced in Figure 2.10 – deposed that 'she is a servant maide & getteth her living therby at service & as yet is but of litle worth'.[67] She was optimistic about either a marriage portion, inheritance, or her earning potential. And servant Elizabeth Bab of Bradninch (Devon) laid out her expectations clearly in 1637, deposing 'that she is not indebted to any and is worth what pleaseth her father to bestow on her'.[68] In 1598, Katherine Tynewell of Morebath (Devon) also gave no cash estimate of her worth but replied 'that she is a servant and unmarried & hath a mother who she hopeth will helpe her for her performent [preferment]', the most explicit reference to marriage an unmarried servant made in stating her worth.[69]

Servants' responses to the worth question also boast of their embeddedness in the linchpin of the early modern economy: good credit. As Table 2.3 shows, nine

[62] DHC, Chanter 857, Susan Hartwell v Henry Hartwell (1615); GA, GDR/121, Agnes Brushe v William Brushe (1613).
[63] GA, GDR/95, Mary Wellins v Jane Tirrett (1605); DHC, Chanter 857, Susan Hartwell v Henry Hartwell (1615).
[64] DHC, Chanter 867, Henry Cockram v Bartholomew Jaquinto (1615).
[65] Erickson, *Women and Property*, p. 93.
[66] SHC, D/D/cd/27, William Tanner and Alice Tanner v Edward Warden (1596).
[67] GA, GDR/148, Eleanor Lane v Thomas Horwood (1622).
[68] DHC, Chanter 866, Alice Stephens v Caleb Saunders (1637).
[69] DHC, Chanter 864, John Lambert v Christopher Tynwell (1598). By 'preferment', Katherine meant advancement by marriage through economic gain from her mother. See 'preferment, n.', OED Online, Oxford University Press, March 2023, www.oed.com/view/Entry/150010 [accessed 24 May 2023].

	Bath & Wells	Exeter	Gloucester	Hereford	Winchester	All courts	Spicksley/ Shepard data
	N	*N*	*N*	*N*	*N*	*N*	*N*
Little or nothing	30	4	12	—	1	47	130
Doesn't know	—	—	1	—	—	1	6
Reference to clothes	24	—	3	—	2	29	53
Reference to wages or labour	19	9	5	—	8	41	22
Poor	6	1	1	1	6	15	16
Dependent on parent or friends	6	4	1	—	—	11	13
Alms	—	1	—	—	—	1	—
Not in debt	7	2	—	—	—	9	35
Not taxed in subsidy	7	—	—	—	1	8	—
Total	**99**	**21**	**23**	**1**	**18**	**162**	**275**

Table 2.3 Female servants' non-monetary estimates of worth (by court)

Note: Table based on eighty-nine observations of non-monetary statements of worth. The totals do not sum to eighty-nine because servants' responses could fall into multiple categories.

reported that they weren't in debt. Thirteen-year-old Jackewina Bickham of West Monkton (Somerset) reported in 1638 that 'shee is indebted to noone'.[70] Many more waved their clean balance sheets. In 1616, Elizabeth Hancox of Coleford (Gloucestershire) deposed that 'she is little or nothing worth *her debtes paied*'.[71] Other witnesses mentioned lending servants money: in 1551, John Smythe of Winchcombe (Gloucestershire) visited servant Margaret Shawe to recover 13*s* 4*d* that she owed him.[72] Humphrey Traye of Barnwood (also Gloucestershire) denied giving servant Elizabeth Flowk any tokens of marriage in 1572, 'saving [he]

---

[70] SHC, D/D/cd/84, Christian Dix v Jacob Richards (1638).
[71] GA, GDR/122 and GDR/127, Humphrey Smart v Roger Higgins (1616). Italics my own.
[72] GA, GDR/8, Margaret Shawe v John Smythe (1551).

sometymes hath lent hir money'.[73] That female servants borrowed money meant they were trusted debtors who participated in credit networks.

They were also moneylenders.[74] Although most held no great wealth, female servants' cash estimates of worth were generally higher than those of labourers, masons, shoemakers, blacksmiths, weavers, and thatchers (to name just a few).[75] With fewer economic responsibilities, single women had more surplus capital. Around half had lost their fathers before they were married and many capitalised on monetary bequests in the moneylending market.[76] Others probably leveraged their wages. Anne Parrie of Frampton on Severn (Gloucestershire) died in 1588, leaving only a nuncupative (oral) will which was disputed in the church court. Anne had lent various sums of money to kin and others. On her deathbed, she allegedly annulled a debt amounting to 20 shillings owed by her still-living father but called in two other debts: £4 owed by 'one Thomas Curtes' and 18 shillings owed by 'one Browning her brother in lawe'. Anne had lent a total of £5 18s, not an insubstantial amount for a female servant to hold. She was industrious, lending her money to generate profit while she had no immediate use for it.[77]

But some female servants *did* express limited access to wealth. Wilmota Ashford of Exeter (Devon) deposed in 1635 that 'shee is not much worth but liveth by her service'.[78] Being of 'little or no worth' was recorded forty-seven times, though Spicksley and Shepard found almost half their servant respondents gave this reply compared with less than a third here. Shepard suggests that

> the relative lack of means, indeed the self-proclaimed poverty, of women and servants and the young and old suggests very strong associations of being 'poor' – particularly in the language of self-description – with social subordination and dependence as much as with hardship.[79]

Although they were among those most likely to describe themselves as 'poor', only fifteen used this word. Joanna Awston of King's Somborne (Hampshire) deposed in 1582 that 'she is a pore mayde & lately was in the service of the said John Allridge'. Perhaps she had been unable to find subsequent work, rendering her 'a pore mayde'.[80] Dionisia Hobbes, a married, elderly servant to Doctor Gammon of Exeter (Devon), didn't describe herself as poor when testifying in 1568 but reported a more desperate (though atypical) economic situation whereby

---

[73] GA, GDR/25, Elizabeth Flowk v Humphry Traye (1572).
[74] Judith Spicksley, '"Fly with a Duck in thy Mouth": Single Women as Sources of Credit in Seventeenth-Century England', *Social History* 32 (2007), 187–207.
[75] Shepard, *Accounting for Oneself*, p. 74.
[76] Erickson, *Women and Property*, p. 93.
[77] GA, GDR/65, Testament of Anne Parrie (1588); GDR/R8/1588/14, Will of Anne Parrie of Frampton on Severn (1588).
[78] DHC, Chanter 866, Mary Blight v Susan Richardson (1635).
[79] Shepard, *Accounting for Oneself*, p. 133.
[80] HRO, 21M65/C3/8, John Allridge v Margaret Grenefelde (1582).

her labour in service was bolstered by parish alms.[81] When their occupation was scrutinised in court, servants more typically pointed to their service and honest labour to preserve their integrity as witnesses. Age had no bearing on the likelihood of servants referring to their limited means. Their alleged 'poverty' was just a trope, signalling their youth, single status, and dependence rather than an approximation of their wealth. Servants weren't expected to be worth much, but their place within someone else's home and their few economic responsibilities shielded most from extreme hardship.

Widespread acceptance of servant youth and dependency did not shield female servants from *others* labelling them 'poor'. Other witnesses routinely leveraged the word in court against them. It was spoken by widow Elizabeth Savory of Brilley (Herefordshire) in 1599, who described widowed servant Sybil Bevor (alias Bowen) as

> a person of litle or noe credit or estimacion, a verie leud and evill disposed person and one that hath an ill name for her bad living. And this examinate knoweth that she is soe poore that oftentimes she and her children doe begge for theire victuals, and other relieffe'.[82]

Poverty, illustrated here in Sybil's begging, was just part of Elizabeth's vitriol against her as a witness. But it was the focus of discrediting strategies against servants Mary Bond and Mary Smithe of Brampford Speke (Devon), who testified in a 1635 defamation dispute. Mary Bond was repeatedly described as 'a poore wenche' and Mary Smithe as 'a poore woman and of little creditt'.[83] Servants were an easy target. The lumping together of the labouring classes, favoured by social commentators such as Sir Thomas Smith, underpinned the strategies of opposing parties to discredit their testimonies.[84] Though few female servants were on the precipice of poverty, disparaging remarks about their poverty were deliberate and calculated. While opposition in court looked to undermine their testimonies, other witnesses in this case defended the integrity of the two female servants, commending Mary Bond and Mary Smithe for being 'honest people'.[85] In 1629, James Sterridge of Wrington (Somerset) reported that servants Priscilla Gooddenow and Jane Wallis in 1629 were 'accompted reputed & taken amongest the inhabitants of Wrington aforesaid to bee woomen of honest lief & conversation'.[86] A master's status could also reflect well upon his servant. In 1610, Richard Smith of Combe Hay (Somerset) deposed that Dorothea Lawrence was 'in the service of one Saunders, an honeste man'. Serving in the right household was important in establishing credit. The

---

[81] DHC, Chanter 858, John Roo v Frances Yarde (1568).
[82] HARC, HD4/2/11, Thomas Hereford v Ann Vaughan (1599).
[83] DHC, Chanter 866, Mary Flood v Dorothy Tucker (1635).
[84] Smith, *De Republica Anglorum*, pp. 64–77.
[85] DHC, Chanter 866, Mary Flood v Dorothea Tucker (1635).
[86] SHC, D/D/cd/65, Agnes Willis v Edmund Heale (1629).

same witness also noted that Dorothy's parents were 'accompted honest people', drawing a continuum of reputation between her parental and surrogate homes.[87] Women in service cannot easily be characterised as 'poor'. That so few female servants described *themselves* as poor reminds us of the generous bandwidth of the labouring population's means.

The finest gradations of wealth can be teased from servant articulations of their material worth. Clothing was mentioned by twenty-nine female servants. After food, clothing made up the largest single category of household expenditure.[88] As 'paraphernalia' it was exempt from coverture laws, meaning a wife could hold considerable wealth in clothes.[89] But clothing was conceded by many female servants as part of a skeletal basket of the worldly goods they possessed. They were worth little but the clothes on their backs, they professed. Elizabeth Prior of Trowbridge (Wiltshire) – who left the distinctive star at the foot of her deposition (Figure 2.13) – was 'worth nothing butt her wearing apparell' in 1625.[90] Ursula Pirrye of Chilton (Somerset) had in 1606 'litle or nothing but her clothes to her back'.[91] Shepard argued that 'to possess nothing more [than clothes] designated the severe limits of a witness's worth' and signified 'a precarious existence'.[92] Clothing was certainly the last possession likely to be sold to stave off extreme hardship. The Tudor government was concerned about masters and mistresses terminating contracts with their servants early, worrying that it forced young men and women without work to sell their clothes, prompting a downward spiral: poor apparel made them unattractive to future masters and therefore they found themselves vagrant.[93] But if clothes were apparently so worthless, why did so many witnesses – and so many female servants – even mention them? And why did some, such as Dorothea Grant of Southampton (Hampshire), who reported in 1584 that 'she liveth by her service & is worth her apparell', refer to clothes as if they were an asset?[94]

A servant's clothes weren't highly valuable, but neither was their value negligible. As Chapter 5 shows, masters and mistresses even attempted to retain their servants' clothes when they tried to leave early. Clothing could be part of a servant's wage: justices of the peace included allowances for clothes or livery

---

[87] SHC, D/D/cd/44, Joanna Kelston v Sara Kelston (1610).
[88] Tim Reinke-Williams, 'Women's Clothes and Female Honour in Early Modern London', *Continuity and Change* 26 (2011), 69–88 at 74; Garthine Walker, 'Women, Theft and the World of Stolen Goods', in Jennifer Kermode and Garthine Walker (eds), *Women, Crime and the Courts in Early Modern England* (1994), pp. 81–105 at 89–90.
[89] Shepard, *Accounting for Oneself*, pp. 120–1.
[90] SHC, D/D/cd/59, Marie Collins v Juliana Blackwell (1625).
[91] SHC, D/D/cd/30, Margaret Huckbridge v Agnes Salter (1606).
[92] Shepard, *Accounting for Oneself*, p. 121.
[93] R. H. Tawney and Eileen Power (eds), *Tudor Economic Documents: Being Select Documents Illustrating the Economic and Social History of Tudor England, Vol. 1* (1951), p. 361.
[94] HRO, 21M65/C3/9, Grant and Mahawlt v Ellery Brock (1584).

in service in their wage assessments. In assessments for Exeter and the county of Devon in 1595, clothing was valued between 5*s* and 6*s* 8*d*, depending on the servant's age.[95] Lack of good clothes was both a practical and an occupational concern for servants. In 1587, Joanne Hull of Exeter was pregnant with her master Roger Chardon's child. He compelled her to leave the city to give birth, attempting to conceal her pregnancy and protect his reputation. The baby died and Joanne returned a year later, despairing at her poverty: 'I canne staye away no longer for I have nether hose nor shoes'.[96] Poorly apparelled servants could also struggle to find service, as discussed in Chapter 5.

No evidence of servant livery as such is identified in the church courts, meaning that the clothes female servants wore bore 'no visual marker of servitude'.[97] But dress might subtly reflect servant status. Fine clothing on a young person might denote service in a way that poor clothing did not; after all, a servant's dress reflected upon the household she served.[98] Gervase Markham advised that the housewife should clothe her family (including servants), providing outward clothing for protection against the cold 'and comeliness to the person', and inward garments 'for cleanliness and neatness of the skin'.[99] Margery Goulding of Burnham-on-Sea (Somerset) remembered Marian Feare (alias Igar) first arriving at her house as a servant in 1603. She was, Margery recalled, 'a poore wenche & verie poore in care in her apparrell'. In serving Margery for a year, Marian's appearance underwent transformation, according to Margery, who deposed that 'as her wages did growe due unto her, she bought of this examinant a hatt, a pettycoate & a band & gorgett som at one tyme & som at another'.[100] We might wonder how far the sartorial bonds between servant and mistress planted seeds of obligation. But clothing was important to servants and should not be overlooked.

Clothing of course was a conspicuous possession. People came to recognise their neighbours' clothes because most owned just a small number. Clothes were intimately bound to a person's identity and held material and sentimental value. They were regularly gifted to servants: in 1551, Gloucestershire servant Joanne Whyfyld deposed that her late mistress, Elizabeth Steynerode, had bequeathed

---

[95] See Exeter and Devon wage assessments in Paul L. Hughes and James F. Larkin (eds), *Tudor Royal Proclamations, Vol. 3: The Later Tudors (1588–1603)* (New Haven, 1969), pp. 143–5, 150–1.

[96] DHC, Chanter 862, Office v Roger Chardon (1587).

[97] Chakravarty, *Fictions of Consent*, p. 22.

[98] Susan Vincent, 'From the Cradle to the Grave: Clothing the Early Modern Body', in Sarah Toulalan and Kate Fisher (eds), *The Routledge History of Sex and the Body 1500 to the Present* (Abingdon, 2013), pp. 163–78 at 167; Reinke-Williams, 'Women's Clothes and Female Honour', 76; Chakravarty, *Fictions of Consent*, p. 40.

[99] Gervase Markham, *The English Housewife*, ed. Michael Robert Best (Montreal, 1986), p. 146.

[100] SHC, D/D/cd/34, John Atwell v Thomas Raynolds (1603). A 'gorget' was a wimple, which women wore to cover their necks. See 'gorget, n.1', OED Online, Oxford University Press, March 2023, www.oed.com/view/Entry/80122 [accessed 21 May 2023].

her 'an old frock'.[101] John Dennys of West Down (Devon) deposed in 1580 that Joanne Deacon, servant of the late Maud Dennys, had been wearing her deceased mistress's cloak, although he didn't know whether it had been bequeathed to her.[102] Other items were gifted and bequeathed to servants but none so conspicuous as her mistress's clothing. As Urvashi Chakravarty argued, even if 'cast' clothing made no obvious proclamation of affinity, it was nonetheless 'a form of bodily mnemonic, marking the wearer's indebtedness' that reminds us of the servant contract and the limitations of freedom, even when outside the term agreed.[103] Female servants also passed their clothes to others when they died. In September 1630, servant Sara Axon of Keynsham (Somerset) bequeathed all her 'wearing apparrell bothe lynnen & woullen' to her sister Fortune.[104] These gifts of clothing weren't trivial and were bitterly fought over in court.

Their value was routinely appraised by others. In a 1617 suit against Richard Lewis of Barrow Gurney (Somerset), deponents debated the credibility of two witnesses, Joanne Sheppard and Edith Scull, who had served in his house. Witnesses agreed they were both worth very little: estimates ranged from 'not worth 40s' to 'not worth any thing'. Neither servant's clothes were worth much. But distinctions were carefully made by witnesses who appraised them in court. Husbandman John Abraham deposed

> Edith Sculls apparell to be hardlye worth xxs [20 shillings] & that to be all that she is worthe. And doth verielye believe the said Joane Sheppard to be worth in her apparell 8s, & to be in all no more worthe.[105]

At 8 shillings, Joanne's clothes were estimated to be worth less than half her fellow servant's. Not all clothes were valued equally and crucially, clothing differentiated the *labouring* poor from the *indigent* poor. It might not have been worth much, but by including it in their statements of worth servants and others pointed to the fine gradations of service.

Masters and mobility

Hiring households

In disaggregating servants and setting out their heterogeneity, it naturally follows that those who hired them were also of mixed status. Mid-twentieth-century scholars told histories of service through letters and diaries penned by gentry

---

[101] GA, GDR/8, Robert Redverne v Henry Stone (1551).
[102] DHC, Chanter 860, John Dennys sen v John Dennys jun (1580).
[103] Chakravarty, *Fictions of Consent*, pp. 22–3.
[104] SHC, D/D/cd/69, Winifred Axon v John Cole (1630).
[105] SHC, D/D/cd/48 and D/D/cd/50, Peter Lane v Richard Lewis (1617).

masters that detailed the activities of their household help.[106] But Roger Richardson pointed out that household servants 'formed a *vertical* feature of the social system, from top to bottom'.[107] Virtually all households required help. In outlining their working lives in their depositions, servants documented who had hired them: 355 female servants could be matched to a master for whom an occupation can be identified either from depositions themselves, surviving probate material, or other sources (see Table 2.4).[108] As Anne Nashe's case described at the beginning of this chapter shows, some households required multiple servants, and in other

	Servant masters		Proportion of all witnesses
	N	%	%
Agriculture	108	30	58
Husbandmen	49	38	(73)
Labourers	2	1	(2)
Other	2	1	(1)
Yeomen and farmers	55	59	(24)
Clergy	52	17	5
Crafts/Trades/Retail	51	14	25
Food and drink	12	18	(12)
Cloth and leather	28	50	(64)
Smiths and makers	11	32	(19)
Gentlemen	93	24	6
Mariners and fishermen	4	2	1
Merchants, professions, and officials	17	6	1
Mining and quarrying	1	1	1
Miscellaneous and unidentified occupations	1	<1	<1
Service sector	29	7	1
Alehouse keepers	4	8	
Innkeepers	24	90	
Tapsters	1	2	
Total	**355**	**100**	

Table 2.4 Female servant masters' occupations

[106] Hecht, *Domestic Servant Class*.
[107] Richardson, *Household Servants*, p. 64.
[108] The highest number of matches was found in the Bath & Wells court (164), followed by the Gloucester (115), Exeter (34), Winchester (34), and Hereford (8) courts.

cases concurrent or consecutive servants (hired over several years) are recorded, meaning that 300 distinct masters with listed occupations were identified.

We find women serving in the homes of husbandmen, clergy, gentlemen, and even occasionally labourers. But the occupational distribution of masters did not mirror the occupational structure of the courts (outlined in Chapter 1). As Table 2.4 shows, female servants appear disproportionately in the homes of the wealthy. Titled men represented 6 per cent of all male witnesses but almost a quarter of servant masters. Easier identification of higher-status masters through probate material and other sources likely inflates their numbers. Multiple servants working in the same gentle or noble household further exaggerates their presence as masters: Thomas Clerck, a Winchester (Hampshire) esquire hired Alice Gilbert, Joan Marvyn, and Ann Jones alongside two male servants, Christopher Gregorie and Henry Marvell (alias Fawconer) in 1597.[109] Many female servants *were* hired in households of status, but record survival inevitably generates a bias towards the rich and exaggerates this trend.

While 58 per cent of male witnesses worked in agriculture, only 30 per cent of female servant masters came from this group. But I show in Chapter 6 that female servants frequently carried out agricultural work. Again, the bias towards high-status masters is likely at play here: husbandmen made up almost three-quarters of all agricultural workers but just 38 per cent of masters. That some husbandmen were mis-recorded as servants themselves in the wider occupational data set partly explains this mismatch in the data: in church courts, 'husbandman' was also a proxy for a male servant. But yeomen masters are also overrepresented here in comparison with their appearance as witnesses; they constituted just under a quarter of those in agriculture but 59 per cent of servant masters. Other middling occupations such as merchants, professionals, and officials like alderman John Jones were also overrepresented as servant masters in relation to their appearance as deponents.

While wealthy masters are easier to identify, those without titles, large households, and significant land also required servants. Masters from the service sector (particularly innkeepers) were prominent, as were those working in the cloth and leather trades. Food and drink producers were also masters, situating women and their work within a service economy in towns and urban centres. Households headed by men in these occupations weren't necessarily poor but they were reliant on trade. At the lower end of the social spectrum, Winchester (Hampshire) labourer Roger Edwards and his wife Marie hired Elizabeth Glose in their service in 1576, and Elizabeth Aishman of Wells (Somerset) served lime burner William Browne and his wife Elizabeth in 1635.[110] These households also required extra labour and perhaps even specialist skills. Women moved between

---

[109] HRO, 21M65/C3/11, John Bragg v Maya Simpson (1597).
[110] HRO, 21M65/C3/7, Elizabeth Glose v Richard Wallys (1576); SHC, D/D/cd/78, Office v George Cooke (1635).

households of the same occupation: in 1591, 20-year-old Margaret Holder of Gloucester served shoemaker Edmund Allen. His servant for four years, she had previously served William Price (alias Mathewes) who was also described as a shoemaker. As I show in Chapter 6, female servants' work was routinely tied to the income-generating activities of the household. Shoemaking wasn't a lucrative trade but perhaps required the specialist labour of this female servant. Edmund Allen likely saw the advantage in hiring a woman who had served a family dependent on the same trade.[111]

Missing from Table 2.4 entirely are mistresses, whose occupations were rarely recorded. Several women identified themselves as being servants to wives, not husbands. Anna Jones of Gloucester described herself as Blanche Cloterbook's servant in 1580, even though Blanche's husband was alive.[112] An additional forty-two widows were mistresses to forty-nine female servants. The Crown inn in Wells (Somerset), where we met servants Joanna Colstone and Margery Sheppard earlier, was run by the widowed innkeeper Mrs Anne Glover in 1624.[113] Widowed women of status were often also businesswomen and those who kept servants were generally wealthy.[114] In her widowhood, Elizabeth Tannor of Wrington (Somerset) not only maintained Agnes Whytton as her household servant but also bequeathed her six silver spoons when she died in the mid-sixteenth century.[115] Elizabeth Stone, a 75-year-old widow of Cirencester (Gloucestershire), and Judith Kilmaster, her former servant, testified in a matrimonial suit in 1639. Asked about her wealth, Elizabeth deposed that 'her husband whilest he lived was taxed at 40*s* in the subsidy booke and that she payeth fower shillings to the poore weekly'. Being a taxed householder indicated some wealth, but Elizabeth refused to 'discover her estate any further'. Her 35-year-old son, Robert (a yarnmaker), however, testified that he was worth £500, suggesting that this was a wealthy family.[116]

Other widows couldn't keep households afloat and, as I show in Chapter 3, were forced to turn to service themselves. But some less prosperous widows *did* find ways to retain servants. In 1570, widow Agnes Fishmore senior of Honiton (Devon) and her servant niece, Rose, testified on behalf of Agnes's daughter in

---

[111] GA, GDR/65, Anne Dobles v Blanche Cloterbook (1591).

[112] GA, GDR/45, Alice Walker v Elizabeth Cookesey (1580).

[113] SHC, D/D/cd/59, Thomasina Vernon v Anna Denbie (1624).

[114] Jane Whittle, 'Enterprising Widows and Active Wives: Women's Unpaid Work in the Household Economy of Early Modern England', *The History of the Family* 19 (2014), 283–300; Mary Hodges, 'Widows of the "Middling Sort" and Their Assets in Two Seventeenth-Century Towns', in Tim Arkell, Nesta Evans, and Nigel Goose (eds), *When Death Do Us Part: Understanding and Interpreting the Probate Records of Early Modern England* (Oxford, 2000), pp. 306–24; Christine Churches, 'Women and Property in Early Modern England: A Case-Study', *Social History* 23 (1998), 165–80.

[115] SHC, D/D/cd/5, Verock v Phelps and Mosse (1551).

[116] Elizabeth was a recent widow; the burial of a '*Mr* Thomas Stone', in Cirencester St John the Baptist church in May 1638 also indicates the family's elevated status. GA, GDR/204, Mary Stone v John Cuffe (1639); P86/1/IN/1/1, Register of baptisms, marriages and burials for the parish of Cirencester (1560–1637).

a matrimonial suit. Agnes was worth the modest (though not trivial) sum of £6 13s 4d. Her worth fell short of the minimum required by the Statute of Artificers to retain a child at home and so her daughter served in another household. But Agnes nonetheless hired her niece. Rose probably received bed and board but no wage for her service: being asked her worth, she responded that she was worth nothing.[117] Those hired by their kin were often unpaid, as I show in Chapter 4.

Servant prospects

While all trace of Anne Nashe is lost in the archives after her master's death in 1631, the lives that other female servants went on to lead are sometimes visible. Across the five courts, wives and widowed witnesses recalled past experiences of service. Added to this are female servants whose subsequent marriages can be traced in the pages of parish registers. Table 2.5 outlines occupations held by fifty-two husbands that were linked to women who (had) served. The occupational distribution of these husbands is very different to the socio-economic distribution of masters. Husbands clustered in husbandry and trades: fifteen female servants (29 per cent) married those working in the cloth and leather trades (tailors, clothiers, and weavers, for instance), and another twelve (23 per cent) married husbandmen. Two Gloucestershire cases in which female servants married weavers are typical examples of matches. In August 1587, 22-year-old servant Sybil Castle (alias Salter) of Bromsberrow testified in a defamation case. Just a few months later, she is recorded in the parish register, marrying a man named Brian Leadington, a 20-year-old narrow weaver who testified in the same case. While Sybil's mark comprised no identifiable letters and no distinctive design, Brian neatly signed his name in full. Turning the pages of the registry book, we find the couple starting a family: a son, Thomas (b. 1590), followed by a daughter, Sybil (b. 1592).[118] Perhaps marrying around the same time as Sybil, Catherine Moore of Bisley served Joan Compton in 1605, not as a single woman but as a wife. Like Sybil, her 1605 deposition was signed with a simple mark. Her weaver husband, William, signed his full name, just like Brian.[119] Brian and William were characteristic matches for women in service, but within these households, male and female literacy was not the same. Differences in literacy were often a product of gender, indicating different trajectories of training and learning for cloth-working husbands and their wives setting up a marital home.

---

[117] DHC, Chanter 857, Agnes Fishmore jun v Thomas Coman (1570).
[118] GA, GDR/65, Sybil Stone v Anne Webb (1597); P63/IN/1/1, Register of baptisms, marriages, and burials for the parish of Bromsberrow (1558–1748). There is an intermission in the entries in this parish register between 1593 and 1597; when record-keeping resumes, no further entries relate to the Leadingtons.
[119] GA, GDR/95, Joan Compton v Edward Townsend (1605).

	Servant spouses		All witnesses
	N	%	%
Agriculture	21	40	58
Husbandmen	*12*	*57*	*(73)*
Labourers	*2*	*10*	*(2)*
Other	*2*	*10*	*(1)*
Yeomen and farmers	*5*	*24*	*(24)*
Clergy	—	—	5
Crafts/trades/retail	23	44	25
Food and drink	*2*	*9*	*(12)*
Cloth and leather	*15*	*65*	*(64)*
Smiths and makers	*5*	*22*	*(19)*
Building and construction	*1*	*4*	
Gentlemen	1	2	6
Mariners and fishermen	2	4	1
Merchants, professions, and officials	2	4	1
Mining and quarrying	—	—	1
Miscellaneous and unidentified occupations	—	—	<1
Service sector	3	6	1
Glass carriers	*1*	*33*	
Innkeepers	*2*	*67*	
Total	**52**	**100**	

Table 2.5 Occupations of female servants' spouses

While Sybil's and Catherine's marriages to weavers represent typical trajectories, partners (like masters) ranged in occupation and associated status. At the bottom of the social ladder, we find them married to labourers and gardeners. At the top, they seldom married gentlemen but sometimes became the wives of yeomen and schoolmasters. Women could seek betterment by working in wealthier households. In 1596, William Baylie, suitor to Marie Farneham of Martock (Somerset), was unhappy about the covenant she had made with Mr Strowde of Stoke-sub-Hamdon. Buying wool from husbandman John Sansome one day, he complained, 'I had thought she shoulde have served a poorer man nearer home'. The one-hour round trip between Martock and Stoke-sub-Hamdon prevented him from seeing Marie as regularly as he would have liked and threatened their relationship. Reading closely between the lines, we see that even in the scarcity of the 1590s, women had the freedom to select whom they served;

presumably Marie was enticed by this household's wealth and the privileges, comforts, and advantages it might bring.[120]

Literacy, training, social connections, and even advantageous marriages were possible in service. Sometimes, depositions capture female servants who married their masters. Servant–master relations loom large in the historiography. Children born out of wedlock were sometimes fathered by masters, bringing the question of consent into conversation with service (discussed throughout this book). But some relationships between servants and masters at least appear consensual and resulted in marriage. Servants could be an obvious choice as second wives to widowed men.[121] At least twenty-one cases across the five courts referred to the formation of a marriage between a master and his servant. Elizabeth Cartwright of Little Washbourne (Gloucestershire) married yeoman Thomas Cartwright after ten years in his service and having previously served William Cartwright, who was probably Thomas's uncle.[122] Shropshire-born Johanna Whittington had served gentleman William Whittington for four years in Bromsberrow (Gloucestershire) before they married.[123] In many cases, it is likely that the socio-economic distance between servants and masters was small. A marriage between them represented a match between social equals rather than a step up the social ladder for the woman in question. However, some female servants actively pursued relationships with their masters in the hope of marriage. In 1618, the Bath & Wells court investigated the relationship between widower John Reeves of East Pennard (Somerset) and his servant, Priscilla Tootle. John's neighbour deposed that Priscilla had 'reported that shee might marrie with the said Reeves her master', though there is no evidence that this marriage ever took place.[124] Depositions like this suggest social discomfort with female servants working for unmarried men or widowers and probably explains why men remarried so quickly. In 1629, David Powell of Churchstock (Herefordshire) was suspected of fathering the child of his servant Margaret Rogers (alias Williams). Witnesses reported their suspicions. But notable in this case was a statement from the memorably named Howell *ap* John (*ap* Caddr), who alerted the authorities to David's unmarried status, deposing that '[D]avid powell hath been and now is a widower and *hath noe wife*'.[125] Given the usual sexual trope of lusty widows, it is significant that this wido*wer* was summoned to court.[126]

---

[120] SHC, D/D/cd/26, Marie Farneham v William Baylie (1596).
[121] Laura Gowing, 'The Haunting of Susan Lay: Servants and Mistresses in Seventeenth-Century England', *Gender & History* 14 (2002), 183–201 at 192.
[122] GA, GDR/95, James Cartwright v Timothy Cartwright (1606).
[123] GA, GDR/32, John Bramedge v Guy Grove (1574).
[124] SHC, D/D/cd/49, Office v John Reeves (1618).
[125] HARC, HD4/2/13, Office v David Powell (1629). Italics my own.
[126] See, for example, Gowing, *Domestic Dangers*, pp. 68–9.

In a handful of cases, female servants left traces of their lives before, during, and after service, allowing us to see service within a full life history. Compare the stories of two Somerset servants, Joanna Gibbons and Joanna Horwood. The two lived in the parishes of Compton Dando and Croscombe respectively, their lives in service separated by about twenty or thirty years. It is difficult to escape a sense of inertia and stagnation in the case of Joanna Gibbons. In 1612, at the age of 63, she testified in a tithe dispute, recalling that forty years earlier she had served in the household of Sir Roger Nicholls, the parish vicar. Joanna had worked there for seventeen years along with her mother. The vicar was unmarried, substituting a wife for this mother and daughter servant duo: Joanna deposed that, 'being a single man', he would show them (instead of a wife) that he had collected tithes from the local millowner, Mother Sutton, and would 'deliver them parte thereof to goe to markett'. His single status explains why he had two servants – as I've argued, female servants working for single male householders could raise suspicion. Joanna and her mother probably weren't wealthy: why else might her mother be in service (and in the same household)? But by 1612, Joanna had married. Her husband, Nicholas Gibbons, testified in the same case, recalling his own service in Mother Sutton's mill. The two servants had probably met in the business exchanges between these two households. Joanna identified Nicholas as a husbandman, but Nicholas introduced himself as a labourer. Serving the parish vicar had introduced Joanna to a husband but it came with no boost up the social ladder. Nicholas deposed that he was worth 'little more then [than] a house over his head & an orchard & garden'. Joanna, meanwhile, said she was worth nothing but her clothes.[127]

In contrast with this gloomy picture of a poor woman's future, others climbed. Joanna Horwood was born in Croscombe (Somerset) on 10 October 1574, the eldest daughter of John and Cicily Horwood, who had married two years earlier. Joanna, her mother, and brother Edward all testified as witnesses. Edward testified in court in 1602, self-identifying as a husbandman and indicating that this family was probably of modest means. We encounter Joanna and her mother in a different dispute eight years earlier in June 1594. Joanna was a 19-year-old servant to Robert Wilkins and her mother, Cicily, was a 52-year-old widow. Cicily told the court that she was worth 40 shillings, her debts paid, while her servant daughter Joanna was worth just 20 shillings. But opposing witnesses scathingly qualified these self-appraisals, claiming that

> Cicylye Horwood of a longe time hath bin and is a verye poore and needy woman, one that is muche relieved and sustained by the allmes of the parishe of Crossecombe … and a woman of little credit or estimacion, and one not knowinge what an oathe meaneth … and thearefore of noe great creditt in her saying.

---

[127] SHC, D/D/cd/42, Richard Davis v Joanna King (1612).

Likewise, Joanna was reckoned 'a verye poore mayden and one not worthe anything moare than her apparell'. Cicily denied receiving money from the parish but admitted that 'when shee was sick [she had] some relief of certaine her frinds in Crossecombe, as nowe and then a meales meate at theire howses'. Robert Wilkins, Joanna's master, leaves virtually no trace in the historical record. He was a married man and witnesses attested to his honesty and integrity, being 'of good conversation' (meaning he was well thought of). His was probably a lower middling household that could afford to hire at least one servant: Joanna.

Fast-forwarding ten years to 1604, Joanna, age 30, was married in Croscombe parish church to a man named Nicholas Clothier. The couple had five children between 1605 and 1617 (three girls and two boys) with four surviving past infancy. In 1647, she was buried in Croscombe and two years later her husband died, leaving behind a will which identifies him as a clothier. The town of Croscombe experienced a wool trade boom in the sixteenth and seventeenth centuries that contextualises a transition in Joanna's economic position. That Nicholas lodged a will in the prestigious Prerogative Court of Canterbury and his bequests (£20 to his daughter, £10 to his son-in-law, and a range of furniture and goods in both the chamber over his shop and house) indicate the couple's relative prosperity.[128] Joanna achieved social mobility, moving from childhood poverty with a poor, widowed mother to running a household built on a prosperous trade.

There is an inherent problem with measuring social mobility as a significant (positive) shift in status. Setting these two cases alongside one another shows the varying fortunes that women in service from similarly poor backgrounds might experience. For Joanna Gibbons, service did not elevate her high above the world into which she was born. But it might have kept her – one of society's poorest – at arm's length from abject poverty. She didn't marry into prosperity, but she *did* marry, and the couple worked to secure a roof over their heads. These small comforts weren't trivial, although many servants must have looked on enviously at the families they worked for. In 1638, Maria Crye of Wellington (Somerset), a 35-year-old tanner's wife, recalled serving Robert Nation and his wife years earlier. She reflected on their relationship with their daughter, Thomasine, deposing that the couple

> tooke great care in bringing [Thomasine] upp ... and kepte her to schoole to bee taught her booke and in godlie and vertuose educacion. And afterwards shee growing to womans estate her sayde father and mother endeavoured to place her in marrage to men of good abilitie & fashion ... and to this deponents certen knowledge ther

---

[128] Cicily was probably widowed around the age of 38. According to the Croscombe parish register, John Horwood was buried on 16 December 1580, just four months after his youngest son Edward was born. SHC, D/D/cd/18, Thomas Snooke v Thomasine Hedges (1594); TNA, PROB 11/216/237, The Will of Nicholas Clothier (1649).

wer divers men att least fower or five very sufficient men of estate and good fashion
that wer suitors to her in way of marriage, and saith that her father would have given
two hundred pounds & upwards with her in marriage.[129]

Thomasine, probably similar in age to Maria, was sent to school and taught to read
(and perhaps write). Maria signed her deposition in two places in 1638. The mark
showed consistency and the ability to reproduce a shape (two circles appended
to one another). This wasn't the first time she had produced a mark. But it also
showed no clear evidence of literacy. Maria may have benefited from her place in
service in other ways, but her marriage to a tanner's wife while Thomasine was
set to receive £200 as a marriage portion indicates the socio-economic gulf that
remained between her and the family she served.

Conclusion

The early modern archive isn't exactly brimming with records that easily allow
labouring women's biographies to be written. Record linkage in undigitised
sources is painstaking work. Lower-status families are difficult to trace. Even when
sources are digitised, spelling variations, changing surnames upon marriage, and
widespread mobility place a wedge between the historian and these women.
Survival of parish registers is patchy, especially for the sixteenth century, and
names of those connected with female servants get us no closer to understanding
their socio-economic circumstances unless an occupation or other identifier
of status can be found. The stories of many lives prove to be threadbare in the
archives. Nonetheless, through meticulous labour, piecemeal stories of a number
of female servants recorded in depositions can be yoked to other sources, moving
us towards a detailed, textured picture of their lives.

It's easy to assume that, like Anne Nashe, female servants were from poor
backgrounds, working in the homes of the wealthy. But these women weren't
socially or economically equal in status, nor was service exclusively an institution
of the underprivileged. Within scholarship of service – and particularly female
service – distinctions and differences are rarely explored. While many of these
women were of humble status and undoubtedly served in households of greater
wealth than their parents', their articulations of socio-economic identity weren't
simply cries of the poor. Many stated their wealth in cash values and owned
clothes that set them apart from the indigent. Others pointed to their labour as
their source of income and self-sufficiency, marking themselves out from those
who lived at home and did not possess their own means. Evidence of female servant literacy reveals that some women could sign in full or with initials. The marks

---

[129] SHC, D/D/cd/87, James Dyer v Robert Nation (1638).

women left on the page also bring us closer to thinking about how they articulated their identities: from perfectly printed initials signifying family names to carefully drawn circles and more complex shapes. They remind us to read these marks as those made by women embedded in labouring cultures that required only semi-literacy. These marks start to peel back the identity 'servant' that was pinned to them when they arrived in court and help us to see other layers to who they were.

Chapter 3

Time for Service

It was two days before Whitsunday in 1592 and the inhabitants of the Hampshire village of Preston Candover was busy at work. Jacob Shackleford, a weaver, had come to the vicarage to deliver a piece of cloth he'd woven for Ann Smith, the vicar's wife. James Guy was erecting a hedge around his meadow which abutted the vicarage ground. And Ann Smith's servants, 20-year-old Christian Marten and 40-year-old Agnes Edwards, were cleaning the hall window, Christian scouring the glass from within while Agnes stood in the garden cleaning the other side. But a peaceful afternoon of work this was not. Heated words gathered pace over the garden hedge. Ann Smith had found her sow's leg broken and was certain that her neighbour, James Guy, was responsible. Denying the claim and defending his integrity, James retorted that he would 'have xx [20] honest men to say [stand up] for [him] and thow shalt goe like a strumpett'.[1]

* * *

The words, their tone, and the blemish they left on Ann Smith's reputation would be the subject of scrutiny in the ensuing defamation suit heard in the Winchester church court. But in the tranquil tableau of rural life (before cross words were hurled over the hedge), we glimpse two servants – Christian and Agnes – at very different stages of the life cycle, busy in their work together. Looking through the glass pane at Christian, 40-year-old Agnes was a less typical servant than her 20-year-old counterpart. Probably widowed or never married, the rest of her life might well have been spent in service. As they cleaned the glass together, perhaps she passed on her knowledge and experience to Christian; her testimony identified this as primarily *her* work, with Christian 'helping'.

The pioneering work of Peter Laslett and Ann Kussmaul has encouraged historians to think of service as a live-in, life-cycle occupation for young, unmarried men and women. Laslett found that around two-thirds of servants in pre-industrial

---

[1] HRO, 21M65/C3/10, Ann Smith v James Guy (1592).

England were between the ages of 15 and 24, and Kussmaul estimated that around 60 per cent of people in this age group worked in service.[2] Explanations for demographic change, economic development, and household formation across pre-industrial north-west Europe are deeply entrenched in the life-cycle model of service.[3] It is credited with producing a higher age of first marriage than in central and southern Europe, as young men and women left service only once they had acquired the skills and capital to form their own households.[4] Tine de Moor and Jan Luiten van Zanden's 'girl power' theory goes further, arguing that service made single women economically independent, which allowed them to marry late. These female agents of precocious economic growth are key in the transition from 'Malthusian stagnation' to 'modern economic growth' as, it is argued, late age of marriage resulted in fewer but *higher-quality* children. Decrease in fertility rates (through service) and increase in human capital unlocked prosperity and, in turn, population growth in north-west Europe.[5]

Studying service in the long run is important but can result in typical or more orthodox experiences being prioritised. Alternative but – crucially – not anomalous circumstances in which individuals entered and carried out service are overlooked. The label 'servant' covered not just those in their late teens and early 20s. It was applied to older women such as Agnes Edwards who were never married, widowed, or sometimes even married, as well as young children who hadn't yet entered the life-cycle phase we refer to as 'youth'. The patriarchal servant–master relationship is predicated on a constellation of power differentials. The life-cycle female servant's youth, gender, and unmarried status heightened inequality within the servant-master relationship. But the nature of this relationship shifts when we insert non-life-cycle servants into the frame. These women came to service for different reasons. Training and the acquisition of means to buy and stock a household upon marriage purportedly underpinned life-cycle service. But these were not the causes that propelled very young children and married, widowed, or older single women into service.

The late seventeenth century has been cast as a period that witnessed a transition away from life-cycle service as day labour took its place.[6] This chapter shows

---

[2] Laslett, *Family Life*, p. 34; Kussmaul, *Servants in Husbandry*, p. 3.

[3] For example, see de Moor and Van Zanden, 'Girl Power'; Cristina Prytz, 'Life-Cycle Servant and Servant for Life: Work and Prospects in Rural Sweden, *c*.1670–1730', in J. Whittle (ed.), *Servants in Rural Europe, 1400–1900* (Woodbridge, 2017), pp. 95–112; Raffealla Sarti, '"The Purgatory of Servants": (In)Subordination, Wages, Gender and Marital Status of Servant in England and Italy in the Seventeenth and Eighteenth Centuries', *Journal of Early Modern Studies* 4 (2015), 347–72.

[4] Laslett, *Family Life*, p. 34; Kussmaul, *Servants in Husbandry*, p. 3; Hajnal, 'European Marriage Patterns', p. 135; John Hajnal, 'Two Kinds of Preindustrial Household Formation System', *Population and Development Review* 8 (1982), 449–94.

[5] De Moor and Van Zanden, 'Girl Power'; Hajnal, 'European Marriage Patterns', pp. 101–47.

[6] Sheila McIsaac Cooper, 'Service to Servitude? The Decline and Demise of Life-Cycle Service in England', *The History of the Family* 10 (2005), 367–86; Graham Mayhew, 'Life-Cycle Service and the Family Unit in Early Modern Rye', *Continuity and Change* 6 (1991), 201–26.

that service in the preceding century may have been a life-cycle occupation for many, but this was not the only way it was experienced. Depositions bring to the fore a range of servant experiences missing from the parish listings that have been used in traditional quantitative studies.[7] This chapter sets out a new agenda for understanding female service in early modern England by moving beyond its characterisation as 'life-cycle'. My aim isn't to reject this model entirely. Certainly, service shaped, determined, and regulated many – perhaps most – experiences of youth. But by shifting the focus to other experiences and placing service within individual life stories, this chapter shows that service was more flexible, contingent, and ambiguous than the life-cycle model allows. Seeing service as an empowering opportunity for many women is both overly simplistic and optimistic. It was sometimes a last resort or even a form of coerced labour. If it was good for economic growth, as the 'girl power' thesis suggests, this doesn't mean it was empowering for individuals.[8]

The age structure of service

The life-cycle model of service is based on 'snapshot' age data, gathered at a single moment in a servant's lifetime. From his selection of six parish listings between 1599 and 1796, Laslett found 67 per cent of female servants were between the ages of 15 and 24, and 82 per cent between 15 and 29. Although around one-quarter of people married over the age of 28, Laslett classified those aged 30 and over as lifelong servants, presupposing they were to remain unmarried and in service until death.[9] Only those between the ages of 15 and 29 were labelled 'life-cycle servants', as they were assumed to be still likely to marry.[10] But servants' futures were less certain than this model allows. A 20-year-old recorded by Laslett as a life-cycle servant may have never married or married much later in life after long-term service. Observing her once in the records at the age of 20, however, she would be categorised as a life-cycle servant rather than a lifelong servant. Individual life histories were more complicated and the implications of making assumptions based on snapshot observations of age are clear: in 1602, Anne Smyth

---

[7] For Laslett's analysis of six parish registers between 1599 and 1796, and Clayworth and Cogenhoe in particular, see Laslett, *Family Life*, pp. 34, 50–101. Marjorie McIntosh and Ann Kussmaul used similar data. See Kussmaul, *Servants in Husbandry*, pp. 70–2; McIntosh, *A Community Transformed*, pp. 53–4.

[8] This chapter expands my earlier work on the age structure of service already published (from a smaller data set). See Charmian Mansell, 'The Variety of Women's Experiences as Servants in England (1548–1649): Evidence from Church Court Depositions', *Continuity and Change* 33 (2018), 315–38.

[9] E. A. Wrigley, R. S. Davies, J. E. Oeppen, and R. S. Schofield, *English Population History from Family Reconstitution 1580–1837* (Cambridge, 1997), p. 146.

[10] Laslett, *Family Life*, p. 34.

of Northleach (Gloucestershire) was 50 years old and married when she deposed in the Gloucester church court. She recalled working in service twelve years earlier at the age of 38. Two scenarios are possible: firstly, at age 38, she was single and only married later (in her late 30s or early 40s). In this scenario, Laslett would have mistakenly classified her as a lifelong servant, her later marriage not anticipated. Alternatively, if at 38 Anne served as a married woman or a widow (following the death of a first husband), then her experience departs from both life-cycle and lifelong models of service entirely.

Reconstructing the age structure of service highlights broad demographic patterns of female service. But attention must be given to individual experiences. While parish listings offer a static picture of service, depositions are more dynamic, containing narratives of servant experiences beyond a fixed point in time. Service carried out in the past was sometimes recalled by witnesses. In 1587, 60-year-old Alice Grene of Tytherington (Gloucestershire) deposed 'that about fyve and thirtie yeres agoe … she this examinate for the space of a yere & no more dwelled in the parsonag[e] of Rockhampton' as a servant.[11] She was therefore around 25 years old while in service. Servant witnesses also sometimes gave the length of their service as well as their age, allowing additional ages in service to be calculated: in 1611, 26-year-old servant Johanna Drinckwater of Cheltenham (Gloucestershire) deposed that she had recently departed from the service of Thomas and Elizabeth Mathewe. Her service spanned ten years, between 1601 to 1611, and from the ages of 16 to 26.[12] Full careers in service can seldom be reconstructed from depositions. But inclusion of recalled or past experiences allows years in service to be reconstructed far more comprehensively than single years given for individual servants in parish listings.

Of the 1,093 female servants recorded between 1532 and 1649, age data is available for 480 (who were almost exclusively witnesses). Over one-third (180) were former servants who recalled service and whose ages in service have been calculated by working backwards from their given age at the time of their deposition. Most (300) were still working in service at the time of their examination, but many instead recalled their experiences. A total of 1,185 servant ages have been collected from these 480 women's accounts. One year in service was recorded for just under half of women (222). Multiple years were recorded for the other 258, corresponding to 960 of the ages recorded. Women giving multiple years typically recalled fewer than five years. Fifteen women who recalled between ten and thirty-one years in service comprise a fifth of the overall data set (of 1,185 ages). Their recalled ages are distributed across the typical life-cycle years of service and do not significantly alter the demography of service represented in Table 3.1 or

---

[11] GA, GDR/65, John Welcock v John Smith (1586).
[12] GA, GDR/114, Elizabeth Mathewe v Thomas Mathewe (1611).

	Age at examination only		All ages recorded	
Age category	N	%	N	%
5–14	1	<1	85	7
15–24	190	63	687	58
25–29	43	14	218	18
30–39	47	16	140	12
40–60	19	6	55	5
Total	300		1,185	

Table 3.1 Distribution of female servant ages

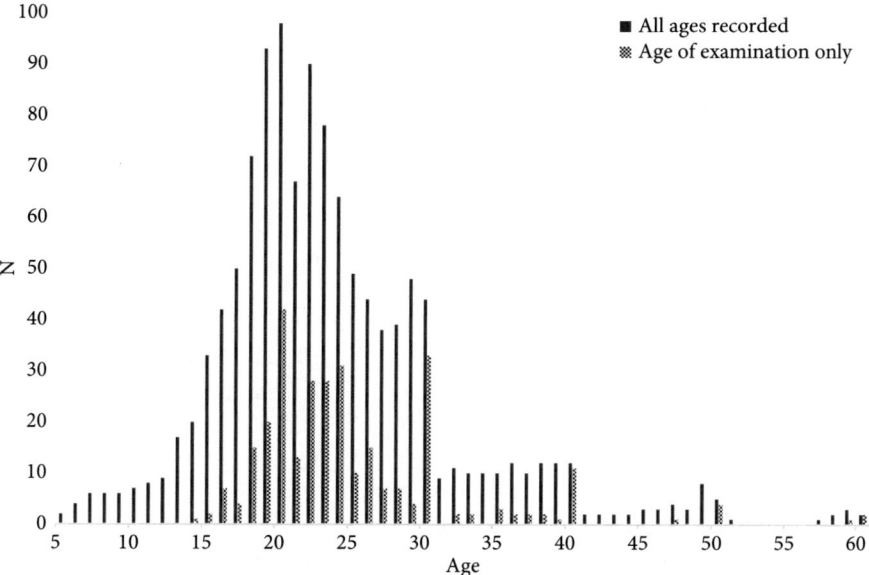

Figure 3.1 Distribution of ages in which women were recorded in service

Figure 3.1. In fact, these examples provide important evidence of complete careers in service (which could last for three decades).

The demographic breadth of female service is clear. Figure 3.1 shows a concentration of female servants between the ages of 15 and 29, and also that service could be experienced at any point between the ages of 5 and 60. By including all recalled ages, Table 3.1 shows 58 per cent working between the ages of 15 and 24, a lower proportion than the two-thirds identified by Laslett. Even if we define life-cycle service as occurring between the ages of 15 and 29 (incorporating the group of 25–29-year-olds who, by Laslett's account, might still marry), around a quarter of women's experiences of service are still unaccounted for. This significant minority experienced service at other times in their lives, demanding that we pay more attention to the full demographic spectrum of women in service in early modern England. The following sections therefore shift the focus from typical experiences to mapping variation across female service and situating experiences of service within individual life stories. The servant institution stretched from childhood to the advanced stages of life.

Early years

The point at which a child left home often represented a transition to youth. This event usually took place in a child's mid-teens and service was a common destination.[13] In studying this transition, Paul Griffiths observed that 'service was not age-specific' but 'was clearly age-related'.[14] Young children were usually maintained at home, where they prepared for working life by running errands and carrying out chores for their parents. When they reached physical maturity and acquired the strength and knowledge to exchange their labour for payment, they left home for service or apprenticeship.[15] Servants continued to be governed by mistresses and masters who acted as quasi parents. But leaving the parental home to work in service represented a moment of change in their day-to-day lives.

Sources recording non-elite childhood are scarce and we have little evidence of how the formative years of the poorest boys and girls in society were spent. Romano-canonical theory prohibited children under the age of 14 from testifying in court and so child witnesses were rare.[16] But although church courts offer almost no direct accounts of childhood, Figure 3.1 records twenty-three children under the age of 15 working in service. By including calculated servant ages from female witnesses' recollections of service, their experiences account for almost 7 per cent of the data set. This almost certainly underestimates the number of child servants, as we generally only encounter child servants in depositions when very young women recalled past positions. Nonetheless, as

---

[13] Paul Griffiths, 'Tudor Troubles: Problems of Youth in Elizabethan England', in Susan Doran and Norman L. Jones (eds), *The Elizabethan World* (Abingdon, 2010), pp. 316–34; Ilana Krausman Ben-Amos, *Adolescence and Youth in Early Modern England* (New Haven, 1994), p. 9; Richard Wall, 'The Age At Leaving Home', *Journal of Family History* 3 (1978), 181–202.

[14] Griffiths, *Youth and Authority*, p. 356.

[15] Kussmaul, *Servants in Husbandry*, p. 70; Ben-Amos, *Adolescence and Youth*, pp. 39, 41; Reinke-Williams, *Women, Work and Sociability*, p. 29.

[16] On child witnesses, see Elizabeth Foyster, *Marital Violence: An English Family History, 1660–1857* (Cambridge, 2005), p. 146; Elizabeth Foyster, 'Silent Witnesses? Children and the Breakdown of Domestic and Social Order in Early Modern England', in Anthony Fletcher and Stephen Hussey (eds), *Childhood in Question: Children, Parents and the State* (Manchester, 1999), pp. 57–73 at 64.

Table 3.1 shows, this evidence would be entirely concealed if we restricted ourselves to servants' ages at examination.

Young girls' point of entry into the world of service can therefore be teased out from church court testimonies. The depositions of Edith Scull and several of her neighbours bear such fruit. Throughout the 1610s and 1620s, Barrow Gurney's minister, Richard Lewis, appears periodically in both the records of the Bath & Wells church court and the Somerset Quarter Sessions. Richard was hardly popular. According to his son-in-law and neighbours, he had been imprisoned in Newgate in Bristol for debt and had fathered several illegitimate children.[17] Edith, his former servant, deposed that she had seen him 'overcome with drink' and accused him of contriving a false trespass suit against his neighbour and unduly impounding his cattle. Edith recalled that eight or nine years earlier, Richard had solicited her twice for sex, desisting only when she pleaded that 'she was but a poore servant, and in so doeinge she should be utterlie undone'. His house wasn't a happy one in which to serve and Edith added her voice to complaints against him only once she had left his service.

Her testimony indicates that she had lived with Richard for approximately twenty-four years. She is recorded as a deponent on two separate occasions in the same year (1620), at the age of 30. Edith would have been just six years old when she first joined Richard's household. She was born in Whitchurch, a parish 5 miles (8 kilometres) east of Barrow Gurney, and one witness, John Hobbes, reported that she 'was a poore wenche in Whitchurch by report, and taken from the parishners by Mr Lewes (by reporte) into his service'. The ambiguous term 'taken' indicates the witness's concern about a child being removed from her poor parents, as well as a grudging acknowledgement that Richard had relieved the parish of the burden of this poor child.[18] This form of poor relief was formalised in the 1598 Poor Law as pauper apprenticeship. In practice, it pre-dated the legislation and aligned with the 1563 Statute of Artificers' vision of remedying the problems of poverty and vagrancy among the young through compulsory service. Pauper or parish apprenticeship lasted for up to thirteen years for girls. Although free to find paid employment elsewhere from the age of 21, some opted to stay with their host families for longer.[19] In Colyton (Devon), children typically entered formal parish

---

[17] SHC, QSR/42, The examination of William Jones (1622); D/D/cd/48 and D/D/cd/50, Peter Lane v Richard Lewis (1617); D/D/cd/54, Office v Richard Lewis (1620); D/D/cd/55, Richard Lewis v William Cooke (1620).

[18] As John was a witness testifying *against* Richard, his statement about how Edith came to live in Richard's household was probably an admission in response to a cross-examination or interrogatory question which sought to present Richard's wardship as benevolent. On the controversial issue of poor children being removed from their homes and parishes, see Steve Hindle, *On the Parish? The Micro-Politics of Poor Relief in Rural England c.1550–1750* (Oxford, 2004), pp. 191–223.

[19] Pamela Sharpe, 'Poor Children as Apprentices in Colyton, 1598–1830', *Continuity and Change* 6 (1991), 253–70 at 253.

apprenticeship at the age of 8.[20] Edith was almost certainly taken into Richard's household as a pauper apprentice, simultaneously providing him with a source of cheap (and probably unwaged) labour and relieving Whitchurch taxpayers of the cost of maintaining a poor child.[21] Richard's connection to Whitchurch is found in its parish registers, where he is recorded as a clerk.[22] Edith's long stretch in 'service' was less free than the term might imply.

The work of female pauper apprentices and servants was probably indistinguishable. Pamela Sharpe suggested pauper apprentices were typically hired for housewifery, although training in crafts was occasionally offered.[23] Church court witnesses unsurprisingly never labelled themselves as pauper apprentices. The very poorest were rarely summoned as witnesses; admission of poverty openly invited testimony to be discredited. Many pauper apprentices instead self-identified as servants in the courts. Upon entering a host family's household, pauper apprentices routinely adopted or were assigned the occupational descriptor 'servant'. But the distinction between service and pauper apprenticeship was not entirely erased. John Hobbes's statement indicates that Edith's childhood poverty and compulsory service remained with her even into adulthood.

There are many indications that the youngest servants in Figure 3.1 were similarly poor children who were bound out to serve, either by an informal reciprocal agreement between households or formally by overseers of the poor. Like Edith Scull, many had remained with the same master for long periods of time. We saw 22-year-old Anne Nashe in Chapter 2 serving Gloucester alderman John Jones from the age of 10.[24] Jane Peeke of Tavistock (Devon) was just 7 years old when she took up service with Dorothy Gaye in the early seventeenth century. She remained for twenty years before leaving to marry in the early 1630s.[25] Joanne Deacon spent thirty years between the ages of 10 and 40 serving Maud Dennys of West Down (Devon), until her mistress's death in 1580.[26] In 1565, Joanna Bonde deposed that she had served John Leach, a farmer of Pinhoe near Exeter (Devon), from the age of 7. She stayed for at least sixteen years before we meet her in the Exeter court at the age of 23.[27] The line between service as income-generating work and poor relief was therefore blurred. That these girls were probably pauper apprentices who subsequently adopted (or were assigned) the occupational identity of 'servant' highlights the elasticity of the term and the range of labour and

---

[20] Ibid., 253. Female pauper apprentices were slightly older in the West Riding of Yorkshire, with a mean age of 9 years and 3 months. See Hindle, *On the Parish?*, p. 214.

[21] Sharpe, 'Poor Children as Apprentices', 253.

[22] Bristol Archives, P.Wch/R/1/a, General register of the Anglican parish of St Nicholas, Whitchurch (1565–1752).

[23] Sharpe, 'Poor Children as Apprentices', 256.

[24] GA, GDR/168, Margaret Hill v Thomas Whittingham (1630).

[25] DHC, Chanter 866, Eustice Peeke v William Carewe (1638).

[26] DHC, Chanter 860, John Dennys v John Dennys jun (1580).

[27] DHC, Chanter 855b, John Leache v Hubert Colwell (1565).

domestic arrangements to which it was applied. More worryingly, the disguising of pauper apprenticeship as service masks the girls' lack of freedom to leave.

One young woman *did* indicate in court that she was a pauper apprentice. We encounter 23-year-old Joanna Fussell in 1633 as a single woman living in Street (Somerset). Eleven years earlier (age 12), she recalled, she had come to live 'as an apprentice with John Ham' for eight years. She was then taken on as his 'covenant servant' for a further year. Joanna evidently saw a contractual difference in being a covenant servant and an apprentice. Ambiguity remains: what did she mean by 'apprentice'? Was she a parish apprentice or apprenticed privately in a particular craft or trade? Clues lie in the parish register of Butleigh, where Joanna was born. The register confirms her baptism took place on 8 June 1611. Her father wasn't recorded; only her mother's name – Marie or Mary Fussell – was listed, suggesting that Joanna was born out of wedlock. Three years later in 1614, Mary's second child (Joanna's brother) Jerome arrived. Again, only Mary is identified as the child's parent. Notes recording payments made to the parish poor in the early seventeenth century were a fortuitous find in the back leaves of the parish register, shedding light on the economic circumstances of this small family. In 1613, when Joanna was just 2 years old, Mary Fussell was given 6*d* from 'Thomas Talbott's legacy to the poor' and a further 4*d* that year from 'Mathelde Knoll's legacy'. The following year, when Jerome arrived and Joanna was 3 years old, Mary received 6*d* from 'Walter Knoll's legacy to the poor'.[28] By 1616, when Joanna was 5, the payments appear to have stopped as Mary's name is no longer among the recipients of relief. This was a family on the knife edge of poverty in the early years of Joanna's life.[29] Parish apprenticeship offered this poor child bed, board, and some experience in the working world, though it could also place the brakes on her potential to earn. Although teenage servants didn't always earn a wage (as I show in Chapter 5), some did. Those in parish apprenticeships surely held less negotiating power to command a wage from masters who had taken them on at least partly out of benevolence.

Evidence of childhood service tells us not only about economic struggles within poor households with small children, but also about labour requirements in the households that hired them. Typically, pauper children were allocated to families that were bereft of labour (i.e. a family in which a marital partner had died) or to wealthy farmers.[30] The cohort of women displaying markers of pauper apprenticeship (through their early years in service) were predominantly hired in relatively prosperous households. Most of the children aged 14 and below in

---

[28] These legacies were left in each of these three individual's wills. Only the 1614 will of Walter Knoll has been identified, in which he bequeathed 20*s* to the poor of Butleigh. TNA, PROB 11/124/346, Will of Walter Knoll (1614); SHC, D/P/butl/2/1/1, Register of Baptisms, Marriages, and Burials for the parish of Butleigh (1578–1653).
[29] SHC, D/D/cd/75, George Ham v Henry Pope (1633).
[30] Sharpe, 'Poor Children as Apprentices', 260–1.

the data set worked in the homes of gentlemen and esquires. In the late 1560s, Margery Hix spent the early years of her life serving esquire George Rodney of Wookey (Somerset).[31] Alice Alsheares recalled working as a young girl in the service of esquire Alexander Ewens in Wincanton in the same county in the 1580s.[32] Maria Cornishe of Dartington (Devon) was taken on by esquire Gawen Champernowne at around 13 years old in the late 1570s.[33] A decade earlier, Barbara Tyll had served a gentleman named Mr Reede for four years between the ages of 13 and 17 in Tewkesbury (Gloucestershire). And Magdalena Rundall of Frome (Somerset) was hired to serve gentleman James Cottington in the late 1620s as a 13- or 14-year-old.[34]

Motivations of the affluent who incorporated young children into their homes were probably mixed, ranging from the political to the economic to the benevolent. They were often those working in official parish capacities. The gentry perhaps led by example: taking children into their homes demonstrated a commitment to remedying poverty through enforced work, which was at the heart of Elizabethan labour and poor laws. Others saw economic benefit to their 'benevolence'. These were homes in which resources were more abundant, but their management required many hands. More girls were bound out as parish apprentices than as private apprentices in a trade; perhaps the high incidence of gentry masters and their demand for domestic labour explains this.[35] But the cost of keeping a young child – an additional mouth to feed and body to clothe – might not be offset by her potential contribution to the household labour force. For households of more modest means, the viability calculation of maintaining a poor child in one's home had to be carefully made. In what was probably a more casual arrangement than a formal parish apprenticeship, Giles Reynolds of Glastonbury (Somerset) maintained John Gillett (and his mother Joanne) in his home following the death of John's father. In the 1630s, Giles attempted to withhold his parish poor rate contribution on the basis that 'his keeping of … Joanne Gillett and her sonne John was a burthen [burden] to him and an ease to the parishe'. The poor rate collectors were apparently unmoved, responding that 'they would take awaie the said Joane and her sonne from him'. But the two remained, indicating that Giles must have decided their work outstripped their cost and that he'd decided to pay the rate after all.[36]

[31] SHC, D/D/cd/28, John Rodnie v Henry Blacklock and John Blacklock (1598).
[32] SHC, D/D/cd/64, Henry Glinn v James Churchaie sen, James Churchaie jun and Anna Churchaie (1629).
[33] DHC, Chanter 861, Gawen Champernowne v Roberta Champernowne (1582).
[34] GA, GDR/25, Johanna Rydge v Griffin ap Thomas (1573); SHC, D/D/cd/76, Robert Powell and Humphrey Yearburie v James Cottington (1633).
[35] See Ben-Amos, *Adolescence and Youth*, p. 82. Sharpe's sex ratios of pauper apprenticeships in Colyton (Devon) indicates a higher percentage of girls than is typical for private apprenticeship. See Table 2 in Sharpe, 'Poor Children as Apprentices', 259.
[36] SHC, D/D/cd/71 and D/D/cd/76, Giles Reynolds v George Stile (1635).

Inherently, the institution of pauper apprenticeship in its sanctioning of compulsory service was an exploitative solution to poverty. In desperate hardship, poor families could be relieved of one extra mouth to feed; another family shouldered the cost of keeping the child but reaped the benefits of their free labour. These weren't the freeborn of which England wanted to boast. Just how far each child was exploited through this system depended on the individual host household and its motivations for taking them into service. Certainly, those who could afford to keep their children at home did so. Typically paid no wages, the youngest girls were placed in service to provide economic relief to their families. They entered service not in the hope of receiving training for marriage but instead to 'get [their] feet under someone else's table'.[37] Their experiences aren't captured by subsuming them into the category of life-cycle servants.

Life-cycle servants

Placing a young child in service was likely a last resort for families navigating poverty and could even have been forced on them by local authorities seeking to alleviate the burden on rate payers. We must be wary of assuming that service was an option or a choice and that the coercive nature of pauper apprenticeship marked it out as entirely unique from other forms of service. Under the buckling pressures of poverty, service was a crutch to be leant on at all stages of life. Because of the concentration of poor relief around either end of the life cycle, this is most apparent in the records at the stages of childhood and old age. But those who fell in the 15–29 age bracket might not work in service entirely through choice either.

Household economies emerge in testamentary disputes concerning orphaned servants who had reached the age of majority (21) and sought legal action against those who had managed their deceased parents' estates. It's worth pausing here to tell the story of Alice Beake of Westonzoyland (Somerset). Alice's mother Joanne was widowed in 1593 and died three years later, leaving behind three young children: Joanne (*b.* 1577), Alice (*b.* 1580), and Thomas (*b.* 1583). In the three years after her husband's death, Joanne seems to have kept at least her two youngest children at home (her eldest daughter's whereabouts during this period aren't mentioned). Things changed when she died. Alice (aged 19) went to live as a servant with husbandman Bartholomew Hyett, a man she had known since infancy who reckoned himself worth £50. Alice's brother Thomas (aged 16) went to live with his elderly uncle John, who later died in 1599.

---

[37] Selina Todd made a similar argument for girls in service in the early twentieth century, using Winifred Foley's recollections of service as evidence. See Winifred Foley, *A Child in the Forest* (1974), p. 141; Selina Todd, 'Domestic Service and Class Relations in Britain 1900–1950', *P&P* 203 (2009), 181–204 at 187.

In 1601, Alice Beake turned 21 and launched a testamentary suit against Thomas Baker, the executor of her mother's estate. Wrangling began over what had happened to the household's finances. The suit reveals the kind of household from which these three children (and particularly Alice, our servant here) came. Witnesses included Alice and Thomas's older sister, Joanne Raynolds, who married in 1599 but two years later, was widowed. Alice's master, Bartholomew Hyett and a range of other men also testified. They had either appraised and inventoried Joanne Beake's goods, bought her goods when she died, or had some other knowledge of her estate's management after her death. We learn that Joanne had £38 and some 'odd monie' at the time of her death. She had three and a half flitches of bacon, nine cheeses, and held just under three acres of land sown with barley, an acre sown with beans, and she left behind sixteen bushels of wheat. She had a cow, a heifer, a steer, and a yearling. Upon her death, the heifer and steer were paid as heriot, a duty levied on the estate payable to the lord of the manor.[38]

The dispute over Joanne's estate boiled down to two contentions: firstly, the handling of the goods and money that legally belonged to her children, and secondly, the economic assets the children had already received from the estate. Witnesses recalled the disbursal of Joanne's goods in the period following her death. Joanne Raynolds (Joanne Beake senior's now widowed daughter) recalled her uncle telling her in 1597 that when her mother had died, Thomas Baker had sold sixteen bushels of her wheat at 'the price of vs viiid [5s 8d] the bushell'. Her uncle was old, dying just two years later, and asked Joanne and her husband to 'beare it [in] minde least his memorie should faile him & hee forget the same yf at any time after the matter should come in question'. The price was important because the 1590s was a decade of bad harvests, scarcity, and rising prices: between the wheat being appraised and its sale, its value had risen, meaning that Thomas was set to profit. When witness Philip Watts later reminded Thomas of this discrepancy, Thomas, allegedly 'growing in collar [colour], tooke up his noates & writings and so went away from him'. On another occasion, witnesses testified, Thomas loaned out 30 shillings bequeathed to Joanne Raynolds, accruing interest of 3 shillings. When Joanne came of age, Thomas parted only with the original 30 shillings and 'denyed her any of the interest saying that it was the executors of the will of the said deceaseds monie'. For his part, Thomas argued he had been at considerable costs maintaining the children in his home following their mother's death, although witnesses responded that the children had stayed no more than a week and had cost him little. At this tipping point, when Joanne's death forced her daughter into service, we see the household economy laid bare.[39] These shifting circumstances changed Alice's life course. Until her late teens, she had lived at

---

[38] The very best animal was usually demanded for this duty. Paul Cavill, 'Mortuary Dues in Early Sixteenth-Century England', *Continuity and Change* 36 (2021), 285–308 at 288.

[39] SHC, D/D/cd/32, Thomas Baker and John Keyser v Thomas Beake and Alice Beake (1601).

home. Suddenly, she found herself a servant. Her age tells us this was life-cycle service, the fate of most women her age. But service surely hadn't been in her future until her mother's death.

This is also apparent in the story of Juliana Davis (alias Key) of Gloucester, a witness in a 1579 testamentary dispute. In September 1578, her next-door neighbours, Thomas and Margaret Crodie, and their two young boys were victims of a bubonic plague epidemic that devastated Gloucester.[40] Living with her parents, Juliana had cared for Thomas Crodie while he was sick. Unsurprisingly, Juliana too had suffered, noting that she 'was sick of yt, but escaped'. Twenty-four years old at the time of her deposition in March 1579, her recovery had been fast but her mother, Joyce, was less fortunate. At some point between September and March, she too had died, and Juliana became household servant to William Barton. Juliana's father's occupation unfortunately isn't recorded but he was literate; witnesses recalled him writing down Margaret Crodie's final will. The rigidity of the term 'life-cycle servant' masks the uncertainty of life. Not all young people expected to serve. Service was a safety net when the family economy was thrown into crisis. Seeing service in this way highlights the various ways different women perceived their time working and living in other people's homes. Throughout this book, the thread of service as a lifeline or a safety net resurfaces time and again.

Married women

More than 16 per cent of all recorded servant ages were 30 and over (see Table 3.1). Laslett acknowledged that 'there were servants at all ages. You could be a nubile unmarried all your life in the West [of Europe] or become a servant again if you were widowed'.[41] Marriage is thought to have been the natural culmination of service and that those aged 30 and over were past the prime of their lives, left with no alternative but to serve. This makes too many assumptions. This age group captures women in their 30s right through to their 60s, making it difficult to generalise their experiences, motivations, and intentions. Advancing calendar age didn't linearly equate to 'old age'. Lynn Botelho argued that women in their 50s were understood to be old.[42] Shulamith Shahar, however, found that old age was as much defined by physical markers (infirmity and functional incapacity) as by a number in the late medieval period.[43] Calendar age increasingly came to fix

---

[40] 'Early Modern Gloucester (to 1640): Population and Economic Development to 1640', in N. M. Herbert (ed.), *A History of the County of Gloucester, Vol. 4: The City of Gloucester* (1988), 73–81. *British History Online*, http://www.british-history.ac.uk/vch/glos/vol4/pp73-81 [accessed 30 May 2023].
[41] Laslett, *Family Life*, pp. 34–5.
[42] Lynn Botelho, 'Old Age and Menopause in Rural Women of Early Modern Suffolk', in Lynn Botelho and Pat Thane (eds), *Women and Ageing in British Society since 1500* (Abingdon, 2001), pp. 43–65 at 59–61.
[43] Shulamith Shahar, 'Who Were Old in the Middle Ages?', *Social History of Medicine* 6 (1993), 313–41.

'old age' as a state of personal decline by the eighteenth century, but even today, the 'boundaries between functional, cultural, and chronological age are themselves very porous'.[44] The prospects for marriage of a woman in her 30s (should she have any inclination towards it) were still relatively high. Women serving in their 40s and 50s may also have gone on to remarry and others even married for the first time. A small but distinct group of married women also served. It's to this group that I now turn.

Advice literature indicated that a married woman was expected to manage her own household. In 1568, courtier Edmund Tilney promoted the importance of good housewifery, instructing the married woman to 'looke well to hir huswifery, and not onely to see that all be done, but that all be well done'.[45] Housewifery, like husbandry, was understood as an important occupation. But wives were engaged in countless other forms of work including textile production, money-lending, running businesses, charwork, and caring for the sick.[46] Amy Erickson emphasised continuity in working experiences for women upon marriage, and Jane Whittle showed that some widowed women had always had successful, independent working lives separate from their husbands.[47] However, it's still assumed that service (especially live-in service) came to an end upon marriage.[48]

But marriage and service were not always incompatible. Married women's labour in service could be a response to household poverty.[49] Patricia Crawford found evidence of married couples in live-in service in the eighteenth century and briefly noted this physical separation of husband and wife as a consequence of economic hardship.[50] Servant Margaret Knowsley, who takes centre stage in Steve Hindle's microhistory of early seventeenth-century Nantwich (Cheshire), was married with four children. Hindle observed that she had probably lived 'a life of grinding poverty', having worked as a casual servant for preachers and ministers for some time.[51] Further evidence of economic distress as a catalyst for a married woman's (re-)entry into service is found in church court depositions. The 1568 deposition of 60-year-old Dionisia Hobbes of Exeter (Devon) records her as both a servant and a wife. She deposed that she 'hath kept Mr doctors howse syns [since]

[44] S. R. Ottaway, *The Decline of Life: Old Age in Eighteenth-Century England* (Cambridge, 2004), p. 18.

[45] Edmund Tilney, *The Flower of Friendship: A Renaissance Dialogue Contesting Marriage*, ed. Valerie Wayne (Ithaca, NY, 1992), p. 137.

[46] Amy Louise Erickson, 'Married Women's Occupations in Eighteenth-Century London', *Continuity and Change* 23 (2008), 267–307; Whittle and Hailwood, 'Gender Division of Labour', 22.

[47] Erickson, 'Married Women's Occupations', 267–307; Erickson, *Women and Property*, p. 193; Whittle, 'Enterprising Widows'.

[48] In eighteenth-century France, married men might continue as servants, but this option wasn't available to their wives as masters disapproved of married women in service. See Sarah C. Maza, *Servants and Masters in Eighteenth-Century France: The Uses of Loyalty* (Princeton and Guildford, 1983), p. 78.

[49] See Todd, 'Domestic Service', 185; Delap, *Knowing their Place*, p. 42.

[50] Patricia Crawford, *Parents of Poor Children in England 1580–1800* (Oxford, 2010), p. 165.

[51] Steve Hindle, 'The Shaming of Margaret Knowsley: Gossip, Gender and the Experience of Authority in Early Modern England', *Continuity and Change* 9 (1994), 391–419 at 396.

he came to be chanon here at Exett[er]'. She was unlikely to have been a live-in servant. Aside from occasional absences from home when required to travel to her master's vicarage in Rockbeare (Devon), she lived in St Catherine's Almshouse in the city with her husband. Their reliance on poor relief and Dionisia's service were part of an economy of makeshifts.[52]

Other couples *were* physically separated by a wife's position in service. In 1605, Catherine Moore of Bisley (Gloucestershire) testified in a defamation dispute on behalf of her former mistress, Joan Compton, a widow of the same parish. We met Catherine in Chapter 2; she was 50 years old and married to 47-year-old broadweaver William. Six months earlier, Catherine had worked in Joan's household as a live-in servant but by the time of her examination, she had left Joan's service, perhaps returning to the marital home.[53] Some clues suggest multiple points of contact between the Moores' household and Joan Compton's. Upon her widowhood, Joan became owner of the Bisley tithes. Recorded as a witness in the Gloucester court on several occasions, William deposed that Joan regularly hired him to gather tithes.[54] Despite the apparent prosperity of cloth-working in the area, it's possible that William's age, fluctuations in trade, or flooding of the market prevented him from earning a sufficient living in broadweaving and he was forced to seek additional work.[55] Multiple income-generating activities appear to have characterised this early seventeenth-century Bisley household. This was a collective household strategy – or, as Maria Ågren et al. refer to it, the 'two-supporter' model – of maintaining a living.[56]

Working in service as a married person wasn't a gender-specific experience. Husbands also served. In 1578, Barbara Lowe of Gloucester described her husband, Roger, as the servant of Mr Pate.[57] Husbandman Richard Windoe of Haresfield

---

[52] DHC, Chanter 858, John Roo v Frances Yarde (1568). The term 'economy of makeshifts' was first coined by Olwen Hufton in her study of the poor of eighteenth-century France. It characterises both the position of families living dangerously close to subsistence levels and their strategies for staying afloat. See Olwen Hufton, *The Poor of Eighteenth-Century France, 1750–1789* (Oxford, 1974), pp. 69–127. See also Pelling, 'Old Age', p. 68.

[53] GA, GDR/95, Joan Compton v Edward Townsend (1605).

[54] See GA, GDR/95, Joan Compton v John Shewell (1604); GDR/95, Elizabeth Robinson v Eleanor Shoell (1605); GDR/106, Christopher Windle v Walter Butt (1608); GDR/148, John Fry v John Gardiner (1622); GDR/148, John Fry v Edmund Snowe (1622); GDR/168, John Sedgman v Walter Masters (1630).

[55] A. P. Baggs, A. R. J. Jurica, and W. J. Sheils, 'Bisley: Economic History', in N. M. Herbert and R. B. Pugh (eds), *A History of the County of Gloucester, Vol. 11: Bisley and Longtree Hundreds* (1976), pp. 20–30. Shepard found that the average worth of weavers in this period was between that of a husbandman and a labourer. See Shepard, *Accounting for Oneself*, p. 74.

[56] Sofia Ling, Karin Hassan Jansson, Marie Lennersand, Christopher Pihl, and Maria Ågren, 'Marriage and Work: Intertwined Sources of Agency and Authority', in Maria Ågren (ed.), *Making a Living, Making a Difference: Gender and Work in Early Modern European Society* (Oxford, 2017), pp. 80–102 at 80. Several works have questioned the existence of the male breadwinner in early modern England. See Jennine Hurl-Eamon, 'The Fiction of Female Dependence and the Makeshift Economy of Soldiers, Sailors, and Their Wives in Eighteenth-Century London', *Labor History* 49 (2008), 481–501; Erickson, 'Married Women's Occupations', 267–307; Shepard, *Accounting for Oneself*, pp. 176, 214–31.

[57] GA, GDR/45, Testament of Margaret Brodie (1578).

(Gloucestershire) described himself as the servant of John Huntly in 1602 and appears to have lived in, while his wife, Joanna, deposed that she 'dwelte at Ipslade in the parish of Strowde with her father'.[58] These male, married servants weren't the wealthy yeomen appointed to manage large rural gentry estates (also notionally labelled as 'servants'). Their labour in service was manual, low-status, and low-paid, indistinguishable from that of the life-cycle servant. Married couples also served together. In summer 1637, Joanna Guilliams and her husband John, a trencher maker,[59] 'with many others were hired servants to Mr Hoxton of Fryarie making of haie in a certaine meade some halfe a myle from the said Mr Hoxton's house'.[60] Witham Friary (where Mr Hoxton's field lay) was around 2.5 kilometres from Trudoxhill (Somerset) where the couple lived. They had married seven years earlier and there was a significant age gap of at least fifteen (but possibly as many as twenty-three) years between them.[61] Joanna and John had no children, expanding their availability to work in service and away from the marital home. Notably, this married couple described themselves as servants even when the work they undertook was temporary and not annually contracted. Their labour was outdoor rather than indoor and more casual than we'd imagine of a servant. The word 'servant' was used in the absence of the term 'day labourer', which became commonplace in the eighteenth century. As I show in Chapter 5, service included 'casual' or non-annual work in this period.

When a married woman served, it was usual to see her husband working in some capacity for the same family. In 1583 in Titchfield (Hampshire), 36-year-old Elizabeth Godderd, a miller's wife, told the Winchester court 'that she hath binn the said Robert Godfrys servant and so yet ys', demonstrating continued economic and occupational dependency on her master. She added that John, her husband, 'is his miller'.[62] Female servants didn't just receive support from their masters in the lead-up to their marriage in the way of gifts and contributions to their marriage portions, as other historians have observed.[63] Connections – and even the promise of labour – continued after marriage. In fact, there is no evidence to suggest that a wife's service was perceived as a disturbance to married life.

---

[58] GA, GDR/89, Hugh Baker v Mabel Elliottes (1602).

[59] A trencher was 'a flat piece of wood, square or circular, on which meat was served and cut up; a plate or platter of wood, metal, or earthenware'. See 'trencher, n.1.' OED Online, Oxford University Press, March 2023, www.oed.com/view/Entry/205528 [accessed 29 May 2023].

[60] SHC, D/D/cd/80, Eleanor Lysnia v Mary Phillips (1637).

[61] Joanna was 33 at the time of their marriage, while John was just 18 (she described herself as around 40 years old at the time of her examination, while he was 25). A Joanne Chanceller (Joanne's maiden name) was recorded as having been baptised in 1589, however, suggesting she was actually around 48 when she came to court, and 41 when she married. No baptisms were recorded for children of the couple in the parish register of Nunney, containing Trudoxhill. See SHC, D/P/nun/2/1/1, Nunney Baptisms, births, marriages, and burials (1547–1703).

[62] HRO, 21M65/C3/9, [Unknown] v [Unknown] (1583).

[63] Diana O'Hara, *Courtship and Constraint: Rethinking the Making of Marriage in Tudor England* (Manchester, 2002), pp. 196–9; Erickson, *Women and Property*, pp. 85–6, 215–17.

We assume it to have been disruptive to normative social and marital behaviour since service meant dependency on a master, whereas a wife was (optimistically) to gain some autonomy or (pessimistically) fall under the rule of her husband. But working in service as a married woman was a practical economic strategy and it's not hard to imagine it fitting within existing frameworks and repertoires of work for married couples. After all, the engagement of poor married women in charwork, a form of daily, non-residential service, is well known.[64] Live-in service was perhaps less usual for married women but in some circumstances could be convenient or necessary.

For other couples, a married woman's service wasn't a response to economic hardship at all but a solution to marital troubles. Lone women who separated from their husbands found work in casual, low-skilled, and low-paid occupations.[65] Live-in arrangements were well suited to estranged wives, as it provided them with refuge and an independent income. Anne Collens of Tregony (Cornwall) sought to annul her union with Edward Pasthawe in 1556, claiming the marriage was unlawful as she was too young to marry (she was, according to witnesses, as young as 12). Witnesses deposed that following the wedding, she refused to live with him and instead offered her service to her godfather, Sir Hugh Trevennon.[66] In 1567, Joanne Corne, a married woman of North Hill (Cornwall), was accused of adultery by her husband, who claimed she had left him for another man. Joanne denied the allegation, responding that she had left her husband to take up a position in service with Sir William Godolphin on board a ship, where she was hired 'to washe the clothinge of the saulderes'. Service offered an escape from abusive husbands: Joanne contended she had left her husband 'by reason that [she] wolld be owt of trouble with her husband [who] was extreme and cruewell unto her'. Upon her return from sea, Joanne moved extensively around Somerset and Devon, her living situation precarious: she took short-term refuge in widows' homes and begged for alms with a baby, who she maintained was her husband's.[67]

While Anne Collens and Joanne Corne turned to service to escape unhappy marriages, the contexts in which they worked were quite different. On the one hand, that Anne's was clearly a forced marriage at a young age indicates her wealthy background. Turning to service may have been socially *and* economically necessary upon her refusal to live with her husband. But crucially, she found protection and patronage from her noble godfather, a Cornish knight, relatively close to home. Joanne, meanwhile, was equipped with far fewer resources and elected for anonymity and the beginning of a new life. She travelled as far from

[64] Eleanor Hubbard noted that these women were 'as respectable as their poverty permitted'. See Hubbard, *City Women*, p. 213.
[65] Joanne Bailey, *Unquiet Lives: Marriage and Marriage Breakdown in England, 1660–1800* (Cambridge, 2003), p. 189.
[66] DHC, Chanter 855, Anne Collens v Edward Pasthawe (1556).
[67] DHC, Chanter 855b, Richard Corne v Joanne Corne (1567).

her husband as possible, opting to take up service on board a ship. She didn't return to Cornwall but instead made makeshift homes in Somerset and Devon. Without the patronage of a wealthy, important master, her escape from marriage was only possible by physically removing herself from any support structures she may have enjoyed in North Hill. Service therefore offered an escape for married women from both economic and physical precarity, but – particularly for Joanne Corne – it can't have been an easy option. If service was a gateway to marriage, it could also be an escape from it.

Never married

For single women, remaining in service meant marriage might also be avoided altogether. It was rare for them to set up their own households and this could only really be achieved with the consent of the community.[68] Some unmarried women were permitted to 'live at their own hands', despite the Statute of Artificers theoretically compelling them to work as covenanted servants on annual contracts.[69] Chapter 5 explores alternatives to service that some never married women explored.[70] But for others, service became their lifelong livelihood and lifestyle. We encounter many older servants who identified as singlewomen in the church courts. Leominster servant Winifred Price was recorded in 1599 in the Hereford court at the age of 40 and identified as a 'spinster', while Dorothy Gater of Northwood (Hampshire) serving in the same year at the same age adopted the same marital descriptor.[71]

How these women navigated service in the later stages of life varied. Those fortunate enough to secure long-term service with a family who took an enduring responsibility for their livelihood as they aged had a stable (though dependant) long-term occupation. Appearing as a witness at the age of 50, Margery Warner of Gloucester had spent twenty-five years serving Thomas and Margaret Weike. Thomas had been the mayor of Gloucester in the 1570s. Upon his death, Margery was taken into service by his daughter, Alice Rainoldes, and her husband Henry. It's possible that Alice's mother, Margaret, also moved in with them. Margery appears in the records in October 1587, working in Henry and Alice's service and testifying to the will that her former master, Thomas Weike, had made. What

[68] Froide, *Never Married*, pp. 23–4.
[69] Tim Wales notes the contemporary usage of this description of the youthful poor living 'outside this ordered world of householders'. See Wales, '"Living at Their Own Hands"', 22.
[70] See also Charmian Mansell, 'Female Service and the Village Community in South-West England 1550–1650: The Labour Laws Reconsidered', in Jane Whittle (ed.), *Servants in Rural Europe c.1400–1900* (Woodbridge, 2017), pp. 77–94.
[71] HARC, HD4/2/11, Eleanor *vez* Howell v Matilda Langford (1599); HRO, 21M65/C3/11, Alexander Harvye v Thomas Barnerd (1599).

is surprising is the apparent turn of events just over one year later. On 4 March 1590, her latest master, Henry Rainoldes was buried in the parish of Holy Trinity, Gloucester, and on 14 April of the same year, a marriage was recorded in the same parish between a Margery Warner and a William Dove. In the 1587 court suit, 85-year-old William Dove senior was Margaret's fellow witness. Her marriage was probably to his recently widowed son, William Dove junior. This may have been a convenient arrangement: Margery had lost her master and William had lost his wife. Margery's long career in service rendered her as experienced at running a household as any widow. Her connections through her extended time in service with this family profoundly shaped her life, culminating in what might be seen as an unexpected marriage in her 50s.[72]

Some made service their career. On 14 October 1601, Ann Huntington, a widow of Bath, was buried. Three months later, two witnesses testified that she had left all her goods to a man named John Miles and a woman named Sybil Lucas before she died. No record of her will survives, but the status of the two witnesses (wives of a gentleman and a yeoman) indicates Ann's affluent social circles and her own wealth. Ann's relationship to Sybil Lucas was elaborated: both witnesses noted that she was Ann's maid.[73] Fifteen years after this suit, Sybil's name appears in the burial register for the parish of Bath Abbey. She was buried on 3 March 1617 and the churchwarden who recorded her death must have known her well. He added to the register that she was 'a maid of above 80 yeares' when she died.[74] Serving Ann Huntington in 1601 before her death, Sybil had therefore been at least 65 years old, and older than any other servant appearing in Figure 3.1.[75] As an unmarried woman, Sybil was a life-long servant.

But for some never married women, positions in service were temporary. In 1592, 50-year-old Bridget Foster of Warnford (Hampshire) testified in a tithe dispute on behalf of her former master that she 'did dwell as covenant servant with ye said Turner from a moneth before Whitsontyde last untill ye tyme of barly harvest last'.[76] This was short-term work and Bridget had to find another position after harvest. Other never married women might have no alternative but to negotiate casual arrangements. In 1592, Agnes Debett of Badgeworth (Gloucestershire) served the parish vicar, Richard Rea. Witnesses deposed that she had given birth to 'foure base children borne out of wedlock' in the previous twelve years.[77]

---

[72] GA, GDR/65, Johanna Wieke v Margaret Wieke (1587).

[73] SHC, D/D/cd/31, John Miles and Sybil Lucas v Thomas Chepman and Margaret Broad (1602).

[74] SHC, D/P/ba.ab/2/1/1, Bath Abbey Register of Baptisms, Marriages and Burial (1569–1743). 'Maid' here didn't necessarily mean 'servant', but an 'unmarried woman, a spinster, esp. one of mature years', as the OED notes. See 'maid, n.1'. OED Online, Oxford University Press, March 2023, www.oed.com/view/Entry/112437 [accessed 29 May 2023].

[75] As her age is imprecisely given by the churchwarden in 1617 and is not stated in the 1601 suit, she doesn't appear in the data set.

[76] HRO, 21M65/C3/10, Parrie v Turner (1592).

[77] GA, GDR/79, John White v John Thaier (1592).

Described as a servant, she didn't live in, residing instead with her mother. Young children and childcare responsibilities could bind a woman to her own home where she might spin, knit, or undertake other income-generating work like service.[78] It's likely that some women entrusted the care of their children to family members, neighbours, or friends while they worked. Perhaps in this household that fell outside patriarchal norms, Agnes's mother carried out the childcare while her daughter worked away from the home.[79]

Live-out service might be essential for women like Agnes whose circumstances placed them within poverty's grasp. Parish alms were reserved for those unable to work. Charwork, taking in laundry, and other live-out service was in theory at least compatible with childcare. In 1637, Mellony Pacey, having given birth to an illegitimate child two decades earlier, was probably around 40 years old. She was hired as 'an ordinary servant' in the house of Emmanuel Sanders in Sampford Peverell (Devon) where she had 'beene dayly' and therefore did not live in.[80] In the early years of her child's life, Mellony – like Agnes – was probably unable to work as a live-in servant because she couldn't be separated from her child. Childbirth outside wedlock occasioned change though only its social stigma is routinely acknowledged, not the necessary upheaval to working life that accompanied the new responsibility of childcare. Mellony no longer lived within a master's household, though she remained dependent on service. Perhaps she even found it difficult to negotiate a place living *within* a family home. Service, then, looks very different from this perspective.

Widowhood

Older female servants weren't exclusively never married women. Depositions recorded several widows who turned to service upon their husbands' deaths. Some men may have faced the same reality upon the death of their wives, but as marital status wasn't systematically recorded for male witnesses, widowers are not easily identified. Widowers were also more likely to remarry than widows, opting for the security that marriage offered.[81] Some widowed women, of course, also remarried but others lived alone. Some 'enterprising widows' were proficient in undertaking market-orientated activities such as moneylending, running farms, and growing existing or new businesses.[82] In Chapter 2, we met widows who

---

[78] Richard Wall, 'Economic Collaboration of Family Members within and Beyond Households in English Society, 1600–2000', *Continuity and Change* 25 (2010), 83–108 at 91; Hindle, *On the Parish?*, p. 26.

[79] Ogilvie, *A Bitter Living*, pp. 140–205.

[80] DHC, Chanter 866, Sanders v Sanders (1637).

[81] Laslett, *Family Life*, p. 200.

[82] Whittle, 'Enterprising Widows', 283–300; Erickson, *Women and Property*, pp. 193–5.

continued to hire servants. But the majority didn't possess such resources or capital, instead carrying out piecemeal work to make ends meet. It's often implied that widows enjoyed economic privileges and autonomy, but this assumes social and economic capital.[83] In 1567, widow Alice Poncherd of Crediton (Devon) described winding corn in Mr Trubbell's field, and Edith Serney, a 35-year-old widow living in Iron Acton (Gloucestershire), went from being Cressett Cox's servant (perhaps before marriage) to being her charmaid in 1612.[84] Those no longer able to afford to run their own homes upon the death of a spouse turned to live-in service as another option. As Laura Gowing has pointed out, it 'was likely to be a last resort, not a stage of the lifecycle'.[85]

Analysis of widowed women's probate inventories suggests that on average, they lost their husbands around age 52.[86] Younger women were perhaps more likely to remarry than older widows, but their prospects ultimately depended on their resources. Edith Serney turned to charwork upon her widowhood, but other young widows returned to live-in service. In 1631, 26-year-old widow Jane Woolley was hired to serve Walter Dansey of Romsey (Hampshire). That service was a response to her recent widowhood is indicated in her explanation that Walter was 'her master whom she *nowe* liveth withall'.[87] Just a year earlier, she had been living in Southampton. Being widowed at such a young age was of course a personal tragedy. At 26, Jane was less likely to have children, and without dependants her return to service must have seemed a logical transition. It nonetheless masks the personal trauma of having socially leapfrogged her unmarried friends upon marriage, only to regress to service and the restricted liberties of a singlewoman.

The marital descriptor 'widow' indicated more autonomy on paper than in practice. In 1634, widow Katherine Phillips of Wells (Somerset) deposed against John Horler, who had attempted on several occasions to sexually assault her. Katherine was just 34 at the time and came from Monmouthshire in Wales. She had lived for only one year in Wells, taking up service in the house of another widowed woman who was probably older, named by other deponents as 'Widdow Perry'. Katherine's fellow servant, 16-year-old Maria Doddrell, deposed that she had seen John Horler come to her mistress's house many times and that 'assoone as he cometh in he goeth to this deponents fellow servant [Katherine] & there

---

[83] See, for example, Froide, *Never Married*, p. 29.

[84] GA, GDR/114, Cressett Cox v Silvester Nayle (1612); DHC, Chanter 856, Katherine Spenser v William Dearle and Agnes Dearle (1567).

[85] Gowing recounts the story of Susan Lay, referred to as 'gammer' (grandma), who was probably in her 30s or 40s when she fell pregnant as a widowed servant. See Gowing, 'Haunting of Susan Lay', 187.

[86] This calculation is based on Whittle's finding that the average length of marriage was 26.5 years and Wrigley and Schofield's estimation that the average age of first marriage was 26. See Whittle, 'Enterprising Widows', 291–2; Wrigley and Schofield, *Population History*, p. 255.

[87] HRO, 21M65/C3/12, Ann Dansey v Christopher Hide (1631). Italics my own.

will strive and struggle with her to have the carnall knowledge of her boddie'. Katherine herself added that half a year earlier, while brewing, she was

> loding out the woort of the said furnace [when] he came to her & there desired he might have the use of her bodie & withall strived with her, that his heeles slipped & fell backward & fell into the furnace, soe that [she] was forced then to helpe him out otherwise he had byn there then killed.[88]

Such treatment may have been especially hard to bear as a widow in service. Although accusations of sexual assault were also levelled by married women, the protection that marriage had once offered must have seemed to have run dry upon widowhood.

Others enjoyed the freedoms that widowhood brought in relative comfort: in 1570, servant Joan Sprowse of Dummer (Hampshire) recalled that her mistress Joan Grant had 'upon a certeine day in her widowhoode called all her servants together & … saide, Now I am a widow & Mr of my owne, I may give what I like', before going on to make several bequests to her servants.[89] But maintaining a household wasn't always possible when its economic foundations buckled with the death of a partner. In 1606, 41-year-old widow Margery Addams deposed that she had served Alice Knight in Bulley (Gloucestershire). Upon Alice's husband's death, Margery's service ended as Alice herself was forced to 'g[i]ve over her house keepinge att Bulley, and came to service in the cytie of Gloucester with Margarett Wodcocke'. The relative security that the Knight household had offered Alice as a married woman and even Margery as a widowed servant suddenly disappeared upon the patriarch's death. No longer able to hire Margery, Alice was forced to dis-assemble her household and return to service herself. Alice's deceased husband's occupation wasn't recorded, but (despite hiring Margery Addams as a servant) the household probably wasn't wealthy. Witnesses described the items that Alice took with her when she entered Margaret Woodcocke's service: the word 'old' was used to describe six of the twelve separate household items recorded, which included 'one overworne coverlidd' and 'two olde clokes'.[90] She served Margaret Woodcocke for two years before her own death. The court records offer no clue to the fate of Margery Addams after she left Alice's service.[91]

In the absence of wage-earning children or a favourable portion to support them, few widows were legally absolved of the requirement to return to service. In theory, the 1563 Statute of Artificers could compel any labouring person under

---

[88] SHC, D/D/cd/131, Office v John Horler (1634).

[89] HRO, 21M65/C3/4, Joan Sprowse v Thomas James (1570).

[90] GA, GDR/100, Mary Syer v Margaret Wodcocke (1606). William Gorway, a weaver, deposed that Margaret Woodcocke possessed 'one flock bedd twoe bolsters one old overworne coverlidd two olde clokes an old gownde an old petticoate three payre of sheetes twoe coffers twoe pynneis, twoe partlettes & an olde hatt and apron one candlesticke & certen writings'.

[91] GA, GDR/100, Mary Syer v Margaret Woodcocke (1606).

the age of 60 to serve.[92] Some older widows continued to work in service: Margaret Powell of Castle Frome (Herefordshire) was 60 years old and widowed when she appeared before the Gloucester court in 1596 and had served Henry Hooper of Bromsberrow (Gloucestershire) for at least two years.[93] But if compulsory service was enforced in any way systematically, it was against the young.[94] Old age, meanwhile, might affect a woman's ability to serve.[95] Older widows might be considered deserving poor and allowed careers as parish pensioners.[96] In 1616, 60-year-old widow Elizabeth Howell, lifelong resident of Kentchurch (Herefordshire), told the Gloucester court that 'shee is a very poore woman litle or nothing worth & sometymes receave the almes of the parishioners of Kentchurch where shee dwelleth'. But younger widows were unlikely to receive parish relief and instead were expected to serve. Witnesses in the same suit, Mary Wyeman and Margaret Netherlock, were 30 years younger than Elizabeth. Despite Margaret similarly describing herself as 'a very poore woman of litle or nothing worth', they had no access to poor relief and instead took up positions in service in widowhood. The sources of economic support that widows relied on therefore differed according to age. Although fellow parishioners surely looked on sympathetically, Mary and Margaret were expected to eke out their own living through labour. Elizabeth, as a senior widow, was unlikely to have been entirely exempt from work but was granted intermittent parochial aid.[97] The Statute of Artificers' age cap of 60 on compulsory service perhaps partly explains why almost no examples of women over this age were identified in service. By law, older women couldn't be compelled to serve; but economic hardship nonetheless produced lifelong servants.

Conclusion

Service was carried out by women across the life cycle. It was predominantly an experience of youth but extended to young children and older, married, unmarried, and widowed women. Exposing the many points at which women entered service reveals its contingency, functioning as a safety net when the household economy or marriage failed. We see strategies and ways of navigating working life that fell outside the typical narrative of household formation. Women's service also

---

[92] 'The Statute of Artificers (1563)' printed in Tawney and Power, *Tudor Economic Documents* p. 340.
[93] GA, GDR/79, Henry Hooper v Richard Mathewes (1596).
[94] See 'The Statute of Artificers (1563)', pp. 340–1; Griffiths, *Youth and Authority*, p. 356. On the patchiness of enforcement, see Mansell, 'Female Service and the Village Community', pp. 77–94; Charmian Mansell, 'Objecting to Youth: Popular Attitudes to Service as a Form of Social and Economic Control in England, 1564–1641', in Jane Whittle and Thijs Lambrecht (eds), *Labour Laws in Preindustrial Europe: The Coercion and Regulation of Wage Labour, c.1350–1850* (Woodbridge, 2023), pp. 185–205.
[95] Froide, *Never Married*, p. 90.
[96] Hindle, *On the Parish?*, p. 26.
[97] GA, GDR/122, William Heywood v Mary Wyeman (1616).

challenges the roles we think women held as single women, wives, and widows. Observing a married woman living under two masters – one she had married and the other she served – complicates the institutions of both marriage and service by undermining the patriarchal structures upon which they rest. Single women could also be mothers, a role which shaped their working lives. Live-in service was less likely for those juggling childcare with earning a living, and hiring households were less amenable to accommodating both servant and child. These unmarried women – working as live-out servants – are not the life-cycle servants we expect to find. The tripartite schema of 'singlewoman', 'wife', and 'widow' cannot accommodate the spectrum of roles women held. The economic positions of women overlapped in ways we have yet to fully uncover.[98]

The extent to which women had *choice* is also questionable. Life-cycle service is predicated on the idea that young women served until they had saved enough to self-support and marry. This freedom and financial independence are at the heart of de Moor and van Zanden's girl-powered theory of economic growth. Women *did* have access to the labour market and some may even have had choice. But that a quarter of the women identified here fell outside life-cycle years suggests that their labour wasn't as free or boundless in choice as the girl power argument supposes. Many served out of economic necessity, and young children in pauper apprenticeships were compelled to serve for many years before they were granted liberty. This also isn't just a history of *girls*; servants in their advanced years were *women* (as were the life-cycle servants in their 20s). To argue that the early modern history of female service in England is 'an unhappy history of wretched girls', as Judith Bennett suggested for the late medieval period, takes too oppositional a stance.[99] But we cannot ignore the fact that for many women, service was not empowering. It was not straightforwardly an institution that young women filtered through on their way to marriage. Service functioned in myriad ways, which raises questions about how far it operated as an 'institution' with its own set of standardising rules and apparatus (such as hiring fairs and hiring patterns). In the next two chapters, the variability of hiring practices moves us further away from service as a highly regulated and structured form of labour.

---

[98] On the problems with marital descriptors, see Rebecca Mason, 'Women, Marital Status, and Law: The Marital Spectrum in Seventeenth-Century Glasgow', *JBS* 58 (2019), 787–804; Jennifer McNabb, '"She Is But a Girl": Talk of Young Women as Daughters, Wives, and Mothers in the Records of the English Consistory Courts, 1550–1650', in Elizabeth S. Cohen and Margaret Reeves (eds), *The Youth of Early Modern Women* (Amsterdam, 2018), pp. 77–95.

[99] Judith M. Bennett, 'Wretched Girls, Wretched Boys and the European Marriage Pattern in England (c.1250–1350)', *Continuity and Change* 34 (2019), 315–47 at 316.

Part II

Chapter 4

On the Move

It was 1 February 1607 and exactly fourteen days since Joanna Daingerfield had joined Maurice Dawncye's household as his servant. And she already needed to ask for a day off. Mr Birche, the parson of Uley, had asked her to come to the Gloucester church court to testify that she'd witnessed Thomas Payne hurl abuse at him at morning prayer one Sunday, and she could hardly say no. She hoped her master wouldn't mind. She was pleased he'd agreed to keep her on until Michaelmas. She knew that people talked about her, about how she was a 'poore lame gerle' who 'stragleth upp and downe to gett worke'.

* * *

Joanna's 'straggling' in search of work hadn't taken her far. She was born in Uley (Gloucestershire) and had lived there for the last three years with Thomas Whitorne. But broadweaver Hugo Salter – himself a newcomer to the parish, having only lived there two years – painted her as an outsider. She was, he claimed, of 'smale [small] reputacion & of weake & smale discrecion'. He cemented her status as an outcast by depicting her as a temporary inhabitant, 'one that hath noe certen habitacion that worketh sometimes with one & sometimes with an other'. Others perhaps thought Hugo's assessment was uncharitable. Broadweaver John Browneinge was 'perswaded that she will not speake an untruith upon her oathe for favor or affection'. But he agreed that she 'straggleth upp and downe to gett worke'. Thomas Parker, another broadweaver in this cloth-working parish, had the same opinion that she 'hath noe certen habitacion or dwellinge but goeth from one to another to gett worke'. He too, however, conceded she wasn't dishonest and lived 'by her heard [hard] labor'. These witnesses depicted a woman whose physical disability made securing stable work difficult and necessitated a life on the move.[1]

---

[1] GA, GDR/100, George Birche v Thomas Payne (1607).

Of the ten Uley parishioners who testified on both sides of this suit, only four were born in the parish. Early modern society was highly mobile.[2] This mobility, however, was not consistent across place or social group. Topography and settlement type as well as gender and occupation shaped patterns of mobility. In rural regions, 'champion' or corn-growing parishes (where land use was less flexible) discouraged long-term settlement in times of dearth and often housed less stable core populations than areas with mixed agriculture.[3] The movements of rural and urban society were different: urban men and women migrated further than their rural counterparts but moved less often.[4] Across England, women moved more, but not as far as men. And while sixteenth- and seventeenth-century Kentish gentlemen and yeomen moved less than craftsmen, servants, and labourers, these same socially privileged groups were among the *most* mobile parishioners of Terling (Essex).[5]

Servants were among society's most itinerant, which seems paradoxical considering state and popular attitudes to their mobility.[6] Disability of course physically restricted Joanna's movements: if she was 'lame', as opposing witnesses claimed, it is unsurprising she hadn't left her parish of birth. But objections to her testimony were largely founded on her uncertain habitation. Itineracy was a threat to the early modern state. The Statute of Artificers sought to pin women to a master and control movement through service, stipulating that contracts should be annual or at least half a year long.[7] In tandem with this labour legislation, vagrancy laws (consolidated in the 1662 Settlement Acts) formally controlled movement and instructed parochial xenophobia.[8] Vagrants and the migrant poor were barred from settling in parishes, forced to return to their birthplace or most recent place of residence. Welfare was locally managed; 'outsiders' (those without settlement rights in the parish) had no access to parochial relief and could be returned to their parish of birth or last habitation if they became economically burdensome.[9] Itinerant living, without the steady rule of a master, bred vice.

[2] Between 1618 and 1628, population turnover was around 52 per cent in Cogenhoe (Northamptonshire), and between 1676 and 1688, around 62 per cent of the population of Clayworth (Nottinghamshire) had left the parish. Laslett, *Family Life*, pp. 65–7.

[3] Christopher Dyer, 'Were Late Medieval English Villages "Self-Contained"?', in Christopher Dyer (ed.), *The Self-Contained Village? The Social History of Rural Communities, 1250–1900* (Hatfield, 2007), pp. 6–27 at 17–19.

[4] See Clark, 'Migration in England', 64–8.

[5] Clark, 'The Migrant in Kentish Towns', pp. 122–3; Wrightson and Levine, *Poverty and Piety*, p. 81.

[6] Laslett observed that in Clayworth, 'servants shifted more often than anyone else' and that 'after a decade scarcely a servant name was the same'. Ann Kussmaul showed that eighteenth-century servants in husbandry were mobile (but rarely travelled more than 15 kilometres). Jane Whittle identified a similar picture of servant mobility in sixteenth-century Norfolk. See Laslett, *Family Life*, p. 72; Kussmaul, *Servants in Husbandry*, p. 52; Whittle, *Development of Agrarian Capitalism*, p. 273.

[7] Tawney and Power, *Tudor Economic Documents*, pp. 338–50.

[8] Paul Slack, *The English Poor Law, 1531–1782* (Basingstoke, 1990), p. 28; K. D. M. Snell, 'The Culture of Local Xenophobia', *Social History* 28 (2010), 1–30.

[9] See Hindle, *On the Parish?*, pp. 300–60.

Sexuality was a continual worry to early modern magistrates, and concern about children born out of wedlock led to stringent enforcement of labour laws in some parts, particularly against women.[10]

But servants *did* move, raising questions about service, movement, and regulation. Joanna Daingerfield doesn't appear to have moved from her parish of birth, but hers was (at least according to witnesses) *too* mobile a life. Church court depositions offer ample opportunity to study female servant mobility at both micro and macro levels and within the context of broader migration patterns exhibited by other witnesses. Each witness was asked questions about their migration, though some were asked more questions than others. Compare the statements given by Cornish servant Beatrix Hawkes in the Exeter court in 1580 and servant Eleanor Philpott in the Gloucester court in 1606:

> Beatrix hawkes of Launceston where she has lived since birth and was born there.[11]

> Ellinore Phillpott of Hope Mansell in the county of Herefordshire where she has lived for the space of 3 months last past and previously in Bowson in the parish of Newent in the county of Gloucestershire for 2 years last past, born in Hope Mansell.[12]

In the Exeter court, scribes rarely captured anything more than where the deponent lived. Only occasionally was place of *birth* recorded, usually when it matched the witness's place of *residence*. Witnesses in the Bath & Wells, Gloucester, Hereford, and Winchester courts, meanwhile, routinely reported their current place of residence *and* place of birth. They also often included other places they had lived in between, thereby outlining a fuller (if not complete) migration history. From this information, we can chart the extent and distance of mobility. Servants also offered information about their movements between households, not just parishes, regularly reporting how long they had served a particular master. We learn (and can also infer) the time of year they switched masters, which in turn tells us about patterns of hiring. As an itinerant group of labourers, female servants navigated both laws around movement and cultural challenges of being mobile.

This chapter quantitatively analyses evidence of servant mobility between parishes and between positions in service. The extent and distances that early modern servants travelled was highly variable, directing our attention to the importance of understanding not only how mobility affected experiences of service but also how service helped create interconnected networks and communities across geographically disparate places. The chapter explores the mechanisms by which servants moved between positions, taking the irregularity of servant hiring and contract length identified as evidence of the prevalence of informal processes

---

[10] Wales, "'Living at Their Own Hands'", 32–3, 35.
[11] DHC, Chanter 860, John Lucas v Joanne Simons (1580).
[12] GA, GDR/100, Milberrowe Berrowe v John Crockett (1606).

of labour exchange and the relative absence of formal mechanisms such as hiring fairs. In identifying the informality of servant hiring, I ask whether the institution of service can really be considered an institution at all.

Migration patterns

Beyond the parish

People in the pre-industrial south and west of England were highly mobile. Of the 27,584 witnesses who testified in the five courts, enough information was recorded for 72 per cent to identify them as 'movers' or 'stayers' (see Table 4.1). Across all regions, men were less mobile than women (61 per cent compared with

	Bath & Wells		Exeter		Gloucester		Hereford		Winchester		All courts	
	N	*%*	*N*	*%*	*N*	*%*	*N*	*%*	*N*	*%*	*N*	*%*
Stationary ('stayers')												
F	445	29	266	32	322	29	13	10	44	12	1,066	28
M	2,563	35	1,751	36	2,054	39	162	27	960	30	6,274	39
All	3,008	34	2,017	35	2,376	37	175	24	1,004	29	7,340	37
Female servants	*45*	*22*	*22*	*26*	*20*	*16*	*1*	*8*	*8*	*14*	*96*	*20*
Mobile ('movers')												
F	1,105	71	572	68	792	71	115	90	327	88	2,713	72
M	4,770	65	3,148	64	3,179	61	438	73	2,189	70	9,696	61
All	5,875	66	3,720	65	3,971	63	553	76	2,516	71	12,409	63
Female servants	*158*	*78*	*64*	*74*	*106*	*84*	*12*	*92*	*48*	*86*	*388*	*80*
All 'movers' and 'stayers'												
F	1,550		838		1,114		128		371		3,779	
M	7,333		4,899		5,233		600		3,149		15,970	
All	8,883		5,737		6,347		728		3,520		19,749	
Female servants	*203*	*42*	*86*	*18*	*126*	*26*	*13*	*3*	*56*	*12*	*484*	

Table 4.1 Female, male, and female servant witness mobility (by court)

72 per cent). Female servants were among the most mobile of all women: across the courts, between 74 and 92 per cent had moved from their parish of birth. On average, just 20 per cent of women serving across the region had stayed in the same parish, compared with 29 per cent of all women. Women were significantly more likely than men to have moved at least once from their parish of birth in Gloucestershire, Herefordshire, and Hampshire. Herefordshire and Hampshire witnesses were the most mobile: just 10 and 12 per cent of women and 27 and 31 per cent of men were 'stayers' respectively. These were thoroughfare counties: Herefordshire and Gloucestershire were gateways between Wales and England and bordered several other counties, while people passed through Hampshire on their way to London. Fewer travellers journeyed through Somerset, Devon, and Cornwall by comparison. Mobility was lower in the diocese of Exeter; dispersed settlements were more typical in Cornwall and Devon and rather than promoting migration to bigger settlements, these places may have nurtured intensely local loyalties.[13] Parishes here were also large, accommodating more movement *within* rather than *between* parishes.

Table 4.2 shows how long people had stayed in the same parish. Most people didn't move regularly, especially later in life. But many had moved at least once during their lifetimes, eventually staying put for long periods. Women, again, were

Length of residence (years)	F		M		F and M		Female servants	
	N	%	N	%	N	%	N	%
< 1	219	6	598	3	817	3	111	20
≥ 1 and < 5	671	18	2,749	13	3,420	14	198	36
≥ 5 and < 10	386	10	2,129	10	2,515	10	74	14
≥ 10 and < 15	346	9	1,891	9	2,237	9	31	6
≥ 15 and < 20	497	13	2,602	12	3,099	13	22	4
≥ 20 and < 30	151	4	802	4	953	4	8	1
≥ 30 and < 40	205	6	1,334	6	1,539	6	1	—
≥ 40 and < 50	164	4	1,199	6	1,363	6	2	—
≥ 50	37	1	319	2	356	1	4	1
From birth	1,040	28	7,268	35	8,308	34	94	17
Total	**3,716**	—	**20,891**	—	**24,607**	—	**545**	—

Table 4.2 Female, male, and female servants' length of residence in the same parish

[13] H. Fox, 'Medieval Farming and Rural Settlement', in Roger Kain, William Ravenhill, and Helen Jones (eds), *Historical Atlas of South-West England* (Exeter, 1999), pp. 273–80 at 277–9.

the more mobile sex: a higher proportion of women than men had lived in the same parish for less than five years (24 per cent compared to 16 per cent). Female servants moved even more regularly. Of the 219 women who had spent less than a year in a parish, 111 were female servants (just over half). Across the cohort of women in service, 20 per cent had spent less than a year in the same parish and a further 36 per cent less than five years. In any given parish, female servants were likely to have been among its newest members.

Younger people reported more mobility because their movement was more recent in their memories; older witnesses may have moved regularly in their youth, but it became less important in the grand narratives of their lives. Just under half of over-70s had either never moved or hadn't moved in the last fifty years (see Table 4.3). Our oldest witness, 103-year-old Nicholas Cornworthie (whom we briefly encountered in Chapter 1) had lived in Halberton (Devon) for a century in 1570.[14] Witnesses under 30 were significantly more likely to have spent fewer than five years in the same parish than those 30 and over: 38 per cent compared with 13 per cent. Those in the earlier stages of the life cycle were the most mobile, settling more permanently later in life, and often upon marriage.

As I showed in Chapter 3, service was not only an experience for young people. But they nonetheless comprise a majority, and we can contrast their mobility with that of a broadly comparable cohort of people aged between 10 and 29. Within this cohort, some were servants, others carried out alternative forms of itinerant work, several had married and settled, and others lived with their parents. Over 50 per cent of female servants had lived in the same parish for less than five years, compared with just 38 per cent of these witnesses aged 10–29. Around 37 per cent of this age group had never moved but only 17 per cent of female servants followed the same pattern. Again, we are reminded here that experiences of youth differed widely: spatial horizons could be much wider for servants than for unmarried girls and boys living at home.

Older servants' mobility aligned more closely with that of other women their age not in service. Once servants reached the age of 30, they moved less regularly. We encounter Catherine Moore again, a 50-year-old married woman, who secured temporary service in 1605 in her home parish of Bisley (Gloucestershire): she had lived in the parish for twenty-four years.[15] Grace Warde of Tavistock (Devon) was the 40-year-old servant of Peter Russell of the same parish in 1618 and had lived there for twenty years.[16] Older servants didn't display the same living and working patterns as their younger counterparts; mobility became a less attractive prospect

---

[14] DHC, Chanter 857, John Pyle and Thomas Sweteland v Robert Whytefylld (1570).
[15] GA, GDR/95, Joan Compton v Edward Townsend (1605).
[16] DHC, Chanter 867, Elizabeth Drake v Robert Wills (1618).

Length of residence (years)	10–19		20–29		30–39		40–49		50–59		60–69		70+		All	
	N	%	N	%	N	%	N	%	N	%	N	%	N	%	N	%
< 1	50	11	375	9	202	4	96	2	47	1	36	1	11	1	817	3
≥ 1 and < 5	132	29	1,137	28	1,016	20	607	11	309	7	157	5	67	5	3,425	14
≥ 5 and < 10	41	9	541	13	855	17	575	10	291	6	149	4	65	4	2,517	10
≥ 10 and < 15	20	4	247	6	647	13	737	13	379	8	153	4	56	4	2,239	9
≥ 15 and < 20	11	2	223	5	525	10	1,077	20	800	18	380	11	83	6	3,099	13
≥ 20 and < 30	—	—	49	1	80	2	227	4	359	8	182	5	54	4	951	4
≥ 30 and < 40	—	—	—	—	104	2	264	5	518	11	524	15	119	8	1,529	6
≥ 40 and < 50	—	—	—	—	—	—	110	2	348	8	562	16	325	22	1,345	5
≥ 50	—	—	—	—	—	—	—	—	39	1	106	3	197	13	342	1
From birth	199	44	1,470	36	1,667	33	1,817	33	1,463	32	1,208	35	490	33	8,314	34
Total	453		4,042		5,096		5,510		4,553		3,457		1,467		24,578	

Table 4.3 Length of residence in the same parish by age

as people aged, irrespective of their occupation in service. Perhaps they were also more likely to find work in parishes where they were known; their age may have been less agreeable to strangers.

If so many young people were on the move in search of service, where did they find it? The historiography of early modern servant mobility is dominated by the story of London's huge influx of migrant servants.[17] But other urban centres offered labour opportunities for young people. Relatively high numbers of servants worked in urban centres. To take Gloucester as an example: 16 per cent of Gloucestershire female servants lived in Gloucester at the time of their examinations. But even by 1660, only around 5 per cent of the population of Gloucestershire lived in the diocesan capital.[18] A disproportionate number of female servants therefore lived and worked in the city, even accounting for the inflated proportion of cases originating from the city (8 per cent). Between the mid-sixteenth century and 1801, Gloucester itself barely doubled in size. Its importance in the county's wool trade was as a distributor rather than as a producer, requiring fewer hands.[19] But while the wool trade offered few opportunities in Gloucester, the city nonetheless provided much work for servants.

In tracing their migration routes (place of birth to place of residence), it's possible to categorise *types* of movement (and non-movement) between settlements for 273 female servants (as Table 4.4 shows). Women living in urban centres more easily found service where they lived than their rural counterparts: only around a quarter of rural servants recorded in Table 4.4 were 'stayers'. By comparison, half of urban dwellers hadn't left the cities in which they were born. In fact, seventeen of the twenty-four urban-born servants found work within a city, and fourteen of them stayed in the *same* city. Sisters Joanne and Martha Mason were born in Gloucester. They testified in a 1591 defamation dispute and had previously held apprenticeships (possibly pauper apprenticeships) with the defendant, Dionisia Sursbye. Following some animosity with their mistress, both left their apprenticeships early and took up service, changing jobs but staying in the city.[20] Twenty-year-old Margaret Diaper, servant to widow Margaret Pynnock of Southampton, had also lived in the city since birth.[21]

But for rural-dwellers, urban spaces did not have quite the same pull as London. A rural servant's home parish might have no work available, but a neighbouring parish could offer a convenient opportunity. Many rural servants *did* move to the city, but many more – 60 per cent of mobile servants – found work in other rural

---

[17] See Gowing, *Domestic Dangers*, pp. 18–20; Finlay, *Population and Metropolis*, p. 140; Brodsky Elliot, 'Single Women', p. 88.
[18] Broadberry et al., *British Economic Growth*, p. 25.
[19] Rollison, *Local Origins*, p. 40.
[20] GA, GDR/65, Blanche Cluterbook v Dionisia Sursbye (1591).
[21] HRO, 21M65/C3/10, William Robyns v Richard Bonyfante (1592).

	N	%
Stayers	**85**	**31**
Rural	49	58
Small town	22	26
Urban	14	16
Movers	**188**	**69**
Rural to rural	113	60
Rural to small town	20	11
Rural to urban	13	7
Small town to rural	14	7
Small town to small town	9	5
Small town to urban	9	5
Urban to rural	4	2
Urban to small town	3	2
Urban to urban	3	2
Total	**273**	—

Table 4.4 Female servant migration routes (by type of settlement)

parishes. Inter-rural migration was also appropriate for servants accustomed to and skilled in carrying out husbandry work; the labour of servants in cities and even small towns could look quite different.

For the eighteenth century, Ann Kussmaul found that most servants moved a distance of less than 15 kilometres.[22] In fourteenth-century Yorkshire, Jeremy Goldberg found 'a day's walk' (or 'between twelve and twenty-four miles [9 and 38 kilometres]') to be the threshold for most migration.[23] This radius from home has loosely been defined as one's 'country', delineating a region that saw similarities in 'migration patterns, kinship links, credit networks, gossip, folklore, commerce, marriage horizons, labour markets, administrative divisions, intercommoning arrangements and road and river networks', which reinforces the idea that a sense of belonging in a parish close to home was easy to attain.[24] Across these five courts, gender made little difference to distance travelled: Table 4.5 shows that 45 and 46 per cent of men and women had migrated fewer than 15 kilometres

---

[22] Kussmaul, *Servants in Husbandry*, p. 57.

[23] P. J. P. Goldberg, *Women, Work and Life Cycle in a Medieval Economy: Women in York and Yorkshire c.1300–1520* (Oxford, 1992), p. 282.

[24] Andy Wood, *The Memory of the People: Custom and Popular Senses of the Past in Early Modern England* (Cambridge, 2013), p. 99.

Distance (km)	F		M		All		Female servants	
	N	*%*	*N*	*%*	*N*	*%*	*N*	*%*
> 0 and < 15	1,398	*46*	6,003	*45*	7,401	*45*	235	*39*
≥ 15 and < 30	719	*23*	2,858	*21*	3,577	*22*	174	*29*
≥ 30 and < 50	490	*16*	1,902	*14*	2,392	*15*	95	*16*
≥ 50	461	*15*	2,577	*19*	3,038	*19*	105	*17*
Total	**3,068**	*19*	**13,340**	*81*	**16,408**		**609**	

Table 4.5 Female, male, and female servant distances migrated

Note: The central point of each parish is taken and Euclidean 'as the crow flies' distances are calculated, though actual journeys undoubtedly exceeded these 'straight line' measurements (travellers rarely move in straight lines, instead navigating paths, roads, and natural features of the landscape).

respectively.[25] For female servants, this proportion was lower: just 39 per cent remained within this 15-kilometre radius. Servant Edith Welsteed, testifying in 1602, lived in Rodborough (Gloucestershire) and had moved barely 3 kilometres from Woodchester, where she was born.[26] Margaret Allen's 1568 deposition recorded her service with William Cloterbooke of Eastington (Gloucestershire). She was born in Frampton on Severn, 5 kilometres away.[27] Joan Silvester, servant to Amy Yates of Tadley (Hampshire), was born in Baughurst, less than 3 kilometres away.[28] Within these examples of local migration, regional similarities of neighbouring parishes probably eased the transition. Geographical shifts were less monumental over short distances where existing support networks were readily accessible.

But Table 4.5 shows that a significant proportion of *people*, let alone female servants, had migrated further, beyond the perimeter of their 'country'. John Powe, the rector of Langridge (Somerset), had travelled the furthest, deposing in 1615 that he had moved almost 375 kilometres from Crosby (Cumbria), where he was born.[29] Servant Elizabeth Adkinson had the longest migration path of all women. Deposing in 1644, she had moved around 263 kilometres from her birthplace, Sandwich (Kent), to Slimbridge (Gloucestershire), where she served Nicholas Richardson until his death.[30] Around a third of men, women, and female servants had migrated over 30 kilometres.

---

[25] Peter Clark, meanwhile, found that women were more mobile but over shorter distances than men. Clark, 'Migration in England', 68.
[26] GA, GDR/89, Stephen Cooke v Margaret Dudbridge (1602).
[27] GA, GDR/24, Margery Cloterbooke v John Batte (1568).
[28] HRO, 21M65/C3/11, Stockton v Robert Grene (1598).
[29] GA, GDR/122, Christopher Wise v Dalamore Gittis (1615).
[30] GA, GDR/205, Elizabeth Parke v Margaret White (1644).

Long migration paths like Elizabeth Adkinson's were not commonplace, but many others travelled over 15 kilometres between their parish of birth and new opportunities in service. Within local consciousness, places just a couple of miles away could be seen as 'distant' if they lay beyond the neighbourhood or typical spaces of work and social interaction. But servants probably had different expectations of how far they might travel for work compared with other members of society. It was an occupation in which itineracy was expected. Around two-thirds of female servants had covered less substantial distances, and at least 20 per cent had migrated more than a day's walk (39 kilometres). Younger servants may have found the prospect of uprooting and moving such considerable distances from kinship networks daunting. We might assume they initially stayed in the same parish, accustoming themselves to living away from parents before moving further afield.[31] But depositions indicate only weak correlation between age and distance travelled. Journeys exceeding 40 kilometres *did* tend to be made by slightly older servants. For example, Alice Spurrier was 33 years old and servant to Thomas Marten of Bath (Somerset) in 1637. She had lived there for five years and was born 50 kilometres away in Sherborne (Dorset).[32] But only nineteen of eighty-five female servants (22 per cent) for whom *no* mobility was recorded were under the age of 20 and the age distribution of this group of 'stayers' was wide.

Moving further afield could generate opportunities. In 1612, 30-year-old Elizabeth Howard made a 185-kilometre journey from Stamford (Lincolnshire) to Frampton Cotterell (Gloucestershire) to serve Sir Thomas and Lady Anne Seymore.[33] Geographically wide aristocratic networks may have promoted a long-distance move for this high-status servant. I am reminded here of Isott Riches of Rockbeare (Devon), who I noted in the opening page of this book had loftier expectations of service, complaining in 1568 that she had not come to her mistress to be her drudge. Isott, too, was migratory, and I return to her later in this chapter. We also met Marie Farneham of Martock (Somerset) in Chapter 2, who opted to delay her marriage in favour of service. Her decision to move further away to serve Mr Strowde rather than staying nearer home to serve 'a poorer man' led to the breakdown of their marriage agreement, according to her rebuffed suitor. Securing better prospects in service further afield might have been most important to women of means. Marie was probably not a poor servant. Her husband-to-be had capital, hiring servants of his own (including one who testified on his behalf). Marie's decision to travel further afield to work in a wealthy home may have been important in styling her own sense of status. Not all household positions were equal; there were better options in service for women who were willing to move.

---

[31] Clark, 'Migration in England', 71.
[32] SHC, D/D/cd/133, Thomas Marten v Adrian Ireland (1637).
[33] GA, GDR/114, Anne Seymore v Thomas Seymore (1612).

Patterns of service

Length of employment

Movement between parishes is one way of looking at servant mobility. At a more granular level, we can also map out the extent of local movement *between households*. How frequently a servant moved was shaped by the length of her agreed term in service. The annual contract has come to underpin a cyclical understanding of how hiring worked. This idea is rooted in law: the 1563 Statute of Artificers promoted contracts between servants and masters of one year or half a year as a minimum.[34] But it is also found within scholarship: Marjorie McIntosh noted that 'some adolescents remained in a given … household year after year, becoming virtually a member of the core family, while others moved on every year or two'.[35] For the eighteenth century, Kussmaul found that over three-quarters of male agricultural servants moved annually between households, failing to renew contracts at each year's end.[36]

Depositions offer new evidence of sixteenth- and early seventeenth-century servant mobility at the household level. The length of time a female servant had served in each household was sometimes recorded in the biographical opening to her deposition, as in this example from 1567:

> Margaret Nyblett of the parish of Painswick in Gloucestershire the servant of Thomas Jackette who she has served since the feast of Saint Michael the Archangel.[37]

Alternatively, comparable information may have been a brief line in the deposition itself: in 1578, Elizabeth Wotton of St Thomas in Exeter (Devon) deposed that she 'did dwell a dosen yeres in the house of Mr Castle as a servante with Mr Castle and came from thence about v [five] yeres agoe'.[38] Occasionally, service histories were detailed: in 1565, Hampshire servant Margery Gryffythe had joined Thomas Read's household just a fortnight before her examination in court. In her deposition, she added that she had previously served Thomas Shepherde for a year and John Webbe for four years.[39]

Table 4.6 records only *completed* posts in service (Margaret Nyblett's service with Thomas Jackette isn't recorded here as she was still in his service). Two key findings emerge. Firstly, female servants stayed for relatively long periods with the same master: the median length of time in service was between 1.5 and two years. Half of female servants worked for the same master for under two years,

---

[34] 'The Statute of Artificers (1563)' printed in Tawney and Power, *Tudor Economic Documents*, p. 340.
[35] Marjorie K. McIntosh, 'Servants and the Household Unit in an Elizabethan English Community', *Journal of Family History* 9 (1984), 3–23 at 12.
[36] Kussmaul, *Servants in Husbandry*, p. 52.
[37] GA, GDR/23, Jones v Thomas Ducke (1567).
[38] DHC, Chanter 860, Raymond Wadland v Blanche Apworthie (1578).
[39] HRO, 21M65/C3/3, Margaret Cocketryce v Agnes Page (1565).

Years in service	N	%
<1	43	28
≥ 1 and < 2	33	22
≥ 2 and < 3	23	15
≥ 3 and < 4	10	7
≥ 4 and < 5	8	5
≥ 5 and < 6	4	3
≥ 6 and < 10	16	11
≥ 10 and < 15	11	7
≥ 15 and < 20	3	2
≥ 20	2	1
Total	**153**	

Table 4.6 Number of years of continuous service in a household

but 35 per cent stayed for over three years. Servants were itinerant but many experienced relative continuity in the same home. Secondly, while some servants were hired on an annual basis (as the Statute of Artificers stipulated), others were not. Twenty-eight observations were for *exactly one year* and an additional sixty-three were for full-year terms (e.g. one year, two years, six years), totalling only 60 per cent of all observations of length of service. Servants (and especially long-standing servants in the same home) likely rounded their terms to full years rather than reporting partial years: two years and nine months, therefore, became three years. The 40 per cent who served for fractions of a year is therefore a *minimum* proportion. Little uniformity in length of service is found here, and the eighteenth-century annual turnover pattern that Kussmaul identified doesn't emerge from the data. Change was likely prompted by the 1662 Settlement Act, which entitled servants to claim settlement in a parish if they had lived there for over a year. By the eighteenth century, servants were routinely hired for one day short of a full year to prevent claims of settlement.[40] Longer periods in service were therefore more common *before* 1662 than *after*.

I showed in Chapter 1 that different cultures of witnessing prompted different types of testimony. These trends in witnessing make small waves in the length of service data: female servant witnesses in defamation and matrimonial suits served for a median length of one year and just under a year respectively, compared with

[40] K. D. M. Snell, *Annals of the Labouring Poor: Social Change and Agrarian England 1660–1900* (Cambridge, 1987), pp. 73–7; Michael Roberts, '"Waiting upon Chance": English Hiring Fairs and Their Meanings from the Fourteenth to the Twentieth Century', *Journal of Historical Sociology* 1 (1988), 119–60 at 134.

two years for those testifying in tithe disputes and 4.75 years for testamentary suit witnesses. Tithe disputes relied on witnesses' recall of parish customs. The long-serving female servants testifying in these cases were settled residents, sometimes recalling their time in service rather than outlining current experiences. Testamentary disputes brought even longer-serving women as witnesses (some of whom never married).

These trends were not fixed and different types of suits bring an array of servant contract lengths to the fore. Long-serving women were not all lifelong servants. Forty-year-old Catherine Pepet of Ludlow (Shropshire) had long been married when she was asked in 1599 to recall the contents of her former master's will made fifteen years earlier. She had served in his house for sixteen years.[41] In 1612, 50-year-old glover's wife Eleanor Shepheard of Blaisdon (Gloucestershire) recalled the will of Elizabeth Hampton of the neighbouring parish of Westbury-on-Severn in whose service she had spent eighteen years. Eleanor had lived in Blaisdon for eleven years, probably since marriage. She had likely left Elizabeth's service around age 39, following almost two decades of service.[42] Women like Catherine and Eleanor had moved little during their lifetimes, establishing strong, persistent connections to both household and parish. If service was a form of training, these women were well versed in managing the rhythms of a particular home as well as the practices of their parish. At the same time, we should be wary of reading long-term service as wholly positive. For some (especially older servants), long residence in the same home may indicate a lack of better options or even economic or social entrapment. The long service of very young servants who were bound to a household through pauper apprenticeship or other coercive means might also be read as less than free. These children remained in the same home for years on end without a wage to offer even a hope of liberty from their situation.

More than a quarter of women remained in the same household for between two and five years. They were mobile but the word 'itinerant' is an uncomfortable fit. In some cases, these women had negotiated an initial period of one year and, by mutual agreement, had continued beyond this term (perhaps even on a rolling basis). Both masters and servants might come to expect the term to be extended. In 1615, George Bannister and his wife of Turkdean (Gloucestershire) accused their servant Elizabeth Gawen of sex outside marriage. Witnesses testifying in Elizabeth's defence implied this suit was retaliatory as Elizabeth had decided to leave the couple's service at the end of the agreed year. Gilbert Hudson deposed that Elizabeth was a

> poore servant & late in the service of M[ist]res[s] Bannester wife of George Bannester of Turkedeane & left theire service after the yeare was out but whether contrary to their wills this respondent knoweth not.

[41] HARC, HD4/2/11, Fox v Mary Hereford (1599).
[42] GA, GDR/114 and GDR/121, Daniel Baineham and Silvester Baineham v William Whitmey (1612).

Elizabeth's reasons for leaving the Bannisters' service at the end of her year's covenant were not recorded.[43] But the case reflects household hopes to retain good servants and in some cases, masters and mistresses could make their lives difficult if expectations were not met. Even upon liberty from the master–servant contract, freedom was not guaranteed. As Urvashi Chakravarty asks: 'Can liberty be prescribed or proscribed through contract, or does it always comprise a form of gift?'[44] Other servants of course did hope to stay on. In a 1574 matrimonial dispute, witnesses deposed that servant Joanne Sybly was thrown out of William John's house in St Germans (Cornwall) at the end of her covenant. The matrimonial suit was instigated by Joanne against her master's son, Thomas, for reneging on a promise of marriage. Thomas's parents evidently didn't approve the match: on the final day of Joanne's covenanted period of service, William's wife 'would not suffer the sayd Joanne Syblie lye in her house for that night'. Joanne's departure was sudden and unexpected; she was forced to seek last-minute overnight accommodation with a neighbour, having anticipated she would be retained in the John's service beyond the agreed year.[45] Those who found working and living conditions that suited them obviously tried to stay put.

While William John and his wife held off on ejecting Joanne from their house until the end of her covenant, others acted faster upon their fears of misbehaviour or disrule. Joanne Loxton agreed to serve Henry Baise in Locking (Somerset) from Michaelmas 1582, but by Christmas she was 'putt out of service by reason they did suspecte her to be with child'. She remained in Locking, staying first with John Crane, the child's suspected father, until Lady Day (March 1583), when she was taken into another home to give birth.[46] Right to settlement moulded collective community attitudes. Unmarried migrant mothers (many of whom were servants) were likely to become a financial burden on the parish. Poor-law legislation encouraged parishioners to assume a collective, inward-looking interest in economic self-preservation, passing the financial costs of supporting a fatherless child and single mother onto another parish. Policing of illegitimate pregnancy forearmed parishioners against the economic burden of a single mother.[47] The system of poor relief defined 'the boundaries of community by the recognition of settlement and entitlement', although, as Chapter 8 shows, these rules weren't hard and fast.[48] Sexual 'misbehaviour' could expedite a servant's departure from not only

[43] GA, GDR/122, Robert Payne v Elizabeth Gawen (1615).
[44] Chakravarty, *Fictions of Consent*, p. 194.
[45] DHC, Chanter 858, Joanne Sybly v Thomas John (1574).
[46] SHC, D/D/cd/17, Robert Tompson v John Crane (1583).
[47] Gowing, *Common Bodies*, pp. 52–81, 117.
[48] Keith Wrightson, 'The Politics of the Parish in Early Modern England', in Paul Griffiths, Adam Fox, and Steve Hindle (eds), *The Experience of Authority in Early Modern England* (Basingstoke, 1996), pp. 10–46 at 21. See also Charmian Mansell, 'Defining the Boundaries of Community? Experiences of Parochial Inclusion and Pregnancy Outside Wedlock in Early Modern England', in Naomi Pullin and Kathryn Woods (eds), *Negotiating Exclusion in Early Modern England, 1550–1800* (Abingdon, 2021), pp. 141–60.

the household, but also the parish and even the county.[49] As a county bordered by several others, Gloucestershire servants were transported to a range of places. In 1625, Susan Fourd of Wotton-under-Edge was sent to Wiltshire, where she was delivered of her illegitimate child.[50] Agnes Debett of Badgeworth was 'removed to one William Whitacres house in Herefordshire where she was delivered' in 1588.[51] In 1614, John Jones of Newent arranged for his widowed sister-in-law, Mary Wyeman (alias Carpenter), a servant who fell pregnant after her husband's death, to give birth in Monmouthshire.[52] And in 1572, William Jackson of Staunton moved his pregnant servant, Elizabeth Godwin, to Worcestershire to live with his cousin, Henry Rogers. This strategy preserved the household's reputation and the parish's pocket. The economic burden Elizabeth Godwin presented was explicitly laid out in this case: despite being bribed with wheat in exchange for Elizabeth's keep, Henry refused to keep her in his house for long (and quickly sold the wheat).[53] Unmarried expectant mothers almost invariably left service: Jane Tayler of Thornbury (Gloucestershire) had 'gon awaie' from her master 'with childe' in 1608, while in 1553 Joan Blyke of Cheltenham 'went away with child beyng servant to the said [Richard] Kemysse'.[54] But the phrases 'gone away' and 'went away' regularly used in depositions often conceal the circumstances of departure.

A handful of masters and mistresses initially overlooked their servants' inappropriate conduct rather than automatically dismissing them. John Edwardes, also of Thornbury, deposed in 1577 that his friends

> wyshed him to putt her [his servant, Margery Carter] awaie which this examinate refused to doe streight waies but saide he wolde keepe her a quarter of a yere longer to trie her an honest woman.

What prompted John's friends to seek Margery's dismissal isn't clear, but her reputation was clearly under scrutiny.[55] In other households, accusations of servant sexual impropriety turned relationships sour and servants themselves took action: in 1600, Sybil Woodward of Holme Lacy (Herefordshire) was accused by her master John Smith of living 'incontinentlie with one Thomas Noren' as well as 'other things'. John reported that 'she, taking displeasure thereat, ymediatly departed this examinates service'.[56] Whether the accusations were true or not, Sybil made her own choice to leave.

---

[49] See Meldrum, *Domestic Service and Gender*, p. 125; Gowing, *Common Bodies*, pp. 61–2.
[50] GA, GDR/148, Dorothy Greene v Richard Greene (1625).
[51] GA, GDR/79, John White v John Thaier (1592).
[52] GA, GDR/122, William Heywood v Mary Wyeman (1616).
[53] GA, GDR/25, Elizabeth Godwin v William Jackson (1572).
[54] GA, GDR/106, George Smith v William Holder (1608); GDR/8, Margaret Kemysse v Richard Kemysse (1553).
[55] GA, GDR/46, Margery Carter v John Edwardes (1577).
[56] HARC, HD4/2/11, Elizabeth Williams v Joan Griffithes (1600).

But illegitimate pregnancy wasn't typical and does not account for the departures of most women who served for less than a year. Many had specifically made these arrangements: a woman known only in the records as 'Julian' was hired to serve John Curtesse of Beckford (Worcestershire) between Shrovetide and harvest of 1551.[57] Alice Hancocks of Wells (Somerset) was hired from Michaelmas 1609 only until Christmas.[58] Eleanor Pallmer of Whitchurch (Hampshire) held a series of short-term positions in service in the 1650s, including a quarter of a year with 'one Barnsdall' and a month in service 'to one White'.[59] Alice Mathewe of Cheltenham (Gloucestershire) agreed to serve Thomas and Elizabeth Mathewe from April 1611 to the following Michaelmas. This short period of less than half a year was shortened further: she stayed just one week as Thomas Mathewe began 'to dislike with her'. Alice's testimony appeared in a case concerning marital breakdown in which Thomas's wife accused him of excessive cruelty. Alice was disliked by Thomas, she believed, because she often 'taketh the part' of Elizabeth when her husband was violent or abusive.[60] But the initial agreed term of Alice's service had been short anyway, and agreements of under a year were commonplace.

While labour laws promoted movement between households only once a year, servant hiring practices were much more varied. Expectations on both the part of master and servant weren't always established before the working relationship began. Length of service was often determined by the ever-changing requirements of the family and the servant. After all, lives were mobile in another sense: horizons, plans, families, and trade shifted as time passed. The rigidity of labour legislation and assumptions about regularity of hiring practices is incongruous with the way in which many masters and servants approached the labour market.

The labour market

On hiring fairs

By what mechanisms did female servants find work? Keith Snell and Kussmaul identified hiring fairs as important sites for job-hunting in the eighteenth century.[61] In the nineteenth century, these fairs were a standard means by which servants found work, with 'servants for hire [lining] themselves down streets'

---

[57] GA, GDR/8, *Office v John Curtesse* (1551).
[58] SHC, D/D/cd/41, *John Force v Joanna Spratt and Alice Wakeman* (1610).
[59] HRO, 21M65/C3/4, *Office v West* (1567).
[60] GA, GDR/114, *Elizabeth Mathewe v Thomas Mathewe* (1611).
[61] Kussmaul, *Servants in Husbandry*, pp. 59–61; Snell, *Annals of the Labouring Poor*, pp. 19–21.

in identical fashion to the horses also available for sale.[62] Hiring fairs require a uniform hiring season. In the south of England, annual contracts were supposed to begin at Michaelmas (29 September), while in the north servants were more frequently hired at Martinmas (11 November).[63] Eighteenth-century settlement examinations tell us that over 90 per cent of hiring took place around these religious festivals.[64] Using sixteenth-century evidence from the east of England, Jane Whittle tested this pattern: firstly, using records of labour law infringements, and secondly, using household accounts recording hiring of servants by gentry families. In sixteenth-century Marsham (Norfolk), where the county's arable economy might have lent itself to a Michaelmas hiring pattern, servants were instead hired irregularly throughout the year.[65] In the Le Strange and Toke households in Norfolk and Kent, she also found 'there was no time of the year when it was impossible for a servant to take up employment or leave'.[66]

Late medieval servant hiring, it's been argued, must have happened at fairs as the regularity of their hiring patterns implies 'some machinery for bringing masters and servants together'.[67] Michael Roberts suggested that statute sessions (courts designed to enforce fourteenth-century labour laws) developed labour markets that provided service with an institutional framework: those not in service, he argued, must have connected with potential masters at these sessions.[68] But the many female servants who spent longer terms in one household scarcely required fairs to find work as their mobility between positions was infrequent. And if women were regularly hired for shorter terms than one year or even six months, how, in practice, would hiring fairs operate? Fairs required servants to be searching for work at the same time, but depositions show this clearly was not the case.

Sometimes female servants explicitly gave the month of the year when they were hired, but it can also be estimated by subtracting how long a servant had worked for her master from the date of her court deposition. For instance, on 4 July 1582, Mary Ware of Dartington (Devon) deposed that she had served Sir Gawen and Lady Roberta Champernowne for two years.[69] Projecting back, we can estimate her service in the Champernowne household began in July 1580.

---

[62] Emma Griffin, *England's Revelry: A History of Popular Sports and Pastimes, 1660–1830* (Oxford, 2005), p. 86.

[63] See Simon Penn and Christopher Dyer, 'Wages and Earnings in Late Medieval England: Evidence from the Enforcement of the Labour Laws', *EcHR* 43 (1990), 356–76.

[64] A different pattern was found only in Lincolnshire, where more servants in husbandry were hired on May Day. See Kussmaul, *Servants in Husbandry*, pp. 50–1.

[65] Whittle, *Development of Agrarian Capitalism*, p. 272.

[66] Jane Whittle, 'A Different Pattern of Employment: Servants in Rural England c.1500–1660', in Jane Whittle (ed.), *Servants in Rural Europe, c.1400–1900* (Woodbridge, 2016), pp. 57–76 at 66.

[67] Penn and Dyer, 'Wages and Earnings', 365.

[68] Roberts, '"Waiting upon Chance"', 124, 130.

[69] DHC, Chanter 861, Gawen Champernowne v Roberta Champernowne (1582).

Some servants were very precise: in March 1576, Margaret Robert of Bulley (Gloucestershire) deposed that she had served William Broke for a year and three months; we can calculate that she started in January 1575.[70] In fact, Margaret was one of sixty-eight female servants who precisely stated the time of year at which they had taken up a new position in service. Time was typically orientated around the liturgical calendar, with Michaelmas overwhelmingly the most frequently cited start date for service. The introduction to Joanna Brayne's 1605 testimony, for example, reads

> Joanna Brayne the servant of John Mawnder of Broadmarston in the parish of Pebworth in the county of Gloucestershire where she has been since the feast of St. Michael.[71]

A smattering of other festivals – Shrovetide, Lady Day, Midsummer, and Christmas – were also given. Others approximated: when deposing in May 1615, Eleanor Weeks of Exeter (Devon) testified that 'she hath beene servant in howse unto Mrs hull *almost* three yeres'.[72] Precision of start dates is variable, but there is sufficient accuracy to reveal broad trends in servant hiring.

Figure 4.1 shows the distribution of female servant hiring across the year. September-to-September contracts were commonplace, and Michaelmas hiring clearly dominated. As the season turned from summer to autumn, many servants must have passed one another on the roadways of southern England as they found new homes. But there was no universal migration. Female servants were hired and left at (virtually) all points of the year, as Whittle also found for the east of England. Even within the same household, hiring could be irregular. In 1615, Henry Hartwell, the vicar of Bishop's Tawton (Devon), hired servants Joanne Osmonde and Salame Freynes at different points of the year: February, June and September. Joanne started work at Shrovetide (February), while Salame was initially hired from Midsummer (June) for three months before being asked again to serve at Michaelmas (September) until Christmas.[73] Perhaps her initial three-month stint was a trial period for both servant and master. As with apprenticeship, in which a trial period was commonplace, this may have given the servant a sense of agency, choice and control in her working life.[74]

As Figure 4.1 shows, September hiring was undoubtedly common. It was recorded in 54 per cent of cases where a servant's start month was *specifically* articulated and accounted for 28 per cent of cases where calculation has been made based on date of deposition and length of service given. Overall, just under 40 per cent of hiring across the south west occurred in September. Roughly one

---

[70] GA, GDR/32 and GDR/45, Elizabeth Addys v John Edwardes (1576).
[71] GA, GDR/95, Hogkins v John Maunder (1605).
[72] DHC, Chanter 867, Henry Cockram v Bartholomew Jaquinto (1615). Italics my own.
[73] DHC, Chanter 857, Susan Hartwell v Henry Hartwell (1615).
[74] Ben-Amos, *Adolescence and Youth*, p. 102.

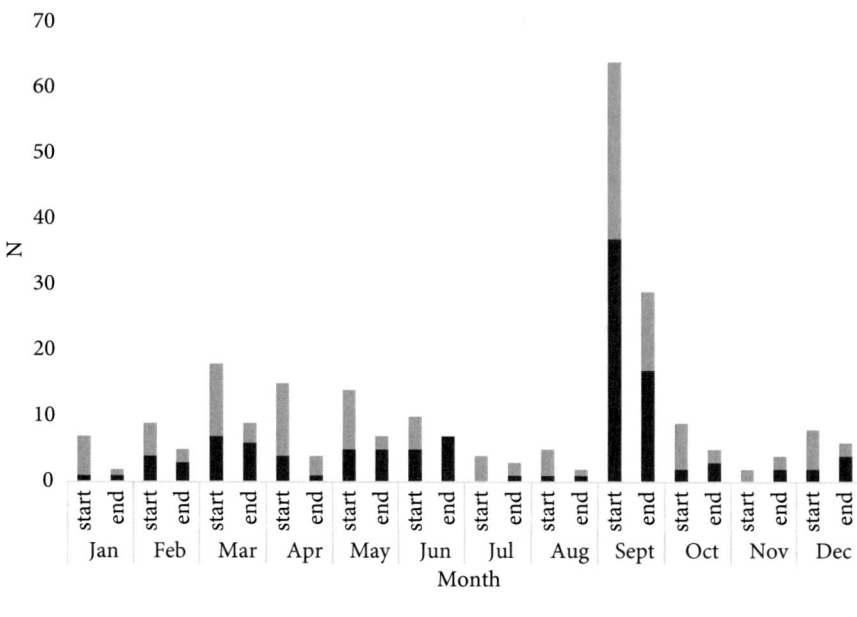

Figure 4.1 Female servant hiring patterns (start and end months of hiring)

third of women also left service in this month. Accounting for approximations and the imprecision of recall (with female servants stating they had served for one year, rather than 1 year and 2 months, for example), we would expect the preceding and following months (August and October) to have seen lots of mobility if Michaelmas really *was* a key time for hiring. But these months saw low levels of activity. Hiring also varied regionally. Very few Hampshire servants explicitly stated when they were hired (only six in total), but none gave Michaelmas or September as their start date. Observations from the Bath & Wells and Gloucester courts, however, suggest more convergence of hiring around September, with around two-thirds of hiring taking place in this month in both cases.

March and April were the next most important hiring months, in which 16 per cent of stated hirings and 23 per cent of calculated hirings occurred. Juliana Walter of Stoke Lane (Somerset), for example, deposed in 1612 that she came to serve Mr Robert Woolfall, the parson of Wanstrow, at 'the feast of the annunciation [Lady Day] next wilbe two yeeres'.[75] Servants may have been paid at quarter days, such as Lady Day (25 March), which helps explain this pattern.[76] Easter and Shrovetide were

---

[75] SHC, D/D/cd/43, Walter Norton v Elizabeth Woollfall (1612).
[76] Whittle, 'A Different Pattern of Employment', p. 64.

also regularly referred to by female servants as points of the year when they first stepped over their masters' thresholds. Hiring in Hampshire more commonly took place around Easter and Whitsuntide (April to May): Elizabeth Glose of Winchester (Hampshire), for example, was hired by Marie Edwards from Easter 1576.[77]

We would expect to find different patterns of hiring in different types of households. In this rural society, agricultural practices likely explain September hiring. Roberts suggested that annual contracts of service were 'orientated by the year of church festivals, itself rooted in the seasonal rhythms of the farming year'.[78] Kussmaul explained the typicality of servant contracts ending in Michaelmas as a phenomenon of arable farming and a requirement for harvest labour. Pastoral farming, meanwhile, required care of animals all year round.[79] The south and west of England wasn't known for its arable economy, although land was of course being cultivated there. Instead, it was a region of woodland and pastoral areas, maintaining strong cloth-working industries and sheep husbandry.[80] Servants were therefore probably required throughout the year in rural farming communities, which may explain year-round hiring (though Whittle's findings for the highly arable east of the country still prompt questions about the connection between farming and September hiring). Those whose service did not appear to be agricultural were hired at other times. Grace Sparck of Kilmersdon (Somerset) started her period of service to baker John Hippie in June 1631.[81] But in cities and large towns, several masters also hired around Michaelmas. In 1579, Anna Elie deposed that she had served John Horne of Gloucester since the Feast of St Michael.[82] Isabella Rogers of the market town of Tewkesbury (Gloucestershire) had been Thomas Kyldermore's servant since the feast of St Michael in 1604.[83] Elizabeth Ellen (alias Willis) of Gloucester was hired around October 1586 to serve pewterer Henry Rainoldes and his wife, Alice.[84] No obvious reason presents itself for this craft-based household to hire at this time of year. Michaelmas hiring may have been a tradition; convention determined it to be the start of many female servants' contracts. But the *necessity* of September hiring in this overwhelmingly pastoral landscape – dotted with cloth-working towns and cities housing servants in artisanal homes – is less evident and explains why hiring patterns were so varied.

Irregular hiring patterns support two conclusions. Firstly, servant hiring wasn't exclusively for a full year (as length of service data also shows). The ability to find

[77] HRO, 21M65/C3/7, Elizabeth Glose v Richard Wallys (1576).
[78] Roberts, '"Waiting upon Chance"', 124.
[79] Kussmaul, *Servants in Husbandry*, p. 97; Whittle, *Development of Agrarian Capitalism*, p. 256.
[80] Joan Thirsk, *England's Agricultural Regions and Agrarian History, 1500–1750* (Basingstoke, 1987), p. 28; Rollison, *Local Origins*, p. 25.
[81] SHC, D/D/cd/71, Jacob Aishton v John Hippie (1634).
[82] GA, GDR/45, Thomas Weekes and Thomas Key v Richard Crodie, Eleanor Davys and Alice Dove (1579).
[83] GA, GDR/89, Thomas Kyldermore v Agnes Quarrier (1604).
[84] GA, GDR/65, Joanne Wieke v Margaret Wieke (1587).

work throughout the year allowed female servants to serve for shorter periods, potentially with less formal arrangements. Secondly, with servants hired at virtually all points of the liturgical calendar, hiring fairs couldn't have been the ordinary route by which servants found work. Across the depositions, not a single servant recorded finding work at a hiring fair.

Finding work

As I've shown, some women travelled considerable distances to find service. In 1622, Jane Wheeler found work in Gloucester, nearly 26 kilometres from her place of birth in Kemble (Wiltshire).[85] Johanna Whittington, former servant and subsequent wife of William Whittington, deposed in 1574 that she was born in Whitchurch (Shropshire) but moved over 100 kilometres to William's household in Bromsberrow (Gloucestershire).[86] How these two women found their positions in service is unclear. Perhaps Jane deliberately opted to travel to a city where opportunities were rumoured to be high. But anonymity could prove challenging for the female servant who sought work further afield. Despite its unusual context, a 1572 matrimonial dispute pursued by Lucy Deane against her master Hugh Tunckes, the parson of Penton Mewsey (Hampshire), is suggestive of these challenges. Thomas Rede, a witness Lucy invited to court, recalled being approached by Hugh, his neighbour:

> Neighboure Reade, I have ben bo[u]nde to put your hand to a certaine bill for to testifie the behaviour of the woman in my house & me, for (quod [said] he) I am called [a] Papist. And soe he noted that nowe I am disposed to marry. It is very well, quod [said] this deponent, I praye let me knowe what she is that yowe meane to marry with all. Mar[r]y, quod [said] he, it is she, in the house here.

Though the language of this scrap of reported speech makes it difficult to follow, we essentially learn that Hugh approached his neighbour to sign a piece of paper confirming nothing untoward had occurred between the servant (Lucy) and her master (Hugh). This 'bill' was important in Hugh's plan to marry her, according to Thomas. From other depositions, we see Lucy tangled in Hugh's religious predicament. His motivation to marry likely emerged because he was under considerable religious scrutiny, suspected of papacy. In 1572, when this suit took place, persecution of Catholic recusants in England was growing. Marriage was one way Hugh might avoid being labelled a papist (as the Catholic faith prohibited ministers from marrying). But as this matrimonial suit against him suggests, he evidently

---

[85] GA, GDR/148, Rebecca Lane v Elizabeth Bick (1622).
[86] GA, GDR/32, John Bramedge v Guy Grove (1574).

changed his mind. In his response to Lucy's accusation in the church court of an unfulfilled promise of marriage, Hugh told an alternative story about his request for a testimonial of Lucy's behaviour. He deposed that

> the saide Luce beinge suspected of an evill name whilest she dwelled with him, at hir first cominge this respondent caused hir to goe to hir friends & fetche a testimonial of her good report & honestie & she the sayde Luce brought such a certificat.

Lucy's brother nonetheless contested that the testimonial procured had been on the promise of marriage, 'under the hands of the parishioners wher she was bred of her good & honest bringing yp [up] & conversation *viz* of half of dosen'. Witnesses made no mention of Lucy's 'evill name'; rather, the testimonial was required for Hugh's confidence in the marriage. Whatever the story here, Hugh's defence indicates it was plausible that when a servant was distant from home, questions could be raised about her reputation. Hugh and Lucy came from distant communities. Lucy was probably born in Farcombe (Hampshire), over 80 kilometres from Penton Mewsey, where Hugh lived and where she had found work.[87] The anonymity that came with being far from home was not helpful when one's integrity was at stake. Whether Hugh's story about the testimonial was believed or not, his will from 1580 indicates that Lucy's suit was unsuccessful: the couple never married. Lucy was not listed as a recipient of any bequest, nor did Hugh list a wife or any children.[88]

Few servants, however, travelled so far for work. Though no evidence of hiring fairs is identified here, other evidence of how service was arranged and agreed surfaces. Some enquired door to door. We met Joanne Sybly of St Germans (Cornwall) earlier in this chapter when she was sent away at the end of her covenant in 1574. She was initially hired around Whitsuntide when, as her master deposed, she 'came to this deponentes wife to seke [seek] service'.[89] In 1568, gentleman John Brooke of Rockbeare (Devon) deposed that he had 'knowne Isott [his servant] by the space of ii [two] yeres for she came to Staverton from Overbryen and offered her service to this deponentes wiff'. Travelling to the next parish over from her home, Isott Riches had secured work with the couple without any apparent connection to them; this was the first time they were acquainted. That both Isott and Joanne offered service to their mistresses highlights the role of the wife in selecting the women that came to be part of the household.

Other women were sought out by masters. Later, Isott was offered a position in Frances Yarde's house; he came to the vicarage where she worked and had 'communicacion with the sayd Isott, for to have her into his service'.[90] In

---

[87] HRO, 21M65/C3/5, Lucy Deane v Hugh Tunckes (1572).
[88] TNA, PROB 11/62/573, Will of Hugh Tunckes (1580).
[89] DHC, Chanter 858, Joanne Sybly v Thomas John (1574).
[90] DHC, Chanter 858, John Roo v Frances Yarde (1568).

1545, Henry Tremynge of Ringwood (Hampshire) was accused of reneging on a promise of marriage he had made to Alice Churcher. Responding to the allegation, Henry argued he had never given her 'a grote in token of matrimony ne [neither] any other quyene [coin] or token'. Instead, he insisted, his father had simply sent him to Alice's father's house in Moortown (just outside Ringwood) to ask Alice to be his servant. The groat she had received from him was, he claimed, an 'ernest' promise of the arrangement on behalf of his father.[91]

Those who saw opportunity in their masters' households – or at least saw no opportunities elsewhere – might remain with them when they moved. After securing work with the Brookes in Staverton, Isott followed the couple to Rockbeare, 38 kilometres away.[92] In 1594, 24-year-old Elizabeth Roberte of Wrington (Somerset) recalled Margaret Atkins telling her 'that she was then servannte to ... Mr Chock and his wife & thatt shee had soe bin before the cominge of the said Mr Chock to Wringeton'. Margaret's testimony fills in the blanks about the journey she and the family had taken. She had travelled with them to Wrington only half a month before this case came to court, and before that had lived with them in Wells, just under 20 kilometres away.[93] In 1636, Elizabeth Mills of Ilsington (Devon) had lived in the parish for less than a year but had served Mr Done for longer (one year and nine months), her deposition indicating a move from Wiltshire and binding her mobility to her master's.[94] Favourable conditions in service, competitive wages, and good relations with the family may have encouraged young women to join them when they moved. Others saw no such incentives. In 1636, at the age of 30, Maria Androwes of Barrow Gurney (Somerset) testified that she had lived as a covenant servant at Felton Inn in nearby Winford with Thomas Latch five years earlier 'untill the said Thomas Latch and his wife went awaie from thence to live att Langford Inne within the parishe of Churchill'.[95] She did not join them.

Given the irregularity of hiring patterns, women might periodically find themselves without work and – more importantly – bed and board. Temporary solutions were found. Alice and John Garye of Boyatt (Hampshire) took Rose Michenar into their home in 1580 following her departure from service. Rose deposed that she 'stayed with this deponent & her husband till she colde here [hear] of a service', reiterating the importance of word of mouth in finding work.[96] In the late 1620s, Alice Waterman and Richard Daire had served together in Mr Gregorie's house in Taunton (Somerset). Richard had been responsible for drawing beer (suggesting

[91] HRO, 21M65/C3/2, Alice Churcher v Henry Tremynge (1545).
[92] DHC, Chanter 858, John Roo v Frances Yarde (1568).
[93] SHC, D/D/cd/18, Elizabeth Chock v Joanna Foster (1594).
[94] DHC, Chanter 866, William Harries v Audrey Rowell (1636).
[95] SHC, D/D/cd/76, Robert Dibbins v Elizabeth Allen (1636).
[96] HRO, 21M65/C3/8, Avice Hewes v John Wayte (1580).

this house was an inn or alehouse) but left service to marry and practise his trade as a weaver. According to Richard, six or eight weeks after he left, Alice,

> beinge out of service came to this deponent and desired shee might have lodging in this deponents howse untill shee could get some service, att whose request this deponent affooreded her lodginge for some space vizt aboute five or six weekes as hee now remembreth the tyme.[97]

As a 40-year-old widow, Alice may have less easily secured new work. This short-term accommodation could therefore have been vital. In other cases, temporary board while in between things could be a double-edged sword. Eleanor Pallmer of Whitchurch (Hampshire) became acquainted with Mr West in 1565 when searching for work. Living in the same parish, he 'was contented to give her meate and drincke untill she might be retained into service'. Two weeks later, he helped her find a position, though her interactions with him became increasingly sexualised, raising the question of how 'free' his aid was.[98]

Stopgaps between positions in service meant more itineracy and moves between houses. But they also consolidated female servants' relationships within communities. Despite Mr West's sexual advances, he had initially promised to find her work and he arranged her first post in service. Likewise, in 1602, Philip Hamlin of Glastonbury (Somerset) deposed that Alice Stone came to his house

> very poore, and very badly apparelled, could [cold] and hungry and craved suckor of this deponent ... telling him that shee was utterlie destitute of meate drincke, lodging, and apparel, and that shee knewe not wheare to be received in to any howse within ye towne.

Philip first gave her 'intertainment' in his own home before finding her a position in service elsewhere.[99] The ties of kinship, obligation, and friendship that those willing to help had at their disposal could be restrictive, locking servants into an indebted relationship. But they might also help root servants within the parish. In early Tudor Cheshire, gentleman Humphrey Newton routinely hired local servants from the neighbourhood and through kinship ties: he, too, hired servants at various points of the year.[100] Eleanor Pallmer remained in Whitchurch for at least one of her positions in service, and Alice was taken into a Glastonbury household's service.

While charity and neighbourliness encouraged parishioners to mobilise their networks to help servants find work, social control might also be at play. In Chapter 3, we encountered interventions made by parish officers in setting up pauper apprenticeships. Parish officials similarly intervened when children were

---

[97] SHC, D/D/cd/65, Priscilla Carpenter v John Coleborne (1630).
[98] HRO, 12M65/C3/2, Office v West (1567).
[99] SHC, D/D/cd/32, Henry Sock v Maria Barter (1601).
[100] Deborah Youngs, *Humphrey Newton (1466–1536): An Early Tudor Gentleman* (Woodbridge, 2008), p. 79.

orphaned. Recall Alice Beake of Westonzoyland (Somerset), orphaned when her widowed mother died in 1596. Gentleman Philip Watts was 'one of the collectors for the poore of Weston in Zoiland wheare the said Alice then dwelt, and was acquainted with the placing of her'. Bartholomew Hyett, a man Alice had known her whole life, now became her master.[101] For those teetering on the precipice of poverty (and therefore presenting a threat to the parish), officials intervened to find them a place in service. When servants threatened the reputation of a household, other work might be sourced for them. Joanna Nymo of Launceston (Cornwall) served miller Richard Kingdon in 1580. The pair became shrouded in the suspicions of their neighbours, with one convinced that Joanna was 'like[ky] to parte a man and his wife'. She was sent to Plymouth to work with another miller.[102] It wasn't just servants who kept their ear to the ground; those around them – whether hostile neighbours who sought their removal from the parish or friends and family acting in their best interests – invested their time in securing service for women.

Once embedded in family life as servants, women might find subsequent work with other family members. Margery Warner of Gloucester deposed in 1587 that following her mistress's death, she was taken in as a servant by the deceased's son-in-law, Henry Rainoldes.[103] The same pattern was found in Stonehouse (Gloucestershire), where in 1558 Isabella Orpin agreed to serve William Hiett following the death of his father, her former master.[104] Eleanor Newcombe of Bishop's Cleeve (also Gloucestershire) was a witness in a 1605 tithe dispute. She deposed that she had served Edmund Wallwin for seven years following the death of Edmund's father, her former master.[105] Family members routinely took on hired workers from their late kin's household. All three women – Margaret, Isabella, and Eleanor – had served the deceased for long periods: these were women who had proved themselves to be capable and loyal. Eleanor's deposition recorded continuity in her experiences of service: she collected tithes for Edmund Wallwin, and later his son, a task that required good comprehension of the parish's landscape, economy, customs, and inhabitants. For Edmund, keeping hold of a knowledgeable and dependable servant was surely advantageous.

Family connections

It wasn't just their masters' kin that female servants relied on for work, but also their own. In the south and west of England, servants were hired by a wide range of family. This trend continued well into the nineteenth century.[106] Thirty-eight

---

[101] SHC, D/D/cd/32, Thomas Baker and John Keyser v Thomas Beake and Alice Beake (1601).
[102] DHC, Chanter 860, Office v Richard Kingdon (1580).
[103] GA, GDR/65, Joanne Wieke v Margaret Wieke (1587).
[104] GA, GDR/65, William Hiett v Thomas Hiett (1558).
[105] GA, GDR/95, Edmund Wallwin v Robert Hobbes (1605).
[106] For a recent, concise summary see Xuesheng You, 'Female relatives and domestic service in nineteenth-century England and Wales: Female kin servants revisited', *EcHR* (2023), 1-28.

women were hired by kin, with an additional eleven working for people with a shared family name. Examples of servants' working within the homes of relatives raises the question of whether these women were true servants; scholarship has questioned whether the designator 'servant' is misleading when attached to men and women working for their kin in the nineteenth century.[107] Here, too, we find servants working for kin, once again problematising what a servant actually *was* in early modern England. As Naomi Tadmor showed, 'kin' had a broader application in early modern England that included social alliances as well as blood relations.[108] In a 1598 tithe dispute originating in Morebath (Devon), Katherine Tynewell deposed that she was 'kinne unto Christofer Tynewell [her master] but in what degree she cannot tell'.[109] Here, 'kin' referred explicitly to a distant blood relationship. She not only shared the same family name as her master but also acknowledged a 'degree' of their relatedness, placing herself and Christopher within the same family tree. Several other servants shared a family name with their masters and mistresses. Richarda Burden of Kenton (Devon) described herself in 1617 as the servant of John Burden, while in 1583, Joanne Wannell of Otterton (also Devon) named Alice Morgan (alias Wannell) as her mistress; Alice was probably her recently married sister.[110] These female servants had lived in the same parish since birth, and found work within a local kin network. Other examples of indistinct kin are littered throughout the depositions; the vagueness of some descriptions of relatedness to kin (like Katherine Tynewell's) might also be read as a witness's attempt to conceal the closeness of their affinity with litigants (to avoid undermining their testimony). Alan Macfarlane proposed that the early modern family didn't rely on kin in selecting and hiring servants, but this doesn't ring true in the communities of the south and west of England.[111]

Within the cluster of servants hired by kin, work was overwhelmingly supplied by either married siblings or aunts and uncles. In 1615 in Quinton (Gloucestershire), 19-year-old Anne Higgens was a 'hired servant to the plaintiff Martha Higgens & the brothers daughter [niece] of George Higgens, husband of the plaintiff'.[112] Seven years earlier, 20-year-old Anne Reynolds of Topsham (Devon) deposed that she was the servant of John and Grace Corbyn, her mother and Grace being 'naturall sisters whereby the saide Grace is aunte to this respondente'.[113] Working in a household headed by kin was a mutually convenient

---

[107] See for example, W. D. Adair, 'Can we trust the census reports? Lessons from a study of domestic servants in Tenbury, Worcestershire, 1851 and 1861', *Family & Community History* 5 (2002), 99–110.

[108] Naomi Tadmor, 'Early Modern English Kinship in the Long Run: Reflections on Continuity and Change', *Continuity and Change* 25 (2010), 15–48 at 24.

[109] DHC, Chanter 864, William Lambert v Christopher Tynewell (1598).

[110] DHC, Chanter 867, Robert Pridham v Combe and Ann Scadlake (1617); Chanter 861, Sprynt v Thomas Wichalse (1583). The addition 'alias Wannell' to Alice Morgan's name suggests her recent marriage, although other uses of 'alias' are found in the depositions.

[111] Macfarlane, *Family Life*, p. 148.

[112] GA, GDR/122, Martha Higgens v Joan Chettle (1615).

[113] DHC, Chanter 865, Grace Corbyn v Joanne Drewe (1608).

arrangement that fostered natural alliances; both Anne Higgens and Anne Reynolds were loyal to their kin-mistresses, deposing against their defamers. But serving a family member could make for awkward negotiations. In 1580, Rose Michenar, who we encountered earlier working in the service of John and Alice Garye of Boyatt (Hampshire), had recently left her aunt's service because 'they colde not agree together for wages'. There were apparently no hard feelings; like Anne Higgens and Anne Reynolds, Rose also testified for her aunt in a defamation case. Rose's new employers, it turns out, were also 'sumwhat of kindred to her', indicating she hadn't been put off serving relatives.[114]

Brothers and sisters routinely hired their younger sisters. In 1602, 20-year-old Averina Ham of Southampton (Hampshire) served her brother William Lile.[115] Kin played a key role in a woman's experience of service, not just in helping them find service, as Tim Meldrum implied.[116] In her late 20s, Eleanor Browne had served her brother Thomas Jones in the Gloucestershire parish of Yate in the 1570s.[117] Her employment arrangements were only possible once her brother had established his own household. Of the same generation, brother- or sister-masters may have left service or apprenticeship only recently themselves. Offering a position in service to same-generation kin may have offered considerable stability (especially for women who didn't marry) and a less formal, more homely workplace. Lucy Hayle of Chirbury (Shropshire) had served her brother Edmund Hill for fourteen years. Following his death in 1599, she testified in court concerning the misadministration of his estate, lamenting the ill treatment of her nephew, William, who was placed in the care of Evan Price after Edmund's death. Age 40 at the time of testifying, Lucy described how William had come to her in distress, she

> being his aunte and complained unto her howe he was used and shewed [her] the printe of the blowes which were uppon his bodie being blacke and blewe by beating with a staffe and howe he was unmeasurablie beaten with a rodd.

Lucy complained to her brother's executor, who then removed William from Price's house.[118] Having a sibling as her master meant that Lucy enjoyed a closeness with his son, even when no longer sharing the same home.

For some women, service might not turn out to be the 'great unknown' that Meldrum suggests.[119] Fifty-six-year-old Paschasius Soper of Dunsford (Devon) hired two of his own daughters as servants in 1585.[120] That this scenario was not

---

[114] HRO, 21M65/C3/8, Avice Hewes v John Wayte (1580).
[115] HRO, 21M65/C3/11, Angelo Stoner v Joan Morrall; Thomasine Stoner v Joan Morrall (1602).
[116] Meldrum, *Domestic Service and Gender*, p. 19.
[117] GA, GDR/89, Thomas Baynham v David Jurden (1604).
[118] HARC, HD4/2/11, Evan ap Edward v William Speake v William Haile (1599).
[119] Meldrum, *Domestic Service and Gender*, p.19.
[120] DHC, Chanter 861 and Chanter 862, John Thomas v James Puddicomb (1585).

so uncommon in late sixteenth-century Devon is hinted at elsewhere. Twenty-eight-year-old Margaret Wattes of Woodbury deposed in 1595 that 'she liveth in house with her father and hathe no wage', and in the same case, 20-year-old Hester Ellyott similarly testified that 'she liveth under her father and hath no wages of him'.[121] Neither of these women were servants but theoretically, their depositions imply, it *was* possible to remain at home and receive a wage from a parent.

Masters also hired a succession of female kin.[122] In 1585, Juliana Wathen of Longney (Gloucestershire), recalled a conversation with Richard Dowdie, her sister's suitor:

> the said Dowdie requested this examinate [Juliana] to come thither to dwell & serve John Walker at Michaelmas following, saieing that he wold then marrie the said Margarett, this examinates sister.

John Walker and his wife Mary were Juliana and Margaret's uncle and aunt. This familial connection provided work for Margaret and, upon her marriage, a position in service for her sister. This must have been an opportune arrangement for both parties.[123] When replacing servants, family connections could be the first port of call: in 1611, Elizabeth Mathewe of Cheltenham (Gloucestershire) sought to replace her servant Alice Mathewe (their shared surnames already indicating a familial link). Elizabeth suggested her niece might fill Alice's shoes, indicating that female kin were an obvious source of additional or replacement labour within the household. Macfarlane's theory of individualism, whereby early modern kinship connections operated only within the nuclear family, doesn't hold in these examples of servant kin-employers.[124]

Conclusion

As a group of workers, female servants were routinely on the move. At least every few years, most moved to a new parish or a new master's household. This high mobility has important implications for how we understand their place within society. Through their work, they became part of many communities, often with a geographical reach well beyond the 15-kilometre radius from home in which Kussmaul assumed servants moved. Through their mobility, they leveraged their networks to generate new employment opportunities, find love, and set up new

---

[121] DHC, Chanter 864, Denys Ellyott v Thomasina Downham (1595).
[122] Between 1628 and 1657, almost 25 per cent of servants in the households of Norfolk gentry, the Le Strange's, shared surnames with former servants. See Whittle, 'A Different Pattern of Employment', p. 67.
[123] GA, GDR/57 and GDR/65, Margaret Wathen v Richard Dowdie (1585).
[124] Alan Macfarlane, *The Origins of English Individualism: The Family, Property and Social Transition* (Oxford, 1978), pp. 98–9, 146–7.

households, as well as fostering broader links between disparate communities. In building a connected state, mobile servants were more important in ways at which we can only guess.

Patterns identified in this chapter also suggest mixed experiences. We assume that the decline of service in the eighteenth century – the transition from annual contracts to shorter terms that led to service being replaced by day labour – began around 1700.[125] But patterns of employment in service had been more mixed before 1650. Not everyone worked for full years in service. And not everyone was highly mobile. Evidence of irregular hiring patterns across the calendar year shows that service for women was much less regulated and uniform than we've supposed. Many servant contracts began and terminated around Michaelmas, but across the south and west, many servants, too, were hired at all points of the year. The scattered evidence of how women found work in service makes no mention of hiring fairs, which chimes with the irregularity of servant contract lengths and start dates. Family connections as well as neighbours and former masters could provide women with access to labour opportunities. But we also find women arranging and negotiating their own positions in service. The widely held perception of female servants as annually hired workers filtering through an organised institution that regulated mobility and hiring practices through fairs does not adequately represent the experiences of many women working in service. Variability in how women found service and their patterns of mobility expose the lack of control around a form of labour that was precisely intended (according to law and moralist literature) *to* control. It's to the question of control that I turn in Chapter 5.

---

[125] Snell, *Annals of the Labouring Poor*, p. 74.

Chapter 5

Navigating Service

In October 1623, Philippa Hooper of Chedzoy in Somerset came to Wells. The only witness brought to testify to the alleged affair of her former mistress, the court wanted to know what she'd seen last summer. As she came into the kitchen of John Gooding's house, Philippa claimed she found his wife, Christian, 'lying upon a winnoweing sheete & well uppon her backe, her cloathes being uppe above her middle, and Henry Seward lying uppon her, his hose being downe about his legs, theire bodies being both naked togeathers'. These weren't innocuous claims, she knew, but could damage both Christian's reputation and her marriage.

Christian, however, drew up a list of interrogatory questions for Philippa that challenged her impartiality as a witness. The Goodings had made a contractual labour agreement with Philippa that had soured, Christian's questions implied. This witness statement was Philippa's retribution. But Philippa shook her head. She admitted that she had 'complaine[d] unto the right Worshipfull Mr Rogers one of his majesties justices of peace against the said Christian Gooding & her husband for that they kepte awaie a partlet & wastcoate from her'. But, she insisted, she had 'never made covenant with the said Gooding or her husband to bee their servant but for a weeke att a time or a daie, or two att a time'. She added that 'whilest shee did worck for them shee did make haie and weede corne & doe other such worck' and 'when shee had no other worck to doe, shee did spin & carde, & had the commoditie theareof her selfe'. She had made covenant as a servant on several other occasions in the past: with Edward Bragg of Westonzoyland, whom she had served for two years; with Mr Bright of Worle, in whose service she had worked for one year; and with John Tuckie of Banwell, whom she had served for seven years. But never with the Goodings.[1]

* * *

---

[1] SHC, D/D/cd/57, John Bussell v Christian Gooding (1623). Italics my own.

Turning away from Christian's alleged affair, Philippa's deposition is a striking commentary on the servant–master labour agreement. Firstly, she raises the possibility of being a *servant* without being a *covenant servant*. She was adamant she had never made covenant with the Goodings but nonetheless referred to working in their 'service' by the day or week. Her testimony hints at what she thought a covenant *was*: her experiences of covenants were for one, two, and seven years. These were long-term agreements, certainly extending beyond seven days. Secondly, Philippa's testimony indicates the word 'covenant' had little relevance on a day-to-day basis. According to her, it was entirely possible to serve without covenant. But her opposition to it being used to describe her labour agreement with the Goodings simultaneously signifies its legal significance. Philippa's recourse to the justice of the peace to restore her clothing was an admission of her interaction with legal channels of labour dispute resolution that were reserved for those with formal agreements. Her admission of this suggests she had left service before her covenant had elapsed; the couple had withheld her clothing in compensation. Finally, Philippa's deposition lays bare the working life of a 30-year-old woman which ranged from covenanted service to service without covenant and periods of independent work.

Philippa's experience wasn't unusual, as this chapter shows. The flexibility of her labour nonetheless seems surprising given that heavy regulation of service was repeatedly stressed in early modern labour laws. Between the mid-fourteenth and late sixteenth centuries, a series of legislation implemented maximum wages that servants could be paid, imposed minimum contracts of one year, and limited access to the casual labour market.[2] From as early as 1349, able-bodied men and women under 60 could be legally compelled to serve.[3] Two years later, the 1351 Statute of Labourers made a clear distinction between casual labour and annual service, ordering that servants were to be 'hired to serve by the entire year, or by other usual terms, and not by the day'. Two hundred years later, this legislation was consolidated in the 1563 Statute of Artificers, which ruled that

> every person between the age of twelve yeres and the age of threescore yeres, not beinge laufullie reteyned, nor [an] apprentice … nor beinge reteyned by the yere or half the yere at the leaste … be compelled to be reteyned to serve in husbandrye by the yere.[4]

Only the relatively wealthy were exempt from compulsory service: those who owned (or whose parents owned) land worth 40 shillings per year or goods to

---

[2] The labour laws are printed in the following publications: The 1349 Ordinance of Labourers and 1388 Statute of Cambridge in P. A. Brown, R. H. Tawney, and A. E. Bland (eds), *English Economic History: Select Documents* (1920), pp. 164–7 and 171–6; the 1351 Statute of Labourers in R. B. Dobson, *The Peasants' Revolt of 1381* (New York, 1970), pp. 63–8; the 1563 Statute of Artificers in Tawney and Power, *Tudor Economic Documents*, pp. 338–50.

[3] Brown, Tawney, and Bland, *English Economic History*, pp. 164–7; Dobson, *Peasants' Revolt*, pp. 63–8.

[4] 'The Statute of Artificers (1563)' printed in Tawney and Power, *Tudor Economic Documents*, pp. 338–50.

the value of £10 were outside the legislation's remit. Maximum rates of pay were set locally by justices of the peace each Easter at the Quarter Sessions, and even mobility was controlled: servants were forbidden to leave a parish without a letter or certificate of good character.[5] Social and economic control of the 'masterless young' was at the centre of this legislation, which sustained the state's nascent ideology that young people *should* be placed under the rule of a master.[6] But the 1563 Act in fact made no mention of the catalogue of perceived vices of 'sexuality, disobedience, lust, and excess' that moralists and magistrates levelled against young people at the time.[7] Its preamble explained only that it wished to 'banish idleness'.[8] The Statute has nonetheless been interpreted as part of an arsenal of laws designed to remedy England's economic and social problems.

Enforcement of these laws was the responsibility of secular courts. Though evidence of their operation on a national scale is thin on the ground, regular petty sessions were supposed to be held at various locations across each hundred. It was here that servant contracts and wages were to be registered, and those who refused to accept the authority of a master were to be compelled.[9] Despite limited surviving evidence of prosecutions, scholarship on service as a labour contract has centred on these records of law infringement and enforcement. Enforcement is understood as piecemeal, with heavier policing in East Anglia than in other parts of the country.[10] A 1572 memorandum complained that many masters hired servants without requesting certificates, suggesting that the widespread regulation of service that the state had hoped for had not yet been achieved.[11]

But records of enforcement tell only a partial tale. These archives are records of non-compliance. We shouldn't read examples of men and women brought before the court for breaking agreements or breaching the law as evidence that this was the consequence for *all* men and women whose working lives deviated from the path laid out in legislation. Instead, we need to know: how many women (and men) lived quietly among their neighbours working to contracts made informally outside legal conventions? How many like Philippa made agreements to serve for short terms at daily or weekly negotiated rates? How many left service before their agreed term but faced no legal repercussions? The archive of labour law enforcement is axiomatically silent on the experiences of such women. But

---

[5] Whittle, *Development of Agrarian Capitalism*, pp. 291–2.

[6] Griffiths, *Youth and Authority*, pp. 351–89, esp. p. 356.

[7] For more on these perceived vices, see Griffiths, *Youth and Authority*, p. 60.

[8] 'The Statute of Artificers (1563)', p. 339.

[9] Whittle, *Development of Agrarian Capitalism*, p. 299.

[10] See ibid., pp. 225–304, esp. 298; R. K. Kelsall, 'Wage Regulations under the Statute of Artificers', in W. E. Minchinton (ed.), *Wage Regulation in Pre-Industrial England* (Newton Abbot, 1972), pp. 93–197 at 113, 151.

[11] See Capp, *When Gossips Meet*, pp. 131–2. See also 'Proposals for the Better Administration of the Statute of Artificers (1572)' printed in Brown, Tawney, and Bland (eds), *English Economic History*, pp. 333–6.

looking elsewhere we find plenty of them. The silences in enforcement records aren't therefore evidence of absence, nor should we see them as dead ends or irretrievable histories about broader experiences of servant–master agreements. Instead, they invite us to look beyond the strict parameters of legislation to other archives that record how service (and other forms of labour) was experienced, negotiated, and navigated in early modern England.[12]

Although service and casual labour were clearly differentiated from one another in law, how early modern people understood service is more complex. By the sixteenth century, service had replaced forms of bonded labour in England. This didn't mean that service was 'free' in the modern sense of the word.[13] Masters were undoubtedly placed above their servants in legal and social hierarchies. They could lawfully punish their servants and had the right to prevent them from working for anyone else. Unlike casual labourers and artificers, a servant was at their master's disposal at any time. Teasing out incidental evidence of hiring patterns, practices, and conditions of employment in service from depositions like Philippa's, this chapter interrogates what service meant in this period. It explores the nature of servant–master labour relations and the conditions under which women agreed to serve. In doing so, the 'flexible' servant institution we've observed so far is placed under the microscope. The chapter asks: under the legislative shadow of the Statute of Artificers, to what extent did consent and freedom of choice underpin young women's labouring lives? What did service mean in early modern England and what alternative options were available to labouring young women? The chapter then turns to issues of contract, exploring the format and contents of a covenant and the rigidity of the agreement. How far were servants (and masters) free to renege on agreements? While service could be flexible and informal in some contexts, this didn't always equate to greater or unlimited freedom.

Patterns of labour

What labour options were open to women in early modern England? In their categorisation of early modern work, economic historians have distinguished between wage labour and annual service. Service came with the security of a yearly

---

[12] Jessica Johnson's work on black enslaved women in the eighteenth-century Atlantic World reframes the silences of imperial archives around these women. She sees their absence in records ('null values') as an opportunity to think about what colonial administrators were and weren't recording and systematically sets out to reconstruct from other sources what isn't found there, thereby 'imbuing absence with disruption and possibility'. See Jessica Marie Johnson, *Wicked Flesh: Black Women, Intimacy, and Freedom in the Atlantic World* (Philadelphia, 2020), p. 76, and also chapters 4, 5, and 6.

[13] Urvasi Chakravarty examined the place of service in the pre-slavery economy and argued that ideas of consent in service were 'fictional'. See Chakravarty, *Fictions of Consent*.

wage, a contract, bed, board, and sometimes other perquisites such as clothing or tips (known as vails). Casual labour was more flexible but less secure, paid by the task, day, or week. It rarely included lodging, food, or clothing. The latter supposedly replaced the former between the sixteenth and nineteenth centuries as the agrarian economy transformed.[14] Such distinctions between annual service and daily wage labour are foundational to English labour history.[15]

Both contractually and culturally, however, it's less clear what contemporaries meant by 'servant'. As Naomi Tadmor noted, 'most forms of labour in sixteenth- and seventeenth-century England were understood in terms of service'.[16] The inconsistency with which court scribes recorded service (see Chapter 1) and ambiguities in how the term 'servant' was used (see Chapter 2) loom large. Its sporadic appearance in depositions also speaks volumes. There is a sense that distinctions between those in service (serving kin or non-kin) and non-servants living and working with non-kin didn't always matter. Distinctions between live-in servants and casual workers who paid to lodge were not routinely expressed. In 1608, Thomas Lydyat, a butler living in Thornbury (Gloucestershire), deposed that 'he knoweth certenlye that … Jane Tayler dwelled in house with … William Holder for a twelve moneth'. It's only later in his examination that we learn that Jane was William's servant.[17]

A defamation case heard in the Exeter court details the assortment of arrangements by which young people could live under the same roof. Joanne Pittman (age 20), Mary Thomas (also 20), and Robert Sweete (age 24) all lived and worked in John and Joan Bennett's house in Kentisbeare (Devon) in 1634. Joanne deposed that she 'did spynne at the howse of the said Joane Bennett & her husband [John] by the weeke'. She provided a detailed breakdown of the number of weeks she had worked and the value of her weekly wages (to which we'll return). When asked by the defendant to outline Mary's and Robert's roles within the home, Joanne responded

> that Mary Thomas did live in howse with John Bennett about 3 quarters of a yere as a servant to the said John Bennett for wages as she thincketh but now liveth with one Edward Hart, and Robert Sweete hath lived there a while by the day as she thincketh at husbandry labour.

This part of Joanne's testimony was a response to the interrogatory questions posed by the defendant, aiming to discredit Joanne and her words. The Statute of Artificers

[14] Kussmaul, *Servants in Husbandry*, p. 133.
[15] Recently, Jane Humphries and Jacob Weisdorf compared the economic trajectories of these 'two distinct forms of female employment: *daily wage labour*, often on a casual basis, and *annual service*' by charting female wages from 1260 to 1850. See Jane Humphries and Jacob Weisdorf, 'The Wages of Women in England, 1260–1850', *Journal of Economic History* 75 (2015), 405–47 at 407. Italics my own.
[16] N. Tadmor, *The Social Universe of the English Bible: Scripture, Society and Culture in Early Modern England* (Cambridge, 2010), p. 83.
[17] GA, GDR/106, George Smith v William Holder (1608).

called for compulsory service of the young and didn't promote the casual labour arrangements that Joanne had made. But the requirements for what constituted a good witness in court posed a challenge. Close affinity (i.e. service) to the plaintiff wasn't a helpful thing to admit here. If Mary, Joanne, and Robert were identified as the plaintiff's servants, their economic loyalties cast them as unreliable witnesses. Testifying under oath, Joanne's admission of her fellow witness's service may have undermined *their* testimonies, but she left her own intact. So, too, did Robert, who offered a similar response to the same question. These were gradations of freedom and contract that mattered principally to the legal progress. Joanne's description of their employment arrangements within the Bennett household needed to be stated only within this legal framework and were rarely expressed incidentally.[18]

The compulsory service clause laid out in the Statute of Artificers clearly wasn't rigorously enforced in this east Devon parish. Joanne was hired to spin by the week, which may have been relatively profitable as demand for spinning labour increased in the seventeenth century.[19] She wasn't a servant and was by no means the only woman whose source of income lay outside the servant institution. We encounter 32-year-old Mary Malin of Brockworth (Gloucestershire) as a witness in a 1612 testamentary dispute. Countersuit deponents contested her impartiality, claiming she was a servant to the testator's father (the plaintiff in the suit). Mary had once been his servant but insisted that now she 'did worke for her selfe ... *& not as a servant*'. Fellow witnesses confirmed this: Henry Hallier deposed that she 'did worke at [his] howse in Brockworth at her owne handes'. Establishing the labour relationship that underpinned Mary's work was again essential to assessing the reliability of her testimony.

On the surface, these examples suggest that freedom to testify was only available to those outside service. Servants more readily spoke out against masters and mistresses once they had left their service (as I showed in Chapter 1). But reading against the grain, the evidence also opens a window onto alternative options to service for unmarried women. They could move between annual live-in service and the casual labour market.[20] The point of contention was not that Mary was living at her own hands. It was at the very least *plausible* and therefore *acceptable* that Mary might generate her own income through her casual labour. The labour laws have been the yardstick against which young people's working lives have been measured. But prescription and practice don't neatly align. Working outside service didn't reduce Mary's position within the community. Nobody appears to have taken issue with her casual labour and even opposing witnesses characterised her

---

[18] DHC, Chanter 866, Joanne Bennett v Joanne Deymont (1634).
[19] Craig Muldrew, '"Th'ancient Distaff" and "Whirling Spindle": Measuring the Contribution of Spinning to Household Earnings and the National Economy in England, 1550–1770', *EcHR* 65 (2012), 498–526 at 520.
[20] Carolyn Steedman noted the multiple roles eighteenth-century servants held. See Steedman, *Labours Lost*, p. 31.

as a woman 'of good creditt & estimacion'.[21] Seniority was also not a decisive factor in permitting unmarried women to work at their own hands, either.[22] Mary was 32 while weekly spinner Joanne Pittman (discussed above) was just 20 years old.

Unmarried women often found themselves between a rock and a hard place in advocating for themselves as witnesses. Paradoxically, they were cast as unsuitable precisely *because* they were in the plaintiff's service, but their credibility also came under attack if they *weren't* in service. Casual work was not always comfortably accommodated within the early modern parish. We met Mary Smith of Brampford Speke (Devon) earlier in this book. Testifying in a 1635 defamation dispute, Mary was a servant but not in the household of the plaintiff on whose behalf she deposed. Unable to leverage her servant status as an objection to her testimony, the opposing party found another way to malign her. Edward Paine deposed that she

> was questioned & convented [brought] before Sir Nicholas Marten a justice of peace for not living with a master. And then the said Sir Nicholas did enjoyne her to procure a master within one moneth following which she did then accordingly but did not long tarry with him by reason whereof shee was againe brought before a Justice. And was threatened to bee punished if shee did not live with a master. And since that tyme shee hath lived in service.

Mary's reputation was tarnished by lack of stable employment. Jerome Upton added that she was 'such a one as doth use to wander upp & downe the conntry and not live in service' and therefore 'little credit is to bee given to what shee sayes'.[23] But one woman spoke in her defence. Widow Katherine Mogridge deposed that Mary had left her service a year earlier to live

> with her mother (who was then very sicke) in Brampford Speke. And there tarryed neere aboute a quarter of a yeere as shee remembreth till her mother's recoverye. And then afterwards a complainte was made by some of her neighbors unto a justice for not living with a master.

Poverty tipped the scales of freedom of choice. Katherine's tale is of a daughter returning home to care for her sick mother. It's likely that her mother was unable to work and was reliant on poor relief. Recipients of poor relief whose children remained at home risked being denied relief and placed in the house of correction.[24] Here, Mary (not her mother) was threatened 'to be sent to Bridewell for not living in service'. By the time of her examination, she had returned to Katherine's home as her servant.[25] Similar objections were raised in 1611 against

---

[21] GA, GDR/121, Agnes Brushe v William Brushe (1613). Italics my own.
[22] This line of argument was suggested by Amy Froide. See Froide, *Never Married*, p. 90.
[23] DHC, Chanter 866, Mary Flood v Dorothea Tucker (1635).
[24] Hindle, *On the Parish?*, p. 199.
[25] DHC, Chanter 866, Mary Flood and Dorothea Tucker (1635).

Joanna Manshipp of Mark (Somerset). Responding to the opposing party's interrogatory questions, she admitted that she

> hath byn but these 6 weeks in Mark parishe with her mother and otherwise hath dwelt out of the parish at service and lived by her labor somewhat. And in that 6 weeks her mother to this examinant's knowledge had xii d [12*d*] of the poore man's box out of the church stock and she had noe more in xii [12] monethes before as she told this respondent. And saith that she stayeth ... at home but to comforte her mother, and doth worke at spinning for her living.

Access to poor relief was contingent on inability to work. It was granted to support the sick, *not* their able-bodied children remaining at home. Joanna's response to this accusation was that she *wasn't* living idly at home but that she spun for her living.[26]

Living at home with parents raised eyebrows when the family household was on the knife edge of poverty. It's possible that enforcement of compulsory service and restricted access to poor relief for the able-bodied may have ramped up following the introduction of the Elizabeth Poor Laws.[27] But enforcement seems occasional in the regions of this study. Legal action was taken by magistrates only when parishioners perceived that a poor family's labour resources weren't being fully exploited. While young women who were too mobile were criticised in court and cast as unsuitable witnesses (as we saw in Joanna Daingerfield's case in Chapter 4), they do not appear to have been prosecuted so long as they were self-sufficient and in some form of work.

Other women from humble backgrounds lived at home with parents without repercussions. Stay-at-home daughters could be a convenient source of labour, depended on by a family trade or simply to help make ends meet. In 1585, 24-year-old Joanne Cheese of Crediton (Devon) recalled being 'at worke in a certen shop of this deponent's fathers house' with her mother.[28] No mention was made of what kind of shop her family ran. In 1596, Clara Jorden deposed that she lived in St Tudy (Cornwall) with her father, describing him as 'a poor man'. She laboured casually at husbandry outside the family home, deposing that 'between whitsontyde and mydsomer last past' she was 'wedding [weeding] in a certeyne p[i]ece of ground within the parish of St Tudy that Edward John then held'.[29] These weren't affluent women whose means placed them beyond the purview of the Statute.[30] But they stayed at home anyway. Others moved between service and home. In 1639, 18-year-old Judith Kilmaster of Cirencester (Gloucestershire) testified in

---

[26] SHC, D/D/cd/28, Richard Hobbes v Cicilia Whiting (1611).
[27] Froide, *Never Married*, p. 36.
[28] DHC, Chanter 861, Rogers v James Tremlet (1585).
[29] DHC, Chanter 864, Elizabeth Trevethicke v Edward John and Petronella John (1695).
[30] For further discussion of alternative labour options for young women, see Mansell, 'Female Service and the Village Community', pp. 82–6.

a matrimonial suit. She had served the plaintiff's mother a year earlier but had left by the time of her deposition. Another witness described Judith as 'then servant' and Judith herself deposed that she lived at home, being 'maintained by her father'.[31] Like Clara, Judith probably lived at home and carried out casual work by the day. This transition from service to living at home gave no rise to accusations of idleness as the labour laws suggest. Judith clearly felt at liberty to divulge in court that she was maintained by her father. If her neighbours protested, their objections had little material impact.

In many of these examples, service was one possibility among a range of options for labouring women. Choice is implicit in freedom. But it's been suggested that female labour became more casualised as women aged: servants became charmaids or workers hired by the day, week, or task. Sheila McIsaac Cooper found that these women 'suffered serious erosion in status'.[32] Eleanor Hubbard imagined that having to call their employers 'mistress' and 'master' must have been 'a painful concession for adult women, [who] did not enjoy the relative security of maidservants, who received meals and lodging'.[33] This transition was a reality for some women. In 1584, 40-year-old Joanna Nutlie of Southampton (Hampshire) deposed that 'she liveth by helping the people of the towne of South[amp]ton wash & doe such thinges & yt [that] she is worth her apparell on her back'. This was effectively charwork. Joanna's own testimony revealed that she had previously been a servant.[34] Only a handful of *young* women were recorded as charwomen in the depositions. Cicilia Frances of Wedmore (Somerset) was 30 and single when charring in Robert and Temperance Hole's house in 1626.[35] In 1593, charwoman Marie Ronney of Gloucestershire was also 30 but married.[36] More unusually perhaps, Joanne Knight of Slimbridge (Gloucestershire) was a 16-year-old servant in 1596, but recalled that previously she 'did many tymes doe chareworke for the sayd goodwife Cowley [the plaintiff in the suit]'. Perhaps this charwork was a gateway to service.

Hubbard noted a distinction between the treatment of adult women as charwomen and young women as charmaids in London. She argued that 'charmaids were objectionable because of their youth and maiden status; their work could be seen as a cover for prostitution. Charwomen, on the other hand, were as respectable as their poverty permitted.'[37] The term 'charmaid' was undoubtedly used

---

[31] GA, GDR/204, Mary Stone v John Cuffe (1639).
[32] Sheila McIsaac Cooper, 'From Family Member to Employee: Aspects of Continuity and Discontinuity in English Domestic Service, 1600–2000', in Antoinette Fauve-Chamoux (ed.), *Domestic Service and the Formation of European Identity: Understanding the Globalization of Domestic Work, 16th–21st Centuries* (Bern, 2004), pp. 277–96 at 280.
[33] Hubbard, *City Women*, p. 211.
[34] HRO, 21M65/C3/9, Grant and Mahawlt v Ellery Brock (1584).
[35] SHC, D/D/cd/51, Eleanor Hodges v Nicholas Baker (1626).
[36] GA, GDR/79, Alice Wiseman v Jane Richardson (1593).
[37] Hubbard, *City Women*, p. 213.

pejoratively. But in these rural areas, it was almost always a shorthand for female poverty, not prostitution. In 1624, 40-year-old Elizabeth Sparckes of Upton St Leonards (Gloucestershire) was described by witness Robert Nelme as

> a singlewoman of no creditt or accompt, an ordinary and common chare maide and hireling here to day and in another place hired to drudge for reward to morrow of no certaine place or abode and is beggarly not worth agroate.[38]

Other charmaids self-identified as poor or were described by others in language denoting poverty. Edith Serney of Iron Acton (Gloucestershire) had moved from service to charwork in 1612 and was described as 'verye poore' and 'beggarly', with others claiming she was 'of no credit'.[39] But if charwork was carried out by the impoverished, these women's credit was not so reduced that it made them entirely unreliable; their appearance in the pages of court depositions indicates that they weren't automatically dismissed as witnesses.

It's noteworthy that 'servant' and 'charmaid' or 'charwoman' were repeatedly used synonymously in depositions. John Crockett of Newent (Gloucestershire) attempted to discredit two female witnesses in 1606, claiming that

> Margery Dawe and Ellinor Phillpott have bin or are the chare maydes or servantes unto the foresayde Mathewe Berrowe & that they are not worthe fortye shillinges apeece but are soe sillye & simple that they cann scarcelye rehearse the Lordes prayer.

Both women described themselves as servants. Eleanor was 19 years old, while at 40, Margery was more than twice her age.[40] In line with distinctions between service and casual work, daily labour within the home has been seen as quite discrete from service. Bridget Hill noted that charmaids worked for a household on a casual basis and weren't live-in employees like servants.[41] Sue Wright characterised charmaids as 'daily helps' who were 'frowned upon by the authorities' for living by such unreliable labour.[42] But the occupational descriptor 'servant' was regularly attached to those carrying out day labour and was used interchangeably with 'charmaid' and 'charwoman'. In 1638, Arthur Lewes was charged by the Bath & Wells court for adultery with Agnes Burrowe of Badgworth (Somerset). One witness described her as a married woman who lived apart from her husband. Another added that she 'often frequents his [Arthur's] howse' where she 'worketh as a churer or servant'.[43] Casual work was demarcated very clearly from service in

---

[38] GA, GDR/148, Richard Atkins v Giles Boyse (1624).
[39] GA, GDR/114, Cressett Cox v Silvester Nayle (1612).
[40] GA, GDR/95, Milberowe Berrowe v John Crockett (1605).
[41] Hill, *Servants*, p. 12.
[42] Sue Wright, '"Churmaids, Huswyfes and Hucksters": The Employment of Women in Tudor and Stuart Salisbury', in Lindsey Charles and Lorna Duffin (eds), *Women and Work in Pre-industrial England* (1985), pp. 100–21 at 104.
[43] SHC, D/D/cd/131, Office v Arthur Lewes (1638).

law. But to early modern people, such distinctions weren't always drawn. The language of service was still in flux.

Attitudes to young women working outside service seldom reflect the preoccupation of lawmakers with regulating young people's employment in service. Though legal documents, depositions are an (imperfect) guide to everyday speech: casual service was routinely elided with annual live-in experiences of service by witnesses, broadly concurring with Alexandra Shepard's verdict that 'wage labour remained conceptually indistinct from service in the seventeenth century'.[44] 'Servant', 'charmaid', 'worked by the day', and 'lived in the house of' were less rigid in meaning than labour legislation leads us to believe.

With or without covenant

So far, I've painted a picture of working life for many young, unmarried women as somewhat free. They could move between different forms of labour with relative ease and unless they were in abject poverty, their working lives were generally unbounded by the labour laws. While these principles hold true, let's pause to consider what is meant by 'free'.

Diarmaid MacCulloch pointed out that early modern English people had a 'distaste for personal unfreedom'.[45] From the late sixteenth century, the idea of the 'freeborn' Englishman was gaining currency.[46] Serfdom had virtually disappeared in England and being 'freeborn' – born outside slavery or bondage – was celebrated. But this didn't make the labouring poor 'free' by modern definitions. Compelling young people to serve and imposing restrictions on their service robbed them of freedom of choice and underscored their subservience. Agreeing to serve or carry out labour for a master was deeply hierarchical. Some wage security was gained but at the price of self-government. As Robert Steinfeld argued, the labourer 'restricted his liberty to the extent of his undertaking'.[47] But state policies were apparently reconciled with 'freedom' in two important ways. Firstly, the idea of 'consent' made sense of restricted freedoms. Minister Richard Baxter saw the servant–master agreement as a consensual one, in which a servant 'temporarily

---

[44] Alexandra Shepard, 'Poverty, Labour and the Language of Social Description in Early Modern England', *P&P* 201 (2008), 51–95 at 55–6.
[45] Diarmaid MacCulloch, 'Bondmen under the Tudors', in Claire Cross, David Loades, and J. J. Scarisbrick (eds), *Law and Government under the Tudors: Essays Presented to Sir Geoffrey Elton, Regius Professor of Modern History in the University of Cambridge, on the Occasion of His Retirement* (Cambridge, 1988), pp. 91–110 at 99.
[46] Christopher Hill, 'Pottage for Freeborn Englishmen: Attitudes to Wage Labour in the Sixteenth and Seventeenth Centuries', in C. H. Feinstein (ed.), *Socialism, Capitalism and Economic Growth: Essays Presented to Maurice Dobb* (Cambridge, 1967), pp. 338–50.
[47] Robert Steinfeld, *The Invention of Free Labour: The Employment Relation in English and American Law and Culture, 1350–1870* (Chapel Hill and London, 1991), p. 40.

alienate[d] their freedom'.[48] Secondly, a tradition of placing service and slavery in two different categories emerged in treatises, sermons, conduct literature, and religious and polemical texts: the move from slavery to service was accompanied by a semantic shift.[49] Nonetheless, early modern society wasn't oblivious to the inconsistencies of the labour laws and ideas of freedom. Instead, as Steinfeld pointed out, legal freedom lay on a spectrum: 'villeins continued to be more unfree than apprentices, apprentices more unfree than servants ... artificers and labourers were more free than servants but less free than yeomen, burgesses, and others'.[50]

As categories of labour are elided and what was meant by 'service' appears murkier, this spectrum becomes a less relevant framework upon which to hang freedom. 'Servant' and 'service' were used to describe a range of labour arrangements, many of which weren't annually contracted or paid. How, then, were agreements of service made and what were the parameters of freedom within the arrangements?

Early modern service and apprenticeship involved binding oneself to a master or mistress for an agreed term. Apprenticeship indentures captured this formal agreement on paper. But early modern culture was still largely oral. Agreements – for sales of goods, deathbed bequests, day labour – all took place without being written down and without the signatory consent of all parties. Jane Whittle noted that servants and labourers were required to appear at petty sessions 'to swear an oath of compliance to the labour laws and declare their terms of employment'. It was also compulsory for masters to attend 'to show they were hiring servants for legal wages'.[51] Mechanisms were theoretically in place to enforce servant–master contracts, and Christopher Hill flagged the Statute of Artificers as an important milestone in reconceptualising labour.[52] But there is scarce evidence of petty sessions operating in the south-west (or elsewhere). Even where records of their operation survive, they don't tell us how many men and women made informal agreements outside official approval. Nor do they tell us how many broken agreements *weren't* legally enforced.

The word 'covenant', used to describe the contract between a female servant and her master, appears only a handful of times in depositions of the Exeter, Hereford, Gloucester, and Winchester courts. It was used more routinely in the Bath & Wells court as a precise description of service arrangements ('covenant service'). But we also saw at the beginning of the chapter in Philippa Hooper's testimony that it was possible to be a 'servant' without being a 'covenant servant'. What did this mean? A legal distinction is made here that other testimonies

---

[48] Baxter, *A Christian Directory*, pp. 588–60.
[49] Tadmor, *Social Universe of the English Bible*, p. 90.
[50] Steinfeld, *Invention of Free Labour*, p. 104.
[51] Whittle, *Development of Agrarian Capitalism*, pp. 276, 284.
[52] Hill, 'Pottage for Freeborn Englishmen', p. 340.

clarify. Questioned in 1577 about the terms by which Joanna Jones of Kenton (Devon) agreed to work for John Evans, Richard Wise deposed that Joanna 'was servant to John Evans but when she went awaye or whether she be yet in covenant or no he cannot tell'.[53] William Wells of Poundstock (Cornwall) clarified in his 1580 deposition that 'Joanna Iago was not covenant servant to Sidwell Callerd at the speaking of the [defamatory] words ... but now she is'.[54] Making a covenant had legal implications and could be leveraged in court to measure a witness's affinity with a plaintiff or defendant. If there was uncertainty over whether a covenant had been made, a non-relative living in the plaintiff's or defendant's home couldn't easily be discredited by the opposing party as an unreliable witness (as the litigant had no legal responsibility for them). In depositions, the covenant was therefore a legalistic device. This isn't to say they were never made. But witnesses who admitted being in service while batting off the identity of 'covenant servant' were at pains to show it was entirely plausible (and therefore possible) to serve *without* covenant. Arrangements were not as tightly fixed or well defined as the labour laws demanded.

Terms of agreement

At its most basic level, a covenant was an agreement to do something for someone else in the future.[55] In negotiating labour exchange, *some* kind of consensual agreement had to be made. The covenant, in theory, protected both master and servant. Both could rely on the law to remedy tensions. But for this protection, the servant (and master) handed over liberties to each other. The servant gave up more – most significantly, her freedom of self-rule during the set period of service and her right to leave at any time. The master took on legal responsibility for the *person* (not just their labour) and relinquished the ability to dismiss them without just cause, ill-treat them, or withhold wages unfairly.[56] I return to the extent to which these freedoms were exercised later.

Urvashi Chakravarty noted that seventeenth-century people wondered whether a verbal contract was binding. Did a person's conscience truss them to their agreement or was material evidence required as proof?[57] It's been suggested that the traditional 'hiring penny', 'fastening penny', or 'God's penny', a token payment made at the point of contract, may have made an agreement binding.[58] Virtually no evidence of this is found in the volumes of court depositions: only

---

[53] DHC, Chanter 859, Joanna Jones v Jacob Escourt (1577).
[54] DHC, Chanter 860, Sidwell Callerd v Elizabeth Markes (1580).
[55] Steinfeld, *Invention of Free Labour*, p. 74.
[56] Ibid., p. 40.
[57] Chakravarty, *Fictions of Consent*, p. 183.
[58] Kussmaul, *Servants in Husbandry*, p. 32.

Henry Tremynge of Ringwood (Hampshire) recalled giving Alice Churcher a groat on behalf of his father in 1545 to secure her service (and this claim was made in objection to the allegation of the groat being a marriage token).[59] But women weren't serving on a promise alone. Though wages were seldom paid upfront, they were also not paid on completion of service. Rather, they were disbursed in instalments. The testimony of one female servant witness in a 1606 Bath & Wells defamation suit survives only partially and without record of her name. This anonymous servant deposed that she received 'wages which she *hath* by service', the present tense of 'hath' suggesting that payment was ongoing and periodic.[60] Margery Lewes of Backwell (Somerset) deposed in 1638 that 'she [is] covenant servant to the producent & *hath* wages from him or his wief'.[61] Gentry household accounts show that servants were routinely paid on 'quarter' days: Lady Day (25 March), Midsummer (24 June), Michaelmas (29 September), and Christmas (25 December). This payment structure allowed regularity of servant payment and may even have accommodated the irregular, non-annual hiring arrangements we saw in Chapter 4.[62]

Burrowing deeper into individual depositions, we get closer to what service agreements looked like and what they included. Philippa Hooper indicated that covenants were usually long term. Where service was described as 'covenanted', the agreement was typically made for one year with the possibility of renewal. In 1635, Isabella Shepperd of Portbury (Somerset) testified that she lived with John Buck of Kingston Seymour as a covenant servant 'for the space of a yeare or thereaboutes ending att or aboute Michaelmas last was two yeares'.[63] We might assume bed and board was almost always included. But in 1628, Stephen Garman of Shepton Mallett (Somerset) stood accused of adultery with his servant, Margaret Olliver. Maintaining innocence, Stephen incidentally noted that Margaret lived in his house as 'his covenant servant', where she had worked for the last six months or more. But husbandman Alexander Watts added that

> she liveth with him all the daye tyme as his servant but doth not lye in howse at night unles he be out of towen then she lyeth with his wiffe & at other tymes she cometh to this deponents where he hath rented [her] a chamber.

This point was laboured over in light of the accusation of sexual deviance and to clarify sleeping arrangements. But even if untrue, Stephen Garman still had to present a plausible defence to the court.[64] It was probably uncommon, but

[59] HRO, 21M65/C3/2, Alice Churcher v Henry Tremynge (1545).
[60] SHC, D/D/cd/30, Margery Huckbridge v Agnes Salter (1606). Italics my own.
[61] SHC, D/D/cd/86, Joseph Crossman v Richard Debden (1638). Italics my own.
[62] Whittle, 'A Different Pattern of Employment', p. 64.
[63] SHC, D/D/cd/81, Grace Swaine v John Buck (1635).
[64] The detail about sharing a bed with Stephen's wife when he was away from the house resonates with other depositional evidence of women not lying at home alone. SHC, D/D/cd/66, Office v Stephen Garman (1628).

covenants at least *could* be made between masters and live-out servants. Bed wasn't always part of the deal.

A covenant gave the master exclusive rights to the servant's labour. In apprenticeship agreements, the indenture logged service as property belonging to the master.[65] It could be sold or traded. In household or farm service, this principle seems broadly applicable. When a master died, the servant's labour – the master's 'property' – routinely passed to his wife or heirs. Richard Arpewoode and Agnes Munke had both served Mr Alexander Oldfelde in Twyford (Hampshire) before his death in 1580. They then became the servants of Mr Rowland Oldfelde, who appears to have been Alexander's son.[66] Whether this reassignment to kin was automatic or a new consensual agreement is unclear, but it was a transfer recorded time and again in the pages of depositions.

In agreeing to serve, women consented to assist the household in its economic strategies. But in several cases, we find servants carrying out work for those *not* living within the household-family unit. Marjorie McIntosh found that servants might be 'loaned to another employer for a day or week'.[67] Such arrangements appear throughout the depositions and beg the question: what did a servant actually consent to when she agreed to serve? Around Lent 1631, John Hyte of Drayton (Somerset) persuaded John Knighte's wife to 'let her maide to come upp [to his house] and make his bedd', his wife being away from home and he presumably professing ignorance of how to do it himself.[68] Here, the hiatus to this servant's normal work was brief, but the servant contract was nonetheless being somewhat stretched. Was the servant paid for this additional work? In 1605, Margaret Gibbins was sent to care for John Barne, who lay sick in his house in Cromhall (Gloucestershire), she being 'a neighbours servant'. She stayed from Sunday morning through the night until the following morning, when someone else was found to step in.[69] This extra-household work could be regular. In 1574, Richard Tanner of Hampshire deposed that he 'sumtymes borowed' Joan Sturte, the servant of Winchester yeoman Richard Edes, 'to do him worke'.[70] Even within an agreed contract of service, the labour female servants carried out wasn't always for their master and his family.

Could female servants *refuse* to work for another? Did they receive monetary reward for temporarily working for someone else? Steinfeld pointed out that if a servant was hired out to a third party, the wages she accrued undertaking that labour were owing to the master. The labour 'was quite literally the master's not

---

[65] Olive Jocelyn Dunlop and Richard Douglas Denman, *English Apprenticeship and Child Labour: A History* (1912), p. 57.

[66] HRO, 21M65/C3/8, John Weke v Alexander Oldfelde (1581).

[67] McIntosh, *A Community Transformed*, p. 61.

[68] SHC, D/D/cd/71, John Hyte v John Staple (1631).

[69] GA, GDR/100, Thomas Barnes v Elizabeth Maunsell (1606).

[70] HRO, 21M65/C3/6, Richard Tanner v Richard Widge (1574).

the servant's, and not available for hire without the master's permission'.[71] In 1575, Alice Jaye, a defamation suit plaintiff, approached Robert Webb of Wells (Somerset) to ask whether his servant Maria Johnson might testify on her behalf. Maria deposed that Alice promised that 'she woulde see this respondentes Mr pleased therefore' (i.e. she would pay him for Maria's missed labour).[72] The cost of testifying was to the master, not the servant.

The Winchester court depositions capture a rare case where money for a female servant changed hands between two men. In 1564, Elizabeth Yonge was passed from her master Henry Bayley of Romsey (Hampshire) to John Barnarde, who paid 26s 8d

> to thuse of the said Elizabeth being his servant and with this agreement the said Elizabeth did grannte her self to be throwglye [thoroughly] and well agreed with the same Barnarde for all demandes.[73]

Why this evidence was presented in court is unclear; this was a tithe dispute pursued by Henry Bayley against John Barnarde. The sum of 26s 8d indicates this was a long-term labour agreement and renegotiation of Elizabeth's position in service, not the temporary 'borrowing' of a servant we've seen elsewhere. Barnarde's payment compensated Bayley for wages and clothing he had probably already stumped up for Elizabeth. Sale or transferral of service required the servant's consent in England. This practice has been contrasted with the forceable and non-consensual sale of indentured servants (and later enslaved people) in British America.[74] Consent *is* stressed in this deposition, but whether Elizabeth was in fact as 'well agreed' with the arrangement as the witness (John's brother) assured the court is impossible to verify. The security that a covenant was supposed to offer a servant could be compromised.

On the other side of the coin, female servants occasionally paused their service of their own volition to take up temporary work elsewhere. Their departure was not always clearly sanctioned. Marie Robins worked for husbandman James Pippett and his wife Elizabeth in their home in Evercreech (Somerset) around 1604. When her suitor visited to entreat the couple to allow Marie to 'com over to her to abyde with' his widowed mother, they responded that 'they could not spare her'. But Marie went anyway, returning after a month.[75] Marie's service with James and Elizabeth probably wasn't covenanted and might not have even been service at all (though she later went on to serve elsewhere). She was able to effectively come and go as she pleased, so long as the couple were willing to take her

---

[71] Steinfeld, *Invention of Free Labour*, p. 71.
[72] SHC, D/D/cd/15, Alice Jaye v Peter Lane (1575).
[73] HRO, 21M65/C3/3, Elizabeth Yonge v John Barnard (1564).
[74] Sonia Tycko, 'Bound and Filed: A Seventeenth-Century Service Indenture from a Scattered Archive', *Early American Studies: An Interdisciplinary Journal* 19 (2021), 166–90 at 169.
[75] SHC, D/D/cd/41, Marie Robins v John Sheppard (1609).

back. We also catch Devon servant Wilmota Rogers pitching hay with her master in 1556, but when he attempted to pay her for sex, she took the money, named a time and place, but 'keapt not appointment with him but went the same wensday to reap with one Norley'.[76] This was hay harvest; perhaps Wilmota shrewdly leveraged his solicitation of her in the field to get what she wanted, threatening to expose his sexual advances if he didn't comply or perhaps she was a casual rather than covenanted servant. A master's exclusive rights to a servant's labour were contingent on contract. But the examples of third parties acting as surrogate masters outlined here show that we need to see many master–servant contracts as informal agreements, not legally binding, enforceable covenants.

Informal negotiations made after the expiry of a covenant illustrates the mutual trust that might develop in the first year of the servant's employment. The end of a covenant offered the chance for renegotiation. Catherine Lawnsdowne (alias Petheram) lived with John Cock of Wedmore (Somerset) 'as a covenant servant for a yeeres space ending aboute three yeares agoe'. John deposed that

> after her covenant was expired, she was verie earnest to dyett in howse with this deponent & to live att her owne hand, & not as a servant, and then she preferred this deponent xvi*d* [16*d*] by the weeke for her dyett and lodging, & was verie importunate with this deponent to take itt, but hee refused her proferr telling her he would not dyett & lodge her under xx*d* [20*d*] a weeke, the said Catherine being then a verie froward wench.

Negotiations broke down, but what this case reveals is that Catherine wasn't afraid to capitalise on her position as his former servant to make new living arrangements. Chakravarty noted that for a master, perfect service was found in the servant's gratitude; even when free, servants should still show gratitude (even though this undercut their manumission).[77] Here, Catherine achieved her freedom but in doing so, she appeared less than grateful. John's unwillingness to retain her in his home was not just based on its economic infeasibility. Her 'frowardness' (disobedience) unsettled the performance of covenant and shattered the illusion of the willing servant.[78]

Wage negotiations

The Statute of Artificers stated that maximum wage rates should be set locally by magistrates. Wage assessments weren't a novelty in 1563; examples survive from as early as the fifteenth century.[79] In surviving late sixteenth- and

---

[76] DHC, Chanter 855, Office v Wilmota Rogers (1556); Office v Richard Stone (1556).

[77] Chakravarty, *Fictions of Consent*, p. 180.

[78] SHC, D/D/cd/51, Charity Lawnsdon v Roger Petherham (1631).

[79] Whittle, 'Attitudes to Wage Labour', p. 43.

early seventeenth-century examples, both annual and day wages were listed for servants.[80] Although service was supposed to be annual, even wage assessments acknowledged that it could be agreed – and paid for – on a more casual basis. Weekly or sometimes daily payments for service were made for those serving for shorter periods than one year. In October 1604, Elizabeth Greene served John Sheile in his Gloucester home. Being asked her worth, she replied that

> she is little or nothinge worth more then [than] the cloathes she useth to weare, and that she doth worke taske worke with John Sheile in his house in bargaine by the weeke tell [till] Christmas next.

Elizabeth's agreed term lasted just three months, and accordingly was paid by the week.[81] The phrase 'in bargaine' indicates that this short-term arrangement *was* nonetheless an agreement. It also signals the power women could hold in negotiating the terms of their work.

Elsewhere we find servants attempting wage negotiation, sometimes successfully. Martha Langdon, servant to Thomas Spracklyn of Westonzoyland (Somerset), fell pregnant with her master's child in 1611. She and other witnesses claimed Thomas had promised to marry her and had given her money and wool to make a coat. Thomas denied these things had been given upon the promise of marriage. Rather, he 'gave the said Martha money and woolle over and above her wages, because she sayed her wages was too little'.[82] Perhaps Martha used her pregnancy as a bargaining chip. Other masters in similar positions to Thomas bestowed money and gifts on their servants in exchange for silence or even as a vague apology. Whether Thomas's gifts were made in the way of marriage or not, his own claim once again speaks to the plausible: it was *conceivable* that servants might successfully negotiate their wages.

Others had less luck. In 1635, Richarda Cock of Churston Ferrers (Devon) had served John Tayler for four years. On the day of her testimony in court, however, she lived at home with her mother. She was 'not to retourne to his [John's] service againe so far as she knoweth nor hath made any promise thereto, but parted from him because he refused to geve her such wages as she demannded'.[83] At the age of 30, Richarda had worked for several years for the same master. Her appeal for higher wages was probably on the grounds of her age, length of service, and the skills and experience she had acquired. John's refusal had soured the relationship: Richarda's testimony was against his wife, who she alleged had spoken defamatory words against her neighbour. John clearly felt their fractious labour relationship prevented her from being an impartial witness; the withdrawal of her

---

[80] See, for example, the Exeter wage assessments in Hughes and Larkin, *Tudor Royal Proclamations, Vol. 3*, p. 19.
[81] GA, GDR/95, Sheile v Thomas Bishopp (1604).
[82] SHC, D/D/cd/44, Martha Langdon v Thomas Spracklyn (1611).
[83] DHC, Chanter 866, Joane Penny v Joane Taylor (1635).

labour was revealed only in interrogatory questioning, directed by John and his wife. Negotiations weren't always successful, but women did not simply resign themselves to the life and lifestyle set out by their masters or the law.[84] Richarda was prepared to walk away, even without a new position in service to turn to. She returned home rather than accept a wage she deemed inadequate. Service for Richarda was not obviously coercive; she had other options. Failed wage negotiations did not always end acrimoniously either. As we saw in Chapter 4, Rose Michenar's disagreement over wages with her aunt-mistress in Otterbourne (Hampshire) in 1580 led to her serving John Garye and his wife, Alice, instead, after six years of service.[85] But Rose nevertheless testified on behalf of her aunt and former mistress in the church court.

How much more money Martha, Richarda, and Rose were asking for isn't stated. In theory, penalties could be imposed on those who paid or accepted more than local wage assessments stipulated.[86] But wage controls do not appear to have been adhered to or stringently enforced. In 1618, 23-year-old servant Mary Hayne of Silverton (Devon) testified in a defamation dispute. She had served John and Elizabeth Faryes 'in the tyme of Christmas last past by the daye and by the weeke'. This casual arrangement meant her wages fluctuated: William Trowte deposed that

> he this deponent did aske the said Merria what sorte she was abiding with the forsaid Elizabeth Farye and the said Marria tould this deponent that some tymes the said Elizabeth Farye promised her vi*d* [6*d*] a weeke and sometimes viii*d* [8*d*] a weeke for her service as she could make her bargine.

Again, the language of bargaining suggests a collaborative discussion between servant and mistress in the agreement of a suitable weekly wage. Maria had some agency in determining her pay, although other factors were likely at play, too (such as the Faryes' economic situation or the level of skill or physicality the work required each week). At the rate of either 6*d* or 8*d* per week, Mary's annual wage ranged between 26*s* and 34*s* 8*d* if she worked five days a week (or 260 days of the year).[87] Devon wage assessments for the year 1595 permitted only those over the age of 24 to legally earn 20*s* a year in service, while those below this age could only earn up to 16*s*.[88] By 1654, this had barely risen to 23*s* 4*d* for those

---

[84] Deborah Youngs found similar flexibility in the servant contracts of Humphrey Newton's household. See Youngs, *Humphrey Newton*, p. 80.

[85] HRO, 21M65/C3/8, Avice Hewes v John Wayte (1580).

[86] R. H. Tawney, 'The Assessment of Wages in England by the Justices of the Peace. (Schluß)', *Vierteljahrschrift für Sozial- und Wirtschaftsgeschichte* 11 (1913), 533–64 at 534.

[87] Robert Allen and Jacob Weisdorf initially proposed a 250-day working year while Humphries and Weisdorf more recently adjusted this to 260 days. See Robert Allen and Jacob Weisdorf, 'Was There an "Industrious Revolution" before the Industrial Revolution? An Empirical Exercise for England, *c.*1300–1830', *EcHR* 64 (2011), 715–29; Humphries and Weisdorf, 'The Wages of Women in England', 412–13.

[88] Hughes and Larkin, *Tudor Royal Proclamations*, pp. 150–1.

aged between 18 and 30.[89] This was below Mary's *minimum* earning potential as a servant to the Faryes over the course of a year.[90] Though insecure, her casual service provided an opportunity to earn a higher annual income than was (at least legally) possible in yearly service. Whether Mary was able to unlock such earning potential by stringing together a series of casual positions in service or other labour is unknown.

Monetary wages of twelve women in service were captured, taken between 1585 and 1634 and ranging from 16*s* to 40*s* per year (with a mean of 24*s* 7*d* and median of 26*s*). Perhaps this was a region of low wages; 40*s* was probably a typical wage for early modern servants.[91] Though only a few observations, these rates of pay are illuminating. To return to a case introduced earlier: one of the servants earning the highest wage during the period was 20-year-old Mary Thomas of Kentisbeare (Devon), who in 1634

> did live a servant in howse to the said Joane Bennett & her husband with whome she lived 3 quarters of a yere for wages after the rate of xl*s* [40*s*] per ann.

The calculations and negotiations involved in her hiring are set out. The Bennetts set an annual rate of pay (40*s*) which they divided according to the number of quarters worked. That Mary knew the annual rate indicates the transparency of the negotiations.[92] Mary's wage of 30*s* for nine months of work was above the maximum wage set by Devon justices of the peace (even twenty years later in 1654, female servants between 18 and 30 could legally be paid only 23*s* 4*d*).[93] In 1598, 20-year-old Mary Tanner of Crediton (Devon) deposed that 'shee servith with William Osbourne … and hath xx*s* [20] a yeere wages'. In 1595, just three years before Mary's appearance in court, the maximum legal wage for an Exeter female servant remained unchanged from the 1588 assessment which stipulated that no female servant between 16 and 24 'shall take above 16*s* by the year, or for her vesture or garment 5*s*'. Only those over the age of 24 could legally earn as much as 20*s* per year.[94] Twenty years old, Mary was paid more than the maximum wage that masters could legally offer.[95] As a means of regulating service and the labour of young people, wage assessments were unlikely to have been effective. R. H. Tawney argued that the 'legal rate often differed considerably from the market rate' and that the law could probably be 'evaded without much difficulty'.[96] Wages

---

[89] Alexander Henry Abercromby Hamilton (ed.), *Quarter Sessions from Queen Elizabeth to Queen Anne: Illustrations of Local Government and History Drawn from Original Records (Chiefly of the County of Devon)* (1878), pp. 163–4.

[90] James E. Thorold Rogers, *A History of Agriculture and Prices in England* (Oxford, 1866), p. 694.

[91] Humphries and Weisdorf, 'The Wages of Women in England', 431–2; Whittle, 'Servants in Rural England', p. 92.

[92] DHC, Chanter 866, Joanne Bennett v Joanne Deymont (1634).

[93] Hamilton, *Quarter Sessions*, p. 163.

[94] Hughes and Larkin, *Tudor Royal Proclamations*, pp. 19, 144.

[95] DHC, Chanter 864, Mary Eve v Margaret Leach (1598).

[96] Tawney, 'The Assessment of Wages', 564.

also weren't regularly assessed and in both these examples, masters and servants appear to have gotten away with paying and receiving wages above maximum legal rates.

Among the lowest earners were the two daughter-servants of Paschasius Soper of Dunsford (Devon) whom we met in Chapter 4. Their wages were mentioned in a rare dispute concerning personal tithes on wages that householders in this parish were allegedly required to pay. Paschasius (their father) deposed that he had 'two mayd servants his daughters serving in Dunsford whom have received xvi*s* [16*s*] a peece by the yeere for their wages'. At Easter, he

> compounded and agreed with Mr Thomas [the vicar] for the tenth of the one half of their wages and paid him sometymes i*d* [1*d*] and vii*d* [7*d*] at a tyme in full payment of the tenth of the halfendeale [half] of every of their wages.

Here, we are reminded of less visible outlays of hiring a servant: masters and mistresses paid dues *on top of* wages in Dunsford. Custom dictated that householders with 'covenante servants there recyving yerely wages' paid a tithe at Easter.[97] We don't know the ages of Paschasius's daughters, but their 16*s* wage was commensurate with the maximum rate female servants between the ages of 16 and 24 could legally be paid in Devon. Pachasius's daughters weren't the only ones earning this low wage. Maria Lane of Curry Rivell (Somerset) deposed in 1628 that 'shee is a servant and doth serve for sixteene shillings a yere'. She gave her age imprecisely as just 15 or 16 years old.[98] Age could therefore be a barrier to high wages for female servants, though Paschasius's servants were also his daughters; perhaps little more than 16*s* each could be afforded or perhaps their low wages came with promises of money from their father-master upon marriage.

Wages also weren't guaranteed and younger servants might serve for just bed and board.[99] Exeter justices of the peace wrote in 1588 that

> no woman servant under the age of 16 years shall have any wages but only meat and drink and other necessaries as shall be agreed between their master, mistress, and the servant.[100]

Being unwaged during minority was raised in two testamentary cases in the courts. In 1584, Juliana Knorle (alias Hardinge) of Ottery (Somerset) deposed that following the death of her parents, she

> was servant unto John Croydon ... and did his worke by all which tyme she believeth as she saieth that she did earne her meate and dricke and apparell and that he did finde her meate drinke and apparell for her woorke and that she had no other wages of him.[101]

[97] DHC, Chanter 861 and Chanter 862, John Thomas v James Puddicomb (1585).
[98] SHC, D/D/cd/65, Maria Traverse v Maria Crowte (1628).
[99] Whittle, *Development of Agrarian Capitalism*, p. 302; Kussmaul, *Servants in Husbandry*, p. 37.
[100] Hughes and Larkin, *Tudor Royal Proclamations*, p. 19.
[101] SHC, D/D/cd/17, John Croydon and William Hobbes v Juliana Knorle (alias Hardinge) (1584).

In 1584, Margaret Peerse likewise appeared before the Exeter court as an orphaned daughter. She had been placed in the service of William Peerse at the age of 13 or 14 but wasn't paid a wage. In both cases, these women were litigant parties who, upon reaching 21, sought to prove they hadn't received their due inheritance from their fathers' estates. Both Juliana and Margaret argued that those entrusted with their care had no legitimate claim that they had been financially burdened by taking them in (and that their inheritance had been required to offset the costs). The labour they had carried out, these two women argued, had covered the costs of their food, drink, and clothing, and they had received no wages. Margaret's testimony in particular records her objection to being an unwaged servant; she believed she was both due and entitled to payment.[102]

Evidently, Exeter wage assessments said otherwise: at 13 years old, Margaret was too young to receive a wage. But this age condition doesn't account for all non-payments. Alice Inwood of Portishead (Somerset) was 18 in 1597 when she served her master for only 'meate drinke and apparel'.[103] In Otterton (Devon) in 1585, Joanne Wannell deposed matter-of-factly that 'she is Thomas Morgan's servant and hath of him no wages but meate drinke and clothes'. She was 18 years old. Not all servants in Thomas Morgan's household were unwaged. Mary Tayler and Melison Solye both received wages (the amounts unspecified) for their service. These women were all similar in age: Melison was the youngest at 17, followed by Joanne at 18, then Mary, at 19 years old.[104] Another explanation for these wage differences is found in the bonds of kinship.[105] As we saw in Chapter 4, Joanne shared a family name with her mistress, Alice Morgan (alias Wannell). Joanne's lack of wages might therefore be explained by this kinship bond. Some kin may only have had the means to clothe, feed, and lodge their relatives; servants sacrificed wages in favour of the familiarity and comfort a familial setting might offer. Kinship ties determined not only the amount that female servants were paid (as we saw earlier in the case of Paschasius Soper), but also whether they were paid at all. If kin were a form of support, they could also force young women into a position of economic dependence whereby liberty wasn't so easily within reach.

Other material benefits were included as part of a servant package for both the waged and the unwaged. For some, the offer of clothes, food, and lodging were far from trivial. In 1602, cordwainer Philip Hamlin of Glastonbury told the Bath & Wells court of his encounter with 21-year-old Alice Stone. Alice had come to his house, 'very poore, and very badly apparelled, could [cold] and hungry and craved suckor of this deponent', saying 'shee was utterlie destitute of meate drinke, lodging, and apparell' and didn't know of a house in the town that

---

[102] DHC, Chanter 860, Thomas Peerse v Margaret Peerse (1584).
[103] SHC, D/D/cd/27, William Tanner and Alice Tanner v Edward Warden (1596).
[104] DHC, Chanter 861, Sprynt v Thomas Wichalse (1583).
[105] Bridget Hill identified a similar pattern in the eighteenth century. See Hill, *Servants*, p. 255.

might receive her. Philip arranged for her to serve 'one Barter' and, as Alice was 'weake and sickly', her new master 'bestowed a whole yeeres wages before hand in apparell uppon her'. A quarter of a year passed before Alice ran away.[106] As Chapter 2 showed, clothing was valuable and wage assessments included provision for servants' clothes. As we'll see, they were also withheld when servants left their contracts early.

Breaking agreements

For all the flexibility that service offered, a covenant theoretically entailed a loss of freedom. Steinfeld pointed out that even when the labouring poor 'freely' made a contract of service, it was legally binding, and their freedom was curtailed. They couldn't leave and were therefore compelled to serve.[107] Contraventions of the labour laws recorded in petty sessions offer limited evidence that servants and masters alike were indicted for breaching contracts. But the evidence stops short of explaining *how* such agreements were proven.[108] Church courts weren't sites of enforcement, but examples of female servants and masters bringing issues of covenant to justices of the peace occasionally crop up.

A covenant gave masters and servants responsibilities but also rights. Female servants have been cast as vulnerable members of the household, with little agency or freedom to challenge not only patriarchal rule but also its abuses. These abuses ranged from withholding pay to unfair dismissal, violent punishment, and sexual assault. Some masters clearly thought their rights over servants were boundless. In 1620, Peter Poole of Withycombe (Somerset) was charged with a litany of offences, including blasphemy and adultery with his servant. One witness reported Peter's speech as follows:

> Althoughe it bee written thou shalt not covet thy neighbours howse thou shalt not covet thie neighbours wief, nor his servant, not his mayde, nor his oxe, nor his asse, nor anie thing that is his; yeat a man may doe what hee will with his owne: but I protest I ame cleere, and free from my servant.[109]

Peter believed he shouldn't covet his neighbour's servant but saw his own servant as his property. In any case, he professed, his relationship with her was no longer as servant and master for he was 'free' from her. His freedom surely looked very different from hers. It's undeniable that like the unnamed woman who served Peter, female servants were vulnerable to sexual violation. Examples

[106] SHC, D/D/cd/32, Henry Sock v Maria Barter (1601).
[107] Steinfeld, *Invention of Free Labour*, chapter 2, esp. p. 24.
[108] Whittle, *Development of Agrarian Capitalism*, chapter 5.
[109] SHC, D/D/cd/55, John Kempe v Peter Poole (1620).

in the church courts of servants becoming pregnant by their masters are abundant. Economic reasons kept these women in the grip of licentious masters: they needed the work. But the threat of sexual assault did call some women to action. In 1617, Elizabeth Edwards joined the household of John Burges of Wells (Somerset). She had served for just five or six weeks when he began to solicit her for sex. She could

> not bee in quiet in his service scarse one daie, to an end shee made her complainte unto one John Sadler of Weeke being a frend of her fathers & desired that hee would bee a meanes to right her, wheareuppon complaint was made unto the worshipfull Thomas Southworth esquire one of his majesties justices of the peace for the countie of Somerset, who sent forth his warrant against the said John Burges, and beeing apprehended was by him examined about it.

John was bound over to appear at the next general (quarter) sessions. Perhaps no resolution was found in the secular court, but it clearly wasn't the end of the matter: this evidence surfaces because the parish churchwardens levelled an allegation of sexual assault in the church court against John. Allegations of sexual assault often cartwheeled between ecclesiastical and secular courts. In response, John claimed that *he* in fact had instigated secular court proceedings against Elizabeth, accusing her of theft and having her examined by the Justice. He insisted hers was a false allegation. John, it seems, was backed into a corner. Elizabeth had acted first and so he responded with his own accusation. Witnesses gathered, testifying that Elizabeth wasn't the only victim of John's attacks: Joan Jones had been promised a cheese worth 12 pence 'if thou wilt lett mee occupie thee three times', and it was reported that John had boasted that Marie Brokenburrowe had given *him* 12 pence 'to have the carnall knowledge of her bodie'.[110] Elizabeth's rationale for initially appealing to secular law is tricky to set down. Was hers a rare allegation of rape (which, if pursued, would have been tried in the assizes)?[111] Or did she see this as an issue of contract and improper labour relations? In either case, the patriarchal hierarchy that underpinned the servant-master agreement was not unswayable. Reporting her ill treatment to a family friend had ensured its route into not just secular legal channels but ecclesiastical ones too.

She was not alone in employing this strategy. In 1618, Joanna Selway of Rowberrow (Somerset) deposed that her master, Edmund Dirrick, regularly attempted to sexually assault her. On Midsummer Eve in 1617, he had 'forceably tooke upp her clothes and handled her by her secret parts, insomuch that this

---

[110] SHC, D/D/cd/51, John Atwell v John Burges (1619).

[111] We assume accusations of rape were rare because they seldom reached the Assizes, whereas allegations of sexual assault appear regularly in defamation, bastardy, and infanticide cases in the church courts. See Miranda Chaytor, 'Husband(ry): Narratives of Rape in the Seventeenth Century', *Gender & History* 7 (1995), 378–407 at 378.

examinate cryed out, and toulde him shee woulde tell his wief of it'. Joanna didn't leave the couple's service but

> continewed dwelling with them until Michaelmas day now last past, when as her dame woulde have covenanted with her for another yeere, but in regarde her Mr had so dealte with her, shee not knowing how hee woulde deale with her yf shee shoulde dwell longer with him, refused to make covenante for anie longer tyme, and so departed from them.[112]

Joanna honoured her covenant, avoiding legal recourse to withdraw from service. But she *did* report Edmund's abuses to both her mistress and her neighbours, setting in motion a chain of proceedings as her grievances were once again picked up by the churchwarden and brought to court.

Likewise, Ursula Daniell of Walton (Somerset) first tried to manage the situation in house. After her master, John Tutton, attempted to rape her while she was milking cows early in the morning, she informed his wife 'that shee would no more go abroade about his busines without some company'. For a while this worked, but something must have happened to make Ursula report the matter within the parish. Hearing this news, John then 'putt her out of his service'. Ursula lost her job but must have felt some consolation that this wasn't the end of the matter: he, too, was hauled before the church court.[113] Servants' complaints against masters do not regularly turn up in secular court records, but this doesn't mean there were no available channels for complaint. Neighbours and friends offered support and helped them pursue cases against sexually abusive masters in the church courts. Power was of course imbalanced within the home, and countless women must have put up with their masters' advances. But female servants facing this unwanted attention strategised carefully over how to break covenant and leave. Avenues of resistance, however limited, were therefore available to some.

At the same time, the imbalance of power in this labour relationship is clear. Servants who had sex out of wedlock through *choice* were regularly dismissed by their masters, although the point at which dismissal came varied. In 1604, Henry Ley of West Buckland (Somerset) found

> John Dummett and Frances Downe his servants, sporting, playing and kissing togeathers, and especiallie at one tyme he found them together verye late at night in his howse incontinentlie, and that therupon he putt the said Frances Downe out of his service.[114]

John Dummett, it seems, was spared. Pregnancy outside wedlock was a sure-fire covenant breaker, and was widely acknowledged as a legitimate cause for dismissal. Thomas Barber of Brambridge (Hampshire) pointed out in no uncertain

[112] SHC, D/D/cd/49, John Atwell v Edmund Dirrick (1618).
[113] SHC, D/D/cd/34, Office v John Tutton (1602).
[114] SHC, D/D/cd/34, John Atwell v John Dummett (1604).

terms that 'the said Amy Dance cam grete with childe to him & *as sone as he perceived it* he putt her away from his service'.[115] Thomas' swift actions sought to forestall his household becoming entrenched in the scandal of Amy's illegitimate pregnancy. In 1569, Richard Thomas of Portbury (Somerset) allegedly backed out of marrying Matilda Methewaye, his father's servant. Reading between the lines, marriage was initially on the cards: he deposed that he and Matilda (or 'Mawd') were very 'familer together', and one day, working in the fields, they began talking about an unmarried pregnant neighbour, Joanne Ashman. Richard told Mawd that he wished her 'belly weare as bigg as Joanne Ashmans' and that if Mawd fell pregnant by him, he would marry her. Months later, finding out that the couple had had sex under his roof, John, Robert's father, 'willed Mawd Methewaye to departe his house'. Richard claimed he 'made intreatye to his father to kepe her in service till her covenante was oute'. But his father's mind was made up; he had 'often tymes' wanted Mawd to leave his house and he finally had the excuse he needed for her dismissal.[116] John Thomas toed a more careful line in exercising his rights under covenant, dismissing Mawd only when he was sure he had reasonable grounds. Less typically, John Huddle of Dunster (also Somerset) was more ruthless. He testified that in Michaelmas 1621, Alice Nicholls had joined his home as a covenant servant. According to John, she was regularly absent for 'three dayes & nightes togeathers', visiting a man named William Amerie. Seeing no good in their relationship, John 'about our Ladie day last past putt his said servant out of his howse & service notwithstandinge hee had made covenant with her for a whole year'.[117] His grievances were likely both Alice's work ethic and her reputation.

Other complaints that led to agreements being called off related to property. Quarter Sessions examinations are replete with theft cases in which servants took away their master's or mistress's property: silver spoons, cash from coffers, items of clothing, and even bags of wheat. The temptation of the goods surrounding them was, for some women in service, too much. A stereotype of the thievish servant emerged. We've already seen that John Burges attempted to lever a charge of theft against Elizabeth Edwards when she complained to the justice of his sexual advances. Other masters and mistresses fabricated similar accusations. Agnes Barons of Ilsington (Devon) found herself being questioned by Mr Cabell, a justice of the peace in 1636. Her master, Mr Done claimed Agnes had broken covenant by leaving before her year's service had ended, while Agnes maintained they had only agreed a term of six months. Mr Cabell dismissed the issue, telling Mr Done that 'he had nothinge to doe with her service, except [unless] he could chardge [her] with any wronge she had don in her service, or

---

[115] HRO, 21M65/C3/7, Anthony Snow v John Weekes (1577). Italics my own.
[116] SHC, D/D/cd/12, Matilda Methewaye v Robert Thomas (1569).
[117] SHC, D/D/cd/56, Office v William Amerie (1623).

had stolen any thinge'. The terms of their agreement couldn't be proven; how *could* any oral agreement ever be proven unless witnessed? Agnes testified that Mr Done initially responded that he could charge her with nothing but then returned with an accusation of theft of a small piece of beef which Agnes had given to a poor woman begging at the door. Unconvinced and seeing 'how he was abused by hearinge such a brable', Mr Cabell was 'very angry with Mr done' and action against Agnes was dropped.[118] This was a power play and, on this occasion, Agnes emerged victorious.

While alleged misbehaviour in service – theft or sex outside marriage – was evidently safe grounds for early dismissal, masters were on shakier ground when claiming that servants had left before their contract had ended. The 1349 Ordinance of Labourers stipulated that a master was entitled to forcibly take back a servant who left before the end of an agreed term under pain of imprisonment.[119] This legislation was consolidated in the 1563 Statute of Artificers, and Whittle found it *was* being enforced in the sixteenth-century Norfolk Quarter Sessions.[120] But the meaning of service was in flux during this period, its definition difficult to pin down, making legal action against early departure difficult.

Among a catalogue of reasons why women in service might leave early, was that marriage was round the corner. In 1639, with marriage on the cards, Joanna Syms of North Petherton (Somerset) had left the service of her master, Mr John Wrath. Testifying on her behalf, Thomas Hall deposed that her pro-spective husband, William Marshall, 'desired this deponent she [Joanna] might live in howse with [Thomas] and his wife in North Petherton & promised to give [him] satisfaccion for her dyett'. Whether Joanna carried out any work there is unclear. She anticipated marrying imminently, but after two years she sought out service again, perceiving that the marriage wasn't happening any time soon. However, the possibility was raised again when she 'made covenant with Mrs Morlie wife of Mr John Morlie then & yet vicar of North Petherton'. Finding out about her contract, William asked Thomas to

> get her off from her said service, declaring he was unwilling she should goe to service againe, & that in a short tyme he intended to marry with her. Uppon whose request this deponent went to Mrs Morlie & gott her off from her intended service, Mrs Morlie declaring that if she intended marryedg she would not be against itt.

The prospect of a servant who might leave midway through her covenant wasn't appealing to Mrs Morlie. Hiring a servant required financial outlay as well as

---

[118] DHC, Chanter 866, William Harries v Audrey Rowell (1636).
[119] 'The Ordinance of Labourers 1349' printed in Brown, Tawney, and Bland (eds), *English Economic History*, p. 165.
[120] Whittle, *Development of Agrarian Capitalism*, p. 281.

time to invest in their training. The opportunity to void the agreement came before it had started, and Mrs Morlie was presumably optimistic about finding a replacement.[121] In 1560, upon her betrothal to William Baker, Rabigia Bennett of Buckland-in-the-Moor (Devon) 'desire[d] that [she] miyght tarrye here meaning yn Exeter untyll her covenand yn Exeter with her sayde Mr wer expired'. But she hadn't ruled out leaving service early to be married and said she would 'comme home at his [William's] request'.[122] A contract could be amicably broken with the agreement of both parties.

Other masters were less accommodating. A defamation case heard in the Gloucester court in 1610 was in many ways a satellite case orbiting a larger labour disagreement over a broken contract. Elizabeth Flann of Stoke Orchard had served Alice and Ciprian Wood in 1609

> and soe continued until Allhollowtide laste past for neare as this deponent remembreth, at which time the sayd Elizabeth Flann retorninge from Tewxbury home to the howse of the said Ciprian Wood … demanded of Alice Wood the said Ciprians wife her the said Elizabeth Flannes cloyes [clothes] for she sayed that she did not intend to serve ye said Ciprian for she said she intended very shortly to marry.

The Woods, however, weren't happy. They withheld her clothes and witnesses reported that Ciprian (presumably in rage) had defamed her, calling her an 'arrant whoare'. Labourer Richard Yarnton deposed that 'he the said Ciprian would first know whether she might not be by law compelled to serve him the said terme before she the sayd Flanne should had [have] her cloyes or apparrell from him'. In Ciprian's mind, a covenant of sorts existed and he withheld Elizabeth's clothes while seeking advice on whether he could compel her to serve for the remaining time of her covenant. Evidently, even he wasn't sure their agreement was legally binding.[123] Whether Elizabeth successfully recovered her clothes without returning to Ciprian's service is unfortunately not recorded.

At the heart of all this is the question of contract. What did it mean? How could it be proved? The rights and responsibilities of servant and master were likely acknowledged by both parties and an agreement was probably generally respected. But when things went wrong, no single strategy could ensure that justice was served. Covenants and contracts had long been a means of regulating labour agreements. But this was problematic in a society and economy built on verbal promises. Without concrete proof of contract, labour disputes were not easily resolved in petty sessions. Other strategies had to be taken. Initial steps were to negotiate; the final straw was dismissal or departure.

---

[121] SHC, D/D/cd/88, Joanna Syms v William Marshall (1639).
[122] DHC, Chanter 855, Rabigia Bennet v William Baker (1560).
[123] GA, GDR/109, Elizabeth Flann v Ciprian Wood (1610).

Conclusion

For early modern women working in south and west England, there was no typical experience of service. Distinctions between service and casual work were not always clear. Some women left service to work by the day or week or returned to their parents' homes with no legal repercussions. Occupations weren't static and while legislation and conduct literature laid a neat path for young women in its rhetoric about the virtues of service, it certainly wasn't the only path that young women took. Labour laws may have been established to control masterless young men and women, but they do not appear to have been enforced rigorously in the south and west of England. Within the same parish and even the same household, women were hired on different contracts, for different lengths of time, and were paid at different rates. Whittle argued that servants 'should be distinguished from labourers, who were hired for shorter terms, often a day at a time, lived apart from their employer, and might be married householders'.[124] But the term 'servant' was so fluid that it was used to describe those Whittle would label as labourers. In this period, labour relations and notions of labour were shifting and incipient. Early modern labour laws certainly played a part in solidifying what service was to be. But it wasn't yet a done deal.

Whether this fluidity offered servants choice or freedom is trickier to pin down. Ultimately, freedom is found in the capacity to escape the labour agreement with little or no resistance. This wasn't the case for many women in service who lacked the economic means to leave. Those who tried to leave and live with parents who were economically stretched were threatened with correction. As I showed in Chapter 2, service stretched across the social pyramid and the labouring women who served were not all the same. Even if freedom lay on a spectrum, it was contingent on wealth and socio-economic position, meaning that not everyone could access it equally.

Contracts were easily challenged because they were oral (though conscience surely kept many people to their word). This meant that both masters' and servants' power to seek justice was limited. In locating service within the complex cultural and legal positions on early modern freedom, I find that limited power to enforce labour legislation gave women in service scope to negotiate the parameters of service. In this sense, freedom to negotiate contract length and even wages was available. But women didn't enter those negotiations on an equal footing: existing hierarchies – social status, employment relations, and gender – all placed restrictions on their bargaining power. While contracts weren't easily enforceable, masters used their socio-economic privileges to secure what they

---

[124] Whittle, *Development of Agrarian Capitalism*, p. 253.

wanted: they levelled accusations of theft when facing accusations against themselves or when women tried to leave their service earlier than they'd hoped. Though servants faced greater limitations in these power struggles and freedoms were hard earned, they weren't entirely power*less*. With the right networks of support, servants could – and did – challenge these power dynamics and bring masters to answer for abuses in service. Patriarchal control could never be absolute, as I show in Chapters 6 and 7.

Chapter 6

Working Lives

The people of Meare in Somerset were fed up. Each Sunday morning and afternoon, they trudged into church to listen to their minister, George Calvert, deliver long, droning sermons, which at times were frankly inaudible. The Sabbath was of course a day of worship but there were things to be done. By 1602, their patience had worn thin and they broached the matter in the church court. Among the complainants was yeoman Giles Ball, who protested that Calvert's services 'detained his parisheners untill verie unseasonable hours so that theire servants can not goe about those necessarie busines which must after eve[n]song be don'.[1]

* * *

What was the 'necessarie busines' that servants took care of? Nebulous phrases such as this are often used to describe the work of servants. Alice Underhill of Widecombe-in-the-Moor (Devon) was 'going in and oute *about her busines'* when she overheard her mistress accuse their neighbour of adultery in 1586.[2] In 1631, husbandman Christopher Gorwood of Stogumber (Somerset) deposed that 'Charitie Wood & Richard Steeven … *doe theire service as servants oughte to do'.*[3] Following a terse conversation with her father in 1580 about her intentions for marriage, Hampshire servant Edith Legatt 'departed a little while [from him] for the space of half an hower *abowt her mres [mistress's] business'.*[4] The 'maid-of-all-work' – a woman hired as the household's sole servant – is assumed to have been lumbered with all menial household chores.[5] But without a detailed study of what women in service *actually* did, we can't know this was true.

---

[1] SHC, D/D/cd/34, William Clerk v George Calvert (1602).
[2] DHC, Chanter 862, William Wiche v Marie Hamlyn (1586). Italics my own.
[3] SHC, D/D/cd/71, Ursula Towte v Marie Hosgood (1631). Italics my own.
[4] HRO, 21M65/C3/8, Anthony Dalbye v Edith Legatt (1582). Italics my own.
[5] In late seventeenth- and early eighteenth-century London, most households hired just one or two servants and job specification increased over the century. See Peter Earle, *The Making of the English Middle Class: Business, Society, and Family Life in London, 1660–1750* (Berkeley, 1989), pp. 218–20.

Since the early twentieth century, debate over the nature and importance of women's work has ebbed and flowed among social and economic historians.[6] We know women carried out a range of labour in the past, but a deep-rooted assumption lingers that women in service principally carried out housework or domestic labour (meaning cooking, cleaning, and childcare).[7] The terms 'domestic servant' and simply 'domestic' are regularly used interchangeably with 'female servant'. But there are problems with this. Firstly, 'domestic servant' seldom appears between 1530 and 1650. Nearly all women in service were simply labelled 'servant'. I found no instances of 'domestic servant' in the diocesan courts of Exeter or Winchester and it was used only four times across the other three courts. Court scribes attached the Latin *famula domestica* to the names of Isabella Rogers of Tewkesbury (Gloucestershire) in 1604 and Maria Johnson of Wells (Somerset) in 1575.[8] When witness Elizabeth Sherwoode of Ditcheat (Somerset) was questioned about her worth in 1609, the scribe wrote that she was the *famula domestica* of William Addams.[9] Only in the 1597 testimony of Margery Harris of Burford (Shropshire) did 'domesticall servant' appear in English.[10]

By comparison, *famulus domesticus* (male domestic servant) appeared in the biographical preambles to five male depositions in the Bath & Wells court, clustering in the 1570s and 1580s when it was the preferred occupational lexicon of one Somerset court scribe.[11] It didn't distinguish household service from agricultural service, however: *famulus domesticus* Henry Haule gathered tithes for his master, so at least some of his work related to husbandry. By extension, we likewise shouldn't assume that a woman labelled 'domestic servant' exclusively undertook indoor work. And in the case of Hampshire servant Sybil Baynham, who was atypically labelled *servian agri* in 1532, we cannot assume she was hired only for husbandry.[12] Records seldom distinguish between domestic service and service in husbandry in the way that scholarship

---

[6] See Alice Clark, *Working Life of Women in the Seventeenth Century* (1982 [1919]); Ivy Pinchbeck, *Women Workers in the Industrial Revolution, 1750–1850* (Abingdon, 2005 [1930]).

[7] For example, Marjorie McIntosh's discussion of female servants largely fell within a chapter titled 'Domestic and personal services', while Craig Muldrew referred to female servants almost exclusively carrying out 'domestic' work. See Marjorie K. McIntosh, *Working Women in English Society, 1300–1620* (Cambridge, 2005), pp. 46–61; Craig Muldrew, *Food, Energy and the Creation of Industriousness Work and Material Culture in Agrarian England, 1550–1780* (Cambridge, 2011), p. 235.

[8] GA, GDR/89, Thomas Kyldermore v Agnes Quarrier (1604); SHC, D/D/cd/15, Alice Jaye v Peter Lane (1575).

[9] SHC, D/D/cd/41, Katherine Knighte v Alice Cooper (1609).

[10] HARC, HD4/2/11, Richard Evans and John Cheese v Edward Evans (1597).

[11] The term was used in the depositions of Cardiff servant Robert Rycharde, William Owsley of Pilton, John Quyke of Stogursey, Robert Mytchell of Bridgwater, and Henry Haule of St Decumans. See SHC, D/D/cd/25, George Roberts v Marie Sheperd (1571); D/D/cd/25, Clare Hawkens v Agnes Vanner (1572); D/D/cd/15, John Standefaste v Elizabeth Stephens (1575); D/D/cd/15, John Holworthie v Margaret Chete (1575) and D/D/cd/19, Hugo Norris v Humphrey Wyndham (1586).

[12] HRO, 21M65/C3/2, Office v Robert Barton and Sybil Baynham (1532).

(mistakenly) does. 'Servant' was shorthand for a variety of labour relationships and 'service' encapsulated many forms of labour.

Secondly, the 'domestic' labour that female servants were supposed to have done is often dismissed as unimportant. Housework has been disparaged as easy labour, or in fact not labour at all. In the twentieth century, even feminists contributed to its degraded status, perceiving domesticity as an 'emotional snare' in which women were caught, 'believing themselves uniquely responsible for making the home a warm and inviting place for husbands and children'.[13] As today, non-market work or housework – such as cleaning, food preparation, laundry, and household management – was often unpaid and carried out by women in early modern England.[14] Its invisibility in the pre-industrial economy is due to the fact that it isn't easy to systematically study (as paid work is more consistently recorded) and it doesn't easily fit with modern conceptions of what counts as work.[15] Alexandra Shepard summarises the issue:

> Too often women appear as shadowy bystanders in such assessments of early modern economic development on account of their relative 'invisibility', and their work is disregarded owing to its characterization as piecemeal, irregular and difficult to compute.[16]

Domestic work is seldom properly integrated into models of occupational structure or included in calculations of British economic development.[17] What 'domestic' meant in pre-industrial England is also not straightforward. As Jane Whittle pointed out, 'domestic' takes on multiple meanings: firstly, it describes the nature of work (typically the care of the family); secondly, it accounts for the location of work (the home); and thirdly, it refers to the market orientation of work (for home or domestic consumption, rather than for the market).[18] Dismissal of

---

[13] On the dismissal of domestic labour as 'non-work', see Jane Whittle, 'A Critique of Approaches to "Domestic Work": Women, Work and the Pre-Industrial Economy', *P&P* 243 (2019), 35–70 at 35. On feminist critiques of unpaid housework, see Helen McCarthy, *Double Lives: A History of Working Motherhood* (2020), p. 139.

[14] Whittle, 'A Critique', 35–70.

[15] Women's identity was frequently characterised by marital status rather than occupation. For men, systematic use of these descriptors enables historians to reconstruct occupational structure. See, for example, E. A. Wrigley and L. Shaw-Taylor, 'Occupational Structure and Population Change', in Roderick Floud, Jane Humphries, and Paul Johnson (eds), *The Cambridge Economic History of Modern Britain, Vol. 1: 1700–1870* (Cambridge, 2014), pp. 53–88. Calculating the size, importance, and value of unpaid domestic work, conversely, is no easy task. Female labour participation is assumed to be around 30 per cent. See Broadberry et al., *British Economic Growth*, p. 348.

[16] Alexandra Shepard, 'Crediting Women in the Early Modern English Economy', *History Workshop Journal* 79 (2015), 1–24, at 2.

[17] For important contributions on how women generated income in early modern England through food production, running businesses, moneylending, and textile production, see Whittle, 'Enterprising Widows'; Amy Erickson, 'Coverture and Capitalism', *History Workshop Journal* 59 (2005), 1–16; Spicksley, "Fly with a Duck in thy Mouth"'; Muldrew, "'Th'ancient Distaff" and "Whirling Spindle"', 498.

[18] Whittle, 'A Critique', 39.

women's work is 'often accompanied by its designation as "domestic", without any detailed consideration of what domestic might mean in an economy in which most production was located in or near the home'.[19] Separating out paid or waged work from unpaid domestic work implies that the latter isn't part of the economy. Not only is this wrong today, it also doesn't sit well with early modern ideas of labour.[20] Thomas Tusser wrote in 1573 that 'though husbandry semeth, to bring in the gains, yet huswifery labours, seeme equall in paines'.[21] Housewifery, like husbandry, was an occupation. William Whately's *A bride-bush: or, A Wedding sermon* (1619) promoted good housewifery and good husbandry in a marriage: 'both must apply themselves to their vocations painefully, and both bee ready to dispatch those businesses, for which themselves and families must fare the better'.[22] Good housewifery was essential to the household's profit and comfort. People saw it as economically valuable and laborious ('painefull').

Female servants generally exchanged labour for payment. But the *value* of their domestic work is routinely set against the income-generating husbandry work carried out by their male counterparts. Ann Kussmaul defined servants in husbandry as those 'hired not to maintain a style of life, but a style of work, the household economy'. Within this dichotomous gendered framework, male servants' work in the fields was 'productive' while female servants' work in the home was not.[23] These distinctions are often meaningless. As early as 1919, Alice Clark pointed out that service to the family was equally as productive.[24] Even if female servants' work *did* revolve around the personal care of the family, it still had economic value insofar as it freed up other members of the household for income generation. Domestic production (i.e. milking or making cheese for home consumption) was also 'productive', enabling household economies to bypass the market for basic goods.[25]

This chapter offers a comprehensive reappraisal of the working lives of women in service. It provides new data on their work, showing both its variety and significance to the (household) economy. Characterising their work as 'domestic' misunderstands what that meant in an economy in which home-based work was the norm and misrepresents the working lives of these women. Analysing over

---

[19] Whittle, 'Housewives and Servants', 52.

[20] As Robert Eisner argued, 'clearly, nonmarket household labour adds a major and varying amount to total output'. See Robert Eisner, 'Measure It to Make It Count', *Feminist Economics* 2 (1996), 143–4 at 143.

[21] Thomas Tusser, *Five Hundreth Points of Good Husbandry United to as Many of Good Huswiferie*, ed. Geoffrey Grigson (Oxford, 1984), p. 157.

[22] William Whately, *A Bride-Bush: Or, Direction for Married Persons: Plainely Describing the Duties Common to Both, and Peculiar to Each of Them* (1619), p. 84.

[23] Kussmaul, *Servants in Husbandry*, p. 4.

[24] Clark, *Working Life* (1982 [1919]), p. 290.

[25] See Whittle, 'A Critique', 67–70; Alexandra Shepard, 'Family and Household', in Susan Doran and Norman Jones (eds), *The Elizabethan World* (Abingdon, 2011), pp. 352–71 at 367.

300 work tasks carried out by women in service, this chapter holds a magnifying glass to the contexts in which their labour was carried out and unpicks the economic exchange between female servants and their masters and mistresses. It proposes a more granular approach to considering work recorded in court testimony than recent scholarship has applied. Other influences on the type of labour female servants carried out – from the type of household in which they served to the time of year – are interrogated. Close reading of depositions highlights the skills and knowledge women applied and learned in the households in which they served.

Counting and categorising labour

Although 'necessarie business' and nondescript expressions of work are plentiful in church court depositions, so too are specific descriptions of work tasks. Mary Smithe and Mary Bond are captured spinning in the hall of their widowed mistress, Katherine Mogridge in Brampford Speke (Devon) in 1635.[26] Alice Lybbye of St Creed (Cornwall) 'did often tymes mylcke the sayd kyene [cows]' in 1575.[27] A verb-oriented approach sidesteps many challenges of studying women's work in the past. Occupational descriptors in early modern records are scarce for women and overlook the multiple forms of labour that people – especially women – undertook.[28] Women in particular have long been known to have worked within an economy of makeshifts.[29] Mining court records for verbs or tasks ('to milk', 'to reap', 'to wash') is more illuminating. Spearheaded by Sheilagh Ogilvie in her study of early modern German women's working lives, the verb-oriented approach has been extensively applied elsewhere: Uppsala University's Gender and Work project on Swedish work adopted a similarly quantitative approach, and Whittle and Mark Hailwood recently employed this methodology to study work tasks recorded in English courts between 1500 and 1700.[30] Their study adopted economist Margaret Reid's third party criterion: 'if an activity is of such character that

---

[26] DHC, Chanter 866, Mary Flood v Dorothy Tucker (1635).
[27] DHC, Chanter 860, Richard Hawkye v Thomas Beale (1580).
[28] On the limitations of occupational descriptors, see Shepard, 'Crediting Women', 11; Rosemarie Fiebranz, Erik Lindberg, Jonas Lindström, and Maria Ågren, 'Making Verbs Count: The Research Project "Gender and Work" and Its Methodology', *Scandinavian Economic History Review* 59 (2011), 273–93 at 278–9. For critiques of occupational titles in signifying female employment in more modern contexts, see Jane Humphries and Sara Horrell, 'Women's Labour Force Participation and the Transition to the Male-Breadwinner Family, 1790–1865', *EcHR* 48 (1995), 89–117; Carmen Sarasua, 'Women's Work and Structural Change: Occupational Structure in Eighteenth-Century Spain', *EcHR* 72 (2019), 481–509. Humphries also argued that occupational titles were rarely assigned to women *because* their incomes were comprised of so many different forms of labour. See Jane Humphries, 'Girls and their Families in an Era of Economic Change', *Continuity and Change* 35 (2020), 311–43.
[29] See Hufton, *The Poor of Eighteenth-Century France*, pp. 69–127.
[30] See Ogilvie, *A Bitter Living*; Fiebranz et al., 'Making Verbs Count'.

it might be delegated to a paid worker, then that activity shall be deemed productive'.[31] Despite gendered patterns in labour tasks, they found that rural women contributed to all key areas of the early modern English economy.[32]

Quantitative aggregate studies of women's work are impressive, but in their necessary breadth, they tell us less about the working patterns of specific groups of women. There are also challenges in turning court testimony into robust, comprehensive data. Recollections of work were anchored to both time and space in depositions. Remembering a disagreement that took place in the fields one hot June afternoon could prompt a witness to recall details of the activity that took them to that space at that time. Or it might not. The examples of carrying out 'necessary business' are shadows of unreported work – either the deponent couldn't easily set down precisely what they were doing, or the work required too much prior knowledge or context to merit an explanation. Desire for privacy or lapses in truthfulness due to servant embarrassment might also affect the recording of work tasks. The approach also sometimes misses labour that isn't captured by a verb. In 1580, Joanne Nymo was hired as a servant to two Cornish millers in succession. No work activity (i.e. 'milling') was recorded, but Joanne's employment with these millers suggests her capability in this line of work.[33] Not all work tasks were equal; more laborious or strenuous work such as milking cows, washing clothes, or reaping crops was perhaps more frequently recalled. Shorter, simpler tasks – heating a kettle of water or dressing a child – might be forgotten or omitted from testimonies (though many fleeting tasks like these *were* woven into depositions). Some recalled tasks were part of wider processes: dusting malt, for example, was one of a series of steps required for brewing. Both the complete task (brewing) and its constituent parts (dusting malt, loading wort,[34] etc.) were recorded in depositions and it is difficult to assign a weighting or value to a constituent part's share of the complete task to allow for accurate quantitative study. This reminds us that a task-based approach offers insight into the *kinds* of work individuals did, but cannot produce a precise time study of how their days were spent. Quantification opens our eyes to broad patterns and trends but reduces experiences to numbers. Taking a narrower lens in analysing the work activities solely of female servants, alongside a wider approach of considering household-level and temporal contexts of work, I aim to avoid (or at least account for) these challenges.

Table 6.1 outlines a taxonomy of work tasks recorded in depositions. Agricultural labour comprises both arable and pastoral husbandry. Care work

---

[31] Margaret G. Reid, *Economics of Household Production* (New York, 1934), p. 11.
[32] Whittle and Hailwood, 'Gender Division of Labour'.
[33] DHC, Chanter 860, Office v Richard Kingdon (1580).
[34] Wort was a sweet liquid produced by steeping ground malt in hot water and fermenting it to produce beer. See 'wort, n.2.', OED Online, Oxford University Press, March 2023, www.oed.com/view/Entry/230372 [accessed 1 June 2023]

Category of work	Examples of tasks
Agriculture	Carrying crops, cocking barley, cutting rye, driving cattle, feeding animals, gathering apples, gathering fern, gelding a boar, milking, pitching crops to a cart, raking, reaping, setting out tithes, winnowing wheat
Care	Attending the sick, childcare, attending employers
Commerce	Attending a shop, buying mutton, selling bread
Errands	Collecting tithes, delivery, delivering a message, paying or delivering tithes, running an errand
Housework	Cleaning, fetching wood, heating a kettle, household management, making a fire, making the bed, preparing or serving food/drink, sweeping, washing clothes
Production	Baking, brewing, grinding corn, making butter/cheese, spinning

Table 6.1 Classification of work tasks recorded in church court depositions

covers childcare as well as personal care of household members and others, while commerce encompasses tasks relating to the buying or selling of goods for the household. Errands are broadly defined to include delivery and collection of messages, people, household provisions, and goods (and invariably took female servants outside the home). Cleaning, laundry, and making beds are categorised as housework in line with our modern conception of domestic chores. The processing of raw materials into items for consumption is categorised as 'production', including both textile work and food and drink production. I make no distinction between production for the household and the market. These categories are indicative, and some tasks inevitably fit more than one. The categories allow conversations between this data set and other comparable studies of women's work but, by necessity, decisions are data driven.[35] Some categories used elsewhere aren't relevant to the labour of female servants; no tasks relating to 'mining and quarrying' or 'military', for example, were recorded and therefore they are excluded as categories of analysis.

Work tasks were recorded across all types of cases heard in the courts. Table 6.2 shows that certain litigation lent itself to the reporting of certain types

---

[35] Whittle and Hailwood used similar categories, with the additions of 'transport', 'mining and quarrying', and 'crafts and construction'. 'Management' tasks were also placed in a separate category, whereas 'errands' weren't categorised separately. The Swedish Gender and Work group made more extensive use of categories amounting to fourteen different groupings of tasks, including 'hunting and fishing', 'military', 'teaching', 'theft and misappropriation', 'trade in real estate', 'administration and justice', and 'credit'. Ogilvie added other categories such as 'mill operation', 'spinning', and 'tavern keeping'. See Whittle and Hailwood, 'Gender Division of Labour', 11; Jonas Lindström, Rosemarie Feibranz, and Göran Rydén, 'The Diversity of Work', in M. Ågren (ed.), *Making a Living, Making a Difference: Gender and Work in Early Modern European Society* (Oxford, 2017), pp. 24–56 at 30–2; Ogilvie, *A Bitter Living*, p. 116.

Type of case	Agriculture		Care		Commerce		Errands		Housework		Production	
	N	%	N	%	N	%	N	%	N	%	N	%
Clerical offence	5	10	2	5	—	—	2	3	—	—	—	—
Defamation	12	24	4	11	2	14	14	19	35	46	17	29
Illicit sex	10	20	3	8	—	—	5	7	16	21	18	31
Matrimonial	3	6	2	5	3	21	9	12	14	18	8	14
Testamentary	1	2	24	63	5	36	14	19	8	10	4	7
Tithes	18	36	—	—	4	29	31	41	1	1	10	17
Other	1	2	2	5	—	—	—	—	1	1	1	2
Unknown	—	—	1	3	—	—	—	—	2	3	—	—
Total	**50**		**38**		**14**		**75**		**77**		**58**	

Table 6.2 Female servant work activities (by type of case)

of labour – agricultural work was frequently recorded in tithe disputes, and care work was identified predominantly in testamentary cases, for example. But the effect of this is less acute than we might suppose. Only 35 per cent of agricultural tasks were found in tithe suit depositions; almost two-thirds were identified elsewhere. Almost two-thirds of care work tasks were recorded in testamentary disputes and almost all pertained to end-of-life care; but over a third of care tasks were recorded in other disputes.

The 312 verb-based tasks carried out by female servants were varied, stretching across the economy. Half of the observations were taken from the Bath & Wells court, reflecting its larger volume of surviving witness testimony (not a greater proclivity for work!). Fewer tasks were recorded in the Exeter, Hereford, and Winchester courts as fewer female servants were identified there. The data also indicates some regional variation, although these differences were not pronounced. Unsurprisingly, agricultural work was scarcely undertaken by urban servants: just two examples – Elizabeth Aishman of Wells (Somerset), who reported milking in 1635, and Alice Gilbert of Winchester (Hampshire), who recalled weeding in 1597 – surface.[36] The Winchester example took place in a garden, not a field, and inhabitants of the small city of Wells were very much connected to its rural hinterland, moving between busy streets and fields. More female servants in Somerset, Devon, and Cornwall carried out agricultural tasks than in Gloucestershire, Hampshire, or Herefordshire, reflecting the landscapes and economies of these

---

[36] SHC, D/D/cd/78, Office v George Cooke (1635); HRO, 21M65/C3/11, John Bragg v Moya Simpson (1597).

counties. Devon, for instance, was an area of extensive pastoral farming. By contrast, Gloucestershire and Hampshire housed mixed economies, perhaps requiring less husbandry work of female servants. Female servants in the far south-western counties also undertook a higher proportion of production tasks, with dairying and food and drink production especially common in Somerset.

The largest categories of work tasks were 'Agriculture' (28 per cent), 'Housework' (25 per cent), and 'Errands' (24 per cent). In this largely rural study, almost 30 per cent of tasks related to husbandry. Dairying accounted for 44 per cent of this work (and 12 per cent of *all* work activities). Women in service were regularly found in the fields: reaping, gathering, and winnowing were key tasks in their labouring lives and were central to the farming household's economy. Of housework duties, laundry was important, accounting for almost two-fifths of this labour. Few instances of cleaning were identified – just ten of the 312 tasks were cleaning or making beds. This isn't surprising. Some servant-hiring households were small, containing just a couple of rooms that were spatially undifferentiated.[37] Cleaning took little time. John Crowley noted that in the late medieval period a 'man's physical requirements for comfort were clean clothes, a well-appointed bed, a fire, and someone to serve him these amenities'.[38] As Table 6.3 indicates, these requirements were delivered by women in service. But housework and the care of the family couldn't – and didn't – occupy all their time. Though Marjorie McIntosh found care work to be an important form of female service, auxiliary support (often older women) was regularly brought into homes when someone fell ill.[39] Live-in household servants couldn't always be spared; those who lived in were often secondary actors in the care of a household member.

Almost two-thirds of work tasks carried out by female servants fell outside the categories of housework or care work. In addition to carrying out agricultural labour, female servants regularly ran errands. Tithe disputes comprised a significant proportion of reported errands – 40 per cent related to the delivery, payment, or collection of tithes – but forty-five errands weren't tithe-related. Accounting for their overrepresentation in tithe cases, it is nonetheless clear that errands were an important part of the female servant workload. Women in service also spent their time baking, brewing, grinding corn, sewing, and spinning. The corn they milled was made into bread. The beer they made was tasted and consumed within or without the household. The wool they spun was made into clothes, which were worn, and sometimes sold.

---

[37] Jane Whittle, 'The House as a Place of Work in Early Modern Rural England', *Home Cultures* 8 (2011), 133–50 at 145.
[38] John E. Crowley, *The Invention of Comfort: Sensibilities and Design in Early Modern Britain and Early America* (Baltimore, MD, 2000), p. 5.
[39] McIntosh, *Working Women*, p. 79.

Category	Subcategory	Bath & Wells		Exeter		Gloucester		Winchester		Hereford		All courts	
		N	%	N	%	N	%	N	%	N	%	N	%
Agriculture	Field work	20	39	6	46	4	33	4	33	—	—	34	39
	Animal husbandry	5	10	1	8	3	25	—	—	—	—	9	10
	Milking	23	45	5	39	4	33	7	58	—	—	39	44
	Gathering produce	3	6	1	8	1	8	—	—	—	—	5	6
	Gardening	—	—	—	—	—	—	1	8	—	—	1	1
		51	33	13	32	12	19	12	28	—	—	88	28
Housework	Laundry	11	31	5	39	8	47	4	67	2	50	30	39
	Food/drink provision	7	19	5	39	4	24	—	—	1	20	17	22
	Light and fire provision	8	22	1	8	3	18	—	—	—	—	12	16
	Cleaning and making beds	6	17	1	8	—	—	2	33	1	20	10	13
	Management	1	3	1	8	2	12	—	—	1	20	5	7
	Attending guests	1	3	—	—	—	—	—	—	—	—	1	1
	Other	2	6	—	—	—	—	—	—	—	—	2	3
		36	23	13	32	17	26	6	14	5	71	77	25
Errands	Tithe collection/payment/delivery	4	15	5	63	14	58	6	38	1	100	30	40
	Delivery/collection of goods	10	39	1	13	4	17	4	25	—	—	19	25
	Delivery of message	5	19	1	13	5	21	5	31	—	—	16	21
	Errands	7	27	1	13	1	4	1	6	—	—	10	13
		26	17	8	20	24	37	16	37	1	14	75	24

(Cont.)

		Bath & Wells		Exeter		Gloucester		Winchester		Hereford		All courts	
Category	**Subcategory**	**N**	**%**	**N**	**%**	**N**	**%**	**N**	**%**	**N**	**%**	**N**	**%**
Care	Healthcare	13	65	2	100	7	70	4	80	1	100	27	71
	Personal care	5	25	–	–	1	10	–	–	–	–	6	16
	Childcare	2	10	–	–	2	20	1	20	–	–	5	13
		20	13	2	5	10	15	5	12	1	14	38	12
Production	Food/drink production	11	73	1	25	1	100	–	–	–	–	13	65
	Textile production	4	27	3	75	–	–	–	–	–	–	7	35
		15	10	4	10	1	2	–	–	–	–	20	7
Commerce	Selling	3	38	1	100	–	–	1	25	–	–	5	36
	Running/serving in a shop	5	63	–	–	–	–	–	–	–	–	5	36
	Buying	–	–	–	–	–	–	2	50	–	–	2	14
	Moneylending	–	–	–	–	1	100	1	25	–	–	2	14
		8	5	1	2	1	2	4	9	–	–	14	5
Total		**156**	**50**	**41**	**13**	**65**	**21**	**43**	**14**	**7**	**2**	**312**	

Table 6.3 Work activities carried out by female servants (by court)

Some work categories are conspicuous by their absence. Commerce didn't feature regularly in the repertoire of work activities recalled by female servants, despite retail being integral to the workload of London female servants.[40] Rural homes, too, were not disconnected from retail and the market.[41] Underreporting of this work is likely a quirk of the evidence and the limits of the verb-oriented approach. Servant *were* entrusted with valuable produce as well as money. At Christmas in 1630, Winifred Oliver bought a couple of turkeys on behalf of her mistress from James Yate of North Waltham (Hampshire).[42] In 1568, Margaret Allen of Eastington (Gloucestershire) deposed that 'uppon mydsomer yeve last past in the morning, yearlie [early] she this deponent … went unto her dame for money'.[43] More servants were identified selling than buying: Marie Edwards of Chew Stoke (Somerset), for instance, sold corn weekly in the market for her master in 1604.[44] Others served in inns and contributed to the running of these businesses: Margery Stevens was a servant in the Three Crowns in Taunton (Somerset) in 1637 and attended guests 'with beare & tobacco'.[45] Without the labour of servants like Margery, the innkeeping household could not generate its income. As discussed in Chapter 2, servants were also at the forefront of moneylending in early modern England. With disposable income and fewer responsibilities, they extended credit to their families, neighbours, and employers and derived income from the interest they charged.[46] Just two instances of female servant moneylending were explicitly identified in depositions but this type of evidence was sparse across all social groups. Credit habits changed over the seventeenth century as single women increasingly received cash from parental bequests (rather than a combination of cash, livestock, and other assets).[47] Female servants *did* take part in this commercial activity in south and south-west England, but opportunities to lend money expanded in the period after 1650.

Female servants' labour wasn't simply to enhance the family's lifestyle. It contributed to the household economy in two important ways. Firstly, the goods they produced were sold for profit or consumed within the household, generating income or allowing the family to sidestep the market. Secondly, the domestic or

---

[40] Meldrum, *Domestic Service and Gender*, pp. 153–8; Reinke-Williams, *Women, Work and Sociability*, p. 104.

[41] In 1620, Berkshire farmer Robert Loder paid his female servants 6*d* a day for selling cherries. See Robert Loder, *Robert Loder's Farm Accounts, 1610–1620*, ed. by G. E. Fussell (1936), p. 185.

[42] HRO, 21M65/C3/12, Mason v Yates (1631).

[43] GA, GDR/24, Margery Cloterbooke v John Batte (1568).

[44] SHC, D/D/cd/36, Thomas Jenkins v John Webb (1605).

[45] SHC, D/D/cd/84, Christian Dix v Jacob Richards (1638).

[46] Spicksley, '"Fly with a Duck in thy Mouth"', 187–207; Erickson, *Women and Property*, p. 81.

[47] Judith Spicksley, 'Usury Legislation, Cash, and Credit: The Development of the Female Investor in the Late Tudor and Stuart Periods', *EcHR* 61 (2008), 277–301 at 280–2. From the 1650s onwards, witnesses more frequently referred to income generated through loans and investments. See Shepard, *Accounting for Oneself*, p. 295.

household labour they carried out freed up other family members for income-generating work. Hiring a servant had to make economic sense. The value of their work *had to* exceed the wages they received (including bed, board, and indirect costs). Live-in service survived until the late eighteenth century (and well beyond in some parts of the country) *precisely because* it had a cost benefit to the early modern household.[48] As I show in this chapter, these labour calculations were explicitly made by masters and mistresses.

Time for work

Toiling throughout the cold month of December was different to working on a rainy April day or in the blistering heat of August. Wednesdays were spent differently to Sundays, and a morning's work may not have mirrored an evening's. Understanding the working lives of female servants requires us to attend to seasonal and horological patterns of labour. Service was not uniformly experienced in early modern England, and how the working day, week, or year was spent differed from servant to servant. Some were hired for shorter periods that coincided with pinch points when additional labour was required in particular households. Their labouring year, week, and day may have looked quite different to those of servants covenanted to serve for full years running from Michaelmas to Michaelmas. The rhythms, patterns, and routines of the working day leave an imprint on very few historical documents. Diaries, autobiographies, and letters occasionally logged daily routines. But life writings were rarely penned by women, and never by women in service.

Hans-Joachim Voth's work extended the verb-oriented methodology to estimate the amount of time spent on particular work activities; in weighting the reporting of activities by internal inconsistences in the data (memory and time lag, the likelihood of particular crimes (and therefore work) occurring at different points in the day, for example), he was able to estimate working hours in eighteenth-century London.[49] While systematic reconstruction of the working day isn't possible for these women because too few activities were accompanied with temporal information, many work tasks recorded in depositions *were* anchored to a point in time. Reporting of events in relation to the liturgical year was commonplace. Almost 200 work tasks were accompanied with the time of year in

[48] Jacob Field, 'Domestic Service, Gender, and Wages in England, *c.*1700–1860', *EcHR* 66 (2013), 249–72 at 267. See also Snell, *Annals of the Labouring Poor*, pp. 85–6; Kussmaul, *Servants in Husbandry*, pp. 113, 120–1; Jane Humphries, 'Household Economy', in Paul Johnson and Roderick Floud (eds), *The Cambridge Economic History of Modern Britain, Vol. 1: Industrialisation, 1700–1860* (Cambridge, 2004), pp. 238–67 at 253.

[49] Hans-Joachim Voth, 'Time and Work in Eighteenth-Century London', *The Journal of Economic History* 58 (1998), 29–58.

which they took place, and it's possible to assign them to a month in the year. For example, Joan and Winifred, two servants of Leominster (Herefordshire), described washing clothes in a well in 1599 about 'a fortnight before the Feast of Sainte Michaell the Archangell' (September) while Joan Cantor of Tavistock (Devon) collected a roasting pig for her mistress in Lent (February or March) 1556.[50] Fewer pinpointed a specific day or time: day of the week was included in eighty-three examples and time of day (including both specific clock time and signifiers such as 'morning' and 'evening') was attached to a quarter (seventy-eight) of the 312 activities.[51]

Seasonality of work

Shaping weather and light levels, the seasons codify our everyday practices including labour and the spaces in which it is carried out. As Amanda Flather noted, winter drew early modern workers inside the home, while spring brought them back to the fields.[52] It's useful, then, to think spatially and seasonally about female servants' labour. Table 6.4 divides the 150 instances in which a work activity was recorded with a month or time of year into 'indoor' (i.e. inside the servant-master's home) and 'outdoor' labour.

Examples of indoor and outdoor work were roughly equal in winter and spring, but outdoor work tasks outnumbered indoor by more than three to one in the summer months (and two to one in autumn). Summer saw more work activities carried out by female servants, particularly outdoor work often recorded in tithe litigation but also elsewhere.[53] Some tasks were carried out throughout the year: the labour of care, for instance, was constant, with no indication that sick-care carried out by servants was seasonal or dipped in the summer, as mortality patterns suggest.[54] Examples of wood gathering and fires lighting turn up in February, May, June, July, and November depositions. When Eleanor Philpott of Newent (Gloucestershire) lit a fire in November 1604 for a late-night guest in her gentleman master's home, it was as a source of heat and hospitality.[55] Servant

---

[50] HARC, HD4/2/11, Eleanor *vez* Howell v Matilda Langford (1599); DHC, Chanter 866, Office v John Kegell (1556).

[51] In his study of time and labour, Hailwood arrived at a figure of 41.3 per cent of witnesses reporting clock time; his inclusion of Quarter Session examination data (which report clock time more frequently) likely accounts for this higher proportion. See Mark Hailwood, 'Time and Work in Rural England, 1500–1700', *P&P* 248 (2020), 87–121 at 95.

[52] Amanda Flather, *Gender and Space in Early Modern England* (Woodbridge, 2007), pp. 81–2.

[53] No corresponding increase in testimonies during the summer was identified in the courts: in fact, the summer hiatus taken by the ecclesiastical courts meant that few testimonies were recorded in August. On the summer interruption of the courts, see Price, 'Administration of the Diocese of Gloucester', p. 22.

[54] Wrigley et al., *English Population History*, p. 324.

[55] GA, GDR/95, Milberowe Berrowe v John Crocket (1605).

	Indoor	Outdoor	All	
Season	*N*	*N*	*N*	*%*
Spring (Mar, Apr, May)	13	16	29	*19*
Summer (Jun, Jul, Aug)	14	46	60	*40*
Autumn (Sep, Oct, Nov)	11	23	34	*23*
Winter (Dec, Jan, Feb)	13	14	27	*18*

Table 6.4 Seasonality of female servants' work tasks

Grace Combe of Upton Pine (Devon) lit a fire in her mistress's chamber late one May night in 1582; here, the fire was also for warmth.[56] But fires were also a source of energy for cooking. When Marie Allone (alias Smith) was 'mending the fyer in the haule' on the afternoon of St James Day (June) in Lottisham (Somerset) in 1601, she was probably adding fuel for cooking. The house was unlikely to need heating during the summer but fire was still required for food preparation.[57]

Other work took place at specific points of the year. Female servants brewed exclusively in winter. On a 'certen night shortlie after Christmas last past' (December 1641), Margaret Rudgeman of Ilton (Somerset) was 'sett to brue' with her fellow servant Michael Barker.[58] Gervase Markham suggested that house-wives 'do give over the making of malt in the extreme heat of summer'. This was 'not because the malt is worse that is made in summer than that which is made in winter, but because the floors [on which the grain is left to germinate] are more unseasonable'.[59] Indeed, commercial brewing took place all year round, as Markham acknowledged. But female servants brewed only in winter in the depositions, reflecting either their limited capacity to do this in summer or (more likely) that the scale of brewing intensified over winter, thereby increasing the chance of observing them at this type of work in depositions.

Most husbandry tasks that female servants undertook – haymaking, reaping, cutting, and gathering corn, oats, and barley – took place in the summer. Leasing (gleaning or gathering corn) continued into September in Hampshire: Helen Smith was hired to lease corn alongside a female servant of Robert Berkensaw's in Highclere in 1580.[60] Gathering apples was recorded in autumn: Elizabeth Pearse of Stratton (Devon) gathered apples from her master's orchard in autumn 1614, and Taria Heywood of Maisemore (Gloucestershire) recalled gathering apples in

---

[56] DHC, Chanter 858, Office v Nicholas Kelway (1582).
[57] SHC, D/D/cd/34, Office v Thomas Hellier (1602).
[58] SHC, D/D/cd/130, Office v Margaret Rudgeman (1612).
[59] Markham, *The English Housewife*, p. 183.
[60] HRO, 21M65/C3/8, Stephen Whittear v Helen Smith (1581).

her mistress's orchard around Michaelmas 1593.[61] Over winter, husbandry waned. Female servants fed and cared for animals and in spring undertook lighter work such as weeding. Collection of tithes usually took place at two points in line with the rhythms of the agricultural calendar: around Easter and at, or shortly after, harvest. Servant Jane Tyler collected tithe wool in Corse (Gloucestershire) in 1622 after sheep shearing, while the servant of Mr Philpott of Micheldever (Hampshire) received a tithe pig between Shrovetide and Easter of 1597.[62] Tithe crops were paid around harvest time: during the 1596 harvest, Catherine John served William Meredith of Snodhill (Herefordshire) and gathered his tithe wheat.[63] The labour of female servants was integral to agrarian cultivation and its economy.

The natural milking season ran from early May to late September, following the birth of calves in early spring, but Deborah Valenze pointed out that from the later medieval period, 'dairies worked hard to defy obstacles of nature'.[64] In the sixteenth and seventeenth centuries, some milk was available virtually all year and milking regularly fell to female servants. At least one observation was captured for every month except February, April, May, and July. Those milking in winter probably served in households profiting from commercial dairying. Evidence of milking was most concentrated in June, when households with milk cows were likely to have new-born calves.

The working week

Eighty-three female servant work tasks could be linked with a day of the week. As Figure 6.1 shows, women in service didn't enjoy a particular 'day off', though a couple of references to tasks taking place 'on a workday' implies by extension that some days *weren't* workdays. Servant Elizabeth Gifford of Clapton-in-Gordano (Somerset) recalled fetching a pail of water 'uppon a workedaie abowte a sennighte [one week] before midsomer' in 1550.[65] Peaks and troughs in the working week are notable. It was on the weekend that most work activities were recorded for female servants. Hailwood, too, observed a spike in Saturday labour.[66] But by focusing specifically on women in service using a comparable data set, differentiated work patterns emerge.

Saturdays saw the second highest number of work activities carried out by female servants. But commerce and the movement of goods and livestock which Hailwood attributed to this Saturday spike cannot account for the increased labour of female servants on this day. Some surely went to market to sell goods for their

[61] DHC, Chanter 867, Thomas Downe v William Woolfe (1615); GA, GDR/79, Richard Restall v William Danby (1594).
[62] GA, GDR/148, William Lambert v William Webb (1623); HRO, 21M65/C3/11, David Philpott v William Brown (1598).
[63] HARC, HD4/2/11, William Meredith v Roger Weston (1597).
[64] Deborah Valenze, *Milk: A Local and Global History* (New Haven, 2011), pp. 35–6.
[65] SHC, D/D/cd/5, John Arthur v Margaret Arthur (1550).
[66] Hailwood, 'Time and Work', 105–6.

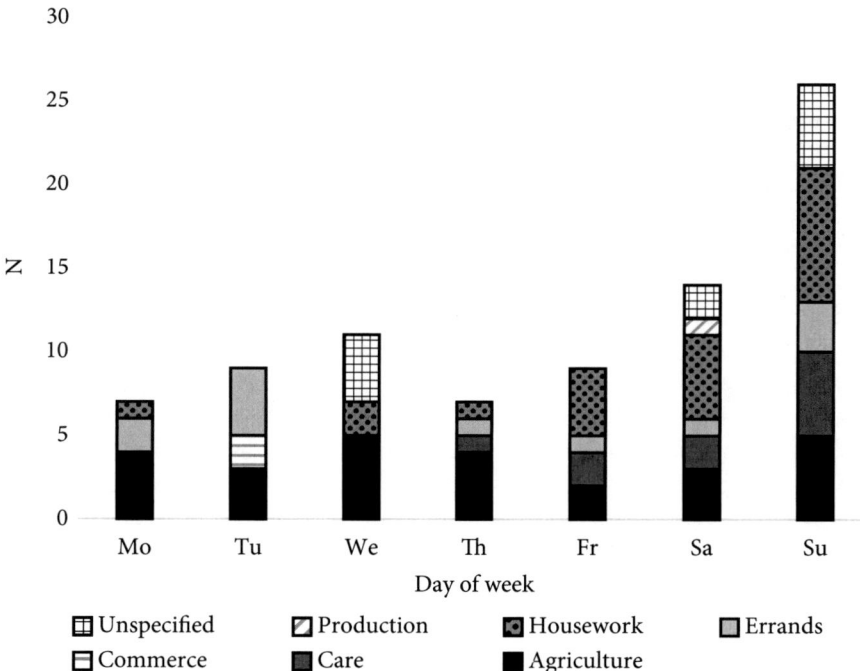

Figure 6.1 Female servants' work tasks by day of the week

masters and mistresses or were involved in other forms of commerce and retail, but these women logged few work activities in this category in their depositions. Saturday labour for them was largely based inside the home, comprising domestic chores and some production. Perhaps they minded the house while their masters and mistresses went to market.

Other differences surface. Hailwood cast doubt on the prevalence of 'St Monday', a custom whereby pre-industrial society observed work-free Mondays. He found no evidence that Monday was even 'a light work day'.[67] Monday similarly wasn't a day off for women in service (as Figure 6.1 shows) but removing instances of milking and animal feeding (jobs that *had* to be done daily) leaves just one instance of washing clothes, a couple of servants running errands, and two carrying out crop husbandry. Fewer work tasks were recorded on this day. For women in service, then, it *was* a light work day.

The Sabbath was supposed to be a work-*free* day. The Third Commandment required Sunday to be kept holy; 'thou shalt not do any work'. People were supposed to attend church throughout the day.[68] Diana Wood found that fifteenth- and sixteenth-century Christians nonetheless broke this commandment

[67] Ibid., 105, 107.
[68] Diana Wood, 'Discipline and Diversity in the Medieval English Sunday', *Studies in Church History* 43 (2007), 202–11 at 204.

and exceptions were made as society became increasingly commercialised.[69] Well into the seventeenth century, parishioners were hauled before church courts for breaking the Sabbath, routinely accused of carrying out income-generating work including husbandry, fitting horseshoes, and tailoring.[70] Hailwood found that although the Sabbath wasn't strictly observed, fewer work activities took place on a Sunday.[71] The pattern is entirely different for women in service. Sunday was when they did *most* of their work; almost one-third of all work activities took place on this day, again concentrated around housework. Put another way, around 42 per cent of all domestic tasks occurred on a Sunday. Sunday wasn't a day of rest for female servants, then, because they were routinely responsible for work that needed to be done for effective household management.

As the case against our droning minister, George Calvert, reminds us, female servants were required to carry out 'necessarie busines' on Sundays. The criteria for determining the permissibility of Sunday work in the eyes of the church was whether it was necessary *on that day*. John Arnold pointed out that parishioners presented to church courts for not attending Sunday services often pled economic hardship: their choice was work or starve.[72] But necessity was defined temporally, not economically, in the church courts. In 1625, Isabella Boultinge described milking cows in a meadow in Westbury-sub-Mendip (Somerset) one Sunday with her daughter-in-law (stepdaughter) Jane. In her deposition, she testified against John Blacklock, whom she had seen making hay for half an hour the same day. Milking was acceptable on a Sunday – it was an unavoidable task that needed to be done – but haymaking could wait.[73]

Some female servants *were* in church on Sundays, and didactic writers stressed the importance of masters and mistresses facilitating the religious instruction of their charges.[74] In 1633, servant Joan Kent of Glastonbury (Somerset) returned home from church one Sunday in late February and saw her neighbour (who had been absent from church) 'carrying of dung and soyle out of his stall into his garden in a wheelebarrowe'. Her attendance at church contrasted with her neighbour's absence.[75] For some servants, going to church *was* work: in 1629, Alice Alsheares recalled almost fifty years earlier 'attending her mistris to church' in Wincanton in the same county. She served esquire Alexander Ewens, and whether for physical support or simply companionship, his wife required her attendance.[76] For this

---

[69] Ibid., 211.

[70] See, for example, SHC, D/D/cd/49 Office v Edward Horler (1618); Office v Richard Ruddock (1618); D/D/cd/66, Office v George Kingman (1633).

[71] Hailwood, 'Time and Work', 105–6.

[72] John Arnold, 'The Materiality of Unbelief in Late Medieval England', in Sophie Page (ed.), *The Unorthodox in Late Medieval Britain* (Manchester, 2010), pp. 65–95 at 84.

[73] SHC, D/D/cd/51, Office v John Blacklock (1625).

[74] Gouge, *Of Domesticall Duties*, p. 667.

[75] SHC, D/D/cd/66, Office v George Kingman (1633).

[76] SHC, D/D/cd/64, Henry Glinn v James Churchaie sen, James Churchaie jun, and Anna Churchaie (1629).

reason servants in wealthier homes may have regularly attended Sunday service. Marie Saunders served Mrs Wadham in 1602 and was among the witnesses who complained about George Calvert, the minister of Meare (Somerset).[77]

But in some middling households, servants' Sunday worship may have been less strictly observed. Joanna Browne of Lottisham (Somerset) described 'dressing of her master's geyes [geese] in the kitching' around 'evening prayer tyme' in July 1601.[78] Instead of being at evening prayer that night, Joanna was busy preparing the family's meal. Her master, Thomas Quarman, was a yeoman and by the time he made his will sixteen years later, he held several tenements and parcels of land.[79] Still, it seemed Joanna couldn't be spared. Gloucestershire servant Margaret Gibbins was sent by her master one Sunday morning in 1606 to care for a sick neighbour. Arriving in the morning, she 'stayed with him all the daye till the next morrowe'.[80] These were exceptional circumstances, but illustrate nonetheless that a female servant's attendance at church could clearly be done away with if necessary. Exeter merchant's wife Prudence Trobridge recalled in 1637 that Daniel Jackson frequently visited to spend time with her servant Elizabeth Moreton, 'and when this deponent hath com from church from moreninge prayer & sermons she hath often tymes found him there, & to slip away at the backe dore that this deponent might not see him'.[81] Perhaps these servants attended church alone at other points of the day, allowing them moments of solitude from the rest of the household.

Time of day

Only eighteen work activities were accompanied with a specific clock time but a further sixty were anchored to a portion of the day – 'morning', 'afternoon', 'evening,' or 'night'. Although imprecise (with some overlap in the hours referred to as 'afternoon' and 'evening', and with some adjustment according to seasonal patterns of light availability), these descriptions of time were generally consistent.

As Figure 6.2 shows, women in service were busiest in the morning: thirty-six of the seventy-eight (46 per cent) work activities took place before midday. Morning work – feeding and milking animals – was habitually part of a female servant's work repertoire. Productivity relied on routine. The 'trustie servants' that Robert Loder required for milk cows to be profitable were expected to be skilled at milking, but this was also a job that required punctuality: cows needed to be milked on time each day.[82] The working day therefore started early for many female servants. John Bartlett was a servant to James Cottington and James's sister Sara Savidge (alias

[77] SHC, D/D/cd/34, William Clerk v George Calvert (1602).
[78] SHC, D/D/cd/34, Office v Thomas Hellier (1602).
[79] TNA, PROB/11/130/11, Will of Thomas Quarman, yeoman of Ditcheat, Somerset (1617).
[80] GA, GDR/100, Thomas Barnes v Elizabeth Maunsell (1606).
[81] DHC, Chanter 866, Daniel Jackson v Elizabeth Moreton (1637).
[82] Loder, *Robert Loder's Farm Accounts*, p. 156.

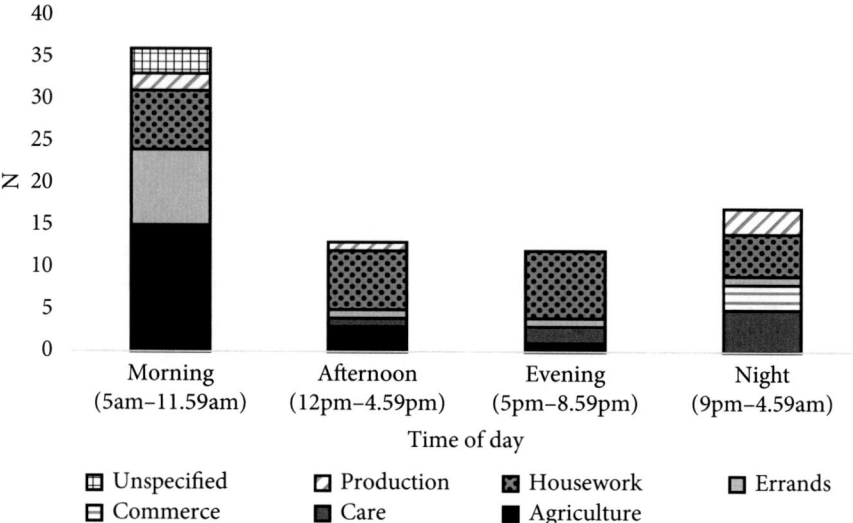

Figure 6.2 Female servants' work tasks by time of day

Cottington) of Frome (Somerset) in the early 1630s. He noted the family's sleeping arrangements: James and his sister slept in the same chamber with a female servant and a girl of about 9 or 10 years of age who shared a truckle bed. John added that the 'woomen servant & childe rose most commonlie everie morning aboute fower or five of the clock when the said James was att home'.[83] Servants were often first to rise.

The archaic term *betines* (meaning very early morning) was used in several Somerset cases. In 1602, Ursula Daniell of Walton 'went betines in the morning before the day did give light to a certaine hayhowse of … her master to serve certaine calves and to milk certaine kyne'.[84] In December, when daylight hours were at their fewest, it was dark when Ursula left the house. Milking usually happened twice a day at set times: Markham advised that cows should be milked between 5 and 6 am and 6 and 7 pm.[85] For reasons that are unclear, very little evening milking was recalled in depositions. Avice Carye, former servant to Alice Beaton of Mudford (Somerset) in 1596, was the only evening milker recorded: she deposed that 'towards the eveninge' she found John Boyce and her mistress alone together in a chamber. Unwilling to leave the two alone in the house, she asked John 'whether hee woulde be gon or no' as she 'was then to goe to milking'.[86]

Animals were fed in the morning and afternoon. Fires were lit by female servants in both the morning and evening, and they required hands to keep them

---

[83] SHC, D/D/cd/76, Robert Powell v Humphrey Yearburie v James Cottington (1633).
[84] SHC, D/D/cd/34, Office v John Tutton (1602).
[85] Markham, *The English Housewife*, p. 169.
[86] SHC, D/D/cd/26, Thomas Bartlett v John Boyce (1596).

going. Other work was ongoing throughout the day and into the night. Joanna Lucks of Curry Rivel (Somerset) described 'dayle & hourlye attending' her dying master, Marmaduke Piper, for seven weeks in the late summer and early autumn of 1613.[87] Care of the sick often required working into the night. Servants described 'watching' with the sick round the clock. In the opening page of this book, we encountered Anna Elie of Gloucester, who 'watched with' her neighbour Thomas Crodie, a plague victim in 1578, 'in his sicknes tyme'.[88] Though the work probably wasn't a regular part of her working day, it indicates the demands that could fall on servants when someone in the house fell sick and required short- or even long-term care. Some activities were inconvenient at night: the servant who rose from bed to care for a child, or the one who fetched her mistress a drink, or another who got up to light a fire for a late guest, were all perhaps frustrated by late-night work. But 'interrupted' sleep (as we think of it) wasn't unusual in early modern England.[89]

Servants in inns and alehouses unsurprisingly found late evenings and night-time busy as they served late into the evening until the last patrons went home. The small hours of the night also appear to have been a convenient time for servants in these households to brew. Innholder George Dowdeny of Hatch Beauchamp (Somerset) was brewing one evening in 1620 with his servants Robert Baller and Joan Ware. At midnight, he went to bed, waking three hours later to check their progress. Rising part-way through the night wasn't uncommon; as Sasha Handley showed, early modern people sometimes slept in two segments. The twilight hours between two sleep cycles might be spent carrying out household activities such as brewing.[90] Instead of brewing, George found his two servants in the parlour, their intimacy alone together in this space raising his suspicions.[91] Thomas Morgan of Frome in the same county described seeing his former mistress Margaret, an alehouse keeper, and her servant Susan Paine brewing one night in 1635. He went to bed, leaving them to it. Given he was charged with attempting to rape Susan, his testimony is unsurprisingly hostile towards the household in which he had served; he claimed Margaret kept her alehouse 'without licence'.[92]

As an antidote to *working* at night, time off for *socialising* was snatched in the twilight hours, too. Servant Alice Stone was spotted by her former master at a Glastonbury (Somerset) inn in 1601 in the company of 'divers young boyes' all 'making merry and at theire pastimes at midnight'.[93] Robert Good of Tiverton (Devon) described being at a 'danncing place' in Crediton on the Sunday after

---

[87] SHC, D/D/cd/45, Joanna Piper v John Gardner (1613).
[88] GA, GDR/45, Thomas Weekes and Thomas Key v Richard Crodie, Eleanor Davys, and Alice Dove (1579).
[89] On early modern sleep culture, see Sasha Handley, *Sleep in Early Modern England* (2016).
[90] Ibid., p. 8.
[91] SHC, D/D/cd/54, Office v Robert Baller (1620).
[92] SHC, D/D/cd/80, John Meeres v Thomas Morgan (1635).
[93] SHC, D/D/cd/32, Henry Sock v Maria Barter (1601).

St Peter's Day in 1594 where 'many maydes and young men did meete thether to dannce about two of the clock in the morning before it was daye'. He noted seeing Agnes Durram, servant to widow Joanna Callow, there.[94] A female servant might gain some freedom at night, either with her master's permission or in secret, while he slept.

Accounting for labour

As we saw in Chapter 2, servant-hiring households spanned the social spectrum. If we peered through the windows of these households, we'd find female servants doing all sorts of labour. Counting and categorising tasks that female servants carried out offers a general picture of what servants did. But the work Charity Lawnsdon of Wedmore (Somerset) did in 1631 may have been quite different to the work Joan Harrys of Wellow (Hampshire) was hired to do in 1584 and different again to the labour Mary Kynvin carried out in Bosbury (Herefordshire) in 1599. In this agricultural village, Mary's working day may have borne no resemblance to Alice Kew's in the bustling city of Gloucester in 1593. We need to look at servants' work at a granular level, accounting for household status and regional economies.

Household economies

Working lives were firstly determined by household size and economy. In choosing to hire servants, masters and mistresses responded to a labour requirement within their home. Occupations present an incomplete picture of the economic activity from which a household's income was derived, but Table 6.5 nonetheless gives a sense of the type of work female servants were doing in households headed by men of different occupations. Differences in the work carried out in homes across the social spectrum are striking. In the houses of gentlemen and minor aristocracy, women in service could expect to do more housework: fifteen of the thirty-two work tasks (46 per cent) identified in these high-ranking households fell within this category. Elizabeth Kyne, the Cornish servant of Mrs Juliana Roughan, recalled 'makinge of the beddes in the parler' in 1559.[95] Servant Catherine Hall of Newent (Gloucestershire) must have regularly made beds in the home of gentleman Guy Dobbins and his wife Jane: in 1604, suspecting her of theft, the couple deliberately planted two 6 pence coins upon a bed. When Catherine went to make the bed, she found the money and stole it (as they had

---

[94] DHC, Chanter 864, Thomas Edbury v Joanna Callowe (1596).
[95] DHC, Chanter 855, Cuthbert Marshall v Juliana Roughan (1559).

Master's occupation	Agriculture		Housework		Errands		Care		Production		Commerce		All work	
	N	%	N	%	N	%	N	%	N	%	N	%	N	%
Husbandmen	8	57	2	14	1	7	3	21	—	—	—	—	14	12
Yeomen and farmers	5	33	5	33	2	13	2	13	1	7	—	—	15	12
Clergy	11	28	5	13	17	44	4	10	1	3	1	3	39	32
Cloth and leather	—	—	4	57	1	14	1	14	1	14	—	—	7	6
Food and drink	—	—	2	18	2	18	3	27	1	9	3	27	11	9
Smiths and makers	1	100	—	—	—	—	—	—	—	—	—	—	1	1
Gentlemen	5	15	15	46	4	12	6	18	2	6	1	3	33	27
Merchants, professions, and officials	—	—	1	100	—	—	—	—	—	—	—	—	1	1
Total	**30**		**34**		**27**		**19**		**6**		**5**		**121**	
No occupation identified	*58*		*43*		*48*		*19*		*14*		*11*			

Table 6.5 Female servants' work tasks in relation to their masters' occupations

anticipated), hiding the coins under some old timber for safekeeping. She was later apprehended and set in the town stocks.[96] The housework that servants in elite homes carried out is therefore commensurate with Kussmaul's depiction of the female 'domestic' responding to the personal needs of the family (though her reading of these tasks being unimportant in the functioning of the household economy is inaccurate).

When a female servant heard of a vacancy or knocked on a door to enquire for work, she must have anticipated what the position would entail and the type of labour the household would require of her. As we saw in Chapter 4, some women travelled far to serve in wealthy homes. Gentry households often hired more than one servant, meaning women shared the workload. In 1607, for example, 27-year-old Maria Perrie described how she, Thomasine Gane, and Agnes Naishe had been 'all three togeathers at a well standing in the open streete of Westharptry [Somerset] waishing of clothes' when Agnes defamed their neighbours who were passing by.[97] Alice Poyntinge of Frome in the same county served gentleman attorney James Cottington (whom we met earlier) in the early 1630s. James's household contained his sister Sara Savidge and a male servant named John Weekes, but 'noe other maide servant … that then lived in howse with them, but one child or girle … being the said Saras daughter & aboute xii [12] yeres old'. Perhaps the daughter later left home, as the year after Alice left service she was replaced by two female servants, Katherine Millerd and Susan Pattrick.[98]

The reality of serving in a gentry household might not correspond with expectations. This mismatch was laid bare by Isott Riches (an ever more familiar servant in this book). Recall that Isott had served gentleman John Brooke and his wife Katherine in 1568, having been hired two years earlier to work in their home in Staverton (Devon). She then followed them to Rockbeare vicarage held by a canon of Exeter cathedral named Doctor Gammon, who was Katherine's brother. The couple appear to have managed the household during his absence. Depositions catch Isott sweeping the house, preparing food, as well as milking and reaping barley. Her discontent with the work she was required to do in this clergy home is captured in the quotation at the beginning of this book: she complained that she came to her mistress 'not to be her drudge'.[99] Evidently, comfortable households weren't all the same and Isott's expectations weren't met.

Across the tasks that female servants carried out in the homes of yeomen and clergy, we see the mixed workload that Isott experienced. In the households of better-known lesser gentry figures such as Henry Best and Nicholas Toke even,

[96] GA, GDR/89 and GDR/95, Anne Harris v Frances Wylson (1604).
[97] SHC, D/D/cd/40, Peter Scriven and Barbara Scriven v Agnes Naishe (1607).
[98] SHC, D/D/cd/76, Robert Powell and Humphrey Yearburie v James Cottington (1633).
[99] DHC, Chanter 858, John Roo v Frances Yarde (1568).

household economies (and therefore the work of their servants) were sometimes geared towards agricultural production.[100] Yeomen owned large farms where female servants carried out agricultural work. Female servants were hired for dairying and specifically milking: four out of five husbandry tasks these women carried out in yeomen's households were milking. Often a specialised role in elite or gentry households, milking was almost exclusively carried out by women in service.[101] In 1576, Thomas Francis deposed that Mr Twine, a Hampshire gentleman, hired a 'deyry [dairy] woman' on his farm, and Joan Collins of Twyford in the same county deposed in 1581 that she had been 'appointed by her Mr & Mres [mistress] to be the dairy mayde' in their gentry household.[102] A relatively high proportion of agricultural tasks were recorded in households headed by clergymen. Many of the links made between female servants carrying out this work and these households were identified in tithe disputes, in which clerical occupations were more prevalent and frequently labelled. The agricultural work their female servants carried out was often crop husbandry: it included loading and carrying hay, raking, and winnowing wheat. But the bulk of their work came under the category 'errands': fourteen out of seventeen of these errands related to the collection of tithes. Joan Silvester, for example, recalled collecting 'tyth peares' from Robert Greene of Baughurst (Hampshire) in 1596, having been 'sent by Amy Yates her dame'.[103] Given the high proportion of clergymen masters identified in tithe disputes, we should be cautious about assuming that female servants in clergymen's households spent most of their time doing this kind of labour. But the importance of female servants in this process also shouldn't be understated and is indicative of the community-facing role these women played. After all, as early modern life was so intrinsically bound to religious experience and practice, the clergyman's house was likely the most visible in the parish.

In Joan Silvester's deposition, we spot her mistress, Amy Yates, coordinating the collection of tithe income in this clerical house. But what else did clergymen's wives do? A couple of examples show that production within these homes was led by wives and probably carried out by female servants, too. In 1594, Margaret Atkins served in the parsonage house of Wrington (Somerset), helping Mrs Chock not only to wash clothes, but also in 'brewing drinke for the said Mris Chock'.[104] The 1615 deposition of Melissa Tawton, who served vicar Henry Hartwell and his

---

[100] Whittle, 'A Different Pattern of Employment', p. 62.
[101] Cultural taboos meant that men were virtually prohibited from milking. See Deborah Valenze, 'The Art of Women and the Business of Men: Women's Work and the Dairy Industry, *c*.1740–1840', *P&P* 130 (1991), 142–69.
[102] HRO, 21M65/C3/7, Gatenbye v Twyne (1576); HRO, 21M65/C3/8, John Weke v Richard More (1581).
[103] HRO, 21M65/C3/11, Stockton v Robert Greene (1598).
[104] SHC, D/D/cd/18, Elizabeth Chock v Joanna Foster (1594).

wife Susan in Bishop's Tawton (Devon), demonstrates further production work in a clerical household. Melissa deposed that

> the sayd Mr hartweswell in greate radge came downe into the dayrie house where this deponent and the wife of the sayd Mr harteswell and a gerle were aboute business.

The presence of these three women in the dairy house suggests they were producing butter or cheese. Three women at different life-cycle stages participated in the same activity, indicating the collaborative nature of some tasks by female members of the household irrespective of status or wealth, as I will discuss later in this chapter.[105]

Husbandmen often set their female servants to farm work. Almost three-fifths of tasks that female servants working in husbandmen's households carried out were in husbandry: half of these examples were milking cows, while the rest involved crop cultivation. Some were hired specifically for this purpose: we earlier met Sybil Baynham of Winchester (Hampshire), who was described as *servian agri* (servant in husbandry) in 1532.[106] Some women were hired for other specialised skills in less wealthy homes. Alice Waterman of Wellington (Somerset) deposed that in the 1620s she had been 'a servant in howse with Jane Guint (alias Carpenter) widow late of Wellington deceased *to draw her beere*'.[107] The occupation of master or mistress shaped not only the type of work a female servant did but also the environment in which she did it. In 1593, Elizabeth Snow, a married woman, and a man named Roger Pile met in a Birdlip inn in Gloucestershire. Visiting the inn, gentleman Richard Fettipeace observed not only the couple's romantic entanglement but also a maid of the house serving food at a banquet there, who 'passed along with the legge of a henne'.[108] Working in an in inn which welcomed patrons from a diverse range of backgrounds, servants were drawn into social and economic interactions with all sorts of people from the poor to the wealthy. The unnamed maid's experience of serving in this Birdlip inn was influenced by her surroundings. Not all households were the same and consequently, neither was the work that women serving within them carried out.

Division of labour

Early modern labour was divided by gender, marital status, and household hierarchies. Female servants appear at the bottom of this labour chain. As subordinate workers in their masters' and mistresses' homes, they were required to

---

[105] DHC, Chanter 867, Susan Hartwell v Henry Hartwell (1615).
[106] HRO, 21M65/C3/2, Office v Robert Barton and Sybil Baynham (1532).
[107] SHC, D/D/cd/65, Priscilla Carpenter v John Coleborne (1630). Italics my own.
[108] GA, GDR/79, William Snow v Elizabeth Snow (1595).

do what was asked of them – the 'necessarie busines' we saw earlier. The relationship was of course never equal. Sara Maza argued that by asking servants to run errands on their behalf, masters emphasized the socio-economic gap between them and their servants.[109] But while eighteenth-century French noble homes may have nurtured such divisions between servants and masters, the working lives and duties of many sixteenth- and seventeenth-century household members overlapped, intersected, and were at times complementary. The picture isn't one of masters barking orders at their downtrodden hires and watching over them as they worked. Errand-running signalled subservience insofar as it was work carried out for another, but being outside the home could also be empowering for servants. As Chapter 7 shows, servants running errands made connections between homes, and as Maria Ågren pointed out, errand-running signifies households sharing resources and services, emphasising the openness and cooperation that servants helped foster between family units.[110] The 'sight lines' and direct oversight by masters and mistresses of their servants' work that Tara Hamling and Catherine Richardson drew up as a blueprint for early modern middling homes could not easily operate within the complex households in which service was carried out.[111] Often, masters and mistresses were too busy with their own work to pay close attention to what their servants were doing. At other times, work took servants outside the home. While their working lives could not be autonomous, nor was it rigorously controlled.

Despite the classic representation of the 'maid of all work', it wasn't so often that servants worked alone. Autonomy was an impracticality in some cases. Most husbandry tasks that female servants carried out were undertaken with others. Three-quarters of the sixty-one examples of this labour (for which it is possible to determine who else was there) were carried out with at least one other person. In 1598, servant Katherine Tynewell of Morebath (Devon) deposed that she 'did helpe to cutt … rye and to bring it home'.[112] Edith Lancaster of Englishcombe (Somerset) was 'one of those who holpe [helped] to reape' the wheat in her master John Beene's field in 1635.[113] On just one occasion, reaping was done by a lone servant: Isott Riches again. This was probably unusual and received comment from another worker: John Warren explained that he was mowing oats in Rockbeare (Devon) in 1568 when gentleman Frances Yarde passed by and said to him 'What mayde is that, that ryppeth all alone barley?', to which John replied 'it is Mr doctor gamons sisters mayde' and noted that 'Francies went to her and loked

---

[109] Maza, *Servants and Masters*, chapter 3.
[110] Maria Ågren, 'Emissaries, Allies, Accomplices and Enemies: Married Women's Work in Eighteenth-Century Urban Sweden', *Urban History* 41 (2014), 394–414 at 413.
[111] Hamling and Richardson, *A Day at Home*, p. 64.
[112] DHC, Chanter 964, William Lambert v Christopher Tynwell (1598).
[113] SHC, D/D/cd/81, Peter Rowswell v John Beene (1635).

upon her rypping and talked with her about the space of half an hower and then departed'. Even while reaping barley, Isott wasn't entirely alone. John was mowing oats nearby.[114]

Milking and feeding animals was carried out alone by women in service. When Joanne Kyng of Badgeworth (Gloucestershire) was accused of an affair with a man named William Lock in 1552, her servant Margaret Burrell deposed that she had seen Joanne in the ox house late one evening. She added that 'on the morowe erly in the mornyng this deponent went as appoynted by her Mr to the oxe howse there to serve [feed] them [the ox] where she sawe a place upon the strawe where some [people] had been lyeng'.[115] She was the only person to give this information, being alone in her work. As I showed earlier in this chapter, female servants regularly milked *alone* early in the mornings. The dark winter months coupled with the solitary nature of this work at such an early hour made it potentially dangerous for female servants. We already encountered Ursula Daniell of Walton (Somerset) milking early in the morning in 1603. The other part of her story is that one morning her master, John Tutton, attempted to rape her. She deposed that it was dark 'so yt shee could not see him, but in the end shee both sawe him and felt him'. In future, when she went to milk the cows, she 'had usually one or another to goe along with her to beare her company for feare what the said Tutton would do unto her'.[116] In some communities, groups of women milked together at set times in the fields, perhaps to avoid this danger. In 1588, servant Margaret Allen of Guiting Power (Gloucestershire) went 'milkinge with divers others into a common field where their kine [cattle] wente all together'.[117]

Making hay, meanwhile, was a group activity. In 1602 Joanne Giblett, another servant in the household of the abusive John Tutton, was found in her master's field making hay with John's son.[118] Female servants reaped and gathered crops predominantly alongside men, and most frequently they worked alongside their masters. In over 30 per cent of cases where a female servant's working companion in husbandry could be identified, it was her master. By contrast, only 13 per cent were accompanied by their mistresses. Carrying out and coordinating agricultural labour, then, was generally the responsibility of the husband. Many rural female servants regularly worked alongside these men.

This working pattern was fairly unique to agriculture. In other areas of the economy, female servants ordinarily worked alongside their mistresses, sometimes in separate roles. Dairying was often hierarchical. Female servants who

---

[114] DHC, Chanter 858, John Roo v Francis Yarde (1568).
[115] GA, GDR/8, John Kyng v Joane Kyng (1662).
[116] SHC, D/D/cd/39, Office v John Tutton (1602).
[117] GA, GDR/65, Elizabeth Wollams v Anne White (1588).
[118] SHC, D/D/cd/32, George Vowles v Joanna Giblett (1602).

were responsible for delivering tithe cheese to their local church, for example, almost never described making the cheese themselves. This was typically carried out by the mistress of the house, though it's likely that some female servants participated.[119] Edith Longden of Hawkesbury (Gloucestershire) recalled paying tithe cheese for her master and mistress in the 1550s and indicated her knowledge of how cheese was made, deposing that 'the said cheeses soe by hir brought to the church were made of every one, of all the mylk that the said nine kyne did geve usually at one meale or mylking as farr as she nowe remembreth'.[120] Edith was probably involved in the cheese-making process. Elizabeth Higdon of Broadmarston (Somerset) recalled that when she served William Cutler 'she did his huswiferie woorke aboute his howse & used to milke his kine [cattle] & make his butter & cheese, other woorke that servants use to doe aboute his howse'.[121] The division of dairying labour is clear in the 1612 deposition of Margaret Addams of Winford (Somerset). For two and a half years, she and a servant in another house milked as many as sixty cows daily between them that grazed on her master's land. The servants milked while Margaret's fellow servant's mistress, Mrs Ingham, 'did help make the cheese and help contriffe [contrive] it'.[122]

The word 'help' surfaces regularly in female servant depositions to describe their labour with fellow workers. As Lindström et al. noted, sometimes the word was used to 'veil relations of hierarchy and dependence, while in other instances it suggests a more equal relationship'.[123] In 1615, Anne Higgens deposed that she had been helping 'Martha Higgens [her mistress] to washe a bucke at her dore' in Lower Quinton (Gloucestershire).[124] Anna Barrie worked alongside her mistress, Mrs Stevens, 'helping' to 'attend the shop' on a market day in Bath in 1611.[125] Perhaps Martha Higgens and Mrs Stevens adopted managerial roles in both scenarios. But their implied physical labour more or less mirrored that of their servants', reducing the distance between mistress and hire. A 1603 deposition outlines in particular detail the joint endeavour of Elizabeth Banwell of Berrow (Somerset) and her mistress in milking a cow. Elizabeth deposed that they were 'in a little plot or peece of ground … the said Marie Hix milking of a cowe and this deponent keeping the said cowe [so] that shee should not start away when shee was milking'.[126] Collaboration and cooperation between Elizabeth and Marie is emphasised, not supervision of a servant by her mistress.

---

[119] Whittle suggested that farmers producing butter and cheese commercially (on a larger scale) would hire at least one female servant. See Whittle, 'Housewives and Servants', 71.
[120] GA, GDR/89, Andrew Thomas v Henry Norris (1604).
[121] SHC, D/D/cd/81, John Allen v William Cutler (1635).
[122] SHC, D/D/cd/43, Meredith Mayde v John Ingham (1612).
[123] Dag Lindström, Rosemarie Feibranz, Jonas Lindström, Jan Mispelaere, and Göran Rydén, 'Working Together', in Maria Ågren (ed.), *Making a Living, Making a Difference: Gender and Work in Early Modern European Society* (Oxford, 2017), pp. 57–79 at 67.
[124] GA, GDR/122, Martha Higgens v Joan Chettle (1615).
[125] SHC, D/D/cd/44, William Stephens v Susan Browne (1611).
[126] SHC, D/D/cd/28, William Hix v Edith Hick (1603).

Calculating labour

The different labour requirements of households mean we cannot generalise about what female servants did. In most homes, they weren't simply hired to support a family's particular style of life. It was an economic decision. How much and what type of labour was needed was calculated according to the size and composition of the household (how many children and of what ages) as well as its economic function(s). Family life-cycle dynamics were important. Childbirth might temporarily remove the wife from a household's pool of available labour, demanding more from female servants and other household members. When Alice Mathewe of Cheltenham (Gloucestershire) left Thomas and Elizabeth Mathewes's service after just one week in 1611, Elizabeth 'did entreate the said Thomas Mathewes her husband to give her leave to goe forth into the towne to his brothers howse to get one of his daughters to come with her into the howse, *having a little child in her hands*'.[127] Elizabeth feared being unable to care for a small child alongside her work duties. Had Alice stayed, her workload was likely to have been high.

We don't learn what specific work Elizabeth Hallowes was asked to do when she served clothier William Harding in Dursley (Gloucestershire) at the end of the sixteenth century. But he calculated that his outlay – including her 'dyet, lodging and washinge' – was 40 *shillings*, while the service she did for him was 'worth xxiiiis, [24s] and not more'. These calculations appear in William's deposition for a testamentary dispute relating to Elizabeth's father's will. His was one of two short depositions recorded, and neither offer much context to the dispute. Probably, upon turning 21, Elizabeth decided to litigate against her father's appointed executor, Edward Trotman, for mismanagement of her father's will. William testified that he had taken Elizabeth (age 14 and a half) into his service upon Edward's promise that he 'should not be a looser [loser] by it'. He claimed he agreed 'in regard of the love he then bore unto the said Mr Trotman'. But Elizabeth, he insisted, didn't carry out sufficient labour to compensate his 40-*shilling* outlay. This hadn't been an economically advantageous agreement for him, William argued, his testimony chiming with a service culture in which the youngest were often unwaged.[128]

Similar labour calculations were recorded in a testamentary dispute heard in the Bath & Wells court in 1625 concerning the will of orphan Elizabeth Bevan, who died around the age of 18. Witnesses claimed she had bequeathed her goods to John Buck, her father-in-law (stepfather). John had kept her in his home in Kingston Seymour (Somerset) throughout her childhood. The extent and nature of her work in his home was scrutinised as the question of recompense hung in the

---

[127] GA, GDR/114, Elizabeth Mathewes v Thomas Mathewes (1611). Italics my own.
[128] GA, GDR/89, Elizabeth Hallowes v Edward Trotman (1601).

air: had Elizabeth earned her keep? If not, John was entitled (witnesses thought) to her goods. These witnesses hint at the household's threshold for requiring female service. They denied Elizabeth's ability to carry out much service for John as she was 'a weeke sicklie and lame maide untill her death'. One neighbour admitted that she 'might some tymes strick or sweepe the said John Buckes howse and after hee had younge children some tymes attend them when theare mother was otherwaies imployed' but that she couldn't perform 'anie greate service or extraordinarie woorke'. Sweeping the house and caring for children didn't, in the eyes of witnesses, amount to 'anie greate service'. But it wasn't that these tasks had no economic value; rather, the extent of this work (carried out only 'some tymes') rendered it negligible in comparison with John's outlay.

As we've seen, female servants frequently milked and therefore labour calculations were often made according to the number of cows a household kept.[129] Witnesses in this same case estimated that John had between ten and twelve cows. Most agreed he had 'never kepte above one female servant [in this case, Elizabeth] att a tyme'. The family unit therefore comprised John and his wife, two young children (aged 3 and 5), and Elizabeth. One witness evidently recognised that milking ten or more cows alongside other household duties was a heavy workload for just one female servant, though he added – almost defensively – that John's wife 'is a lustie strong younge woman and able to doe a greate parte of her woorke her selfe'. Engaging in pastoral dairy farming at this level, with no children of working age to contribute to the family labour pool, required more than one female servant. Implicit, then, was the suggestion that Elizabeth Bevan had milked the cows herself and that the claim that she hadn't done 'anie greate service' was false. Evidently, this was extremely economically valuable work.[130]

How many cows a female servant might be responsible for milking varied, perhaps even regionally; G. E. Fussell found that one Wiltshire farmer estimated six to have been a good number for a maid to milk, while a Norfolk farmer thought a good dairymaid could manage twenty.[131] By the eighteenth century, dairy farming households perhaps hired one milk maid for every ten cows (though with increasing specialisation, perhaps this was the only work they did).[132] In 1631, two Basingstoke women recalled milking Mr Baynerd's cows as his servants. Joanna Dent remembered that in each year between 1619 and 1622, Mr Baynerd had seven cows, which daily produced 3 quarts (or 6 pints) of milk each and annually delivered six calves. In 1622, Mr Baynerd's herd grew to nine. Joanna Hatchett, who took over service from Joanna Dent in 1623, recalled that these nine cows

---

[129] Whittle showed that almost three-quarters of servant-employing households had milk cows in the seventeenth century, though not more than ten. See Whittle, 'Housewives and Servants', 67.
[130] SHC, D/D/cd/59, John Buck v Elizabeth Heyward (1625).
[131] G. E. Fussell, *The English Dairy Farmer 1500–1900* (1966), pp. 162–3.
[132] Ibid., p. 163; Pinchbeck, *Women Workers*, p. 15.

delivered eight calves a year between them, and 35 quarts (70 pints) daily collectively (7.8 pints each). Mr Baynerd's dairy farming had therefore intensified over this four-year period.

The work both servants carried out likely generated a reasonable income for him. In 1618, Robert Loder experimented with keeping cattle. He believed that '3 pints and half a quartune' (3.125 pints) was worth 1*d*. Loder's twelve cows produced slightly more milk than Mr Baynerd's, averaging around 8 pints per day per cow.[133] Though milk prices varied year on year and regionally (although Berkshire and Hampshire are contiguous), we can estimate that Joanna Dent could bring home up to 42 pints of milk daily (6 pints from seven cows), worth around 13*d*. By 1623, Joanna Hatchett was getting as many as 70 pints from nine cows a day, generating an income of around 22*d*. Though milk yields fluctuated across the year, these cows weren't only supplying Mr Baynerd's household with milk, butter, and cheese. There was evidently surplus to be sold for profit. How long the two servants spent milking these seven or nine cows each day is difficult to gauge but it may have taken an hour in the morning and another at night, depending on each cow's temperament, stage of lactation, and the experience of the milker.[134] It was of course only a fraction of these women's daily work. Even considering the costs of buying, feeding, and pasturing the cows, the value of Joanna Dent and Joanna Hatchett's work must have surpassed the wages they received.[135]

Dairy farming was therefore lucrative business. The details given in these cases about labour and productivity indicate that yields and profits were carefully tracked, not just by householders but by servants, too. The economic importance of milking, regularly carried out by female servants, is reflected in this evidence as well as in a comment Loder added to his accounting for 1618. He noted the great profits that might be had in keeping milk cows 'yf I canne have trustie servantes'.[136]

Training and skills

Mr Baynerd's farm was a productive business and its workers acquired practical agricultural knowledge. In the manual repetition of their work, women such as Joanna Dent and Joanna Hatchett also saw the profits to be made. Interestingly, their fellow servant Joanna Addams, serving in the same household between 1614 and 1624, knew how many cows Mr Baynerd had but not their yields. She explained that she was 'but a servant to doe worke within doors & ... verie seldome went abroad to milke the kine [cattle]'.[137] Her knowledge was of a different kind.

---

[133] Loder, *Robert Loder's Farm Accounts*, p. 156.
[134] Fussell, *The English Dairy Farmer*, p. 163.
[135] HRO, 21M65/C3/12, Ambrose Webb v George Baynerd (1631).
[136] Loder, *Robert Loder's Farm Accounts*, p. 156.
[137] HRO, 21M65/C3/12, West and West v Brackley (1631).

Mr Baynerd's servants were far from the only ones who demonstrated practice-based knowledge. In July 1637, Agnes Shipman of West Pennard (Somerset) had been working in Edward Frie's service for almost six years since Michaelmas 1631. Her deposition records no trace of her work if we look for verbs or tasks. But she revealed detailed knowledge of her master's beekeeping. In 1635, she noted, Edward had no honey or wax from his hives. The following year, he had 'but fower hives of bees' (which Agnes evidently deemed a low number) and 'he caused but one to be burnte'. Holding a sulphur match at the entrance to the hive and suffocating the bees, the beekeeper could freely take the honey and wax.[138] Edward's hive contained 'three quarts of honie att utmost & noe more' according to Agnes, and she judged it to be 'badd honie', having seen and tasted it. She deposed that it was 'not worth in this deponents judgment above two shillings a quarte'. At no point can we directly connect Agnes to beekeeping activities through a verb or task. But her deposition locates her at this site of work and is laced with beekeeping knowledge. She noted that three opposing witnesses (who claimed honey to be worth 4s a quart) weren't there at the 'taking of the honie & wax that came from them, for if they had this deponent must needes have seane them *being present thereatt*'.[139] Nineteen-year-old Agnes had been there. She knew how to extract honey and wax from hives. She also knew its price, what 'badd honie' tasted like, and what it was likely to sell for.

Likewise without mentioning her work, Izoda Brayne, servant to David Jorden of Yate (Gloucestershire), knew that in 1603 calves were worth 6s 8d and piglets could fetch 5d. She knew that her master's five loads of hay were each worth 6s 8d.[140] Servant Marie Edwards of Chew Stoke (Somerset) sold corn at the weekly market for her uncle. She deposed that each week 'hee sett her the pace how she should sell it, and received the mony for the same'.[141] We met Agnes Barons of Ilsington (Devon) in Chapter 5, whose former master, Mr Done, complained to the justice of the peace that she had given away 'a peece of beif at his dore to a poore woeman worth 18d'. Recalling this in 1636, Agnes contested the beef's value (just 14d, not 18d) and pointed out that ten people had dined on it before just a tiny scrap had been doled out to the poor woman in charity.[142] Holding knowledge of prices made servants powerful witnesses. In 1581, Agnes Munke, servant to gentleman Alexander Oldfelde of Twyford (Hampshire), recalled milking his twelve cows. She knew how many calves were born and when, but not how much they were worth, as, Agnes replied 'she hath no skyll in process of such thinges'.[143]

---

138 On early modern bee keeping, see Charles Butler, *The Feminine Monarchie: Or the Historie of Bees* (1623), chapter 10.
139 SHC, D/D/cd/84, Peter Coward and George Hipeslie v Edward Frie (1637). Italics my own.
140 GA, GDR/89, Thomas Baynham v David Jorden (1604).
141 SHC, D/D/cd/36, Thomas Jenkins v John Webb (1605).
142 DHC, Chanter 866, William Harries v Audrey Rowell (1636).
143 HRO, 21M65/C3/8, John Weke v Alexander Oldfield (1581).

This tithe case hinged on the value of a tithe cow being correctly appraised. In this case, her master, Alexander, stood accused of non-payment. Agnes, testifying on his behalf, probably feigned ignorance; the fact that she was asked to appraise the value of a calf indicates she was expected to know.

While commerce was scarcely reported by women in service, their knowledge of prices clearly indicates their involvement in this work and further embeds them within the rituals and rhythms of rural life. Prices of food and commodities were picked up from working in households that both produced and consumed. In the account books of gentry wives who meticulously recorded household expenditure and income, we see that these women knew the value of commodities and labour. But while women lower down the social ladder typically lacked the literacy skills to record their finances, they too possessed the same mental index of prices. Service also taught young women economic management and business acumen. Their senses were sharpened to the world around them. Agnes Shipman knew what bad honey tasted and looked like. Izoda could visualise the size of a 'load' of hay and knew what it could fetch. Others fiercely defended their knowledge. Joanna Bonde, long-time servant of John Leach of Pinhoe (Devon), recalled accepting tithe fleeces from Hubert Colwell in 1565 on behalf of her master. Returning home, her master returned then in a sack to Hubert, refusing to accept them on the grounds that he had seen his 'good flock of shepe' and the fleeces Joanna had received were 'all badde'. Hubert was, he claimed, unjustly paying his tithe (the tithe fleece should be comparable in quality with the fleeces he kept for his own commodity). Justifying her actions, Joanna added that Colwell hadn't given her notice to visit the field to view the tithe wool against the rest of the wool sheared from his flock. She was therefore unable to judge the tithe wool's quality.[144] While service wasn't necessarily the training ground for hard skills such as literacy, service nonetheless taught them to shrewdly assess and appraise the goods and commodities around them.

Conclusion

The 'necessarie busines' that the *female* servants of Meare (Somerset) did at the turn of the seventeenth century turns out to be wider ranging and more economically significant than scholarship suggests. The tasks they undertook contributed to more than just maintaining the hiring family's 'style of life'.[145] From evidence recorded in depositions, it is possible to say much more about the work of female servants than simply that it was 'domestic'. The verb- or task-based

---

[144] DHC, Chanter 654, John Leache v Hubert Colwell (1565).
[145] Kussmaul, *Servants in Husbandry*, p. 4.

approach reconceptualises the labour they carried out. The 312 tasks collected and analysed here show that female servants' work was varied, stretching across the early modern economy. The women of south and south-west England reaped and sowed in the fields, dusted malt in the streets ready for brewing, ran countless errands for their masters and mistresses, and washed clothes in rivers. This work was essential to the functioning of the household. In carrying out domestic work, they freed up other family members for income-generating activities. Much of the food and drink they produced was either sold or consumed within the home.

The value of digging deeper into depositions is also revealed in this chapter. Verbs denoting work activities are only a starting point. By placing tasks within their contexts, it is possible to flesh out the labour we read about by understanding who it was carried out with, at what time of day or year, and in whose household. Throughout the year, but especially in summer, much of the work female servants did was based outdoors, often husbandry in the fields. For early modern society, Sunday was a lighter work day. But this wasn't the case for servants, whose workloads shot up on this day. Female servants were often the first to rise, with the working day regularly geared around the rhythms of milking, a task probably undertaken by most female servants (though in many households this was not a specialised form of labour in this period). Reading depositions more closely exhumes evidence of labour that isn't easily captured by the verb-oriented approach. Here, we see households in action, with servants working alongside other household members in the fields and at dairying. It's to the spaces where their work took place and to the interactions they had there that we now turn.

Part III

Chapter 7

The Home and Beyond

In the early spring of 1605, a one-hundred-strong crowd congregated around a bench outside the house of Mr William Locksmith in Southgate Street in Gloucester. Upon the bench was a young baby, rumoured to be the product of an illicit affair between William's unmarried servants, Margaret Gilbert and Anthony Provis. In the crowd was a young woman named Alice Butler, servant of a city alderman. She had a different tale to tell of the child's paternity. Before the crowd and in the open street, Alice declared: 'Well masters, the servant hath the name but the master had the game'.[1]

* * *

These words appear in the witness statements of several members of the crowd who testified in the Gloucester church court to Alice's defamation. By alleging that 'the master had the game', Alice insinuated that William, not Anthony, was the father of Margaret's illegitimate child. These words weren't only defamatory; they also resonate with a well-documented and almost proverbial history of servant vulnerability. Female servants like Margaret endured the sexual advances of their masters, who held a position of privilege and power within the early modern household-family.[2] Male servants like Anthony were coerced into bearing the consequences.[3] Underpinning this household patriarchal order were two interconnected systems of power – rank and gender – which played out simultaneously within the servant-hiring household and were at the root of Alice's words.

But this glimpse into a busy seventeenth-century urban street exposes a different history of female service. Shifting the focus to Alice, a servant herself, decentres not only the concept of patriarchal household order and the

---

[1] GA, GDR/95, William Locksmith v Alice Butler (1605).
[2] The 'household-family' is used here (and throughout) to mean biological family members as well as servants and apprentices. See Tadmor, 'Concept of the Household-Family'.
[3] Amussen, *An Ordered Society*, pp. 1–3.

ideas of subordination and vulnerability that it encapsulates. It also decentres the household context altogether. The city-centre street – Alice's chosen stage for her words – guaranteed a large audience. It was a working and living space containing permanent inhabitants and a thoroughfare through which passers-by flowed, ensuring wide transmission of the rumour. The sense of drama with which Alice delivered the cynical line to the crowd and its mark upon their collective memory is unmistakable. Eleanor Dovety, wife of a Gloucester brazier, recalled that Alice said, 'Come come … here is a greate wondering but the master had the game and the servant had the name'. News of Alice's defamation trickled down the streets of Gloucester and beyond the city precincts. It reached the parish of Hartpury 8 kilometres away, where the vicar repeated the words: 'a yonge woman in Gloucester sayd that the man had the name, and the maister had the game'. The geographical reach of this rumour threatened to damage William's reputation. His appeal to the church court to clear himself of the charges that Alice had laid at his door is unsurprising.

This is a story that situates women in service within the early modern community. Emily Cockayne argued that crowds offered anonymity for those like Alice 'wanting to voice criticism against the powerful', who could then 'retreat into the heart of the mob to avoid identification'.[4] But Alice was familiar to at least some of the crowd, who knew she lived in the Gloucester parish of St John the Baptist, less than a kilometre from Southgate Street where this episode played out. Anonymity was apparently of little concern to Alice: we encounter her in the street, absent from her master's home, offering a frank and sharp-witted commentary on servant–master relations and illegitimacy (issues clearly of great economic and social concern to this early modern community). Evidence like this prompts us to attend to the spatial and social worlds in which female servants lived and worked.

Spaces weren't gender-neutral in early modern literature: we are reminded again of courtier Edmund Tilney's advice in 1568 that 'the office of the husbande is to go abroad in matters of profite, of the wife, to tarry at home, and see all be well there'.[5] Social norms and gender rules theoretically demarcated space in early modern England. But prescription didn't map onto practice. While the spatial turn has upended gendered notions of space, with historians exploring the frequent collision of 'public' and 'private', little headway has been made in rescuing female servants from the rigid 'separate spheres' framework.[6] Women in service

---

[4] Emily Cockayne, *Hubbub: Filth, Noise & Stench in England 1600–1770* (New Haven, 2007), p. 161.
[5] Tilney, *Flower of Friendship*, p. 120.
[6] 'Separate spheres' is a model in which space is gendered: women existed within and controlled the 'private' domestic sphere while men inhabited and influenced the public sphere. See Leonore Davidoff and Catherine Hall, *Family Fortunes: Men and Women of the English Middle Class 1780–1850* (1987). For important rebuttals, see Amanda Vickery, 'Golden Age to Separate Spheres? A Review of the

are frequently labelled 'domestic servants', even though the term 'servant' was much more common in the sixteenth and seventeenth centuries. The footprints of female servants continue to be tracked around the home, perpetuating the myth of the 'great enclosure' of youth.[7] Michael Mitterauer argued that 'in service, there was no such thing as a private sphere independent of working relationships', and that recreation was controlled by the household head.[8] Studies of female servants' working activities, social experiences, and relationships are firmly bound within the home and its patriarchal structures.[9]

This chapter analyses spaces in which we encounter female servants like Alice in church court depositions. Presenting a statistical spatial model of service underpinned by detailed qualitative analysis of the evidence, it challenges our understanding of these women's interactions with space in early modern England. These women weren't confined to the domestic sphere. As Paul Griffiths suggests, they were young people 'on the move, spilling onto fields and streets'.[10] Service embedded them within local communities. And further, their links to the wider community afforded them power and agency – limited perhaps, but significant nonetheless. In analysing the activities that took place within these spaces and the social forces at work in shaping servants' movements, the chapter destabilises the model of the patriarchal household as a structure of governance. If, as this chapter shows, women in service habitually spent time outside their masters' homes and with people outside their household-family, how useful a framework is the patriarchal household for understanding their experiences?

Categorising space

From the depositions of the five courts, I have systematically collected and categorised 939 examples of spaces in which women in service were identified (see Table 7.1). We meet them in these spaces for a variety of reasons and in a range of circumstances. The most frequently heard court grievances – defamation,

---

Categories and Chronology of English Women's History', *The Historical Journal* 36 (1993), 383–414; Paul Griffiths, 'Meanings of Nightwalking in Early Modern England', *Seventeenth-Century Journal* 13 (1998), 212–38; Laura Gowing, '"The Freedom of the Streets": Women and Social Space, 1560–1640', in Paul Griffiths and Mark S. R. Jenner (eds), *Londinopolis: Essays in the Cultural and Social History of Early Modern London c.1500–c.1750* (Manchester, 2000), pp. 130–53.

[7] Griffiths, *Youth and Authority*, p. 112.

[8] By 'private', Mitterauer refers to the sphere of the individual rather than within the context of the 'separate spheres' debate. See Michael Mitterauer, *A History of Youth* (Oxford, 1993), pp. 115, 131.

[9] Elizabeth Ewan noted the independence achieved by early modern Scottish female servants through by-employments (moneylending, brewing, and laundering). See Elizabeth Ewan, 'Mistresses of Themselves? Female Domestic Servants and By-Employments in Sixteenth-Century Scottish Towns', in Antoinette Fauve-Chamoux (ed.), *Domestic Service and the Formation of European Identity* (Bern, 2004), pp. 411–33.

[10] Griffiths, *Youth and Authority*, p. 113.

	N	%
Servant–master/mistress household		
Unspecified	175	38
Chamber	123	27
Hall	65	14
Kitchen	36	8
Parlour	30	7
(Master's) inn	6	1
(Master's) shop	6	1
Loft	4	1
Other	14	3
	459	49
Liminal		
Doorway/entry/gate	32	34
Outbuildings	24	25
Court/yard/backside	20	21
Garden	16	17
Other	3	3
	95	10
Other		
Another's household	143	37
Field/meadow/close	54	14
Church or churchyard	42	11
Street	39	10
Market	16	4
Highway/road	16	4
Unspecified	13	3
River/water/brook	11	3
Fair/church ale	9	2
Parent's house	8	2
Inn/alehouse	8	2
Mill	6	2
Shop	5	1
Barn	4	1
Other	11	3
	385	41
Total	**939**	

Table 7.1 Spaces in which female servants were recorded

	Servant–master/ mistress household		Liminal		Other		All
	N	*%*	*N*	*%*	*N*	*%*	
Defamation	125	*40*	45	*14*	144	*46*	314
Matrimonial	96	*49*	17	*9*	83	*42*	196
Testamentary	100	*79*	7	*6*	19	*15*	126
Tithes	10	*21*	4	*8*	34	*71*	48
Total	**331**	*49*	**73**	*10*	**280**	*42*	**684**

Table 7.2 Spaces in which female servants were recorded (by main categories of dispute)

matrimonial, testamentary, and tithe disputes – indicate some common contexts. The street, for example, is the archetypal site in which insults were hurled back and forth; according to Laura Gowing, defamatory words were rarely spoken inside London homes.[11] But Table 7.2 suggests a different pattern: defamatory words were *regularly* spoken in household spaces as well as streets, at least in the more rural south and south west of England. Audience, not place, was key to setting the scene. To file a successful defamation suit against Alice Butler, William Locksmith had to prove the insult was spoken in public and had significantly injured his reputation. The setting had to be plausible too, dovetailing with a credible narrative of service that permitted Alice's presence in the street. But crucially, the insult had to have been witnessed by several people, and those people didn't necessarily need to be in the street.[12] A much broader constellation of scenarios than standard testimonies of street-based insults, chamber-based will-making, and field-based tithing comes to light. Witnesses' depositions are punctuated with descriptions of work, conversations they had, and social occasions in which they participated.

Adopting a female servant perspective, the examples of spaces collected are categorised as 'servant-master/mistress household', 'liminal', or 'other' spaces. Only *rooms* within the homes in which servants lived are classified as 'servant-master/mistress household'. Spaces defined as 'liminal' were physically and conceptually connected with the servant-master/mistress home but were located on its boundary. They include gardens, doorways, gateways, and stables. 'Other' spaces are sites distinct from servant-master/mistress households, including the street, marketplace, and church. The households of others have been included in this category to mark a sharp distinction between a female servant's place of residence and the households of strangers, neighbours, friends, and kin (where

---

[11] Gowing, *Domestic Dangers*, p. 99.
[12] See K. Tawny Paul, 'Credit, Reputation, and Masculinity in British Urban Commerce: Edinburgh, c.1710–70', *EcHR* 66 (2013), 226–48 at 232.

	Type of space							
	Servant–master/ mistress household		Liminal		Other		All	
Relationship	*N*	*%*	*N*	*%*	*N*	*%*	*N*	*%*
Master/mistress	364	*29*	52	*19*	102	*10*	518	*21*
Other household members	258	*21*	48	*17*	66	*7*	372	*15*
Members of other households	616	*50*	176	*64*	812	*83*	1,604	*64*
Total	**1,238**	—	**276**	—	**980**	—	**2,494**	—

Table 7.3 Identifiable relationships of female servants to those sharing the same spaces

we might assume a master's or mistress's authority was more limited). The categories serve to draw spatial or property distinctions, rather than to impose strict public/private divisions.

In tracking female servants around and beyond the parish, we find less than half within their employers' homes (49 per cent). Women in service were occasionally identified on the boundary between the home and the wider parish, but we regularly (in 41 per cent of cases) encounter them in 'other' spaces. The networks, affinities, and relationships they constructed within their masters' or mistresses' households tell only a partial story of service. As Table 7.3 shows, female servants were often recorded in spaces without their master or mistress and instead with members of other households. Chapter 8 explores these interactions and relationships in more detail; for now, it's important to note that as female servants moved away from the households in which they served, their master or mistress was less likely to be with them. This raises important questions about how, on a practical level, they exercised patriarchal control over their servants.

Imagining space

The home

When a female servant joined a household, it may have looked and felt very different in size, composition, and nature to the one in which she was raised or had last served. Many households were a hive of activity, open to neighbours, visitors, friends, and kin, who entered – sometimes intruded – frequently.[13]

---

[13] Fiona Williamson found that the people of early modern Norwich spent much time in other people's households. See Fiona Williamson, *Social Relations and Urban Space: Norwich, 1600–1700* (Woodbridge, 2014), p. 59.

Although female servants were marginally more likely to be found in the home than outside it, so too were other members of the household-family. The multi-functionality of rooms admitted men, women, servants, and children who went about their daily work.[14] Outsiders crossed the threshold as invited guests: in 1592, Edmund Evenish of Badgeworth (Gloucestershire) was passing by the vicarage on his way home from Gloucester when the vicar, Mr Rea, called him inside for a drink.[15] People worked in others' households: as he was 'at work in Nicholas Shorts house', tailor John Somerwell of Goodleigh (Devon) witnessed Nicholas's sick servant, Walter Blackmore, make his will in 1588.[16] Some came on other business: Cirencester butcher Nicholas Phillipes visited John Hytchins in Down Ampney (Gloucestershire) in 1573 to buy a sheep.[17] Female servants were no different: they, too, were in and out of other people's homes.[18] A Devon servant known only as Clara washed clothes in her neighbour's well in Berry Pomeroy in 1561, servant Katherine Morgan skirted the Herefordshire–Radnorshire border to visit Mr Pension's household in Brilley in 1599, and Agnes Cover stole away from service one day to see Richard Smith (whom she hoped to marry) at his Winchester (Hampshire) home in 1568.[19]

Architecturally, houses were porous and penetrable, though not all company was invited. Open window frames exposed the house to both the elements and the community as glazing became a feature of only town houses from the sixteenth century.[20] In 1579, Gloucester tanner William Conneby heard Margaret Crodie make her will, as he 'stoode in the backside under the windowe, whereat a hole that is in the wall he might putt his hedd into the howse'.[21] As Margaret had contracted plague, it wasn't safe to be inside her home. Holes and chinks in walls and doors that provided windows into household spaces in early modern England regularly furnished court testimony and have attracted much scholarship.[22] The widely-held idea that these domestic imperfections were invented to make eyewitness accounts watertight is compelling. But fissures, slits, and cracks must have been commonplace to render them plausible. Walls were also thin: in 1610, Margaret Wood, also of Gloucester, was in 'a rome next adjoining' when she

---

[14] Flather, *Gender and Space*, p. 43.
[15] GA, GDR/79, John White v John Thaier (1592).
[16] DHC, Chanter 862, Nicholas Short v Hamon (1588).
[17] GA, GDR/32, Eleanor Rowles v John Hytchman (1573).
[18] 'Other household' accounts for around 15 per cent of all spaces in which we encounter female servants.
[19] DHC, Chanter 855a, William Jane v Alice Myller (1561); HARC, HD4/2/11, Thomas Hereford v Ann Vaughan (1599); HRO, 21M65/C3/4, Agnes Cover v Richard Smith (1568).
[20] Crowley, *The Invention of Comfort*, p. 66.
[21] GA, GDR/45, Thomas Weekes and Thomas Key v Richard Crodie, Eleanor Davys and Alice Dove (1579).
[22] See Dolan, *True Relation*, pp. 146–8; Orlin, *Locating Privacy*, pp. 189–92; Ingram, *Church Courts*, pp. 244–5; Gowing, *Domestic Dangers*, p. 71.

'did see and behold the said clay wall shakeinge and heard the said Michaell Paine blowe and puff as yf he had bin out of breath'. Michael's affair with their neighbour, Joan Anslett, was visible and audible even in the next house.[23]

Beyond the home

While Gowing noted that 'the early modern household was not built for privacy', Malcolm Gaskill pointed out that it wasn't necessarily expected.[24] But conceptual boundaries between private and communal spaces existed – fluid perhaps, but identifiable nonetheless. Victualler William Webb testified on behalf of his servant, Joan Dudson, in 1608 that Edith Oram was

> neare this examinates dwelling house in the parishe of St Nicholas within the Cytie of Gloucester and fallinge into hot angrie termes against the saide Joane Dudson, & thereupon the said Joane Dudson comeinge into this examinates house from the said Edith Oram, the said Edith Oram followed and came after her into the entrie of this examinates house which is neare to this examinates hall [he] being then asate by the fier in the said hall accompanied with Alice Web this examinates wife.

Once inside, Edith announced

> if her [Joan's] maister … did knowe as muche by her the said Dudson as she the said Edith Oram did knowe he wolde never keepe her one deye in his house.[25]

Homes weren't impermeable. The women's voices carried from the street, and Edith freely followed Joan into her home, perhaps intending to defame her in front of her master and mistress. But Joan's retreat into the house represents an attempt to shield herself from her defamer. While female servants' access to privacy might be limited, they nonetheless might see their masters' homes as spaces of solace and sanctuary from the outside world. William's and Alice's depositions against Edith further validated Joan's place within their home.

Legally, boundaries of the home were demarcated. In secular courts, defendants in theft cases insisted they had 'found' the goods they were accused of stealing *at the door* of the owner's house, not inside. They thereby avoided charges of breaking and entering but could also claim ignorance of whom the goods belonged to, having found them in this liminal space.[26] Shirley Ardener argued that the empirical boundary between 'private' and 'public' was 'measured

[23] GA, GDR/109, Henry Jones v Michael Paine and Joan Anslett (1610).
[24] Gowing, *Domestic Dangers*, p. 190; Malcolm Gaskill, 'Little Commonwealths II: Communities', in Keith Wrightson (ed.), *A Social History of England 1500–1750* (Cambridge, 2017), pp. 84–104 at 89.
[25] GA, GDR/100, Joan Dudson v Edith Oram (1608).
[26] For example, see SHC, QSR-34, The Examination of Mary French (alias Lawrence) (1620).

primarily by earshot'.[27] William and Alice listened to Joan and Edith's altercation from the hallway of their home, but liminal spaces at the boundaries – doorways, gates, courts, yards, gardens, and 'backsides' – offered better access to the sights and sounds of the community.[28] These semi-public spaces hosted conversations of community significance, including marriage: gardens and courtyards were often sites of betrothal. In 1552 in Meysey Hampton (Gloucestershire), Jane Rook was betrothed to her mistress's son, Thomas Orchard, by their neighbour over a stone wall that divided the 'backsides' of the two properties.[29] Couples chose picturesque or symbolic scenes for their betrothals: Herefordshire couple Anne Vaughan and Roger Prosser made their vows under a hall window one day in April 1598, Cicely Howchins and Thomas White selected a well in Cicely's master's garden in Nursling (Hampshire) in 1561, and servant Edith Leggatt and Anthony Dalby were betrothed in her mistress's orchard at Sydmonton House (Hampshire) in 1582.[30] But these were also sites in which the couples could be seen, if not heard.

Servants standing at the edge of the household could be silent earwitnesses to insults hurled over garden fences. Standing in her master's courtyard in Silverton (Devon), Mary Hayne was one of several witnesses to overhear Grace Luscombe defame her mistress in 1618.[31] Katherine Frynde, too, was standing at the door of her master's house in nearby Crediton in 1576 when she overheard insults exchanged between Elizabeth Lange and Hugo Hempton.[32] We don't know what Mary and Katherine were doing in these spaces: were they already there or were they drawn outdoors by the commotion? Like Katherine, many female servants recorded in liminal spaces lived in large towns such as Cirencester, Tewkesbury, Southampton, and Wells, but rural female servants were also identified in these spaces. In nucleated villages and urban parishes alike, spaces on the peripheries of the home could be as public as streets, lanes, and market squares.

The perimeters of the home functioned as working and social spaces. Indoor light levels were low in winter and at the waning of the day. Poor eyesight, the cost of candlelight, and the smoke of the central hearth therefore drew people outdoors. Women sat in the entries of their homes, taking advantage of the natural light as they spun, knitted, sewed, and gossiped.[33] Women and their work weren't separated from the wider community but were instead at the heart of it. When Jane Paddon insulted Alice Rowland in the street in Shebbear (Devon)

---

[27] Shirley Ardener, 'Ground Rules and Social Maps for Women', in Shirley Ardener (ed.), *Women and Space: Ground Rules and Social Maps* (Oxford, 1983), pp. 11–32 at 12.

[28] Gowing marks these liminal spaces as 'public'. See Gowing, '"The Freedom of the Streets"', pp. 134–7.

[29] GA, GDR/8, Jane Rook v Thomas Orchard (1552).

[30] HARC, HD4/2/11, Roger Prosser v Thomas Hereford (1600); HRO, 21M65/C3/2, Cecilia Howchins v Thomas White (1561); HRO, 21M65/C3/8, Anthony Dalbye v Edith Legatt (1582).

[31] DHC, Chanter 867, Elizabeth Faryes v Grace Luscombe (1618).

[32] DHC, Chanter 859, Elizabeth Lange v Hugo Hempton (1576).

[33] Flather, *Gender and Space*, p. 84; Crowley, *The Invention of Comfort*, p. 8.

in 1575, several witnesses overheard, including 20-year-old servant Joanne Edwardes, who was spinning in the entry of her master's house. Interestingly, two men (aged 19 and 30) kept her company as she laboured, although we don't know what they were doing in the entry.[34] In working alongside their neighbours, female migrant servants who held no long-term standing in the parish, established new connections and could acquire reputations as honest, creditworthy, and neighbourly (as I show in Chapter 8).

Doorways and gardens were specifically pinpointed as being on the fringes of properties. But other spaces were also contiguous to the household. In the countryside, fields and meadows adjoined the home. In towns, doors opened directly onto the street: witnesses referred to the 'streate door' of James Wood's house in the city of Bath in 1637, and Ann White clearly stepped straight out onto Winchester High Street from her home in 1572 to chide James Vibert, who stood in the street.[35] When servant Alice Davys was dusting malt in a Tewkesbury street in Gloucestershire in 1575, she was probably just outside her master's door, and the wood that Andrea Phillips of nearby Cirencester fetched from the street in 1612 was likely propped up against the house in which she served.[36]

Spaces shifted in meaning and use. But stepping outside the home into 'public' or communal spaces nonetheless represents a transition between two different (though overlapping) forms of belonging: to the household and to the neighbourhood. Neighbourhood or 'country' might be geographically larger for gentry than for ordinary people, but for all it signified collectivity and endowed members with a sense of inclusion.[37] Men and women of different sorts were found in the same communal (and private) spaces: servant Alice Kew was in the street passing by the door of Elizabeth Stringer around Easter in 1593 when she overheard Alice Wiseman accuse Elizabeth of adultery with her husband. This Gloucester street contained Anne Parker, the wife of a clothier; John Reignoldes, a cordwainer; and 'a mayde of Mr Garnas'. Anne's superior status was marked by Alice's reference to her as 'goodwyfe Parker'.[38] As Cockayne notes, 'the social classes mixed on the streets: the tattered and torn rubbed shoulders with the well-heeled rich'.[39] The street, fields, churches, alehouses, and inns rooted female servants in the disorder and discord of village and town life. Even when members were several miles from home, communities reassembled at fairs and markets, and neighbourhood squabbles played out on highways and roads. Labourer John Grene of Huntley

[34] DHC, Chanter 859, Alice Rowland v Jane Paddon (1575).
[35] SHC, D/D/cd/72, Thomas Marten v Adlie Ireland (1637); HRO, 21M65/C3/5, Ann White v Jasper Vibert (1572).
[36] GA, GDR/32, Alice Davys v Elizabeth Bundye (1575); GA, GDR/114, Elizabeth Tomes v Anne Vaughan (1612).
[37] Andy Wood, *Faith, Hope and Charity: English Neighbourhoods, 1500–1640* (Cambridge, 2020), pp. 98–100.
[38] GA, GDR/79, Alice Wiseman v Elizabeth Stringer (1593); Erickson, 'Mistresses and Marriage', 53.
[39] Cockayne, *Hubbub*, p. 159.

(Gloucestershire) was accompanying Alice Hemminge home from the city of Gloucester in 1571 when they met their servant neighbour Alice Gilman, who 'spake verye angerlye to … the saied Alyce hemynge' and called her 'an arrant whore'.[40] But communal spaces also encouraged connections, and as I argue in this chapter and Chapter 8, these spaces were equally important to female servants and their relationships.

(En)forcing hierarchies

In the relatively fluid spatial world in which early modern people lived, it's easy to picture women in service moving freely about the parish, chatting with neighbours, fellow servants, and even strangers whose paths they crossed. But other social forces were at play that erode the edges of any rosy picture of early modern life I may have painted so far. At the very least, female servants weren't expected to *belong*, they were expected to *behave*. Domestic rulers were to be as present as possible in governing servants and *control* was stressed rather than *inclusion*.[41] Servants joined the household as hired workers who were transient and only sometimes biologically related to their employers. These factors could bar them from benefitting from any sense of love or belonging the household unit offered its other members.

In a bid to separate servants from the family, servant quarters featured in late seventeenth- and eighteenth-century domestic architecture.[42] Amanda Vickery found that keys were typically held by male heads of households in Georgian England but could be entrusted to kinswomen or one reliable servant, who tightly controlled access to rooms.[43] But in Tudor and Stuart church court depositions, although keys were carefully guarded, they more often locked items into chests and coffers, rather than people from or within spaces. In most homes, female servants accessed virtually all spaces, including chambers and formal reception rooms such as parlours. I have found just one exception: in 1582, Maria Cornishe, servant to Lord and Lady Champernowne of Dartington Hall (Devon), fetched washing from Lady Roberta's chamber. This room wasn't usually closed off to Maria, but Lady Roberta was angry, reprimanding her 'for coming up there while [Christopher] Melhuish was there'.[44] Maria's access to the room was restricted

---

[40] GA, GDR/25, Alice Hemminge v Alice Gylman (1571).
[41] On this, see Hamling and Richardson, *A Day at Home*, p. 64.
[42] Mark Girouard, *Life in the English Country House: A Social and Architectural History* (1980), pp. 136–8. For alternative perspectives on shifting domestic architecture and the demand for privacy, see Meldrum, *Domestic Service and Gender*, p. 78; Amanda Vickery, *Behind Closed Doors: At Home in Georgian England* (New Haven, 2009), pp. 25–48.
[43] Vickery, *Behind Closed Doors*, pp. 43–4.
[44] DHC, Chanter 861, Gawen Champernowne v Roberta Champernowne (1582).

only when her mistress feared being caught in adultery. But while servants weren't generally barred from spaces, household order could nonetheless be displayed in other domestic practices. As this book shows, servants were hired by households across the social spectrum, and where the socio-economic gap between servant and master was greatest, household hierarchies appear more defined. One Saturday night in 1605, John Crockett arrived at the house of gentleman Matthew Berrowe of Newent (Gloucestershire), intending to visit Matthew's daughter. The household had gone to bed, so servant Eleanor Philpott 'did rise out of her bedd & did let the sayde Crockett in doors & made a fyer for him in the hall'.[45] That Eleanor arose to assist the guest displays her lowly rank within the strict hierarchy of this high-status household.

Domestic architecture, too, played an important role in defining and staging order. The family's traditional living area throughout the medieval period until the later seventeenth century was the hall.[46] In the homes of middling sorts and the gentry, halls were large and family members sat according to their position in the household hierarchy.[47] Humble dwellings, meanwhile, had either no hall or a smaller space containing a small open hearth where it's difficult to imagine such rigid practices.[48] The hall was a reception room, and female servants moved in and out, attending to employers and guests. John Hill of Wrington (Somerset) invited a small group of men and women to drink and dine in his hall after evening prayer in 1628, his servant Pricilla Gooddenow serving them.[49] Social (and spatial) distinctions are at their most stark in descriptions of servants performing tasks in the homes in which they maintained – but didn't *participate* in – the family's style of life. Pricilla experienced the hall in a different way to her master and the invited guests. Protocol for dining existed. In a 1641 case which probed the relationship between innkeeper James Napper of Castle Cary (Somerset) and his servant Grace Morgan, dining arrangements in the inn were commented upon. Yeoman John Hoddinott remarked that

> [he] sawe James Napper to sitt togeather at dinner at a table in the hall of his howse in Castle Carie … with Grace Morgan, where he sat at the higher end of the table, & in the inside of the said table next [to] the said Napper, one John Jinkyn a workman, & next [to] him one John Smith a poore boy of the howse. And in the outside of the table first the said Grace Morgan, & next [to] her a poore wentch also a servant to the said James Napper.[50]

---

[45] GA, GDR/95, Milberrowe Berrow v John Crockett (1605).
[46] Overton et al., *Production and Consumption*, pp. 127–9.
[47] Matthew Johnson, *English Houses, 1300–1800: Vernacular Architecture, Social Life* (Harlow, 2010), p. 73.
[48] Open hearths situated in the centre of the hall were gradually replaced by chimney fireplaces during the sixteenth and early seventeenth centuries. See Crowley, *The Invention of Comfort*, p. 8.
[49] SHC, D/D/cd/65, Agnes Willis v Edmund Heale (1629).
[50] SHC, D/D/cd/131, James Napper and Grace Morgan v William Chepman (1641).

The master at the head of the table with servants seated in lesser positions was a ritualised display of patriarchy. Servants shared a position in the household hierarchy with children: Elizabeth Harewood, Margaret Allen, and Catherine Baker ate breakfast with their master William Cloterbooke's children in Eastington (Gloucestershire) in 1568.[51] But in other cases, servants dined with masters but their relative positions at the table are unstated. Tailor John Kyng of Wells (Somerset) was 'accustomed to have all his house holde servants aswell maied servants as men servants sytt att his owen table'.[52] Richard Steven, Charity Wood, and Joan Wood all took supper in the hall with their mistress Agnes Kempe of Brompton Regis (Somerset) one December evening in 1631, alongside their neighbours, Andrew and Marie Hosgood.[53] Formal seating arrangements weren't always strictly adhered to in the homes of ordinary folk. Emmett Jeynes of Cheltenham (Gloucestershire), for example, ate a simple supper of bread, butter, and cheese with only her mistress when her abusive master locked away their food in 1611.[54] These were two women supporting one another in a domestic crisis; hierarchies appear absent. Practicalities such as working patterns also determined whose company servants shared while eating. Servants and workers often ate together. Casual servant Dionisia Hobbes, husbandman John Warren, and live-in servant Isott Riches stopped their harvest work in Rockbeare (Devon) in 1567 to eat bread and cheese together in the field.[55] Visiting her sister Margaret, a servant in her uncle's house, Juliana Wathen of Longney (Gloucestershire) enjoyed a posset in the company of her sister and two other servants in 1585.[56] Seated together at mealtimes, servants and other quasi-family lodging within larger homes fashioned their own sense of domestic belonging and collectivity.

Household order was to be displayed publicly. Contemporaries wrote that responsibility for the moral and religious instruction of servants lay with the household head. William Gouge stressed that

> Masters must cause their servants to go to the publike ministerie of the word, and worship of God, to be further built up thereby, and confirmed in their faith.[57]

Masters should ensure their servants attended church and received religious education, and female servants clearly participated in the rituals of religion, although as I showed in Chapter 6, high Sunday workloads could prevent their

---

[51] GA, GDR/24, Margery Cloterbooke v John Batte (1568).
[52] SHC, D/D/cd/15, John Dewe v Thomasine Kynge (1574).
[53] SHC, D/D/cd/71, Ursula Towte v Marie Hosgood (1631).
[54] GA, GDR/114, Elizabeth Mathewe v Thomas Mathewe (1611).
[55] DHC, Chanter 858, John Roo v Frances Yarde (1568).
[56] GA, GDR/57 and GDR/65, Margaret Wathen v Richard Dowdie (1585). A posset was a syllabub-like drink made from hot milk and often flavoured with sugar. See 'posset, n.', OED Online, Oxford University Press, March 2023, www.oed.com/view/Entry/148370 [accessed 4 June 2023].
[57] Gouge, *Of Domesticall Duties*, p. 667.

attendance at church. In the pages of the depositions, they are nonetheless regularly encountered in the parish church (representing *c.*11 per cent of 'other' sites). Servant Elizabeth Perrycote of Kenton (Devon) crossed paths with John Evans, his wife, and John Morrye one Sunday in 1577 as she 'was going toward the parishe churche to morning prayer'.[58] Servant Anna Ingram of Stow-on-the-Wold (Gloucestershire) recalled a notice of a new tithe owner being announced to the congregation by the parson while she was in church 'uppon a Sundaye or hollidaye att the tyme of divine service' in 1605.[59] Joan Pengelley at least attempted to 'learne the cathechisms' in the vicarage of Hatherleigh (Devon), but her efforts were impeded by the vicar, Sir Thomas Pickering, who repeatedly solicited both her and her mistress.[60] Servants Richard Steven, Charity Wood, and Joan Wood (mentioned above) of Brompton Regis (Somerset) must have been in church at some point around 1631, as Christopher Gorwood testified that he had witnessed them receiving communion.[61]

Some servants attended church with little or no coaxing. Catherine Holman regularly attended in 1615 while her master Richard Moore, the vicar of Bickleigh (Devon), was in Ireland for around three months.[62] Others indicated that church-going was a household activity. Eleanor Browne of Iron Acton (Gloucestershire) was hired in her brother's service sometime before 1604 and told the court that her 'said brother and his howshould did usually come to Yate church to heare divine servyce'.[63] Singling out her brother as household head, Eleanor implied his responsibility in ensuring his family's attendance. Roger Richardson noted that servants must have begrudged masters and mistresses who made them attend church, a resentment further fuelled by spatial segregation of servants in church.[64] Joanne Chepman of Carhampton (Somerset) attended church with her mistress, Christian Moggridge, and noted that she usually sat at the 'peewes *end*', indicating her lowly position in the church.[65] In Chirbury (Shropshire), Oliver Rudge's servants, Margaret Spake and Marie Rudge, spent three full years at the end of the sixteenth century disturbed in church by Margaret Gethin, who pushed her way into the pew, sitting on their laps and forcing them out of the seat with her elbows. A 1598 suit instigated by Oliver eventually sought to allow his servants to enjoy church in peace, although whether they wanted to be there in the first place is anyone's guess.[66]

---

[58] DHC, Chanter 859, Joanne Johns v Jacob Escourt (1577).
[59] GA, GDR/95, Edmund Chamberlen v Richard Perkes and Edward Broughton (1605).
[60] DHC, Chanter 858, Office v Thomas Pickering (1583).
[61] SHC, D/D/cd/71, Ursula Towte v Marie Hasgood (1631).
[62] DHC, Chanter 876, John Wolcombe v Richard Ashe v Collins (1615).
[63] GA, GDR/89, Thomas Baynham v David Jorden (1604).
[64] Richardson, *Household Servants*, pp. 112–13.
[65] SHC, D/D/cd/28, Christian Moggridge v Maria Washer (1606). Italics my own.
[66] HARC, HD4/2/11, Oliver Rudge v Margaret Gethin (1598).

Being liberated from attending tedious and drawn-out services could be an attractive prospect. Servant Marie Saunders of Meare (Somerset) testified in 1602 against the incumbent vicar George Calvert, who we recall from Chapter 6 preaching the same long, dull sermon each Sunday morning and evening. She complained that his preaching was incomprehensible and that despite 'sitting verie neere unto him [she] canot manye tymes understand him, althoughe she have given attentive eare unto him'.[67] For some servants, attendance at Sunday services represented an opportunity to escape the monotony of labour, while for others it placed another burden upon them on an already busy workday. But spiritual guidance may have been far from the minds of some masters and mistresses. Elizabeth Brewer of Stroud (Gloucestershire) missed the commotion in church between her mistress Jane Brewer and Alice Warner over a church pew one Sunday in 1608. She reported that Jane's legs

> were blacke & blewe in manye places & [she] complayned of the payne of her armes & sholders as beinge hurte & punched … but this deponent did not see the said defendant soe hurte beate or misuse the complaintant on the Sunday aforesaid for this deponent was not at churche that daye.[68]

Some servants were left at home to mind the house on a Sunday.[69] They couldn't always be spared, even for divine service.

Policing intimacy

For the godly, Alec Ryrie suggests that bedtime was an opportunity for privacy and private devotion.[70] But it's difficult to imagine how servants snatched either the time or space for such practice. At night, chambers and beds were shared and this was especially the case for female servants. In larger houses, chambers could be used exclusively as bedrooms, increasingly located upstairs in the seventeenth century.[71] In smaller homes, the chamber was often a multi-purpose room, but as the day came to a close, it was almost universally the site of sleep.[72] Sasha Handley noted that 'the sleeping environments of servants were heavily influenced by the wishes of their employers and by considerations of practical economy'.[73] Thirty-six

---

[67] SHC, D/D/cd/34, William Clerk v George Calvert (1602).
[68] GA, GDR/100, Jane Brewer v Alice Warner (1609).
[69] Capp, *When Gossips Meet*, p. 336.
[70] Alec Ryrie, 'Sleeping, Waking and Dreaming in Protestant Piety', in Jessica Martin and Alec Ryrie (eds), *Private and Domestic Devotion in Early Modern Britain* (2012), pp. 73–92 at 81.
[71] Johnson, *English Houses*, p. 150; Overton et al., *Production and Consumption*, p. 133.
[72] Beds were identified in virtually all chambers listed in over 8,000 Cornish and Kentish probate inventories between 1600 and 1750. See Overton et al., *Production and Consumption*, p. 133.
[73] Handley, *Sleep*, p. 119.

women in service described their regular sleeping arrangements. Twenty shared a chamber (and often a bed) with other members of the household, including fellow servants and children, while sixteen shared with their master and/or mistress. An additional four testified to sharing beds with strangers or guests temporarily accommodated within the household, indicating the relative instability of patterns of sleep for female servants. As they moved between positions in service, these women also adjusted to new bedfellows.

Bed sharing could be the most convenient arrangement in households with complex dynamics. Margaret Hawlinge of Cheltenham (Gloucestershire) probably shared a chamber with her master and mistress Thomas and Elizabeth Mathewe, deposing in 1611 that Elizabeth cried out for her in the night as her husband attempted to 'stifle her to death'.[74] In a deeply abusive relationship, Elizabeth relied on her servant's presence for protection, thereby also placing Margaret in a precarious position. In 1567, Eleanor Pallmer of Whitchurch (Hampshire) slept in the loft in a truckle bed at the foot of a bed shared by her mistress, Mrs West, and two of her children. Mr West slept downstairs in the hall.[75] Servants sometimes slept with their widowed mistresses or those estranged from their husbands. While in the service of John and Margaret Arthur of Clapton-in-Gordano (Somerset), Elizabeth Gifford shared a bed with her mistress. The couple weren't on good terms: John accused his wife of adultery and when the separation case came before the court in 1550, they no longer lived in the same house.[76]

Bed sharing was necessary in houses bursting with people, but it also operated as a system of policing. For the female servant in particular, the bedchamber was seen as a sexually charged space: adulterous or premarital affairs were ventured here. Masters and mistresses who invited their servants to share their chamber sought to regulate their behaviour. William Marks and his wife shared a chamber in their home in Stogursey (Somerset) with their servant Cecilia Baker. On New Year's Eve in 1550, Cecilia returned home from a neighbour's 'merry-making' around 11 pm with her suitor Robert Stone. It was late, and William prompted Robert to go home and ushered Cecilia to bed. Time passed, and as he and his wife lay there in the chamber, William 'marvell[ed] that [his] maide cometh not to bed'. Rising again, he found Robert and Cecilia in the next chamber. His suspicions were unfounded: the couple were doing nothing untoward, simply making a marriage contract.[77] But Cecilia's absence from the bedchamber was evidently noticed. Thomas Turner and his brother John shared a house in Bulley (Gloucestershire) in 1575. Sitting by the fire one evening, Thomas's servant, Margaret Robert, overheard John ask his own servant, Elizabeth Addys,

[74] GA, GDR/114, Elizabeth Mathewe v Thomas Mathewe (1611).
[75] HRO, 21M65/C3/4, Office v West (1567).
[76] SHC, D/D/cd/5, John Arthur v Margaret Arthur (1550).
[77] SHC, D/D/cd/5, Cecilia Baker v Robert Stone (1551).

'whether she would come to bed th[a]t night', meaning his own bed. Margaret and Elizabeth were bedfellows and when Elizabeth rose in the night (thinking Margaret was asleep), Margaret

> rose shortlie after her & lighted a chandelle [candle] & went to the chamber of the saied John Turner where she found her the saied Elizabeth Addys in bed with him the saied Turner her Mr & demanding her the saied Addys what she did there she answeared her not & she made as thoughe she had ben slepinge.

Margaret actively policed the chamber. But the next morning, after recounting the story to her fellow servants, she was beaten and chided by John, who feared his affair would be uncovered.[78] The house could be a fraught space for servants.[79]

Shared sleeping quarters could be a double-edged sword for household harmony, facilitating surveillance, but also creating conditions for marital discord. In 1618, John Reeves of East Pennard (Somerset) was accused of adultery with his servant, Priscilla Tootle. According to one witness, 'the said Reeves, his said wief & the said Prisilla did lie nyghtlie & usuallie in one & the selfe same chamber'.[80] But the wife often wasn't the only injured party. Agnes Durram of Silverton (Devon) revealed her personal battle in sharing a bed with her widowed mistress in 1596, who repeatedly allowed her lover John Hunny into the same bed. Agnes's reputation was at stake: she deposed that 'misliking with that behaviour of his, [she] did fynde faulte with him for it' as 'she was troubled three or iiii [four] tymes aboute [by] the sayde Huny'. Her strategy for navigating this difficult situation was to stake a claim on one side of the shared bed, refusing to allow John Hunny 'to goe into the bed by her but made him goe an other waye'.[81] Shared beds and rooms could heighten servant vulnerability.[82]

In a court which routinely delivered justice on cases of sexual deviance, it's interesting that female servants were implicated in illicit sex in only around 15 per cent of instances in which they were recorded in chambers. Martin Ingram suggested that illicit sex between servants and masters and other men 'in halls, *bedchambers*, barns and cowhouses' is only partially captured in church court records. Much sexual activity, he ventured, fell under the radar of neighbours and churchwardens (and, I add, masters and mistresses).[83] There may be some truth to this (and as we shall see, sex happened in other spaces). But historiographical prejudices are exposed by the many more women in service identified in chambers *policing* illicit sex. We met Alice Poyntinge of Frome (Somerset) in Chapter 6, recalling the sleeping arrangements and habits in her gentleman master

---

[78] GA, GDR/32 and GDR/45, Elizabeth Addys v John Edwardes (1576).
[79] See Capp, *When Gossips Meet*, pp. 156–7; Flather, *Gender and Space*, pp. 39–74, esp. pp. 47–9.
[80] SHC, D/D/cd/49, Office v John Reeves (1618).
[81] DHC, Chanter 864, Thomas Edbury v Joanne Callowe (1596).
[82] Laura Gowing, 'The Twinkling of a Bedstaff', *Home Cultures* 11 (2014), 275–304.
[83] Ingram, *Church Courts*, p. 259. Italics my own.

James Cottington's house. She informed on him in the church court in 1633, testifying to his incestuous affair with his sister Sara Savidge (alias Cottington). She recalled that she

> usuallie made the beds wheare they laie in, and when she soe made the said beds she playnelie perceaved that divers tymes there had two persons laine in the said James Cottingtons bedd ... wherefore this deponent veylie beleiveth in her conscience that ... the said James & his sister Sara Savidg laie togeathers in the same bedd for noe bodie else those nights laie in the said chamber but this deponent in the truckle bed.[84]

Alice lived in the house for just six weeks. As a relatively anonymous single woman living far from her Wiltshire home, she couldn't afford her reputation being spoiled by association with this household and so she left Cottington's service earlier than planned. In 1625, Joanne Jeffries of Highleadon (Gloucestershire) deposed that she often found her former master, Richard Greene, and Susan Fourd together in a chamber with the door locked.[85] Sharing the intimate space of the chamber provided female servants with knowledge of their masters' or mistresses' illicit liaisons, but the power to disseminate this information was likely constrained by their position as dependants. Church courts offered an outlet for whistleblowing on masters and mistresses but typically only after a rumour had already surfaced or (as was the case for both Alice Poyntinge and Joanne Jeffries) they had left service. Nonetheless, bedchambers were sites in which control was exercised, but not exclusively by masters and mistresses.

Servant courtship (from sex to keeping company) was of interest to householder and community alike. Diana O'Hara stressed the importance of kin and community as intermediaries in courtship and betrothals but had less to say about the role masters and mistresses played in their servants' courtship.[86] Suitors and admirers were regularly received within the household, but masters and mistresses sometimes complained about these visits. Husbandman John Huddle of Dunster (Somerset) was deeply suspicious of William Amerie's visits to his house in 1623 'to talke with and see ... Alice Nicholls [John's servant] perceavinge & ymagininge the same to bee for no good intent or purpose'.[87] Likewise, in 1567, Exeter merchant Joseph Trobridge complained that 'Daniell Jackson did much frequent [his] howse and the company of the said Elizabeth [his servant] insomuch that [he] and his wife did much dislike thereof and for that cause cheifely (because they were so togeither) ... did put her from their service'.[88] It wasn't possible to monitor servants' behaviour at all times and where freedoms weren't granted, they could be taken. Elizabeth's dismissal represents a clash between the agency she displayed

---

[84] SHC, D/D/cd/76 and D/D/cd/77, Robert Powell and Humphrey Yearburie v James Cottington (1633).

[85] GA, GDR/148, Dorothy Greene v Richard Greene (1625).

[86] On intermediaries, see O'Hara, *Courtship and Constraint*, pp. 99–121.

[87] SHC, D/D/cd/56, Office v William Amerie (1623).

[88] DHC, Chanter 866, Daniel Jackson v Elizabeth Moreton (1637).

in her courtship and her master's patriarchal rule. Her termination was ultimately a failure of patriarchal household control.

Apprehensions centred around two main concerns: labour productivity and morality. In the late 1590s, Agnes Addams of Berkley (Somerset) grew tired of Roger Addams visiting her servant Joanne Vincent so often that 'by meanes thereof she [Joanne] did neglect her busyness'.[89] Once again, permissible behaviour was calculated around the household economy. Elsewhere, household repute took centre stage: in 1608 in Down Ampney (Gloucestershire), John Blunt accused Thomas Kinge of being 'verie bolde to open his chamber dore and goe to bed to [his] mayd [Elizabeth Clerke] she beinge led in her smocke'. John was absent from his house on the night in question. An anonymous telltale had informed on Thomas and Elizabeth. But witnesses contested the report, insisting that Thomas merely came inside and lay waiting upon the bed while Elizabeth got ready to go to 'a merrie meetinge'. Thomas's presence in the space was reasonable as Elizabeth wasn't in the bed and was in her 'weareinge clothes', insisted 26-year-old Eleanor Blunt. Access to the bedchamber by those outside the household operated along gendered lines: the one or two women who invited Eleanor and Elizabeth to the 'merrie meetinge' also entered the bedchamber with no objections from John Blunt, while Thomas's presence *was* contested.[90] This was an issue of surveillance, but also reputation on both sides: John strove to protect the integrity of his home, while Thomas and Elizabeth (via witnesses) fought back to protect their reputations.

Fairs, markets, and other sociable spaces regularly hosted courting couples. O'Hara suggested that spaces of courtship 'allowed transgression, licence and experimentation', albeit within a local context of prescribed space and time.[91] We catch female servants on highways and roads, travelling to these sites of courtship. Servant Margaret Fydler of Abson (Gloucestershire), a plaintiff in a matrimonial suit, outlined her contested courtship with the defendant, William Hyll, deposing that 'they rode togeyther to Bristoll' one Saturday in 1552.[92] Markets and fairs were important nodes of interaction for members of different communities.[93] Servants John Smythe and Margaret Shawe of Winchcombe (Gloucestershire) went to a St Matthew's Day fair together in 1551 before travelling homewards, stopping off at John's father's house in Gretton where they ate and drank.[94] The bounds of community extended beyond the neighbourhood or parish: Tewkesbury, the site of the fair, wasn't far from Winchcombe (just 11 kilometres away). Their neighbours had probably made the same journey, so they were unlikely to have been anonymous

---

[89] SHC, D/D/cd/32, Joanne Vincent v Roger Addams (1602).
[90] GA, GDR/100, Thomas Kinge v John Blunte (1608).
[91] O'Hara, *Courtship and Constraint*, pp. 238–9.
[92] GA, GDR/8, Margaret Fydler v William Hyll (1552).
[93] O'Hara, *Courtship and Constraint*, p. 139.
[94] GA, GDR/8, Margaret Shawe v John Smythe (1551).

at the fair. The couple visited John's father's house afterwards on their journey home. Courtship here took place under the observation and monitoring of both kin and community.

But surveillance could be evaded, especially outside the home. The fair was just one site where servant Isott Riches of Rockbeare (Devon) met gentleman Frances Yarde, the reputed father of her illegitimate child. Katherine Brooke recalled being told by her brother, Doctor Gammon (Isott's master), in 1568 that he suspected Frances and Isott's misbehaviour and had warned Frances that he would 'prove you have ben in other places [in] the citie [Exeter] in Isottes companye'. Frances responded

> never ... but ones [once] at the fayre I mett her and hobbes wiff with her and willed them to come to Stephyns howse to geve her a quart of wyne unto the which place she and hobbes is [his] wiff came in thafter noone.[95]

The testimony of Isott's fellow servant, Dionisia Hobbes (referred to by Frances as 'hobbes wiff'), confirmed that she and Isott had been in Exeter on an errand before they took a detour to 'Stephyns howse' and the fair. Busy masters couldn't always track their servants' movements, especially beyond the neighbourhood. As a migrant servant, Isott also doesn't appear to have had a local kin network to bolster surveillance. Keeping tabs on her wasn't easy.

The depositions from Isott's case tell us what her master may not have known. We follow Isott's courtship to a site closer to home. Witnesses deposed that Isott and Frances spent an hour and a half sitting under a bush in a meadow near the vicarage where she worked. Fields were sites of work and play for women in service, representing 14 per cent of all 'other' spaces recorded. Although fields could be isolated spots, the couple's privacy here was limited; accompanying Isott was Margaret Martyn, who acted as chaperone. Her testimony insists that she 'removed herself from them by the space of 12 paces or ther about', remaining within sight and earshot. When pressed further, she denied the couple had had intercourse, deposing only that she occasionally saw Isott sitting on Frances's knee or between his legs.[96] By remaining in the meadow, Margaret monitored the behaviour that was possible within it.

But fields and meadows could be secluded. In seventeenth-century London, fields were situated on the outskirts of the city, offering relative privacy to poor pregnant women who were 'excluded from the civilising rituals of birth' within the city walls.[97] Illicit sex took place in these semi-private spaces.[98] In rural hamlets and villages, fields were often distant enough from homes, streets, and other

---

[95] DHC, Chanter 858, John Roo v Frances Yarde (1568).
[96] DHC, Chanter 858, John Roo v Frances Yarde (1568).
[97] Gowing, *Common Bodies*, p. 151.
[98] Gowing, '"The Freedom of the Streets"', p. 144.

communal areas. In 1551, Alice Lymbroke of Upton St Leonards (Gloucestershire) was spotted with her master John Hughes in 'a medowe' where she was heard to euphemistically say 'that a thorne did prick her buttock'.[99] Thomas King of Brockley (Somerset) was spotted with his servant Marie Comer in 1623 in a meadow 'neere a haie reeke tumbling and kisseing eache other'.[100] The home clearly wasn't always a private enough space for these master–servant relations. The cover of night, the remoteness, and the emptiness of fields, defended against watchful eyes. In 1556, servant Thomasina Floode of Farway (Devon) testified of a series of sexual encounters in fields near her master's house with several men, including his son, John Coxe, who 'had her in a close … within the nyght this last somer'.[101] These same attributes, however, made fields and meadows unsafe spaces. In Chapter 6, I showed that servants working in these spaces, away from the household at quiet times of the day, could be left defenceless against abuse. Elizabeth Aishman of Wells (Somerset) was milking her master's cows early one October morning in 1635 when George Cooke attempted to rape her in the common.[102] Sadly, she wasn't alone in experiencing vulnerability in this space. Isott Stoane of Walton (Somerset), Marie Allone (alias Smith) of Lottisham (also Somerset), and Elizabeth Kneebone of Saltash (Cornwall), all gave similar accounts of sexual attacks in or nearby the fields in which they milked cows early in the morning.[103] Their tragic narratives record some crying out for help – only sometimes with success in the early hours – and others using all their strength to escape. The appalling consequences of sexually abusive masters and other men preying on these women who were left alone and unsupervised to carry out their work are stark in their depositions.

Discipline and labour

In many homes, the rhythms and requirements of the household economy were as influential in shaping the governance of servants as was the moralistic agendas of their masters and mistresses. As Chapter 6 shows, sometimes masters and servants worked together. In 1576, Edith Gibbens described helping her master sow and turn peas in a close in Clatford (Hampshire).[104] Supervision and direct control accompanies collaborative working, but on a practical level, some

---

[99] GA, GDR/8, Office v John Hughes (1551).
[100] SHC, D/D/cd/58, Office v Thomas King (1623).
[101] DHC, Chanter 855, Office v Thomasina Floode (1556).
[102] SHC, D/D/cd/78, Office v George Cooke (1635).
[103] SHC, D/D/cd/66, Office v Robert England (1631); SHC, D/D/cd/34, Office v Thomas Hellier (1602); DHC, Chanter 861, Sampson Rawlye v Elizabeth Kneebone (1583).
[104] HRO, 21M65/C3/7, Gatenbye v Twyne (1576).

freedoms had to be granted as round-the-clock surveillance of labour and behaviour was impossible. For the most part, trust and a mutually understood rubric of expectations must have existed between masters and servants. Even within the home, their labour wasn't always monitored and sometimes masters and mistresses were entirely absent. In 1615, gentleman George Bannister of Turkdean (Gloucestershire) spent Christmas in Northamptonshire with his family, leaving 'Elizabeth Gawen amongest other his servants to attend his busines and kepe his howse till his retorne'.[105] The household was entrusted to the servants, although it's not clear whether there was an established hierarchy among them. In some households, female servants could be placed in complete charge: in 1577, John Edwardes of Thornbury (Gloucestershire) deposed that he put his servant Margery Carter 'in truste with all the charge of his howse above her felloes'.[106]

As they moved further from the household, female servants were less likely to be accompanied by their masters or mistresses (see Table 7.3). But the extent to which the *conceptual* authority of the household head governed the behaviour of his or her servants is more difficult to establish and trace across spaces. Depositions hand us a couple of rare glimpses. Alice Gilbert of Winchester (Hampshire) was weeding her master's garden with two young men in 1597 when one of her co-workers sought to incriminate her in an illicit affair. Annoyed, Alice 'went owt of the garden & wold work no longer'.[107] No watchful eyes were upon her in this liminal space on the periphery of the home. Alice's refusal to continue weeding went unchecked and she clearly felt at liberty to select her own working pattern. But in 1587, Sybil Castle (alias Salter) of Bromsberrow (Gloucestershire) deposed that she washed clothes in the brook 'not farre from her Mr ... his howse'. The servant-master/mistress household was of significance even outside its doors, imposing upon Sybil's perception of the brook.[108] Spaces outside the home could offer some servants a brief escape from patriarchal control, but the bond of labour was never entirely absent. When women in service left the bounds of their masters' homes and grounds, they were out of their sight and earshot, but not wholly free.

The psychological control a household head held over his servant could extend beyond the boundary of his household, but physical correction rarely spilled outside this space. Andy Wood noted that violent male patriarchs could be 'seen as problematic members of the neighbourhood'.[109] But when violent 'discipline' was contained within the four walls of the home, outside intervention was exercised with caution. For at least the last six months of her five-year marriage, Susan Hartwell of Bishop's Tawton (Devon) was abused by her husband Henry.

---

[105] GA, GDR/122, Robert Payne v Elizabeth Gawen (1615).
[106] GA, GDR/46, Margery Carter v John Edwardes (1577).
[107] HRO, 21M65/C3/11, John Bragg v Moya Simpson (1597).
[108] GA, GDR/65, Sybil Stone v Anne Webb (1587).
[109] Wood, *Faith, Hope and Charity*, pp. 151–2.

In 1615, she sought separation in the church court, calling witnesses – including several female servants – to testify to the breakdown of the marriage. Michael Hilwaye lived just 40 feet from the Hartwell's house and testified that three months earlier, he heard 'som blowes', heard Henry call his wife 'drunken whore', heard Susan 'crie oute', and finally heard Henry call for his sword. Salame Freynes, the Hartwell's servant, fled to Michael's house 'with her hedd bloodye, and sayd that her Mr had broken her hedd' and that she feared for her mistress. But Michael didn't intervene at this point and Salame returned to the Hartwell's house.[110]

Violence within the family often remained behind closed doors. While neighbours regularly chastised scolding wives and blew the whistle on cuckoldry, domestic violence was a stickier subject. Correction was a facet of the patriarchal household: so at what point should neighbours intervene in another man's home life? In 1558, Thomas Langdon of Exminster (Devon) appeared before the Exeter church court, charged with the abuse of his female servant in the house of John Bond. Responding to the charge, Thomas admitted that he went to John Bond's house to 'fetche home' his servant who had run away. She had left after he had given her

> two or three strypes with a lether halter. And fydning her in the said Bondes howse gave her 2 or 3 stripes with a whyte rodde which [… he] had in his hand … And willed her to gett her home again to [his] howse.[111]

Thomas's abuse of his servant was extreme. But to early modern eyes, it was also inappropriate. Conduct literature advised masters to discipline male servants, and mistresses to correct female servants: John Dod and Robert Cleaver specified that a master shouldn't 'meddle with the punishing or chastising of the maide-servants'.[112] But it was the spatial impropriety of Thomas's 'correction' that led to his indictment. Emerging from a chamber in the same house, the local priest chastised Thomas, saying 'you ar to blayme, to beat your servant *in a nother man's howse*'.[113] It was the location of the abuse that the priest took issue with, not the abuse itself. By beating his servant in John Bond's house, Thomas undermined John's authority within his own patriarchal principality.

Neighbours' homes evidently offered ill-treated servants a refuge, particularly at times of crisis. We already met Joanne Sybly of St Germans (Cornwall), who found shelter at William Geyke's house following a heated exchange with her mistress, who refused to let her stay even one night past the end of her covenant.[114] Connections outside the household could be vital when servants were placed in precarious positions, yet forging relationships with neighbours might not be easy.

---

[110] DHC, Chanter 867, Susan Hartwell v Henry Hartwell (1615).
[111] DHC, Chanter 855, Office v Thomas Langdon (1558).
[112] Dod and Cleaver, *A Godlie Forme of Householde Government*, pp. 378.
[113] DHC, Chanter 855, Office v Thomas Langdon (1558). Italics my own.
[114] DHC, Chanter 858, Joanne Sybly v Thomas John (1574).

While going about their work, servants weren't expected to linger in other people's homes. In 1575, William Stubbe testified against Cheltenham (Gloucestershire) servant Alice Hunte, who turned up at his house on an errand and began 'complayning yt she could not have libertye to goe abroad at her pleasure'. Apparently undeterred, she lingered until William warned her that her mistress 'would checke [rebuke her] for staying longe uppon a message'. Seemingly irritated, she then accused her mistress of adultery, although it seems that her curtailed freedom was at the heart of this servant–mistress clash. Such episodes must have represented a crisis point in servant–master or mistress relations: this was a breakdown of social relations (as in other defamation cases) but also a collapse of a labour agreement. By the time William testified in court, Alice had left or been dismissed from her mistress's service. Despite William's testimony against her, Alice nonetheless perceived his home as a site in which she could share her frustrations.[115] She wasn't the only servant to undermine the patriarchal rule of the household by carrying tales and gossip to other homes. In 1571, Anne Jacob, also of Cheltenham (Gloucestershire), went door to door telling her neighbours that her master 'kepith Alice Clerk as commonly as he doth his wyf'.[116] These were deeply damaging words, and as Bernard Capp noted, 'knowledge of the family's private concerns gave servants a powerful weapon'.[117] Most importantly, the words demonstrate connections with other households forged out of sight and earshot of masters and mistresses.

Conclusion

If we study women in service solely within the context of the home and its oppressive patriarchal structure, it's inevitable that a depressing tale emerges. Within scholarship of service, servant vulnerability to sexual abuse looms large, as do the countless tales of servant pregnancy outside wedlock. These accounts are of course important in the history of service, but they mask a variety of experiences and create the misleading impression that all or most female servants were submissive victims of an oppressive household patriarchal regime. It isn't my intention to propose that household patriarchy didn't exist or couldn't be pervasive and oppressive for some women. This was surely the case. However, we need to shape our understanding of early modern female service around evidence not just of the scandalous or immoral, but also of quotidian practices. Female servants spent as much time beyond the home as within it. The home was an important site in which female servants worked and lived. But it wasn't the only site. Other households offered opportunities for sociability with the wider community and

---

[115] GA, GDR/32, Jane Sherford v Alice Hunte (1575).
[116] GA, GDR/25, Alice Clerck v Anne Jacob (1571).
[117] Capp, *When Gossips Meet*, p. 170.

could act as surrogate homes for female servants when relations with those who employed them became frayed. The high mobility experienced by these women on a local level as they travelled between parishes provides further evidence that characterisation of the female servant as 'domestic' is anachronistic and misleading.

The control of a master or mistress was contingent upon the requirements of labour within the household as well as on surveillance. Both within and beyond the home, opportunities for women in service to establish friendships independent of the household family and to exchange news and gossip were abundant. At times, the absence of masters and mistresses gave these women the freedom to pursue their own agendas. Importantly, household patriarchy wasn't the only social system that monitored and regulated servant behaviour; neighbours could be equally influential (as the next chapter will explore in more detail). While servants might be monitored, they too policed spaces in which miscreant behaviour might take place, monitoring the bedchamber, for example, as often as their contemporaries.

Power and patriarchal order could be performed in the household through formal dining seating, discipline, and correction. But this operated with flexibility and there were always opportunities to escape the gaze of masters and mistresses. Tracing the paths that servants took around their masters' homes and beyond doesn't always lead to a reconstruction of the footprints of labour. Nor do we find female servants living a shadowy existence, at the edges of rooms or on the fringes of sociability. For long-term servants, the household must have come to feel like home. Freedom to invite company – including male suitors – into the household indicates a sense of belonging, albeit negotiated. But inclusion was experienced in other forums, too – in sociability that took place in homes, churchyards, and the streets.

When Alice Butler spoke the words 'the servant hath the name, but the master had the game', William Locksmith rallied the support of his community. Their depositions against Alice's defamatory words sought to impose order on this unruly servant. At the same time, her position in service was irrelevant: none of the witnesses noted that she was a servant until explicitly asked by the court where she lived. In fact, only one witness responded that she was a servant to a Gloucester alderman and lived in the parish of St John the Baptist (other witnesses gave only her parish of residence with no other details).[118] When outside the household and sharing communal space with their neighbours, servants weren't just servants – they were part of the community. And even when they were brought to court for defamation or other misdemeanours, they played an active and individual role in community life. By casting our nets beyond the household, we capture a broader range of female servant interactions, friendships, and experiences, which are explored further in Chapter 8.

---

[118] GA, GDR/95, William Locksmith v Alice Butler (1605).

Chapter 8

Neighbours and Networks

Marie Robins was no stranger to moving. At the turn of the seventeenth century, she'd lodged in Richard Barry's house in Ditcheat in Somerset. He was a husbandman and she'd taught his children to knit, staying for three years. She'd briefly returned home to her mother in Shepton Mallett before finding work in Elizabeth and James Pippett's home in Evercreech for about a year. She packed up her things again and moved just up the road to Stoney Stratton, serving Thomas Clarke for a year and a half. She was no longer the 'knittester' that had found work with Richard Barry's family.

Marie's was an itinerant life, but her footsteps padded across familiar ground. Her movements were local, allowing her life to become entwined with John Sheppard's: they went to revels together, he accompanied her in the fields early in the morning and late at night while she milked the cows, and they exchanged gifts. Despite their protestations, Marie even briefly abandoned working in the Pippetts' home to tend to John's mother while she lay sick. Her neighbours were certain the pair would marry. But then John disappeared – evading a debt or a marriage to her, Marie wasn't sure. In his absence, she fell sick for eight weeks and in June 1609 complained to the Bath & Wells church court that he had broken his promise of marriage.[1]

* * *

Service was just one of several occupations Marie undertook as a young woman. She taught children to knit and may also have spent much of her time knitting in the Pippett's household. Here, she was a woman of relative independence, able to build and maintain networks and social contacts as she saw fit. When John came to Elizabeth Pippett's house requesting Marie's help in tending his mother, she told him 'they could not spare her'. But the next morning, she left anyway and stayed

---

[1] SHC, D/D/cd/41, Marie Robins v John Sheppard (1609).

away for a month. The freedoms that Marie enjoyed as a knitster were reduced when she entered service. Maintaining the relationships she'd built across place over time now required negotiation with her master, Thomas Clarke.

Over five years, Marie lived in four different houses, embedding herself in close but disparate communities. It was from these communities that she assembled her witnesses. Elizabeth Pippett deposed that she and Marie had knitted John Sheppard a pair of yarn stockings as a token of matrimony. Thomas Clarke described the couple's courtship: John had regularly come to the house and had asked Thomas's permission to 'suffer' Marie to visit his family and accompany him at feasts and festivities, which Thomas 'grannted'. Joanna Pellye, a neighbour to Marie's mother, recalled Marie giving John 'a paire of garters & a handkercher, which he tooke verie thankfully of hir, and he gave unto her a musk balle'.[2] She remembered them drinking together in alehouses and agreed that the 'neighbors of the saide Marie Robins and her mother … tooke notice of their conversing & companyeing togethers to be a couple that meant marriage togethers'.

The navigation of social relationships that we observe in Marie's story was familiar to virtually all women in service. As society's most itinerant, female servants regularly engaged with a scale of community larger than was common. When leaving a household and moving to another parish, they left behind *people* and *communities*, as well as intricate networks of friendship, sociability, neighbourliness, and support. Physical departure undoubtedly destabilised connections, but emotional bonds, attachments, and friendships weren't altogether lost. Andy Wood argued that neighbourliness was predicated on 'having a sense of place, defined by Christian morality, long residence, common association, credit, trustworthiness and communal entitlement'.[3] Was it possible to be a good neighbour if you were a servant? If belonging was achieved through the status acquired by long residence in a place, how did female servants gain a sense of belonging without such a foothold? The transient, low-status servant appears to be the antithesis of Wood's definition of a good neighbour. But Marie Robins retained – and could therefore mobilise – connections forged across space and time.

The household looms large in scholarship on service while the servant's place within community is routinely overlooked. Part of the problem is that 'community' is regularly rooted in the parish or village, spaces in which female servants are only seen as a fleeting presence. This mobility, coupled with perceptions of their low status, precluded their inclusion in 'community'. These sets of assumptions

---

[2] Musk balls were used to perfume clothes. See Susan North, *Sweet and Clean? Bodies and Clothes in Early Modern England* (Oxford, 2020), p. 266.
[3] Wood, *Faith, Hope and Charity*, p. 199.

rest partly on the theory that pre-industrial communities were a web of extremely local ties. In the sixteenth and seventeenth centuries, 'community' was inward-looking, geographically located in self-supporting settlements, and only gave way to the modern concept 'society' when kinship links were broken by industrialisation, urbanisation, and centralisation.[4] Early modern villages were 'isolated' and assumed to display little evidence of the interconnectivity identified in Chapter 4.[5]

The problems of the teleological theory of social structure in which we moved from community (*Gemeinschaft*) to society (*Gesellschaft*) have been thoroughly laid bare.[6] Institutions such as courts, for instance, were part of a national machinery of justice in medieval England, and men and women participated in legal processes and pursued suits outside their localities.[7] The rose-tinted depiction of medieval village life, organised around the principles of *Gemeinschaft*, ignores myriad ways in which people's lives spilled beyond parish boundaries in pre-modern England.[8] Certainly, for many early modern people, the village or the parish was 'the relevant social system'.[9] But community is not always coterminous with place.[10] Community is created through economic ties, emotional bonds, cultural or religious contacts, and shared friendship groups. The social, political, economic, and religious networks that people belonged to could – and did – lie outside their parish of residence. As Alan Macfarlane warned, '"community" may be geographically based or it may not … it may be mistaken to demarcate the area of interest on the basis of physical space'.[11] Inclusion wasn't always geographically defined: not all parishioners were members of a community and not all members of a community lived in the same parish.

Female service is an opportune lens through which to study the ways in which communities intersected and extended over parish boundaries. Picking up the

---

[4] On the transition from community (*Gemeinschaft*) to society (*Gesellschaft*), see Ferdinand Tönnies, *Community and Association: Gemeinschaft und Gesellschaft* (London, 1887). On the movement from localism to centralisation, see Lawrence Stone, *The Family, Sex and Marriage in England 1500–1800* (1977), pp. 123–50; Keith Thomas, *Religion and the Decline of Magic: Studies in Popular Beliefs in Sixteenth- and Seventeenth-Century England* (Harmondsworth, 1991), p. 672; David Underdown, *Revel, Riot and Rebellion: Popular Politics and Culture in England 1603–1660* (Oxford, 1985), pp. 17–18.

[5] G. E. Fussell and K. R. Fussell, *The English Countrywoman: A Farmhouse Social History: The Internal Aspect of Rural Life AD 1500–1900* (London, 1953), p. 17.

[6] See, for example, Alan Macfarlane, 'History, Anthropology and the Study of Communities', *Social History* 2 (1977), 631–52 at 631.

[7] Richard Smith, '"Modernisation" and the Corporate Medieval Village Community in England: Some Sceptical Reflections', in A. R. H. Baker and D. Gregory (eds), *Explorations in Historical Geography: Interpretative Essays* (Cambridge, 1984), pp. 140–80 at 176.

[8] Alexandra Shepard and Phil J. Withington, 'Introduction: Communities in Early Modern England', in Alexandra Shepard and Phil J. Withington (eds), *Communities in Early Modern England: Networks, Place, Rhetoric* (Manchester, 2000), pp. 1–15 at 4–5. I am currently working on a project titled 'Everyday Travel and Communities in Early Modern England' which uncovers extra-parochial networks and ties.

[9] Thomas Hylland Eriksen, *Small Places, Large Issues: An Introduction to Social and Cultural Anthropology* (2015), p. 103.

[10] Doreen Massey, 'A Global Sense of Place', *Marxism Today* (June 1991), 24.

[11] Macfarlane, 'History, Anthropology and the Study of Communities', 633.

thread from Chapter 4 on servant mobility, this chapter unpicks ideas of belonging and inclusion. Studying the connections that these highly mobile women forged challenges the idea that long-term residence and status were the linchpins of early modern community. Sustained relationships (both good and bad) and evidence of integration – or exclusion – routinely appear and are often discussed at length in church court depositions. The ways in which relationships were articulated varied, allowing multiple points of entry into the nebulous and often slippery concepts of community and belonging. We can look at *whom* female servants talked about and shared spaces with, but we can also look at *how* female servants were referred to by others.

The chapter first focuses on the range of people with whom female servants came into contact and how their relationships with others were represented in depositions. I show the embeddedness of female servants in communities: the connections they described were as long-standing as those of other witnesses. The chapter also shows that servants nurtured friendships (taken to mean both support networks and companionship and sociability). In particular, I shine light on the support others, especially women, offered servants both within and beyond the home. Female servants retained connections *after* leaving a parish, demonstrating that community extended beyond the geographical and administrative boundaries of settlement. They might leverage support from former masters and mistresses, but the lingering spectre of obligation and gratitude of service could also entrench them in unwanted relationships. The final section traces the idea of reputation across parish boundaries. Maintaining a good reputation is seen as key to a successful adult life, and service was to function as a regulating institution. For those whose reputation was less than wholesome, anonymity was surely to be strived for. The chapter shows that in rural society, rumours travelled and severing connections proved difficult. Taken as a whole, the chapter addresses the absence of female servants in histories of early modern community and establishes their place within it.

Familiarity and acquaintance

With whom did female servants interact? Ilana Krausman Ben-Amos observed that those with the most 'direct effect' on young people weren't other young people, their parents, or masters, but

> a host of other people, mostly adults – a neighbour, a 'poor man' who came to the house, 'many people' and 'godly people' in or around the village or town … travelling preachers, godly ministers, and women and men a youth encountered at the local inn, or in his master's shop.[12]

---

[12] Ben-Amos, *Adolescence and Youth*, p. 188.

We've traced the footsteps of many women in service already and seen their mobility within and beyond the parish. But they didn't have to leave home to encounter people. Networks of economic and social exchange brought people to even the most isolated farmsteads. But how well did servants know the people they shared spaces with and vice versa? In some houses, turnover was regular, and even servants could change on a weekly basis. One way to test how well female servants were known by those around them is to look at how they were referred to. What was in a name? Maryanne Kowaleski found medieval servants listed only by their first name and their master's name in the Exeter mayor's court rolls, taking this as indicative of their low status.[13] Jeremy Goldberg argued that an unrecorded surname denoted youth rather than low status.[14] Laura Gowing noted that 'the goodness of a woman's name was contingent on not being spoken of at all – a good name meant no name'.[15] But being referred to by name *was* a marker of inclusion.

Acquaintances

Some female servants were referred to only as 'maid' or 'servant'. In 1582, witness Roger Over of Blisland (Cornwall) deposed that upon 'Easter Eave last past there came a woeman servant to the parsonadge house of Blisland and enquired for Mr parson of Blisland'.[16] Others recalled the servant's first name but gave no surname. Juliana Ware of Driffield (Gloucestershire) deposed in 1587 'that William Hawkins … begot his servant with child whose name was Jane aboute fower yeres agoe'.[17] Often, a missing surname *was* indicative of it not being known; after all, the overwhelming majority of men and women mentioned by deponents were given full names. But it wasn't always the case that the name wasn't known. Elizabeth Savory of Brilley (Herefordshire) pointed out in 1599 that Sybil Bevor (alias Bowen) 'did browe [borrow] of *this examinates maid servant* divers tymes a gowen and a hatt'.[18] It seems unlikely that Elizabeth didn't know the name of her own servant.

Some servants were given no name but a collective identity. Individual servants became anonymous when referred to as part of a group. George Parlor of Newent (Gloucestershire) deposed in 1603 that he heard Anne Harrys call Dorothy Wylson 'a druncken sott, a druncken sockett, and druncken pissepott' in the presence of 'Mrs Suckliffes three maides'.[19] Arthur Rowe of Lamerton (Devon)

---

[13] Maryanne Kowaleski, *Local Markets and Regional Trade in Medieval Exeter* (Cambridge, 1995), p. 169.

[14] Goldberg, *Women, Work and Life Cycle*, p. 181.

[15] Gowing, *Domestic Dangers*, p. 270.

[16] DHC, Chanter 861, John Trelawny v Thomas Robyns (1582).

[17] GA, GDR/65, Thomas Iles v Joanne Addams (1587).

[18] HARC, HD4/2/11, Thomas Hereford v Ann Vaughen (1699). Italics my own.

[19] GA, GDR/90, Dorothy Wylson v Anne Harrys (1603).

heard defamatory remarks made in 1618 by Robert Wills against Elizabeth Drake, 'present also then and there two maydes of … Peter Russells house'.[20] Children were often treated similarly and were rarely referred to by their full names: in 1593, servant Bridget Verne of Churcham (Gloucestershire) noted that 'two little children under eyghte yeares of age' were present when Richard Hammons defamed Eleanor Everett.[21] Alice Combe of Chudleigh (Devon) deposed in 1598 that 'it was reported that Pentecoste Balls mayde had beaten Jane Everies children'.[22] Youth – and the dependency that came with it – could determine how groups of servants were perceived and consequently referred to. As a group, female servants could therefore be infantilised, sometimes losing the identity that a name could give them.

Routinely, female servants who were given only first names were talked about in the context of premarital sex or pregnancy. Sexual misdemeanours and subsequent pregnancies were discussed by witnesses in relation to three otherwise unidentified servants named Abigail, Jane, and Eleanor.[23] Reducing a female servant to her first name – or sometimes even no name – subtly conveyed contemporary judgements of sexually deviant women. In 1591, witness Walter Bicklesse of Cirencester (Gloucestershire) believed that 'John Havland had a bastard by his servant and that the same was conveyed by him into Oxfordshyre or Barkshire'.[24] Others may have deliberately referred to a female servant only by her first name either to protect her identity or to protect themselves from being accused of defamation. Accusations of illegitimate pregnancy frequently resulted in church court litigation. The unknown name of the servant also delimited the witness's relationship to her, bereft of any emotional attachment, or social or economic connection. An otherwise inconspicuous female servant could feature as a topic of news or gossip if she fell pregnant outside wedlock. Yeoman John Goodwyne of Berkeley (Gloucestershire) deposed in 1613 that Robert Lawford's servant 'Jone' was pregnant before she was married, although, he added, 'by whome this respondent knoweth not *nor never heard*'.[25] Yeoman's wife Mary Gearinge, of Lechlade in the same county, deposed in 1628 that William Phippes's servant Abigail

> was begotten with child when she lived with the said Mr Phippes but never heard the said Mr Phippes suspected to be the father thereof but hath heard that one Roberte Butcher alias Joy was the father thereof but whether the said Abigall was ever punished for the same she knoweth not.[26]

[20] DHC, Chanter 867, Elizabeth Drake v Robert Wills (1618).
[21] GA, GDR/79, Eleanor Everett v Richard Hammons (1593).
[22] DHC, Chanter 864, Jane Iverye v Pentecost Ball and Andrew Fole (1598).
[23] GA, GDR/168, William Phippes v Anne Gearinge (1628); GDR/121, Office v William Hall (1613); DHC, Chanter 856 and 857, Henry Dugdale v Margaret Tudde (1564).
[24] GA, GDR/65, John Haveland v Anthony Hungerford (1591).
[25] GA, GDR/121, Office v William Hall (1613). Italics my own.
[26] GA, GDR/168, William Phippes v Anne Gearinge (128). Italics my own.

Although Abigail was referred to only by her first name, this was a story Mary had clearly been following. As Adam Fox noted, 'behind any tale told to the authorities of church and state was this undercurrent and atmosphere of public gossip'.[27] News of behaviour that conflicted with the norms of an ordered society thrived in the early modern village or town and, as we'll see, was transmitted from place to place. Here, the communities in which the servant and witness lived overlapped slightly, but they weren't one and the same. It is important to remember, however, that these unnamed or partially named women were the exception. Of 1,871 witnesses that referred to one or more female servants, only 143 (slightly under 8 per cent) *didn't* provide their full names. Most female servants were known by both first name and surname. They became familiar faces within the communities in which they lived and beyond.

Familiars

Familiarity between servants and the wider community can be studied by another measure. When deposing in court, witnesses were routinely asked how well and for how long they had known the litigant parties. Their responses were recorded in the biographical preambles to their depositions. Responses to this question have received little attention, yet systematic analysis of these responses illuminates the connections that existed between litigants and female servant witnesses.[28] Some witnesses were specific, stating the length of time they had known the litigant. In church court depositions, this was routinely given in years rather than from a certain age. John Hopkins, 33, of Wedmore (Somerset), for example, testified in a defamation dispute between Agnes Russe and Robert Hole in 1626. He told the court that he had known Agnes and Robert for five and three years respectively.[29]

Others reported they had known a litigant since childhood or birth; indicating lifelong familiarity. As witnesses varied in age, comparison of the length of time they had known a litigant is meaningless unless expressed as a proportion of their age (and therefore lifetime); these calculations are shown in Table 8.1. The phrase 'knows the parties well' was sometimes recorded as a response, which is not possible to quantify as what constituted 'knowing someone well' is subjective. But by stating familiarity with a plaintiff or defendant, female servants signified a sense of inclusion within a community. Elizabeth Owyn of Gloucester deposed in 1573 that she knew the parties Elizabeth Mason and John Perkins well. She was the servant of William Braford, a shop-owner in the city, and she had worked there for a

---

[27] Adam Fox, 'Rumour, News and Popular Political Opinion in Elizabethan and Early Stuart England', *The Historical Journal* 40 (1997), 597–620 at 601.

[28] Andy Wood refers to these responses in secular courts, but otherwise little mention of them has been made. See Wood, *Memory of the People*, p. 35.

[29] SHC, D/D/cd/51, Agnes Russe v Robert Hole (1626).

Percentage of lifetime	F				M				Female servants			
	Plaintiff		Defendant		Plaintiff		Defendant		Plaintiff		Defendant	
	N	*%*	*N*	*%*	*N*	*%*	*N*	*%*	*N*	*%*	*N*	*%*
Doesn't know them	59	*5*	33	*2*	265	*4*	310	*4*	15	*8*	6	*3*
≤ 25	540	*42*	673	*48*	3,004	*42*	3,425	*44*	90	*50*	108	*56*
> 25 – ≤ 50	329	*26*	362	*26*	2,062	*29*	2,139	*28*	40	*22*	40	*21*
> 50 – ≤ 75	113	*9*	119	*8*	771	*11*	769	*10*	13	*7*	18	*9*
> 75 – ≤ 100	230	*18*	217	*15*	1,119	*15*	1,106	*14*	23	*13*	20	*10*
Total	**1,271**	—	**1,404**	—	**7,221**	—	**7,749**	—	**181**	—	**192**	—

Table 8.1 Proportion of lifetime that female, male, and female servant witnesses had known the litigant parties

year and a half, having previously lived and worked nearby in the Crypt School in Gloucester. She perceived herself sufficiently integrated within the community to comment on Elizabeth's reputation, deposing that the words spoken by John were 'not of suche credit that they have hurte hir good name but … words of slander may deminishe & take awey hir good name which shee hayth not deservyd'.[30]

Witnesses rarely stated that they didn't know the defending parties at all. Less than 5 per cent of men and women didn't know the plaintiff or defendant, and this figure was only slightly higher for female servants (8 per cent). The similarity between female servants and male and female witnesses in their familiarity with litigants is striking. Somewhere between 40 and 50 per cent of men and women had known the plaintiff or defendant for less than a quarter of their lives. Although 80 per cent of female servants had moved in their lifetimes compared with 63 per cent of all witnesses, their itineracy did not significantly affect their familiarity with litigants. Fifty per cent had known plaintiffs and 56 per cent had known defendants for this same proportion of their lives. The average age of these female servants was 26, meaning that this group had typically known the parties for six or seven years. Female servants are seen as highly mobile, spending one year in service at a time. Yet roughly 40 per cent had known the litigants for more than a quarter of their lives, and almost 20 per cent of them for over half their lives. This is surprisingly high and shows a connectedness to people and communities that we might not expect.

Mobility, age, and the type of dispute work together to offer a partial explanation for the length of time witnesses had known litigants. Tithe and testamentary disputes which relied on knowledge of parish customs, or a will made many years

---

[30] GA, GDR/32, Elizabeth Mason v John Perkins (1573).

earlier, also brought in witnesses that had long-established connections with the plaintiff or defendant. Migration patterns also account for long-resident witnesses being called to testify. Alice Blackaller of Dartington (Devon) deposed in 1582 that she had lived in the parish for just one year and knew the parties (her master and mistress, Lord and Lady Champernowne) for the same amount of time. Alice's short-term residence in Dartington alongside the couple's elevated social status meant that Alice, a servant whose work repertoire included washing laundry, was unlikely to have crossed paths with them before she joined the household.[31] But connections between female servants and others sometimes pre-dated their co-residence in a parish. This was partly because they had connections beyond their parish of residence. But it was also because they weren't the only moving parts. Servant Honor Drynford was a lifelong resident of Sheepwash (Devon). In 1583, she had known Anne Hayne since infancy and Mary Scam for twelve years. At the age of 22, her familiarity with Mary for twelve years indicates her earliest memory of her was at the age of 10. It's likely that Mary, a married woman, had moved to the parish herself twelve years earlier (perhaps when she married).[32]

Networks were sometimes complex. Servant Alice Rowland of Shebbear (Devon) brought a defamation suit against Jane Paddon in 1575. Three witnesses testified on her behalf that Jane had called her 'an arrante whore and a copper nosed drak[e]'. Alice's fellow servant Joanne Edwardes had lived in Shebbear her whole life but had known Alice for just one year, indicating Alice had only recently moved to the parish. Meanwhile, Joanne had known Jane since infancy. The other two witnesses, Richard Norryce and Henry Rackclief, had known Alice for longer. Richard was the master of Henry, Joanne, and Alice. He deposed that Alice 'hathe dwelte in [his] house this xii [12] monethes'. Alice's relationships with Joanne and Richard were clearly created through co-residence in the same household. Henry, however, had lived in Shebbear for just six months but had known Alice for seven years, suggesting an existing connection between them across parishes. Her position in Richard's service commenced six months before Henry's. Perhaps Alice had even helped him secure work within the household.[33]

Familiarity transcended neighbourhood and parish boundaries. Barbara Tyll of Tewkesbury (Gloucestershire) deposed in 1573 that she had known Joanne Rydge and Griffin *ap* Thomas (opposing parties in a defamation dispute) for five and six years respectively. Barbara was born in Tewkesbury but hadn't been stationary: she had served William Cotterell of Tewkesbury for three years, and had previously been a servant to gentleman Mr Reede of Mitton, just outside the town, for four years. Barbara had met both Joanne and Griffin before her stint in service

[31] DHC, Chanter 861, Gawen Champernowne v Roberta Champernowne (1582).
[32] DHC, Chanter 861, Mary Scam v Anne Hayne (1583).
[33] DHC, Chanter 859, Alice Rowland v Jane Paddon (1575).

with William Cotterell; in fact, she had met them while still a servant in Mitton. Even migrant servants who left communities retained connections.[34]

The assumption that their mobility prevented servants from staying in one place long enough to become integrated is problematic. Some servants knew members of a neighbourhood for longer than they had resided together in a parish. Other women in service had lived in the parish for longer than they had known the parties. Servants weren't the only migrants in early modern England and in some instances were fixed features of a community. They, too, witnessed others entering and leaving the parish. Spheres of contact weren't always coterminous with the geographical unit of the parish.

Friendship

In Chapter 7, we found that only around a third of the people with whom female servants shared spaces were members of the same household. A female servant wasn't only part of her master's household but was also a member of the wider community. These links to the wider community often allowed female servants to challenge (or push the boundaries of) patriarchal control. Outside the household, a master's or mistress's power over his or her servant was lessened. This enriched women's experience of service, offering outlets for gossip, leisure, and courtship.

What was the nature of these social interactions and relationships? What did it mean to be someone's 'friend' in early modern England? Who could be counted as a friend and what were the markers of friendship? The term is rarely defined with any precision in church court depositions despite being regularly used. Macfarlane suggested that 'friend' was virtually synonymous with 'kin', describing both related and non-related individuals.[35] Diana O'Hara noted that many intermediaries in brokering marriages – including biological family, masters and mistresses, fellow servants, and other 'fictive kin' – were termed 'friend'.[36] Amanda Herbert noted that early modern women used the word 'friend' to 'describe some of their homosocial bonds', denoting 'positive social relationships between women'.[37] The definition doesn't differentiate between formal alliances of patronage and kin and the informal relationships that developed through proximity, sociability, and other lived experiences. As Naomi Tadmor argued for the eighteenth century, the word 'friend' could encompass a spectrum of interpersonal relationships.[38] Today,

---

[34] GA, GDR/25, Joanne Rydge v Griffin *ap* Thomas (1573).
[35] Macfarlane, *Family Life*, pp. 149–51.
[36] O'Hara, *Courtship and Constraint*, pp. 38, 110.
[37] Amanda E. Herbert, *Female Alliances: Gender, Identity, and Friendship in Early Modern Britain* (New Haven, 2014), p. 15.
[38] Naomi Tadmor, *Family and Friends in Eighteenth-Century England: Household, Kinship, and Patronage* (Cambridge, 2001), p. 171.

the terms 'friend' and 'friendship' aren't usually used to describe such formal alliances. But friendships were nonetheless wide-ranging, based on patronage and economic support, as well as companionship and sociability. It is therefore difficult to disentangle the word's various meanings. This section explores evidence of friendships appearing in church court depositions that female servants relied upon in different ways.

Friendships and alliances

Gowing noted that amity – friendship that went arm in arm with mutual dependability and support – was seen by early modern writers as 'simply unavailable to women'. But this wasn't true.[39] Women's friendships, Gowing and others found, were politically important. Female servants' formal friendships are laid bare within the context of marriage formation. O'Hara identified these 'friends' as typically male, older than the couple, and of gentle or yeoman status. They had known at least one of the parties for a minimum of two to three years.[40] Female servants also used the word 'friend' to characterise relationships with those upon whom their futures depended economically. Joanna Dowell of Bristol (Gloucestershire) deposed in 1630 that 'as yet shee is but a servant; what her *frends* will doe for her shee knoweth not, but hopeth well'.[41] In 1552, servant Margaret Fydler of Abson (Gloucestershire) claimed that she and William Hyll had agreed to marry. But William argued that he would 'not tak[e] her with nothyng'. Testifying on her behalf, her master William Harding responded 'she is not so offered unto the[e] for thow hast had money offered with her *of her frendes* and she shall be made worth xx [20] nobles'. William Hyll, however, claimed that he 'thynck her frendes will not stand to theire word seeing the chance'.[42] Whether they were reliable or not, Margaret's friends were – at least to her – economically key to securing her marriage. Her master was also an important mediator between the couple and was probably included within this formal friendship group.

The precise nature of the relationships between Joanna Dowell and her friends, and Margaret and hers, wasn't specified. In marriage litigation, it's difficult to tease out precisely the basis or degree of friendships. O'Hara suggested that a hierarchy of intervention operated among the 'go-betweens' in arranging courtship and marriage, with intermediaries ranging from 'the aged and respectable, to the marginal characters at the other end of the spectrum'.[43] But these friendships were

---

[39] Laura Gowing, 'The Politics of Women's Friendship in Early Modern England', in Laura Gowing, Michael Hunter, and Miri Rubin (eds), *Love, Friendship and Faith in Europe, 1300–1800* (2005), pp. 131–49 at 132.
[40] O'Hara, *Courtship and Constraint*, pp. 109–10.
[41] SHC, D/D/cd/65, Nicholas Plumer v Nicholas Harvie (1630). Italics my own.
[42] GA, GDR/8, Margaret Fydler v William Hyll (1552). Italics my own.
[43] O'Hara, *Courtship and Constraint*, p. 117.

tied to social status and appear more like bonds of patronage, support, or socio-economic backing than anything like 'a meeting of equals'.[44]

Masters' and mistresses' endorsement of a female servant could be integral if she was pursuing a suit of her own. In 1576, Catherine Bennett of Cirencester (Gloucestershire) brought a defamation suit against a married woman named Jane Winston, who had allegedly called her a whore on several occasions. Innkeeper John Gurney, Catherine's master, testified on her behalf. But she also secured the support of a gentleman named Thomas Monoxe, who told the court that the defamation had damaged Catherine's reputation as it 'is much talked of', though he knew Catherine to be 'an honest mayden'. Thomas wasn't simply a bystander to Jane Winston's defamatory words. He was John Gurney's friend: two years later, Thomas was one of the witnesses to the compilation of John's will. Female servants could therefore draw on support *beyond* the household through their positions *within* it.[45]

Friends were usually more than marriage brokers. They were companions, business acquaintances, members of a shared household and style of life, with the same social, economic, political, and religious experiences, practices, and values.[46] Other moments of crisis for women in service laid the parameters of networks of support bare. Although distressing, cases pivoting around allegations of attempted rape are particularly enlightening. Rape charges were rare in early modern England. There were several very real obstacles to a woman prosecuting for rape, not least the fact that she was male property and therefore not the 'wronged part[y]'.[47] Cases were supposed to be tried in secular courts, but they were seldom recorded.[48] Occasionally, allegations of rape were made in church courts and traces of non-consensual sex are littered throughout the pages of depositions.[49]

Sampson Rawlyn of St Stephens near Saltash (Cornwall) litigated against servant Elizabeth Kneebone in 1583. The charge was defamation as Elizabeth had apparently told others in the parish that he had attempted to rape her on her return home from milking. Witnesses rallied in Elizabeth's defence. In testifying – itself sometimes an act of friendship – they pointed to the importance of her friends in providing support. Ebbot Langmead and Alice Kneebone both deposed that

---

[44] Naomi Pullin, *Female Friends and the Making of Transatlantic Quakerism, 1650–1750* (Cambridge, 2018), p. 157.

[45] GA, GDR/45, Catherine Bennett v Jane Winston (1576); GDR/R8/1578/73, Will of John Gurney of Cirencester (1578).

[46] There is a rich literature on early modern friendship. See for example, Tadmor, *Family and Friends*, pp. 167– 215; Pullin, *Female Friends*, esp. chapter 3.

[47] Garthine Walker, 'Rape, Acquittal and Culpability in Popular Crime Reports in England, c.1670–c.1750', *P&P* 220 (2013), 115–42 at 116–17.

[48] Chaytor, 'Husband(ry)', 378.

[49] F. G. Emmison found that while Essex assize records show very few indictments for rape, several appear in the diocesan ecclesiastical courts. See F. G. Emmison, *Elizabethan Life: Morals and the Church Courts* (Chelmsford, 1973), p. 44.

Elizabeth had struggled with Sampson during his attack and had cried out 'that if he did abuse her so she would … go home to her frendes'. He let her go upon the promise 'that she should not tell anye of her frindes of it'. William Kneebone added that afterwards, 'Elizabeth … made complaint to her frendes against Rawlyn for that he attempted to have carnall knowledge of her bodye'. Elizabeth invoked her anonymous 'frendes' at a time of particular vulnerability and danger. She wielded her integration within a community of friends as a weapon, warning Sampson that his actions would have consequences. Women who brought sexual assault to the attention of others (particularly authorities) were women who belonged, Miranda Chaytor has argued. They were *useful* women who demonstrated their importance in economic and household structures.[50] Elizabeth, who was returning home from milking (important household labour) at the time of the attack, didn't just signify her integration and labour within a household. She mobilised her belonging within an established group of friends, forewarning Sampson of her loyal and steadfast network of supporters.

In referring to her 'frendes', Elizabeth likely counted on Sampson knowing exactly who they were without needing to name them. Her networks were visible. Twenty-four-year-old Alice Kneebone deposed that Elizabeth came to her directly after the attack 'weeping verie bitterlye', and 'she made the like complaint to this deponent and Elizabeth Kneebone this deponentes brothers wife'. Elizabeth's friendship network was largely familial: Alice shared the defendant's surname (and was probably her sister), but she had also told the story to Alice's (who was also probably her own) sister-in-law. Only Elizabeth's fellow servant, 36-year-old Ebbot Langmead, wasn't a member of her biological family, deposing that Elizabeth came directly to her and 'all the tyme she tould this deponent of the abuse of the sayd Rawlyn wept verie bitterlye and often tymes verie sorrowfully wronge her handes'. Shared working patterns and labour created bonds. The language used in Ebbot's deposition was particularly evocative. She described Sampson's 'filthie attempt' to 'defloure her', and we can hear this woman's outrage at the abuse of her friend. We should, as Frances Dolan has warned, be wary of ascribing too much meaning to 'the appearance of a vivid adjective' as it 'might not necessarily signal authenticity'.[51] But comparison of Ebbots deposition to the other two in this same case reveals this crucial difference in tone and language, suggesting a particularly close bond between these two servants.

Two of the three women that Elizabeth told of the assault and leveraged against Sampson as her 'frendes' – Ebbot, who was a servant, and Alice, another young woman, likely to have been her sister – were of similar status to her. The third woman was Elizabeth's sister-in-law, but she didn't testify. Instead, the

---

[50] Chaytor, 'Husband(ry)', 379.
[51] Dolan, *True Relations*, pp. 144–5.

final witness was William Kneebone, who deposed that '*he heard a reporte* that Elizabeth Kneebone made a complaint to her frendes against Rawlyn'. Age 25 with the same family name, William was almost certainly related to Elizabeth and was probably the husband of the missing sister-in-law in this suit. His words as a married man reflect a legal agenda to bolster Elizabeth's defence with the addition of male testimony to what would otherwise be an exclusively female set of depositions. Contemporary ideas of credibility, as we've seen, were gendered. But the depositions nonetheless reveal that the physical support group that Elizabeth turned to – Alice Kneebone and her sister-in-law, as well as servant Ebbot Langmead – was one of female alliances.[52]

In 1603, gentleman Thomas Raynolds was cited for adultery in the Bath & Wells court. Witnesses testified that he was the father of the illegitimate child of servant Marian Feare (alias Igar) who lived in Burnham-on-Sea (Somerset). Among the surviving records of this case is a partial, incomplete testimony given by a female witness. We don't know her name, age, or place of residence because the biographical heading to the deposition doesn't survive. She was probably Marian's sister (Marian referred to her as 'good sister' and asked her not to tell her brother of her pregnancy). Despite it being incomplete, this deposition nonetheless tells us a lot about relationships: between unequal parties as well as friendship between servants and their sisters, other servants, masters, mistresses, and others. One day, sitting on a stool milking a cow with Marian by her side, the witness asked

> I praye the[e] Marian tell me in ernest art thowe with childe in deede, thow knowest I am noe enemye of thyne, but that I wish the[e] well and I am verie sorie for the[e] & I fear thowe wilt be utterlye undon by it

Marian confided that she was pregnant and that it was Thomas Raynolds' child but that he had given her a hat, paid for a new waistcoat, and had also paid for a coat that Marian's mistress had sold her. The female witness saw some consolation in this news, deposing that 'it is all the better, it weare better to be his then [than] a poorer mans, and he is able to keepe the childe and doe somwhat for thee too'. Again, this moment of crisis lays bare Marian's predicament, but also her reliance upon and trust in this woman. She didn't, however, get on with *everyone*. Thomas had apparently advised Marian to go to Gilbert Tutton's house in South Brent for money, but Marian replied 'I will not goe thither because his wife & I be not frends'. Nonetheless, the genuine care for Marian's welfare in the anonymous woman's testimony shines through and in this same case, Marian's master and mistress also deposed, again demonstrating a support network that she could draw upon.[53]

---

[52] DHC, Chanter 861, Sampson Rawlyn v Elizabeth Kneebone (1583). Italics my own.
[53] SHC, D/D/cd/34, John Atwell v Thomas Raynolds (1603).

Witnessing after service

In their migration and everyday 'micro' mobilities, female servants zigzagged the English landscape. Migration and mobility create new communities, but migrant people are also integrated into existing social groups. When they left these communities, sometimes they lost touch with people. But they also maintained nebulous networks across distance. Depositions offer significant evidence of the connections early modern people held and maintained outside their parish of residence. Across the depositions, we find former servants everywhere testifying on behalf of their past masters, mistresses, and neighbours. Plaintiffs and defendants didn't always draw their witnesses from their immediate neighbourhoods nor from within their households. Witnesses were selected from outside, reflecting the extended networks of friends and acquaintances that early modern people constructed. Former female servants were part of these networks. Their testimonies demonstrate the longevity of relationships forged in service. But in the first place, the plaintiff or defendant had to know how to get hold of them: the very act of their testimony being taken signifies that the litigating party had an address for them. A total of 159 female witnesses were identified as former servants who had since left the parish in which the plaintiff or defendant lived. Proximity of these witnesses to the plaintiff or defendant varied greatly. As Table 8.2 shows, while 50 per cent had moved less than 10 kilometres away, the same proportion had travelled further, with examples of women testifying in cases pursued by past acquaintances and friends as far as 67 kilometres away.

When former servants were called by their past neighbours, masters, or mistresses to testify, how had they stayed in touch? Some female servants had only moved to the next parish and connections over short distances were easier to maintain. Eight years before testifying in the Exeter church court in 1578, Christian Collen of Totnes (Devon) had served the defendant John Sparcks of

Distance (km)	N	%
> 0 and < 5	39	25
≥ 5 and < 10	39	25
≥ 10 and < 20	33	21
≥ 20 and < 30	21	13
≥ 30	27	17
Total	**159**	—

Table 8.2 Former female servants' proximity to the place of residence of the plaintiff or defendant requesting their testimony

the adjacent parish of Harberton for nine years. She fell pregnant in his service, which may have caused a rift in their relationship: Christian noted that they had 'bene enemyes, but nowe for her parte she beareth him no yll will'. Although opposing witnesses testified that her illegitimate pregnancy was 'notorious within the parishe of Harberton', Christian was nonetheless requested as a witness by the plaintiff John Morris. Christian deposed 'that Morrys ... did talke with this deponent to understand what she could saye in this matter', indicating that her former neighbour of eight years ago still knew where to find her. She had known him for fourteen years and the defendant, John Sparcks, for thirteen. The short distance from Harberton to Totnes permitted Christian's continued involvement in Harberton community life, even if she had left the parish to escape the shame of her pregnancy. Her deposition details an intricate knowledge of the countersuit witnesses as well as the litigants, who were all resident in the parish. In turn, the opposing witnesses all knew her well; despite their hostility towards her, Christian's connection to the community in which she had previously lived and worked clearly wasn't altogether broken.[54]

In some cases, there's no direct evidence that the plaintiff had directly approached a former female servant. Cases were probably discussed with witnesses prior to their examination in court to ensure that their testimony would uphold the suit. Payment of travel costs and expenses must have also been established prior to the witness's attendance at court. These practicalities of testifying may have been discussed with distant witnesses by a proctor rather than the plaintiffs themselves. But in most cases, female servants made it clear that they *had* physically spoken with the litigant party. Servant Mary Shorte of Slimbridge (Gloucestershire), testifying on behalf of Nicholas Davis of Longney in 1625, deposed that 'she cometh to testify in this cause at the request & procurement of the said Nicholas'.[55] In the same year, Marie Collins of Bath (Somerset) directly asked her former servant, Elizabeth Prior, to testify for her in a defamation suit. Elizabeth had only been gone for a month but had moved around 12 kilometres over the county border to Trowbridge (Wiltshire), where she was born. Her stay in Bath had been for only a year. Elizabeth told the court that she 'came to testifie in this cause att the request of the partie her producing [Marie] without anie citation, and that the said Marie Collins is to paie her necessarie charges'.[56] Evidently, they had been in touch.

In theory, it was possible to turn up to court, testify, and return home without any further involvement in the suit or with those pursuing it. Regular contact between plaintiffs and distant witnesses wasn't necessarily expected. But, as we've seen, being a witness was usually more meaningful than simply reporting

---

[54] DHC, Chanter 860, John Morris v John Sparcks (1578).
[55] GA, GDR/159, John Jacques and Joanne Jacques v Nicholas Davis (1625).
[56] SHC, D/D/cd/59, Marie Collins v Juliana Blackwell (1625).

something you had seen or heard. Most witnesses were involved not only in the case but also in the life of the litigating party, even at a distance. Men and women made quotidian or everyday journeys – to market, to visit friends and family, to work – that took them outside the parishes in which they lived. We see evidence of the connections with people and places that former servants retained even when they had moved away and moved on from service. In 1557, Juliana Burges, a married woman of Tavistock (Devon), returned to Whitchurch where she had previously served William Gooding. The journey wasn't far – perhaps only a couple of kilometres – but it was made deliberately. Juliana's purpose was to 'vysyt a seke [sick] childe' of William's next-door neighbour. She maintained her friendship with the family who lived next door to her former master after she left service, continuing to visit and support her Whitchurch friends. Overnight, Juliana stayed in William's house. She was still in touch with her former master, though their connection was controversial as he stood accused of an earlier extra-marital relationship with her.[57]

Relationships were more permanent than the itineracy of service suggests. In 1605, Marie Edwards of Chew Stoke (Somerset) testified on behalf of her former master, John Webb of Backwell. She had left his service nine months earlier but indicated her continued presence in the parish. Her testimony was required in a tithe dispute pursued against John and she recounted not only what she recalled of tithing while she lived for a year in his service, but also what she had observed since, deposing that she

> hath divers tymes since her departure byn at the howse of her saide Mr, and sawe not the contrarie but that the said Mr continueth in the same as he did when this deponent served him.[58]

Twenty-four-year-old Marie had lived a particularly mobile life. She had lived in Chew Stoke for nine months, before that in Backwell for one year, and before that for nine years in Chew Stoke again. She was originally born in Littledean (Gloucestershire), at least 51 kilometres from her latest Somerset home. This mobility and her one year in Backwell, however, disguise an otherwise long-term relationship with her master, whom she had known for eleven years. Presumably she had met him when she first moved to Chew Stoke, although Backwell was still almost 9 kilometres away. The question of coercion bubbles underneath the surface of servant testimonies on behalf of masters, but there is sometimes more to the relationship than meets the eye. Her initial connection with John had not been as his servant – this came later. Living in a mobile society, early modern people travelled to visit friends and former neighbours who lived outside their parish of residence.

---

[57] DHC, Chanter 855, Office v William Gooding (1557).
[58] SHC, D/D/cd/36, Thomas Jenkins v John Webb (1605).

A handful of female servants had connections to places and people that are unexplained by their migration. Dorothea Lawrence of Rode (Somerset) was a witness in a 1620 defamation case. She had lived there for five years and before that in Wellow in the same county. She had never lived in Combe Hay where the plaintiff, the defendant, and every single one of the other witnesses lived. However, she had known the plaintiff, Joanne Kelston, since infancy.[59] As we saw earlier, servants weren't the only moving parts, and the movements of others they had encountered brought them into networks outside the places they lived. Perhaps their paths had crossed because Joanne Kelston had moved around.

Many female servants retained links with their masters and mistresses after they had left service, especially if they stayed in the same parish. Goodwill was retained between Alice Brent and her former mistress Emma Jones, a grover's wife of Wells (Somerset), six full years after Alice had departed her service. In 1621, Emma deposed that during Alice's year in service

> and soe ever since shee the said Alice did, and hath lived in good credit amongest her honest neighbours the inhabitants of Wells aforesaid & hath byn and is of good lief & conversation during the said tyme, & beleeveth that shee will not speake anie thing more then truth uppon her oathe.[60]

Not all masters and mistresses kept memories of past servants warm in their hearts. John Williams, the vicar of Awre (Gloucestershire), and his wife Johanna deposed in 1573 *against* their former servant Elizabeth Thromer, who had worked for them two years earlier and was now being charged with defamation in the church court by Elizabeth Mychell. Elizabeth Thromer had apparently accused Elizabeth Mychell of having a child out of wedlock, a claim that had impaired her reputation and prevented her from marrying. The couple were probably around the same ages as both litigants; John was 27 years old and Johanna just 22. Recently married, they were perhaps particularly sensitive to the impact of their former servant's words on Elizabeth Mychell and keen to help make amends on her behalf.[61]

As we saw in Chapter 1, female servants' own reputations could be at stake by association. We often assume that a servant's actions had consequences for the repute of the household in which she served – after all, we regularly read of pregnant servants being turned out of their masters' homes. But female servants could be inadvertent vehicles for insults directed at their masters and mistresses. In 1572, Juliana Hewe of Fordingbridge (Hampshire) testified that while milking cows belonging to her master Mr Scot, who was the parish vicar, Francis Fetispase (who was shooting in the same field) approached her and 'sunge unto hir certayne

[59] SHC, D/D/cd/44, Joanna Kelston v Sara Kelston (1610).
[60] SHC, D/D/cd/57, Jewell Watts v Thomas Brent (1621).
[61] GA, GDR/32, Elizabeth Mychell v Elizabeth Thromer (1573).

abhominable & filthy bawdye songs & sayde to [her] these songes are scripture tell thy mr that he must studye such scriptures'.[62] A servant's identity and status were closely tied to the household in which she served, but this wasn't always a good thing. Juliana was the target of Francis's malice by virtue of her association with the vicar. A master's or mistress's ill repute could equally be injurious to a female servant whose socio-economic position was more precarious, especially in a community she had only recently joined. In 1594, Anna Smith defended her mistress, Mrs Morrell of Southampton (Hampshire), who was defamed as an 'old bawde', which Anna considered 'the most vile word'.[63] If Mrs Morrell was a bawd (a woman keeping a house of prostitution), then by extension (as her servant) Anna's own sexual morality and reputation would be called into question.

A defamation case heard in the Winchester court in 1577 brings to light how a servant could face unfounded questions about her reputation by serving a master who had had several affairs. Anthony Snow had been suspected of illicit liaisons with his servants in the past and people were talking about it. To protect his reputation, Anthony litigated against one defamer, John Wekes. Questioned about Anthony Snow's behaviour, husbandman William Ball of Twyford (Hampshire) deposed

> that the said Anthony Snowes wife did mistrust the said Anthony her husband with the said Joan Shoveler when she was his servant, but the said Anthony Snows wife is so unstable hedded & given to ale that ther is no hede to be given to her words for this respondent thinketh in his conscience that the said Joan Shoveler untill she was married was an honest mayde & sithens is an honest wife & so is the common voice.[64]

According to William, Joan was an honest servant; however, her position in Anthony's household gave rise to allegations of improper master–servant relations.

For others, ending service gave women the opportunity to testify *against* former masters and mistresses, a point I return to from Chapter 1. We have met Edith Scull of Barrow Gurney (Somerset) at other points in this book. In 1617, she was finally free from long-term service as a pauper apprentice to Richard Lewis, who on several occasions was summoned to court. One witness noted in 1617 that she had 'depend[ed] on him for her meat and drink and mayntaynance' but once she was 'free from [his] service' she didn't hold back from revealing some home truths. Firstly, she impaired the testimony his defence relied upon, revealing that she knew of a loan agreement between him and one of his appointed witnesses, thereby rendering the latter unfree of obligation to the former. The description she gave of attempted rape three years later was the ultimate nail in the coffin;

---

[62] HRO, 21M65/C3/5, Office v Francis Fetispase (1572).
[63] HRO, 21M65/C3/10, Joan Morrell v Thomasine Stoner (1594).
[64] HRO, 21M65/C3/7, Anthony Snow v John Wekes (1577).

she was sufficiently free of this man to use the power of the court to bring justice against him.[65]

Leaving service, however, didn't immediately pave the way for servants to set out how they felt about former masters. A dispute in the Winchester court illustrates the power that they continued to hold. On 6 June 1573, witnesses testified in two disputes: one pursued by Marmaduke Blake against his former servant Agnes Harvy and the second by Agnes against Marmaduke. Marmaduke brought witnesses who testified that a year earlier, Agnes had told them her master 'would have forced her divers tymes to have had to doe with her'. These stories, Marmaduke claimed, were untrue and defamatory. But Agnes had evidently poked the bear as her suit against him was also for defamation: in the hundred court held at Christmas, Marmaduke had apparently called her 'a strompett and a harlott, for John Gyle had her at his comandement where he would'. Not only was this ruinous to Agnes's reputation, one witness also testified it was economically damaging: he deposed that 'the mayde is like [likely] to lose xx [20] markes which was given to her by the ould parson of Over Wallop to be distributed amongst his kindred which were of good name and fame'.[66] When a female servant left a parish or her master, the relationship between them could continue to be coercive and sometimes acrimonious. Connections were not easily severed permanently at the end of service, reminding us of its longer legacy.

Reputation

Regular interactions and residency within the same parish partly determined belonging. But we've seen that personal networks were maintained over distance. By the same token, a person's reputation travelled too.

For some female servants, movement to another parish offered a fresh start: perhaps a chance to escape oppressive, corrupt, or abusive masters and mistresses, or their own pasts. London – a city full of anonymous people – presented itself as a possible destination for runaway servants seeking both work and concealment.[67] Some privacy must have been possible in smaller urban settlements, too, but it was harder to find and maintain in rural areas. While the parish was an important delineator of individual identity, collective identity regularly extended beyond parochial boundaries. Witnesses frequently referred to their 'country': in

---

[65] SHC, D/D/cd/48 and D/D/cd/50, Peter Lane v Richard Lewes (1617); D/D/cd/54, Office v Richard Lewis (1620).
[66] HRO, 21M65/C3/5, Marmaduke Blake v Agnes Harvy (1573); 21M65/C3/5, Agnes Harvy v Marmaduke Blake (1573).
[67] Capp, *When Gossips Meet*, p. 178; Gowing, *Common Bodies*, pp. 8–9.

1567 John Stowford of Dolton (Devon) deposed that the 'rumour of the contrye is that they [servant Alice Pawe and her intended husband, John Brennelcombe] shulld marry to gather'.[68] In reality, 'country' had no fixed geographical boundary and its definition shifted from place to place and person to person. David Rollison nonetheless defined it as approximately 8 or 10 kilometres in area, 'having more or less definite limits in relation to human occupation e.g. owned by the same lord or proprietor, or inhabited by people of the same race, dialect, occupation, etc.'[69] Rumours and gossip could spread to other parishes and beyond.[70] Knowledge – of local customs and people – had a geography, and some witnesses were even aware of how far gossip and news travelled: Martin Tresteyne of Ruan Langham (Cornwall) testified in 1584 that

> the fame and reporte is not onely in the parish of Ruan Lanyhorne but as [he] thincketh nere within tenne miles compasse That the sayd Joanne Daniell and Richard Rawe live incontinently together and this deponent hathe hard the same diverse and sundry tymes.[71]

Early modern society was reliant on oral transmission of rumour and news. Market crosses, inns, and taverns in provincial centres must have been sites of exchange of news and gossip, much like London's Exchange and St Paul's Walk.[72] Reputations of rural female servants were carried over parish boundaries by masters, mistresses, and other parishioners who criss-crossed back and forth between their homes and these centres of exchange. Ann Kussmaul suggested that eighteenth and nineteenth-century hiring fairs were forums in which servants and masters met as complete strangers and gained knowledge of one another before agreeing a contract of service.[73] In the absence of these hiring fairs, markets and other sites of sociability were more likely venues for strangers to be accredited or denounced.

It could be difficult to shake off gossip or a scandalous past. In 1637, Elizabeth Bab of Bradninch (Devon) testified in a defamation dispute on behalf of her former mistress Alice Stephens. Elizabeth gave a brief history of her service: she currently worked for Alice Stephens's father, Clement Rudley, but had previously served Alice and her husband William. But opposing witness Elizen Cooke, who was the vicar of Dawlish, rewound the clock a few more years in his deposition, testifying that

> Elizabeth Bab the daughter of James Babb of Dawlish aforesaid about 3 yeeres sithence was a servant unto one William Painter thelder of Dawlish and after that was servant to one in Kenton (whose name as this deponent hath heard was Kenwood)

[68] DHC, Chanter 856, Alice Pawe v John Brennelcombe (1567).
[69] Rollison, *Local Origins*, p. 16.
[70] Fox, 'Rumour, News and Popular Political Opinion', 613–14.
[71] DHC, Chanter 861, John Travanian v Joanne Daniell (1584).
[72] Cust, 'News and Politics', 70.
[73] Kussmaul, *Servants in Husbandry*, pp. 64–5.

And saith that by credible report the said Elizabeth Bab was whiles she was servant to the said Kenwood unlawfully begotten with childe and was delivered of a base childe as he hath heard but who was the reputed father thereof he knoweth not.[74]

The spectre of Elizabeth's past didn't just emerge in court. It had taken root in Elizabeth's new home in Bradninch: another witness deposed that she 'had a bastard & so ran away from her owne country'. At 25 kilometres apart, Dawlish or Kenton and Bradninch lay much more distant from one another than Rollison's parameters of 'country'.[75] Tracing the paths these rumours took is virtually impossible: Elizen Cooke had heard of Elizabeth's pregnancy simply by 'credible report' and witnesses seldom revealed the source of their knowledge, remaining deliberately vague to avoid implicating others in defamation.

Like Elizabeth Bab, others sought escape. William Stidman of Ashwick (Somerset) was cited to appear in court in 1632, charged with adultery with his servant Grace Jones. In October that year, Grace had died being 'greate with childe'. Witnesses testifying against William deposed of his desire to leave his wife. On a fair day in Wells that year, gentleman Thomas Hippislie had seen William and Grace together in an inn and noticed them 'to weepe each to the other & she wiped each others eyes'. The cause of their tears was not recorded, but William told Thomas that he 'wished his wiffe deade' and he 'would forsake the countrie & goe into Ireland with the said Grace & there live with her'.[76] Early modern journeys to Ireland were often made in the pursuit of anonymity. William (and presumably Grace) wanted escape from hiding their relationship; they already had to travell to Wells from Ashwick to pursue their relationship in secret. The distinction between right and wrong connections – those that were socially sanctioned versus those that were denounced – was critical. Here, Ireland offered the possibility of anonymity that the couple were not able to achieve within the county – or even country.

Conclusion

Communities were not simply defined by geography. Female servants retained connections and relationships across time and space. While proximity could determine whom people knew, and a neighbourhood was delineated by the physical closeness of a group of inhabitants at a particular time, the boundaries of this community could be stretched when individuals left. Proximity to a neighbourhood or community facilitated connections, but physical separation was not an

[74] DHC, Chanter 866, Alice Stephens v Caleb Saunders (1637).
[75] Rollison, *Local Origins*, p. 16.
[76] SHC, D/D/cd/66, Office v William Stidman (1632).

insurmountable barrier and relationships endured across considerable distances. Female servants established a range of connections, both temporary and enduring, positive and negative.

Even when servants were transient, appearing one year in the parish and disappearing the next, this doesn't mean they didn't lay down roots. Some connections were maintained through the tenacity and resolve of both parties to retain contact. Early modern society was mobile and opportunities to encounter one another – at markets, fairs, and other spaces of contact – were abundant. Other relationships were reignited by the processes of ecclesiastical law and litigation, which inadvertently reconstructed communities within the walls of the church courts and in the pages of depositions. Of course, these connections were being leveraged at critical moments when it served the interests of litigant parties. This doesn't negate those connections – knowing where to find distant acquaintances indicates that ties were rarely severed permanently at the end of service. Even where direct interaction does not appear to have occurred regularly between former servants and litigant parties, shared recollections and memories nonetheless situated the female servant within a community that might reform itself in court.

Chapter 9

Remembering Service

In 1638, Isabella Venn, a 73-year-old widow, travelled to the Wells court from her home in Wedmore in Somerset. Perhaps 1638 marked the beginning of a decline in her health: in the six months before testifying, she had received 6d a week in parish relief 'towards her maintenance' and three years later, her name was to appear in Wedmore's burial register.[1] Isabella was a lifelong resident of Wedmore, spending just one year of her long life outside it. It is a large parish and she had lived in various parts of it. As 'a young woman', she recalled, she had come to live with her father in the hamlet of Heath House when there were 'but to [two] dweling howse[s] standing in the said village'.[2] She had been a servant there. Agnes and John Wall, 'her master & dame', lived in one of the two houses, while her father lived in the other. Access to and departure from this tiny settlement was ruled by the seasons. The principal path to Wedmore church could be taken on foot or horseback but Isabella recalled that 'in the winter season when the waie weare durtie & deepe [it] was not passable on foote without goeing verie deepe in durte not fit for men, women & children to passe through, neither hath it bene since, or now is in winter tyme'. Those on foot chanced only part of the road, turning instead 'into the common field … to the ca[u]sewaie … and soe that waie to Wedmore church'.

* * *

Isabella's testimony overflows with evidence of her deep-rooted and intimate connection to Wedmore – from her detailed and personal knowledge of the church pathway to her application for parish relief. This was a connection partly forged during her time in service. Though servants were an itinerant workforce, we've seen that some women remained with masters and mistresses for long stretches of time. Some, including Isabella, took up service locally in the place they

---

[1] SHC, D/P/wed/2/1/2, Wedmore Register of Baptisms, Marriages and Burials (1611–63).
[2] Heath House contained only nine farmhouses and three cottages even by 1791. See John Collinson and Edmund Rack, *The History and Antiquities of the County of Somerset* (1791), p. 187.

were born. Isabella's recollections aren't unusual, but neither were they randomly selected from her bank of memories. Her testimony documents a fifty-year history of the church path because part of the field through which it ran had recently been occupied by a new tenant who had 'caused parte of the said churchpath or waie to be plowed upp'. Isabella was one of five witnesses called upon by the aggrieved plaintiff to testify that the new tenant's actions were contrary to custom, common usage, and collective practice. In her testimony, Isabella drew a continuum between Heath House's past and its present (though later, when pressed, she acknowledged change, conceding that 'of late years the highewaie … hath bene worse for passage on foote then [than] it was when [she] lived in heath howse').[3]

The landscape of England had been altered dramatically in this period in ways palpable to its people. By the 1640s, before civil war shook the country's landscape once more, England already bore the physical marks of religious, economic, and agricultural change: monasteries and religious houses had been pulled down, church interiors whitewashed, and land enclosed. As parishioners fought against change by pursuing suits in both ecclesiastical and secular courts, collective memory was pinned down on paper in depositions. Court testimony was imperative in collective action to preserve local custom and defend parochial rights.[4] The memories of male, 'ancient' inhabitants were particularly relied upon in local disputes. These men were 'revered as the repositories of ancient wisdom and the custodians of communal memory', their depositions turning custom into right as long-standing practices became codified in law.[5]

Despite appearing less frequently as deponents in these suits, women, too, played an important role.[6] Women like Isabella were expert witnesses; their testimonies were read as evidence of the past alongside men's. Testifying in 1638, Isabella wasn't just reiterating or restating a custom or ritual. She was part of an active discussion about that custom. As Andy Wood wrote, 'custom was not so much a dominant norm as an especially sensitive discursive field within which subaltern groups felt able to make effective claims to land, power, space, rights and resources'.[7] Bronach Kane's work on medieval church courts showed that testimony was a platform from which women could challenge patriarchal norms and narratives.[8] The testimonies of women like Isabella symbolise the

---

[3] SHC, D/D/cd/51, Hodges v Edward Tincknell (1638).
[4] Wood, *Memory of the People*, pp. 70–1; Adam Fox, *Oral and Literate Culture in England, 1500–1700* (Oxford, 2002), chapter 6.
[5] Adam Fox, 'Remembering the Past in Early Modern England: Oral and Written Tradition', *TRHS* 9 (1999), 233–56 at 236.
[6] Nicola Whyte's work on female testimony in Westminster's equity court has been instrumental in integrating women into this history of collective, local memory. See Whyte, 'Custodians of Memory'.
[7] Wood, *Memory of the People*, p. 289.
[8] Bronach Kane, *Popular Memory and Gender in Medieval England: Men, Women and Testimony in the Church Courts, c.1200–1500* (Woodbridge, 2019).

power that former servants held, not just as chance passers-by who happened to overhear altercations between their neighbours, but also as active and long-standing members of a community, with memories of service that stretched far back into the past.

There is a sort of paradox in this. Their position as servants had put them at the bottom of the household hierarchy. But in being asked to remember – *by virtue of* their former servant status, not *in spite of* it – these women became repositories and sharers of knowledge *through* their employment as servants. Their past labour and occupational identity took on new meaning in the courts. Memory isn't simply a storage system; the mind processes information, creating new ideas and reworking and repackaging past experiences.[9] Recalling tithing practices to which they had contributed their labour, or wills they had witnessed their dying masters make, former female servants moved from being peripheral or shadowy figures and stepped to the fore. Their memories held both collective and personal significance.[10] But their memories of service also remind us of the longer bonds of servitude. In the same way that clothing that was passed from mistress to servant represented a bodily mnemonic of service, so too did embodied routines of journeys made on foot between a master's home and church. The 'teleology of liberty' from service that came with departure is in part a fiction.[11]

This chapter interrogates the place and role of service in individual life histories. While service wasn't a career for most, it accounted for a significant proportion of many women's working lives. We need to think of servants as people with entire life histories that stretched from birth to death. As Judith Pollmann noted, 'our memories shape what is known as our "identity"; we need to know who we are, where we belong and what our position is in relation to others'.[12] Exploring memories of service recorded in women's depositions, this chapter traces the importance of service as part of a woman's identity across her life. Formative years spent in service certainly shaped who these women were, and if we understand service as a form of training, we must consider the *outcome* of that training (i.e. who was the person at the end of it?). For men, occupational and social titles such as 'tailor' or 'gentleman' are markers of identity that we as historians latch on to and make much of in telling their life histories. Once a weaver completed his apprenticeship, the title 'weaver' remained attached to any record of him we encounter in the archives, usually until his death. But for a woman, the moment the descriptor 'servant' and the labour and identity bound within it is dropped and replaced

[9] James Fentress and Chris Wickham, *Social Memory* (Oxford, 1992), pp. 16–17.
[10] James Fentress and Chris Wickham write that 'there seems little reason … to suppose that memory itself is divided into two compartments – one personal and the other social'. See ibid., p. 7.
[11] Chakravarty, *Fictions of Consent*, p. 177.
[12] Judith Pollmann, *Memory in Early Modern Europe, 1500–1800* (Oxford, 2017), p. 19.

with a marital status descriptor, the importance of service in identity formation is hidden from view. Memories of service therefore offer a gateway to understanding its lasting impact on women's identities and lives across the life cycle.

Retrieving memories

Keith Thomas argued that past memories and stories that survive are often 'intrinsically memorable', typically amusing, or unusual in some way.[13] This is surely true of memories related in autobiographical writings, chronicles, and cheap print. But church court depositions offer a different representation of memory in which the mundane, routine, or quotidian is habitually recorded. Although 'memory is always at work in our minds',[14] it had a specific function in court testimony. Depositional memories can be false, constructed to serve a legal purpose, and they are often coded to legal conventions. As Peter Burke put it, memories are 'malleable', and it's important 'to understand how they are shaped and by whom'.[15] Precisely how memory operates in a legal context is difficult to pin down, but in addition to the layers of legal manipulation of memories contained within a deposition, memories are also *constructed by* and *coded to* social norms.[16] Anthropological studies show that individuals 'remember in common' and that a village 'informally constructs a continuous communal history of itself: a history in which the act of portrayal never stops. This leaves little if any space for the presentation of the self in everyday life.'[17] An individual life history is therefore embedded within a collective history of a place or community and is difficult to extract.[18] Across all suits in the church courts, former female servant witnesses were asked to remember but their time in service was rarely the primary context for their memories. Questions instead centred on tithing, church seating, and other local practices. In recalling the past, women might collapse their experiences of service into broader, collective memory. Depositional memories might indeed be reduced to events, actions, and behaviours that appear to reflect local, collective values, rather than an individual's recalled or reflective emotions relating to the past.

Former female servants were therefore almost never asked to relay their full career in service or even a complete story of the months or years spent in the

---

[13] Keith Thomas, 'The Perception of the Past in Early Modern England (1989 Creighton Lecture)', in David Bates, Jennifer Wallis, and Jane Winters (eds), *The Creighton Century, 1907–2007* (London, 2009), pp. 181–218 at 186.

[14] Fentress and Wickham, *Social Memory*, p. 5.

[15] Peter Burke, 'History as Social Memory', in Thomas Butler (ed.), *Memory: History, Culture and the Mind* (Oxford, 1989), pp. 97–113 at 100.

[16] Paul Connerton, *How Societies Remember* (Cambridge, 1989), p. 27; Frederic C. Bartlett, *Remembering: A Study in Experimental and Social Psychology* (Cambridge, 1932).

[17] Connerton, *How Societies Remember*, p. 17.

[18] Ibid., p. 21.

household of just one master or mistress. The information they recalled springs from a set of cues or prompts dictated by legal procedure. The detail that we read in modern oral histories or autobiographical works penned about or by servants is therefore absent from the testimonies of these early modern women. After leaving service, these women had space to reflect on it.[19] But depositions rarely give room for emotional reflection. Rambling recollections that digress from a suit's key points, or frank reflections on what it was like to live and work in someone else's household are entirely absent. In being asked to remember in the church courts, former servants weren't invited to divulge their personal or intimate feelings about their time in service. Memories of service presented in court records are therefore void of emotion, leaning towards the neutral or sometimes suspiciously rose-tinted and optimistic.

As historians, then, we are left to read against the grain to excavate feelings and tease out the personal. How each deponent presented their memories – albeit through the lens of legal procedure and its constraints – nonetheless tells us about identity, both collective *and* individual. How these women drew on their past experiences of service to give their testimonies authority and credibility and to make sense of the present reveals much about how they assembled their own personal histories. Service as a framework for their recollections held significance.

The memories that concern us here are those of women who had long left the service of a particular master. In timestamping their recollections, specific dates for service were often given. Joanna Lansdowne deposed in 1629 that she had first come to live in Wincanton (Somerset) as a servant 'threescoare and three yeeres agou'.[20] Abigail Lambol recalled serving the rector of North Waltham (Hampshire) 'about 17 yeares agowe'.[21] These time frames are not likely to be approximate given that they have not been rounded to decadal thresholds. In some cases, specificity was required: tithe suits hinged on how tithing had been performed in specific years. Former servants recalled *precisely* which years they had been in service and therefore had observed or taken part in these practices. Joanna Addams of Basingstoke (Hampshire), for instance, could recall over ten years later that she had been a servant to Mr Baynerd in every year between 1614 and 1624.[22]

Unlike criminal courts such as Quarter Sessions (where the judicial process was often immediate and witnesses testified on the same day a crime was reported),

[19] For twentieth-century examples, see Foley, *A Child in the Forest*; Nella Last, *Nella Last's Peace: The Post-War Diaries of Housewife 49*, (eds) Patricia E. Malcolmson and Robert W. Malcolmson (London, 2008). Of course, the most personal and private memories of an individual's life are generally inaccessible to historians working on any given period, and even when working with modern oral histories. See Pollmann, *Memory in Early Modern Europe*, p. 1.
[20] SHC, D/D/cd/64, Henry Glinn v James Churchaie sen, James Churchaie jun and Anna Churchaie (1629).
[21] HRO, 21M65/C3/12, Mason v Yates (1631).
[22] HRO, 21M65/C3/12, West and West v Bradley (1631).

church court suits could be drawn-out affairs. Rarely were the memories witnesses recounted fresh. They had time to reflect on, process, and perhaps forget certain aspects of what they were asked to recall. The passing of time between deposition and recalled events adds a level of complexity in working with this evidence. Did the deponent remember events accurately? Was a testimony taken shortly after the event more credible than one taken years later? Perhaps surprisingly, testimonies of recent events are generally no more detailed than those outlining distant memories. Omission of information – names, dates, and times – doesn't appear intrinsically related to the passing of time. This is not because time did not erase or erode memory; rather, legal processes muddy the waters. Phrases in depositions such as 'this deponent doth not certaynelye remember' and 'she doth well remember' indicates witnesses expressed the level of detail or certainty with which they remembered. But some claims of inability to remember are undoubtedly dubious. In 1627, David Macie of Weston near Bath (Somerset) recalled hearing that Henry Bristoll and Margery Luellin did 'live incontinentlie' together but claimed he was unable to remember which of his neighbours had told him. David's memory probably hadn't failed him; concealing his neighbour's identity was likely deliberate, to shield them from a potential indictment for defamation.[23] We might take a more generous view of other omissions from depositions: when Maria Taylor, an 80-year-old widow of Wincanton (Somerset), couldn't remember the Christian names of the 'Glinns of Wincanton' whom she had served as a young woman, we might trust that this was the result of ageing and the passing of time. Reading more closely, we might even suppose her forgetfulness was because she never used their Christian names, referring to them instead deferentially. Still many years later, the underlying power differential in how a servant addressed her master or mistress was cemented in her mind.[24]

Table 9.1 summarises the time elapsed since the events recalled in a former servant's deposition. Memories could be as recent as just one year earlier. The length of time that had passed between their deposition and their recollections was often contingent on the type of case for which their testimony was sought. Those testifying when fewer than ten years had passed were witnesses in virtually all kinds of suits. Certain cases required only short-term memory: the hurling of insults over garden walls or across busy streets that were central to defamation suits hadn't usually happened more than three or four months (and certainly no more than a year) earlier. Similarly, a recalled betrothal that might underpin a successful matrimonial suit had rarely taken place more than two years before. Almost three-quarters of those recalling episodes in their service career drew on relatively recent experiences (between one and four years earlier). But just

---

[23] SHC, D/D/cd/61, Office v Henry Bristoll (1627).
[24] SHC, D/D/cd/64, Case 2139, Henry Glinn v James Churchaie sen, James Churchaie jun and Anna Churchaie (1629).

		Bath & Wells	Exeter	Gloucester	Hereford	Winchester	All
< 4 years	N	67	26	35	5	23	156
	%	78	72	67	83	77	74
≥ 4 and < 10 years	N	8	7	8	—	5	28
	%	9	19	15	—	17	13
≥ 10 years	N	11	3	9	1	2	26
	%	13	8	17	17	7	12
Total		86	36	52	6	30	210

Table 9.1 Time elapsed since events recalled by former female servants (by court)

over a quarter of women (typically much older and often married or widowed) remembered being a servant four or more years previously. Their depositions recalled more distant memories of service, stretching as far back as fifty years. Those recalling experiences of service from ten or more years earlier testified almost exclusively in church seating, tithe, and testamentary disputes. In fact, only those with more than ten years' distance between their employment in service and the time of the dispute testified in church seating suits. As this chapter considers the role of service in the formation of identity over a person's lifetime, I focus here on the testimonies of women whose recollections of service stretched further back into the past.

Memories of labour

Across depositions, the authority of a servant's testimony was undermined by opposing witnesses. Objections were raised not only on the grounds that their economic dependency gave them a lack of autonomy, but also because they were perceived to be of limited means.[25] As I showed in Chapter 2, being 'but a poor servant' was a frequent objection to servant witnesses. But later in life, as female deponents were asked for their memories of a parish and its practices, their time in service took on new meaning in court. Once a hindrance, service now proved useful. In part, this new-found authority stemmed from age and the wisdom and experience it brought. But time and again, these older witnesses pointed directly to their experiences of service as grounds for their knowledge. Compared with their younger counterparts (whose testimonies were undermined on the basis that they were young, poor, and dependent), those who had left service much earlier

[25] Shepard, *Accounting for Oneself*, p. 182.

found themselves in a stronger position. Later in life, the labour of service was unquestionable grounds upon which to claim authority.

Memory, therefore, translated the mundane, repetitive acts of labour in service into powerful, authoritative experiences. But these memories also remind us of the continuity of service. A male servant's agricultural labour is seen to form a continuum with his independent identity and occupation as a husbandman years later. For women, the transition from 'singlewoman' to 'wife', from a role of dependency within a household to the manager of her own home is the focus.[26] The connection between time in service and married life is severed. Further, not all women went on to lead married lives. Focusing on recollections of service draws continuity in women's life histories and brings it to bear on their sense of identity.

Edith Longden of Hawkesbury (Gloucestershire) was 73 years old when she testified in a tithe dispute in 1604. She recalled paying the cheese tithe on behalf of her master and mistress while serving fifty-five years earlier in the nearby parish of Horton. Her recollection of her master's dairying was specific and embedded in practice. She told the court that John Hathway (her master) kept nine cows and paid thirteen cheeses as tithes for the year. It is remarkable that over half a century later, Edith remembered these numbers with such specificity. But habit and repetition embed the past in the body, and Edith had taken ownership of and responsibility for this labour. In her deposition, she adds that 'shee well remembreth' these details

> for that shee … by the comandement of the said Mr and dame did bring the same cheese unto Hortons church and there left them for the said parson of Horton uppon a stone or coffer neere the chancel doore in Horton church, and she brought them cheeses fower at the first tyme, fower at the second tyme, and fyve at the last tyme. And the said cheeses soe by hir brought to the church were made of every one, of all the mylk that the said nine kyne did geve usually at one meale or milking, as farr as she nowe remember.[27]

Reading Edith's deposition alongside others, we can imagine conversations that took place before this tithe dispute. Other witnesses had similar recollections of paying tithe cheese, and perhaps the community of deponents reached some consensus beforehand. Yeoman John Walker had been a scholar in the church thirty years earlier and recalled cheeses being left near the chancel door. Jane *ap* Richardes recalled living with her mother and stepfather sixty years earlier. In the thirty years she lived there, they kept cows and paid tithe cheese in the way Edith described. Butcher Thomas Cooper also recalled the practice, adding that thirty-seven years earlier he had lived with his brother, the parish curate,

---

[26] Karin Hassan Jansson, Rosemarie Fiebranz, and Ann-Catrin Östman, 'Constitutive Tasks: Performances of Hierarchy and Identity', in Maria Ågren (ed.), *Making a Living, Making a Difference: Gender and Work in Early Modern European Society* (Oxford, 2017), pp. 127–58 at 140–1.
[27] GA, GDR/89, Andrew Thomas v Henry Norris (1604).

and had watched him write the names of each parishioner on their tithe cheese. But none recalled the practice or the labour with such specificity as Edith. Her deposition gives no indication of how long she served John Hathway, but it's clear the routine and repetition of this task at least three times a year cemented this labour in her memory. Edith didn't just remember the parish custom and how it was practised. Her recollections of service were embedded and coded within it.

Anne Smyth of Northleach (Gloucestershire) came before the Gloucester court in 1602 at the age of 50. She had paid tithes since service (while in her 30s) and continued to pay as a married woman fourteen years later. We see the evolution of Anne's participation in the tithing practice over the course of her life. In service, she had paid an offering or personal tithe of two pence to the vicar. As a married woman, she paid tithes of cabbage, onion, and garlic from her garden. She rooted the legitimacy of her long-standing knowledge of the tithing customs in her time in service. Service is often seen as an interlude, a means of gaining some fuzzy, vague skills and the cash and goods required to set up a marital household. Marjorie McIntosh and Jane Whittle both noted the importance of service as a life-cycle stage for women in acquiring both wealth and skills to set up their own homes.[28] But Anne's experience of service wasn't just a stepping stone on the route to marriage. Her memory reminds us that women's labour stretched across their lifetimes. The labour they carried out during service informed and intersected with their later labouring lives.[29]

Local histories

Though I've shown that female servants forged and maintained connections across time and space with the communities they had served, the geographically stable are more abundant among those who dredged up distant memories of service. Those recalling events ten or more years earlier typically lived in either the same parish as the one in which they recalled their experiences of service or nearby (twenty-three out of twenty-six). Departing from the place where she had served might afford a servant greater freedom from future obligation to her former master. But that would mean removing herself from the networks of support and care she had established within the parish.[30] Only three lived in parishes geographically distant. Eleanor Seaward of Harpford (Devon), who recalled her former mistress's funeral in 1617, had lived and served in Heavitree (just outside Exeter), 16 kilometres

---

[28] McIntosh, *A Community Transformed*, p. 49; Whittle, 'Servants in Rural England'.
[29] GA, GDR/89, Mascall v Myllard (1602).
[30] Urvashi Chakravarty noted that in slavery narratives, captivity 'seems spatially delimited'; freedom should therefore be its opposite. Chakravarty, *Fictions of Consent*, p. 184.

from her current home.[31] Agnes Willes of Glastonbury (Somerset) testified in a 1609 tithe case arising from Sutton Bingham (29 kilometres away), where she had lived more than thirty years earlier.[32] And in 1585, Joan Harrys testified in a testamentary dispute, recalling her deceased master making his will 'in his house at Wellow' (Hampshire), almost 39 kilometres from Portsmouth where she had settled with her husband.[33]

Of the twenty-eight women who recalled experiences of service between four and ten years earlier, patterns were similar. Just four had moved considerable distances: Alice Lybbye, testifying in a 1580 Cornish tithe suit, had moved around 24 kilometres to St Creed from Lanteglos; Joanna Richardes, one of just two witnesses in a 1567 separation case, had moved around 53 kilometres to Eggesford from North Hill (also Cornwall); Alice Cane, a deponent in an incest case heard in the Bath & Wells court in 1633, had moved around 24 kilometres to Middlezoy from Bleadon (Somerset); and Elizabeth Izarde, testifying in a 1569 matrimonial suit, had moved around 32 kilometres from Staunton (Gloucestershire) to Broadway (Worcestershire).[34] These patterns fit with what we know about selecting witnesses, particularly in cases relating to parochial customs in which memory was key: deponents needed a long-established connection with the parish in question.[35]

We've already seen that servants recalled their footsteps around the parish. Isabella Venn's familiarity with the route she took to church demonstrates the intimate knowledge that could be gained from service of the topographies, landscapes, and infrastructures of the places they had worked. But women also remembered the physicality and materiality of the homes in which they served. Idiosyncrasies became etched into the memories of those who inhabited them. Five years after a ten-year stint in the service of Mr Castle, Elizabeth Wotton of St Thomas in Exeter (Devon) cast her mind back to his house and its layout. She deposed in 1578 of

> a hole in the dawbed wall of the buttrye aboute a fote from the grounde, and then one John Kelly a servant in the sayd house did stoppe the sayd hole but whither anie hole were in the same place since the sayd tyme of her being there as a servant which was five yeres agoe she cannot tell.[36]

Her recollections were sought in relation to an accusation against Blanche Apworthie, who was suspected of illicit sex in the house. Other depositions in

---

[31] DHC, Chanter 867, Office v Bridgeman and Henry Ashe (1617).
[32] SHC, D/D/cd/41, Giles Phelps v Frances Abbott (1609).
[33] HRO, 21M65/C3/9, Edward Bennys and Jane Bennys v Thomas Cooper (1585).
[34] DHC, Chanter 860, Richard Hawkye v Thomas Bede (1580); DHC, Chanter 855b, Richard Corne v Joanna Corne (1567); SHC, D/D/cd/66, Office v Agnes Least and Samuel King (1633); GA, GDR/25, Alice Woodwarde v William Izarde (1569).
[35] Whyte, for instance, showed that female parishioners from long-established households worked together with men to set out the 'moral and economic boundaries of the parish', drawing on their knowledge of customs, right, and long-standing practices. See Whyte, 'Custodians of Memory', 158.
[36] DHC, Chanter 860, Raymond Wadland v Blanche Apworthie (1578).

this case haven't survived, but we might assume that witnesses testified to spying Blanche's affair through this alleged hole in the buttery wall.[37] The mental map that Elizabeth drew of her former master's house stitched together place, people, and experiences. She gave the precise location of the hole – a foot from the ground – and stationed her fellow servant John within her memory of the place. Her connection with the spaces engaged memories of both sight and touch. This was especially the case for those who served for a long period in the same home. Spaces are not passive but we can go further: they have agency and can influence and shape the thoughts and actions of those who encounter them. In testifying as former servants in cases relating to space and place, it's those spaces in conjunction with the labour they carried out *in those spaces* that brought them to court and required them to remember.

It's not entirely clear where the house Elizabeth Wotton described was located, but it's likely it was in Northlew (Devon), a parish 42 kilometres from her new home in St Thomas, Exeter.[38] While the geographically stable were more likely to be witnesses in disputes that required long-term memory, connections to the parish weren't always continuous. In 1629, a church seating dispute called several former female servants to recall seating practices in the church of Wincanton (Somerset) in the late 1500s. Alice Alsheares, a 60-year-old widow who had moved from Wincanton to North Brewham six or seven years earlier, remembered arriving in Wincanton forty-six or forty-seven years before. She had taken up service in the household of esquire Alexander Ewens. By the 1580s, then, Alice had served in his home for seven or eight years and could only have been in her mid-teens when she joined the household. Alice recalled where her mistress's sister-in-law sat in church, deposing that

> by reason of her attending her mistris to church, the said Mrs Alice Ewens divers tymes goeing to church with her mistres, this deponent well knew and observed wheare the said Mrs Alice Ewens usuallie sate in the said church … in the woomans seate now in question being erected & builte up in the upper side of the uppermost north piller of the parish church of Wincannton.

Alice's memories of service were circumscribed by the nature of this church seating litigation, but her recollections nonetheless offer insight into the rhythms of service and how her labour intersected with religious practice and social interaction in church. Alice's memory of where people sat in church was vivid, probably helped by her long-term residence in the town. Her story wasn't one of sedentarism, however. She had lived in Ireland with her husband for around three years, and at the time of her examination she lived around 8

---

[37] A buttery was a small room used for storage of victuals and cooking pots. See Overton et al., *Production and Consumption*, p. 131.

[38] Most witnesses in this case listed Northlew as their place of residence.

kilometres north of Wincanton in North Brewham. She deposed that she had been approached by Agnes Glinn, the plaintiff's wife, on the Monday before she testified, 'who enquired of her what shee could saie concerning the matter'. Her mobility appears not to have erased her from the community. Service clearly marked the beginning of her connection with Wincanton. Although she remained in the town for a further forty years, her initial years in service with the Ewens provided her with the strongest claim to knowledge of where the town's elites should sit in Wincanton church.

By comparison, a deposition from the same case presents service as a disruptive rather than instructive experience. Christian Dowden, a 73-year-old widow, deposed that she

> was borne in the parishe of Wincannton aforesaid and there lived until shee was aboute eighteene yeeres of aige, when she went abroad to service, and was absent att service for neere about eighte yeeres.

In her testimony, we enjoy a glimpse of how this woman experienced and felt about moving from the parish in which she had grown up. Christian situated her time in service within a longer life arc. She drew a timeline of her life in the parish that was divided into two episodes: the first before she left for service and the second following her return after eight years 'abroad'. She deposed

> that Mr Thomas Ewens was marryed unto Mrs Glinn ... in the tyme this respondent was abroad att service ... And therefore this respondent knoweth that itt is above three and fortie yeers agou that shee was soe married.[39]

Her migration for service interrupted her direct experience and observations of parish customs and practices and her recollections are framed around this absence. She saw her eight years away from Wincanton while working as a servant as a period of dislocation and disconnection from the town. Nonetheless, despite being geographically distant, she clearly remained connected during this absence, perhaps kept abreast of local goings-on by friends and family, or maybe she even returned home for Thomas Ewens's wedding. Despite the different ways in which service contributed to or limited the knowledge that Alice Alsheares and Christian Dowden could give in their depositions, in both cases service shaped their narratives in important ways. It was a personal point of reference for how they identified their own place within the communal history of Wincanton.

Permanent settlement and continuous residence tell only part of a story that connects people to places. Some former servants who had moved away since service *were* called to testify, as we saw in Chapter 8. In a testamentary dispute heard in the Bath & Wells court in 1630, Alice Waterman of Wellington (Somerset)

---

[39] SHC, D/D/cd/64, Henry Glinn v James Churchaie sen, James Churchaie jun and Anna Churchaie (1629).

deposed what she remembered of the will her former mistress, widow Jane Guint of the same town, had made before her death. Alice's memories stretched back nine or ten years, but she had moved from Wellington between leaving service and her former mistress's death. The biographical introduction to her deposition tells us she had lived in Crediton and Exeter (Devon) for the last two years or so. In fact, her return to Wellington was very recent: she had arrived on the Sunday before her examination. Had her testimony been taken one week earlier while she was still resident in Devon, we might overlook what appears to be a long-term connection with the small Somerset market town of Wellington, situated near the Somerset–Devon border.[40] Alice was a woman on the move for reasons that the pages of her depositions can't tell us. She likely moved around this region and perhaps travelled back and forth between Somerset and Devon. Her mobility appears to have played a key role in maintaining her connection with Wellington and specifically the house in which she had previously worked. Seemingly local recollections of former female servants, therefore, are sometimes more complex. How we understand 'the local' might be expanded in surprising ways.

National horizons

We are accustomed to thinking of the worlds of female servants, especially those working in rural households, as isolated or detached from broader national affairs. Depositions often lean towards this, routinely pertaining to local, collective memory. Sixteenth- and seventeenth-century England experienced significant religious, political, economic, and social upheaval in the hundred or so years of this study. Society lived through these events, and so it's unsurprising that witnesses' memories are occasionally embedded within broader contexts that speak to *national* rather than local memory. A handful of female servants framed relatively unextraordinary memories of service within more exceptional contexts and are the focus of this section. Privileging these exceptional or unusual depositions over the more typical might be read as cherry-picking; after all, these types of memories are numerically few. I argue, however, that these women weren't necessarily exceptional for conceiving of their lives in these wider contexts. After all, analysis of the incidental has already shown that female servants' footsteps and their interactions took them further afield than is supposed. These women therefore were only exceptional for articulating these contexts in their testimonies.[41] References to broader contexts were scarce across *all* depositions, not just those of

---

[40] SHC, D/D/cd/65, Priscilla Carpenter v John Coleborne (1630).
[41] Frances Dolan suggested that 'self-expression [might] occur through rather than despite convention'. On privileging the exceptional over the everyday in court testimony, see Dolan, *True Relations*, p. 145.

female servants. There is no reason to suppose that the female servants discussed here aren't, therefore, representative of the small number of deponents who similarly situated their recollections within broader national events. They tell us something about how these flashpoints in early modern England shaped their experiences of service and vice versa. This section focuses on the stories of three former servants: Judith Webb, Lucy Hayle, and Joan Good.

Beginning a new position in service was bound to be a major life event, whatever comforts or familiarities a servant might take with them to their new home and workplace (for example, remaining in the same parish or being hired by neighbours, friends, or relations). But the temporal intersection of this change with a sudden social or economic crisis must have been a particularly unsettling experience. In 1630, 54-year-old widow Judith Webb was one of twenty witnesses called to testify in a dispute over seating arrangements in St Cuthberts church in Wells (Somerset). Unlike her fellow witnesses, however, Judith's memory of where particular families had sat in the church forty years earlier took her back to the plague years. She deposed that

> in the yeere when the greate sicknes was att Wells which was as this deponent remembreth aboute fortie yeeres agoe [she] came to live in howse as servant with the deceased Mr Edward Smith.

Her memory of her service to Edward Smith was shaped by the epidemiological circumstances of the time and the consequences it had for the city. This was a time of upheaval and uncertainty in a city in which Judith had spent her whole life. But her reference to the 'greate sicknes' wasn't just a local one. In the early 1590s, plague had broken out in the south-west, devastating the populations of several Devon towns including Tiverton and Totnes, before spreading across England, eventually reaching London in the autumn of 1592.[42] Judith's memory situated her own experience within a country ravaged by a life-threatening disease while also giving texture and individuality to her deposition: she testified to her recollections of going to church with her master's wives over the years, adding the detail that his first wife, Joanne, died of the disease 'some what upwards of a yeere after this deponent's soe coming to live with them'.[43] Judith hinted at the shifting composition of the household in which she worked, the adjustments that had to be made, and the impact of plague on her experience – and memories – of service. At first glance, her deposition appears to be one of many formulaic accounts of where people sat in church. But the legal veneer wears thin in places, allowing a fleeting glimpse of the complexities of service at a time of death, disease, and uncertainty.

---

[42] Charles Creighton, *A History of Epidemics in Britain from A.D. 664 to the Extinction of Plague* (Cambridge, 1891), p. 352. Paul Slack found that between 1589 and 1593, almost 60 per cent of parishes with surviving burial registers recorded evidence of plague as being responsible for mortality. See Paul Slack, *The Impact of Plague in Tudor and Stuart England* (1985), p. 85.

[43] SHC, D/D/cd/65 and D/D/cd/66, Marie Smith v Susan Meade (1630).

Judith wasn't the only former servant who recalled the 1590s as a time of crisis. Lucy Hayle of Chirbury (Shropshire), testifying in October 1599, identified the final years of her fourteen-year stretch serving Edmund Hill as a time of economic crisis and food scarcity. Deposing in a dispute over her former master's will, Lucy set out in considerable detail his belongings at the time of his death. His possessions, she noted, included cattle, sheep, goats, corn, malt, clothing, and household goods including pewterware. She appraised their value meticulously. The corn, she deposed, was 'rie and muckorne' to the quantity of 'six strikes and a half worth x*s* [10*s*] a strike *considering the scarcitie at that time*'. The malt, amounting to three bushels, was worth 'vi*s* viii*d* [6*s* 8*d*] a bushell at least *being in the deare yeares*'. We don't know the precise year of Edmund's death, but Lucy's recollections of 'the deare yeares' situate it squarely in the 1590s and probably 1596–7, when failure of harvests across the country led to staggering increases in the price of grain and other crops.[44] Dearth, famine, and surplus mortality followed as prices soared and there wasn't enough food to go round. Shrewsbury, just 26 kilometres away, as well as several other towns in the west of England including Chester, Gloucester, Worcester, and Tamworth had to turn to the international grain market in these years, sourcing it from as far afield as Denmark and Poland.[45] Significantly, like Judith's mention of the plague in Wells, Lucy's reference to these years of 'scarcitie' is unusual. Of the fourteen witnesses in the case, only she and two others (including one other woman who also worked in Edmund Hill's household) referred to this period of dearth in a way that marked it out as *different* or out of the ordinary.[46]

The flattening effect that the legal process had on a witness's testimony means we can only guess at the physical and emotional impact this period of extreme economic hardship had on Lucy's experience of service. Perhaps living in this household where corn and malt was being stored gave her a sense of safety in this time of economic insecurity. Perhaps her overriding feeling was guilt as others around her struggled. What Lucy's deposition makes clear, however, is that this was a departure from the norm. The deposition offers no clue as to what happened to Lucy after her master's death. Finding service when the price of food was inflated couldn't have been easy. Rather than facing the customary accusation from opposing witnesses of being a 'poor servant', Lucy was described instead as a 'verie poore woman', 'a poore begger', and was even accused of having embezzled goods (though whether this alleged embezzlement was recent or historic isn't clarified). Perhaps Lucy's reference to the 'deare yeares' alludes to the personal

---

[44] W. G. Hoskins, 'Harvest Fluctuations and English Economic History, 1480–1619', *Agricultural History Review* 12 (1964), 28–46.

[45] R. W. Hoyle, 'Shrewsbury, Dearth, and Extreme Weather at the End of the Sixteenth Century', *Agricultural History Review* 86 (2020), 22–36 at 31–2.

[46] HARC, HD4/2/11, Evan *ap* Edward v William Speake and William Haile (1599). Italics my own.

economic cost of this period of dearth and its impact on the labour market. Her ability to earn an income may have been limited as households cut back on hired labour to make ends meet and ensure that biological family members were fed. Perhaps the 'deare yeares', therefore, marked the end of her career in service.

The specific or individual impact of wider national events recalled in witness testimony isn't, therefore, always easy to locate. But as we've seen, depositions leave clues. In 1564, 50-year-old Joan Good of Colyton (Devon) testified in a matrimonial suit. She recalled a betrothal that had taken place between her mistress's nephew and a woman named Joan Ham 'a bowt a eyre [year] after the commocion'. The word 'commotion' here refers to a series of rebellions that had taken place across the country fifteen years earlier in 1549 against Edwardian religious reform but also in response to increasing socio-economic polarisation.[47] We might assume that Joan's frame of reference was a relatively local one. She likely pointed specifically to the Western Rebellion, which had taken place in Cornwall and Devon, rather than to any national wave of unrest. Colyton, where Joan was a lifelong resident, wasn't far from Fenny Bridges and Honiton, where rebels and the king's men clashed.[48] She was 35 years old in the year of the uprising.[49]

Devon witnesses seldom mention these rebellions. In the first two surviving deposition books from the diocese of Exeter following the rebellion (covering the years 1556 to 1564), witnesses in only five of the 602 cases referred to the time of 'the commotion'.[50] Each rebellion timestamp appeared in the earliest depositions available (in 1556 and 1557), making Joan's testimony in 1564 even more intriguing. Why, then, did this small handful of people refer to the commotion? It's worth considering similar references to the commotion in detail. References appear to have been thinly veiled attempts to signal to close observers a political or religious leaning. In his 1556 examination, rector Bartholomew Cowde timestamped his recollection as 'the yere next *after the commotion in thies west parties* [parts] whiche was abowt a syx yeres agowe'. A defendant in the Exeter court, Bartholomew faced a litany of charges of clerical misconduct including holding multiple benefices, absence from his flock, and – crucially – the complaint that he was 'a maried prest'.[51] During Edward VI's reign (1547–53), priests were allowed

---

[47] See 'commotion, n.', OED Online, Oxford University Press, March 2023, www.oed.com/view/Entry/37277 [accessed 31 May 2023]. Insurrection against Edwardian religious reform was targeted initially at the fear of confiscation of church goods, but then at the dissolution of chantries, and the introduction of services read from the English Prayer Book. See Diarmaid MacCulloch and Anthony Fletcher, *Tudor Rebellions* 7th edition (Abingdon, 2020), p. 58; Mark Stoyle, '"Fullye bente to fighte oute the matter": Reconsidering Cornwall's Role in the Western Rebellion of 1549', *English Historical Review* 129 (2014), 549–77.

[48] MacCulloch and Fletcher, *Tudor Rebellions*, p. 63.

[49] DHC, Chanter 855a, Office v Leonarde Evered and Joanne Ham (1564). Italics my own.

[50] DHC, Chanter 855, Office v Bartholomew Cowde (1556); Roger Ireland v Anthony Bowden (1556); Gold v James Salter (1557); Office v William Gooding (1557); Richard More v Thomasina More (1557).

[51] DHC, Chanter 855, Office v Bartholomew Cowde (1556). Italics my own.

to marry: approximately seventy clergymen in the diocese of Exeter had married (*c.*15 per cent), indicating their leanings towards reformed thought. Under Mary I's Catholic rule (1553–8), all were ejected from their benefices, though many ended their relationships or kept them secret and took up new positions.[52] Two years after Bartholomew had been appointed to Jacobstow, Eggesford, and Widworthy, the parishioners evidently hadn't accepted him as a Catholic minister.[53] The atypical framing of his testimony within the context of the commotion time appears to reflect this man's personal religious conflict at a turbulent time.

Religious nonconformity runs through each of the cases in which the 1549 rebellion was referenced. William Gooding of Whitchurch (Devon) told the Exeter court in 1557 that 'his said wiff went from [him] & was absent by the space of two yeres next *before the commotion* and beleavith that she went not away for this respondentes adulterie'.[54] But the court's questions strayed beyond his extra-marital relations, instead interrogating his religious practice and beliefs. Doubts were raised about the frequency with which he attended church, with William contending 'that he walketh theare sondrie tymes in mattens & evynsong tyme'. Questions were also asked about the improper use of a tabernacle he had purchased seven years earlier, presumably as Edwardian reform stripped parish churches of such furnishings. William insisted he had 'syled [furnished] his parlure [with the tabernacle] *not contemptuoslie'*. The references deponents like William Gooding and Bartholomew Cowde made to the commotion time were therefore subtle *yet intentional* reminders of their religious insecurity at a time when Protestant thinking and practice had become unlawful.

The religious reform and economic change that prompted the 1549 rebellion certainly shook Devon society, as Eamon Duffy showed for the village of Morebath, 42 kilometres from where Joan Good lived.[55] Returning to Joan's reference to her time in service during the 'commocion', we can only speculate on its significance to her own religious beliefs and practice. We must be cautious in overstating the significance of word choice in depositions; as Judith Butler wrote, '[t]he "I" has no story of its own that is not also the story of a relation – or set of relations – to a set of norms'.[56] The framework for understanding the events of 1549 was already cast and set within a vernacular culture of 'commotion'. That Joan's recollections were made in 1564 (when the rebellions were long absent from

[52] Vage, 'The Diocese of Exeter 1519–1641' (Unpublished thesis, University of Cambridge, 1991), pp. 92, 105, 113.
[53] For Bartholomew Cowde's appointment to the parish churches of Jacobstowe, Eggesford, and Widworthy in Devon in 1554, see https://theclergydatabase.org.uk/jsp/persons/DisplayPerson.jsp?PersonID=95674 (accessed 31 May 2023).
[54] DHC, Chanter 855, Office v William Gooding (1557). Italics my own.
[55] Eamon Duffy, *The Voices of Morebath: Reformation and Rebellion in an English Village* (New Haven and London, 2001), pp. 127–51.
[56] Judith Butler, *Giving an Account of Oneself* (New York, 2005), p. 8.

Devon depositions) is nonetheless interesting: the convocation of 1563 had taken place just one year earlier, consolidating the Elizabethan religious settlement and further entrenching Protestantism in the country.[57] Perhaps referring explicitly to the rebellion was no longer politically and religiously subversive, at least to legal eyes. However Joan felt about the events of 1549, when she thought about her time in service, the rebellions had clearly become intertwined with that memory.

Religious upheaval, dearth, and plague are all major focal points around which histories of early modern England pivot. Yet the localised – even household-centred – stories of female service we read give no indication of these women's place within a period of so many monumental changes. Joan's 1564 reference to the Western Rebellion, Judith's recollection of plague in Wells in the final decade of the sixteenth century, and Lucy's acknowledgement of the same decade as the 'deare yeares' indicate that these women were acutely aware of their place within wider narratives of change. These descriptions marked these events as personal, local, and national in their memories.[58] Although unusual in their explicit articulation, the broader contexts of these three women's memories of service help us to connect their working lives to the changes that took place around them, changes that they both observed and experienced. In turn, their memories of these changes were inextricably bound to their employment and experiences as servants.

Conclusion

In the absence of life writings or memoirs penned by sixteenth- and seventeenth-century female servants, we can nonetheless unravel their memories of service in court depositions. Their recollections open up their perceptions of events of the past. They show how they came to see and draw upon their experiences of service – as a source of knowledge and authority – later in life. These snippets of autobiographical reflections shed light on how people from the lower rungs of society thought about and remembered their lives.[59]

Communal practices and national changes – plague, rebellion, and local custom – have long dominated histories of memory. But service itself makes sense as a framework for remembering the past. Spending a long time away from their families, women in service were very mobile and their time in service represented a departure from their normal world. Being 'absent att service', for Christian

---

[57] Duffy found strict enforcement of the Elizabethan settlement across the diocese of Exeter in the early 1560s. See Duffy, *The Voices of Morebath*, pp. 169–81.

[58] Pollmann noted that local memory could be 'used both to distinguish that community from other communities and the world at large and to forge virtual relations to it'. See Pollmann, *Memory in Early Modern Europe*, p. 96.

[59] Brodie Waddell, 'Writing History from Below: Chronicling and Record-Keeping in Early Modern England', *History Workshop Journal* 85 (2018), 239–64 at 239–41.

Dowden of Wincanton (Somerset), was an inconsequential shift in the macro sense, but a large one in her world.[60]

As a form of identity, service wasn't fleeting or temporary. These formative years weren't just significant in teaching women the skills they needed to run households or even manage businesses. They were also important in shaping the connections these women made to other people and to the landscape around them. Once married and with an established household, one's identity became more fixed. Pollmann argued that personal development at this point was 'complete' for the memoirist and that 'they rarely recorded memories of personal change'.[61] The very fact that older women – never married, married, or widowed – referred back to their time in service reflects their emphasis on the importance of service in the creation of their identities. Service gave context or texture to their recollections. When asked to cast their minds back to a particular time or event, service for the most part was surely the main thing that rose to the surface of their recall. Service helped make sense of and organise their life stories – stories which grounded their working lives within national epidemics, economic crises, local practices, and customs.

---

[60] SHC, D/D/cd/64, Henry Glinn v James Churchaie sen, James Churchaie jun and Anna Churchaie (1629).
[61] Pollmann, *Memory in Early Modern Europe*, p. 37.

Conclusion

I bring my focus back to the four women with whom this book began: Matilda Bates, gathering apples high in a tree, listening to women arguing at the river; Sybil Bevor, dressed in borrowed clothes as she testified in court; Anna Elie, watching over her master and mistress's neighbour in his sickness; and Isott Riches, complaining at her neighbour's door that she had never agreed to be her mistress's 'drudge'. I started with a simple question: who were these servants?

Simple questions rarely have straightforward answers. In the history of service, the early modern period has been bookended by periods of change, leading us to assume that women like Matilda, Sybil, Anna, and Isott experienced service as something rigid, static, and *un*changing. At an aggregate level, service in Tawney's century (the period studied here) appears stable. Court depositions indicate that numbers of servants remained constant: Table 10.1 shows that the number of female servants identified across the period broadly aligns with record survival each year; no economic change or fluctuating opportunities for women are identified. Service had experienced a boom in late medieval England as Black Death labour shortages empowered workers and eroded the coercive labour bonds between landlords and serfs. By the sixteenth century, bonded labour had all but disappeared here, paving the way for the freeborn Englishman. Service was the epitome of free labour. Men and women made contracts and agreed terms. They were free to leave, no longer bound to the lord and land. By the beginning of the eighteenth century, agrarian transformations altered the economic climate once more. Large-scale farmers found it more profitable to hire wage labour than live-in servants. Social difference between servants and employers grew and by the nineteenth century, service remained only on smaller farms in the north of England and in large gentry households.

As economic and social historians, we routinely search for change over time. Of course, a woman in 1532 likely experienced service differently to her 1649 counterpart. Broadly, the evidence suggests that differences across this long century, however, were small: change is virtually imperceptible. As Andy Wood noted, a macro-historical perspective and focus on the '*long* view does not *of itself* help

Decade	Female servants in work		Deposition-generating cases	
	N	*%*	*N*	*%*
1530s	5	*< 1*	84	*1*
1540s	23	*1*	145	*2*
1550s	71	*4*	496	*6*
1560s	155	*9*	1,268	*15*
1570s	218	*13*	1,244	*14*
1580s	188	*11*	893	*10*
1590s	205	*12*	809	*9*
1600s	292	*17*	926	*11*
1610s	207	*12*	1,083	*12*
1620s	160	*9*	785	*9*
1630s	175	*10*	891	*10*
1640s	20	*1*	116	*1*
Total	**1,719**	—	**8,740**	—

Table 10.1 Female servants identified in depositions *c*.1530–1649

us to appreciate the lived experiences and mental worlds of the generations who lived under this great arch of capitalist evolution'.[1] But by looking closer at lived experiences rather than macro change, we find early modern service was anything but stable.

This was a time when what it meant to be a servant was in flux. Close analysis of the experiences of over one thousand women like Matilda, Sybil, Anna, and Isott disrupt traditional narratives: that they were life-cycle, annually hired, domestic workers whose labour was carried out within the home. This book has stretched open the prescriptive codes of servant conduct. It has shown that the lives and labour of these women were much more varied than previously thought. Female servants in early modern England weren't a homogeneous group. Much of what we thought we knew about them has piggy-backed on well-established tropes of their gender, youth, and dependent status. These tropes were perpetuated in both law and contemporary writings. This book has found that these tropes do not always hold.

Other sources and studies have been quiet about the range of socio-economic backgrounds from which early modern servants came. It is assumed that wealth 'saved' women from service and that poverty necessitated dependence on this

[1] Wood, *Memory of the People*, p. 196.

work. But it wasn't just the poor who served. Digging deeper into the life histories of servants, this book has shown that service was a vertically gradated occupation. Penniless children, orphaned teenagers, young women of modest means, and daughters of gentlemen *all served*. While labour sometimes flowed from poor to rich, it also flowed between households of similar status. Many women encountered in this book worked in the households of gentlemen and yeomen, but servants were hired even by those occupying the lower rungs of England's socio-economic ladder.

For some, service was a 'limbo' state. When questioned about their worth, female servants revealed expectations of inheritance or referred to sums of money they had already received from deceased parents. Others were only too aware of their economic adversity, characterising themselves as 'of little worth', though few readily admitted to being poor. Those of little worth pointed to the wealth they *did* hold – their wages or the clothes they owned. As most servants were young, this wasn't evidence of their poverty; they had no dependants and few responsibilities, so their belongings could indicate economic capacity. Women in service articulated their identities in different ways that reveal the capaciousness of the term 'servant'. A small group signalled their education, training, and upbringing with sophisticated signatures and initialling at the foot of their depositions. Others made elaborate designs that reflected education of a different sort: their experience in using a pen and making marks, as well as their recognition of the importance of a mark that was both an individual expression of their identity and personally reproducible and recognisable. These were women embedded in social practices and legal cultures. We saw in Chapter 1 how servant Marie Brimpton of Walton (Somerset) treaded carefully in 1609 with her prospective marriage, reminding her suitor that she 'must deal wearily' and have witnesses to their betrothal.

We also met Anne Nashe, servant of Gloucester alderman John Jones, in Chapter 2. She was conceived out of wedlock into a family of little wealth. But in 1630, she was working in one of the most literate households in the city, herself able to leave her shaky initials on the page of her deposition. Some women like Anne gained training and education in service that may even have stimulated social mobility, but this wasn't a universal experience. Others were forced into service when their household economies failed. How far orphans, widows, and even married women experienced service as an opportunity is questionable. For them, it was regularly a safety net, there to catch women or girls who fell on hard times. It was little more than a lifeline to the very poorest who might otherwise be dragged down by their circumstances.

Seeing service as contingent reminds us that children as young as 7 and women as old as 60 worked for families in exchange for wages, bed, and board. Service spanned the life cycle, providing work for single, married, widowed, and never married women, who entered, re-entered, and sometimes remained in service.

As a form of labour, service was flexible and accommodated several economic arrangements. The very young children placed in service were likely unfree, bound out as parish or pauper apprentices. This coercive strategy eased the burden on rate payers in supporting a poor household but forced service upon children, with no prospect of liberty until they reached adulthood. Entering service was often a response to economic hardship for widowed and even sometimes married women. The demographic range of service highlights the very different experiences that women might have, even working in the same household. Remember Christian Marten, age 20, and Agnes Edwards, age 40, of Preston Candover (Hampshire)? The shared act of cleaning the window as servants in the vicarage house in 1592 united two women who might otherwise have had little in common.

Servants are rightly characterised as the most mobile members of early modern society. Eighty per cent of female servants had moved at least once in their lifetimes. But while mobility was common and a handful had travelled considerable distances, others remained in their place of birth or migrated only short distances to adjacent parishes. Few travelled further than a day's journey from where they were born. This book has shown that female servants weren't always transient. While only a small proportion had never moved, some stayed in the same parish for several years, allowing them time to integrate into community life. Those who were more mobile also retained connections with people among whom they had lived and worked.

Mobility was normal for female servants but discouraged in law. The law, in fact, sought to limit mobility and ensure servants remained for at least six months in the same position. We met Joanna Daingerfield of Uley (Gloucestershire) in Chapter 4. Described by opposing witnesses in 1607 as a 'poore lame gerle' who 'stragleth upp and downe' for work, Joanna had in fact remained in the same parish but, at times, presumably struggled to find labour. The 1563 Statute of Artificers stipulated that servants should expect to make annual contracts with their masters. But the length of time servants remained in households varied considerably: many stayed for exactly one year; others stayed much longer and became established, almost permanent members of the household; and a significant number carried out much shorter periods of service, even as little as one week. As contract length varied, so too did start dates. While Michaelmas marked the beginning of service for many women, female servants were hired at virtually all times of the year. Hiring fairs that were commonly referred to in eighteenth- and nineteenth-century records couldn't have been widespread in the preceding two centuries and no evidence is found of them being held in the depositions. Word of mouth, familial connections, and general enquiry were more common paths taken in seeking service.

Regulation of service, then, is generally found lacking. Only in pauper apprenticeship and among the very poorest in society do we see hints that service could be coercively extracted from young women in the ways that Judith Bennett identified for the late medieval period.[2] Labour laws theoretically required contracts to be annual, pay not to exceed locally assessed rates, and masters and servants to appear at petty sessions to declare the terms of their agreements. But adherence to and enforcement of the labour laws appears piecemeal, at least in the south and west of England. Early modern labour laws saw service as preferable for young women, placing them under the patriarchal rule of the household, itself a microcosm of the state. But in practice, women carried out different forms of work without repercussion. Society saw limited difference between service and other forms of wage labour. Even the language of service was in flux during this period. We see 'servant' used to describe live-in, annually contracted workers as well as women hired on a casual basis. Some who were described as servants negotiated their pay on a weekly basis: strictly speaking these were casual workers, but society made no such differentiation. As early as 1962, C. B. Macpherson argued that when people in seventeenth-century England used the word 'servant', they included all wage earners.[3] Pay sometimes exceeded maximum wage rates. A covenant had a strict legal meaning that formalised labour relations between servants and masters and mistresses. It ratified the employer's responsibility for his or her servant, and gave each recourse to the law should things go wrong. But in a society where agreements were overwhelmingly oral, how could a covenant easily be enforced? Agreements were only as good as the people. In Chapter 5, we eavesdropped on the testimony of Philippa Hooper of Chedzoy (Somerset), a witness in an adultery case against her former mistress in 1623. She protested that she had never been in covenant as her servant. Many women worked in service without covenant at all, challenging the equation of service with stability and security. In this period of flux, freedom was not necessarily fictional, but nor were both parties equal in labour relations.

With all this flexibility, these really *were* women who attended to the vague 'necessary business' that the parishioners of Meare (Somerset) complained their servants couldn't get round to after their vicar's lengthy, droning sermons at the beginning of the seventeenth century. Short, casual contracts reflected the sometimes unpredictable, ad hoc needs of households, and the work these women carried out wasn't easily defined. If working in service as a woman is usually accompanied by the assumption that she exclusively tended to domestic work – cooking, cleaning, washing, and personal care of the family – this book has also proven this to be untrue. Work included running errands, carrying out husbandry tasks, milking, brewing, and other 'productive' labour. Depending on time of day, week, month, and the socio-economic status of

---

[2] Judith Bennett, 'Compulsory Service in Late Medieval England', *P&P* 209 (2010), 7–51.
[3] C. B. Macpherson, *The Political Theory of Possessive Individualism: Hobbes to Locke* (Oxford, 1962), pp. 107, 282.

the hiring family, households varied in the types of labour they required. The idea that male servants were *productive*, generating income for the household economy, while female servants' labour was *reproductive* and had no real monetary value, is wrong. These women were rarely described as domestic servants, and never as 'domestics' in this period. Literally meaning 'of the home', there is no intrinsic problem with using the term 'domestic servant' so long as we qualify what we mean by it.[4] The 'domestic' work these women carried out had economic value: it freed up other members of the household to participate in market labour. I prefer to describe these women simply as 'servants' or 'household servants'.

This isn't to say that women in service were confined to the physical building of the home. Contemporary writers encouraged female servants (like the rest of their gender) to remain at home. This was of course impractical. Female servants worked outdoors, but their social, economic, and religious lives also played out beyond the home. In Chapter 7, we encountered Alice Butler, a Gloucester servant in 1605 standing in the street before a hundred-strong crowd to masterfully defame her fellow servant's master with the memorable phrase, 'When the master has the game, the servant has the name'. Many other women in service were recorded outside their masters' homes for more innocuous reasons: running errands, meeting friends, and participating in community practices.

In spaces within and beyond the walls of the household, female servants were an integral part of community life. Friendships were created with members of the community as well as within the household. This evidence forces us to challenge the marginal status that servants have been accorded within early modern communities. Their ubiquity is well known, but their invisibility is assumed to the point that they are rarely included in discussions of community. As an itinerant work force, servants frequently moved between communities. But the important friendships and connections they maintained once they left remind us that communities were neither isolated nor geographically limited. Communities could stretch across landscapes. Inclusion and exclusion weren't entirely determined by geography. Pregnant women were turned away from parishes and rumours followed women as they moved, potentially barring access to communities: connections weren't always positive. But this was no truer of female servants than of other members of society. Church court depositions remind us of the networks of connectivity that stretched across the many parishes of the five dioceses, networks that female servants very much belonged to. Marie Robins of Ditcheat (Somerset), whom we met in Chapter 8, mobilised these networks when she came to court. Her mobility between occupations and also around a local area revealed the relationships she had built and could call upon when she brought a matrimonial suit to court in

---

[4] Whittle, 'A Critique', 39.

1609. Service constructed communities, networks, and relationships. It wasn't just a fleeting or transient experience.

In fact, service was a defining feature of many women's lives. By studying the testimonies of women *remembering* service, it's possible to see the importance of their work in their lives as a whole. In Chapter 9, we met Isabella Venn of Wedmore (Somerset), who testified in 1638 to her footsteps to the parish church. Service was a formative experience and the training it offered wasn't just in household management and work. Life events – national, local, and even individual practices – were embedded within memories of service (and vice versa). Service was remembered in different ways by different women. Its longevity was not always positive; throughout the book we are reminded of the long-term obligations to masters and mistresses that could accompany service. But service had temporal significance that its appointment as 'life-cycle' overlooks.

* * *

What should we make of this variation in experiences? What can we say about service if the very language used to describe it makes it *less* not *more* tangible? Service proves to be much slipperier than we've assumed. At its core, the only thing 'servant' signified was a labour relationship: *doing something on another person's behalf*. This is the only truth that holds for every single servant in this book. Many – but crucially not *all* – features or markers of service might also be present: live-in arrangements, payment of a wage as well as bed and board, and a contract or agreement (although its length might be short and its terms unenforceable). The servant might or might not be in her late teens or early 20s, unmarried, and poor.

Diversity of servant experience in early modern England raises questions about how we understand its decline in the eighteenth and nineteenth centuries. While the period 1532–1649 doesn't appear to have been a century of transition for service, service was also not the rigid, life-cycle, annually contracted occupation we thought it was either. In the early modern period, the line between service and casual labour was more blurred than we've thought. Perhaps, then, the shift over the eighteenth and nineteenth centuries from service to day labour was not so abrupt after all. Of course, much of the story of decline in service and rise in day labour has focused on male labour. This study raises questions about how female labour fits into this picture of change. A deposition-based study of a similar kind (for both male and female service) of the later period would be beneficial in answering these questions.

Of course, studies of women's work tend to hinge on injecting female labour into male-centric models of the economy. Acknowledgement of the significant contribution women made to the early modern economy is important. Female service tends to be dismissed as 'domestic', which I've shown to be meaningless without studying the actual tasks and repertoires of their working days. But the one way in which female servants *have* been integrated into a picture of broader economic change is in Tine de Moor and Jan Luiten van Zanden's 'girl power' argument. Based on the late age of marriage in northern Europe, which meant that unmarried people remained in the labour market for longer, their argument centralises the labour of single women in grand narratives of an increasingly commercialised economy over the early modern period.[5] The flexibility of service that we observe in English church court depositions seems to pave the way for a more commercialised economy. We've seen female servants hired to carry out work that directly contributed to the household's primary economic activities, and we've explored the labour calculations that early modern society made in weighing up the value of servants' labour. 'Hiring and firing' wasn't seriously obstructed by the law (and likewise, the law may not have been able to seriously hinder servants who wanted to leave). Shorter contracts enabled shrewd householders to hire servants only when they had economic need. Hiring for a full year was not always economically necessary, particularly in an agrarian economy where work was tied to the rhythms of the farming calendar.[6]

The girl power argument assumes the value of labour at a particular stage of the life cycle (i.e. before marriage). It assumes women were saving up for marriage, but we don't know this was always true. The evidence presented here breaks the clear relationship between service and setting up a household, because not all servants were of that age. Significantly, the argument is an optimistic take on the history of women's work. It implies there was choice and freedom. But if the work I've iden-tified in this book really was so central to fuelling modern economic growth, we must be cautious in seeing it as an 'opportunity' for all women. Certainly for some, ability to move between positions offered freedom and opportunity to grow and develop. Some gained skills and through their labour, human capital development (which de Moor and van Zanden argued accompanied this burgeoning labour market for women) was possible. But for others who were regularly dismissed or who could barely make ends meet, the lack of regulation of service brought inse-curity. Freedom to leave and to choose a path can be good for economic growth but not necessarily good for individual people. The flexibility of service and other forms of female labour may have been 'empowering' in an economic sense but also detrimental to the lives of individual women in service. Freedom, at the heart of this economic model, came at a cost.

---

[5] De Moor and Van Zanden, 'Girl Power', 1–33.
[6] This argument finds parallels in the nineteenth century, when employers may have hired day labourers for short periods and passed on the cost of outdoor relief to the rural middles classes during periods when they weren't required. For discussion of this, see George R. Boyer, *An Economic History of the English Poor Law, 1750–1850* (Cambridge, 1990), p. 124.

This raises the following question: did the state have the capacity to regulate? England's power was becoming more centralised, and the sixteenth- and seventeenth-century laws around labour and settlement, for example, were a gradual consolidation of various acts and ordinances from centuries past. But the machinery of the state was still fledgling. To enforce its laws, the state relied on local magistrates to rule and discipline, but more importantly on community policing – society's willingness to report young people living outside service or working on short contracts of service. But casual living and working arrangements were not inherently problematic to early modern society. Certainly, greater labour turnover put parishes at higher risk of supporting those without work. But until such risk became reality, communities appear not to have challenged the labour arrangements that young women negotiated for themselves, at least not in the south and west of the country. The Statute of Artificers suggests that the state's appetite to regulate their labour was high. But evidence littered throughout court depositions tells us that locals didn't meet this appetite with the same enthusiasm.

Legally, service was endorsed as an institution. There was no guild or company of servants, but service was promoted as an establishment that regulated and controlled youth and their labour. The premise of service being an institution is partly based on the idea that its members conformed to rules and that there were criteria for belonging. It is also based on the idea that the labour market was highly regulated through labour laws and statutes. But in practice, there was a great deal of variety in working practices and experiences of service and very little regulation on the ground. With practice failing to correlate with prescription, it's not so meaningful to talk of service as an institution.

Desire for an ordered society has been the bedrock of our understanding of the early modern social, economic, religious, and political landscape. But it's possible that casual – and therefore less ordered – labour served the needs of both young women and early modern households. As Tawny Paul argued for eighteenth-century middling-status men, multiple occupations and the movement between different work, may even have – at least for some early modern female servants – been central to their identities.[7] Hiring a servant for a week or a month was also less of an economic commitment for households. Households that hired servants on a casual basis presumably themselves took on some of the labour that an annual, live-in servant would otherwise do. These arrangements were a different kind of household management and order.

With greater fluidity and flexibility in early modern female service, we return to the question of the household patriarchy that apparently underpinned it. The fatherly authority of household patriarchy wasn't supposed to be directly oppressive, but the overlap of household patriarchy with patriarchy as a complete

---

[7] K. Tawny Paul, 'Accounting for Men's Work: Multiple Employments and Occupational Identities in Early Modern England', *History Workshop Journal* 85 (2018), 26–46 at 46.

system of male dominance has muddied the waters. Of course, household patriarchy – rule over the family by the male head – could be particularly oppressive for female servants, and examples of sexually abusive masters testify to this.

The world in which these women lived was undoubtedly one in which men ruled, just not in the way that we thought. We've paid too much attention to the moralists and lawmakers. Patriarchy and particularly household patriarchy were in full swing in the sixteenth and seventeenth centuries. But we've come to assume that any instance in which a woman displayed any behaviour or agenda that was even remotely at odds with patriarchal privilege made her unique or rebellious. 'Agency' when ascribed to early modern women is too often presented as something oppositional. But it needn't have been that way. Loose regulation of service, the ability to move regularly between masters, to make casual labour agreements, and the frequency with which servants were recorded outside the patriarchal home indicates that household patriarchy was less rigid than we might think.

Finding women in service in the pages of depositions is needle in a haystack work. They represent just 540 of 27,584 witnesses (only 2 per cent) and 186 of 16,247 litigants (just over 1 per cent) who came before the courts in this 117-year period. But this approach has shown the value of close examination of a group whose experiences we otherwise would know very little about. This statistical approach to using church court depositions offers a unique opportunity to understand and observe trends quantitatively while analysing these trends in conjunction with narrative evidence. The application of these methodologies to studying church court depositions opens up opportunities to seek new perspectives on various aspects of early modern life. How female servants' experiences compared with those of their male counterparts might be the next fruitful area of enquiry along these lines.

* * *

We return one final time to Isott Riches of Rockbeare (Devon), the one who refused to be beaten or to be a drudge. In writing history, we are supposed to avoid cherry-picking examples in favour of more impartial selection processes. But sometimes it's hard to resist. I unapologetically choose Isott now because – for some intangible reason – I was drawn to her when I found her story in the book of Exeter court depositions taken in 1568. I've no sense that her story was exceptional, but she has stuck with me throughout the ten years or so I have spent studying these women (which counts for a lot). We've come to 'know' Isott throughout the book. She is virtually a model example of a servant who conforms to the tropes we find across other sources. She was almost certainly a young 'life-cycle' servant who had served John and Katherine Brooke for a couple of years. Her stay in their house ended when she fell pregnant and was sent away. But her story encapsulates the complex history of early modern female service that I have set down in this book. When her neighbour Joanne Large deposed that Isott told her that she didn't come to Katherine Brooke's service 'to be beatyn, nor to be her drudge and that she wolde not tary long', these words at least in part defy the powerlessness that female servants could experience within the household patriarchal structure. She felt ill-treated and had decided she wouldn't stay. Isott was mobile, considerably more so than most. She had moved across Devon to follow her master and mistress to the scattered settlement of Rockbeare. Her expectations of work were at odds with what she experienced, despite the tasks being routine in the repertoires of so many others: she saw drudgery in the varied but perhaps heavy workload of milking, reaping barley, and food preparation.[8] While Isott bears some of the hallmarks of a stereotypical early modern servant, her story of service – like so many others recorded in court depositions – ultimately resists its easy characterisation as domestic, fleeting, or temporary.

---

[8] DHC, Chanter 858, John Roo v Frances Yarde (1568).

Appendix

	Probate (PCC 1653–60)											Gloucester Muster Survey (1608)	
	Somerset		Cornwall and Devon		Gloucestershire		Herefordshire		Hampshire		All		Gloucestershire	
	N	%	N	%	N	%	N	%	N	%	N		N	%
Agriculture	1,016	66	1,387	57	548	54	193	61	408	52	3,552		6,671	41
Husbandmen	414		387		103		14		99		1,017		3,774	
Labourers	3		8		4		4		1		20		1,831	
Yeomen and farmers	599		987		437		175		307		2,505		137	
Other			5		4				1		10		929	
Clergy	34	2	61	3	30	3	14	4	35	4	174		4	—
Crafts/trades/retail	296	19	462	19	255	25	33	10	143	18	1,189		5,808	36
Building and construction	4		21		12		3		7		47		319	
Cloth and leather	194		270		149		19		71		703		3,760	
Food and drink	33		67		30		5		25		160		586	
Smiths and makers	65		104		64		6		40		279		1,143	
Gentlemen	109	7	282	12	72	7	63	20	108	14	634		430	3
Mariners and fishermen	10	1	87	4	19	2		—	33	4	149		221	1
Merchants, professions, and officials	22	1	94	4	36	4	3	1	18	2	173		57	<1

(*Cont.*)

	Probate (PCC 1653–60)											Gloucester Muster Survey (1608)	
Mining and quarrying	2	*<1*	11	*<1*	1	*<1*	–	–	–	–	14	167	*1*
Miscellaneous and unidentified occupations	10	*1*	34	*1*	8	*1*	3	*1*	16	*2*	71	22	*<1*
Servants and apprentices	1	*<1*	9	*<1*	1	*<1*	–	–	3	*<1*	14	2,640	*16*
Service sector	36	*2*	26	*1*	42	*4*	10	*3*	23	*3*	137	228	*1*
Total	**1,536**		**2,453**		**1,012**		**319**		**787**		**6,107**	**16,248**	
No occupation given	*411*	*21*	*648*	*21*	*181*	*15*	*69*	*18*	*198*	*20*	*1,507*	*2,248*	*12*

Table A.1 Male occupations recorded in PCC wills (1563–60) and the Gloucester Muster Survey (1608)

Bibliography

Manuscript sources

Bristol Archives

Parochial Records

P.Wch/R/1/a   Parish Register of St Nicholas, Whitchurch (1565–1752)

Devon Heritage Centre

Diocese of Exeter Church court

Chanter 855–867   Depositions (1556–1640)

Gloucester Archives

Diocese of Gloucester Church court

GDR/3–205   Depositions (1549–1649)

Parochial Records

P62/IN/1/1   Parish Register of Brockworth (1559–1780)
P63/IN/1/1   Parish Register of Bromsberrow (1558–1748)
P86/1/IN/1/1   Parish Register of Cirencester (1560–1637)

Wills

GDR/R8/1578/73   Will of John Gurney of Cirencester (1578)
GDR/R8/1588/14   Will of Anne Parrie of Frampton on Severn (1588)
GDR/R8/1638/53   Will of Francis Smith of Coberley, yeoman (1638/9)

Hampshire Record Office

Diocese of Winchester Church court

21M65/C3/14   Depositions (1531–1635)

Hereford Archive and Records Centre

Diocese of Hereford Church court

HD4/2/11–14   Depositions (1545–1610)

Somerset Heritage Centre

Diocese of Bath & Wells Church court

D/D/cd/5–129   Depositions (1549–1648)

Somerset Quarter Sessions

QSR/34   Examination of Mary French (alias Lawrence) (1620)
QSR/42   Examination of William Jones (1622)

Parochial Records

D/P/ba.ab/2/1/1   Parish Register of Bath Abbey (1569–1743)
D/P/butl/2/1/1   Parish Register of Butleigh (1578–1653)
D/P/nun/2/1/1   Parish Register of Nunney (1547–1703)
D/P/wed/2/1/2   Parish Register of Wedmore (1611–1663)

The National Archives

Wills

PROB 11/124/346   Will of Walter Knoll (1614)
PROB 11/130/11   Will of Thomas Quarman (1617)
PROB 11/159/495   Will of John Jones (1631)
PROB 11/216/237   Will of Nicholas Clothier (1649)

Online resources and data sets

British History Online https://www.british-history.ac.uk
Oxford English Dictionary https://oed.com
The Clergy Database https://theclergydatabase.org.uk
Spicksley, J., and Shepard, A., *Worth of Witnesses in the English Church Courts, 1550–1728* [data collection] (2020), UK Data Service. SN: 5652, http://doi.org/10.5255/UKDA-SN-5652-1

Printed primary sources

Contemporary printed books

Baxter, R., *A Christian directory, or, A summ of practical theologie and cases of conscience directing Christians how to use their knowledge and faith* (1673).
Butler, C., *The Feminine Monarchie: Or the Historie of Bees* (1623).
Carter, T., *Christian Commonwealth* (1627).
Chamberlayne, E., *Angliae Notitia: Or, the Present State of England* (1669).
Conset, H., *The Practice of the Spiritual or Ecclesiastical Courts to which is added a brief discourse of the structure and manner of forming the libel or declaration* (1685).
Dod, J., and Cleaver, R., *A Godlie Forme of Householde Government for the Ordering of Private Families* (1612).
Favine, A., *The Theater of Honour and Knighthood* (1623, translated from the French of 1620).
Gouge, W., *Of Domesticall Duties: Eight Treatises*, 3rd edition (1622).
West, W., *The Second Part of Symboleography* (1604).
Whately, W., *A Bride-Bush: Or, Direction for Married Persons: Plainely Describing the Duties Common to Both, and Peculiar to Each of Them* (1619).

Editions of manuscripts

Brown, P. A., Tawney, R. H., and Bland, A. E. (eds), *English Economic History: Select Documents* (Bell, 1920).
Chandler, J. (ed.), *John Leland's Itinerary: Travels in Tudor England* (Stroud: Sutton, 1998).
Given-Wilson, C., Brand, P., Phillips, S., Ormrod, M., Martin, G., Curry, A. and Horrox, R. (eds), *Parliament Rolls of Medieval England* (Woodbridge: Boydell, 2005, *British History Online* www.british-history.ac.uk/no-series/parliament-rolls-medieval/may-1413 [accessed 3 May 2023]
Hamilton, A. H. A. (ed.), *Quarter Sessions from Queen Elizabeth to Queen Anne: Illustrations of Local Government and History Drawn from Original*

Records (Chiefly of the County of Devon) (Sampson Low, Marston, Searle & Rivington, 1878).

Hughes, P. L., and Larkin, J. F. (eds), *Tudor Royal Proclamations, Vol. 3: The Later Tudors (1588–1603)* (New Haven: Yale University Press, 1969).

Husband, W. (ed.), *Depositions in the Consistory Court of the Bishop of Bath and Wells, Vol. 1: Office Depositions 1601 to 1605* (Croydon: List and Index Society, 2019).

Last, N., *Nella Last's Peace: The Post-War Diaries of Housewife, 49*, Malcolmsen, P. E., and Malcolmson, R. W. (eds)(London: Profile, 2008).

Loder, R., *Robert Loder's Farm Accounts, 1610–1620*, (ed.) G. E. Fussell (Offices of the Camden Society, 1936).

Luders, A. (ed.), *The Statutes of the Realm* (1810).

Markham, G., *The English Housewife*, (ed.) M. R. Best (Montreal: McGill-Queen's University Press, 1986).

Smith, T., *De Republica Anglorum*, (ed.) M. Dewar (Cambridge: Cambridge University Press, 1982).

Tawney, R. H., and Power, E. (eds), *Tudor Economic Documents: Being Select Documents Illustrating the Economic and Social History of Tudor England, Vol. 1* (1951).

Tilney, E., *The Flower of Friendship: A Renaissance Dialogue Contesting Marriage*, (ed.) V. Wayne (Ithaca, NY: Cornell University Press, 1992).

Tusser, T., *Five Hundreth Points of Good Husbandry United to as Many of Good Huswiferie*, (ed.) G. Grigson (Oxford: Oxford University Press, 1984).

Secondary works

Place of publication is London unless otherwise stated.

Adair, W.D., 'Can we trust the census reports? Lessons from a study of domestic servants in Tenbury, Worcestershire, 1851 and 1861', *Family & Community History* 5 (2002), 99–110.

Ågren, M., 'Emissaries, Allies, Accomplices and Enemies: Married Women's Work in Eighteenth-Century Urban Sweden', *Urban History* 41 (2014), 394–414.

Ågren, M. (ed.), *Making a Living, Making a Difference: Gender and Work in Early Modern European Society* (Oxford: Oxford University Press, 2017).

Allen, R. C., and Weisdorf, J. L., 'Was There an "Industrious Revolution" before the Industrial Revolution? An Empirical Exercise for England, *c.*1300–1830', *EcHR* 64 (2011), 715–29.

Amussen, S. D., *An Ordered Society: Gender and Class in Early Modern England* (New York: Columbia University Press, 1993).

Amussen, S. D., *Gender, Culture and Politics in England, 1560–1640: Turning the World Upside Down* (Bloomsbury, 2017).

Ardener, S., 'Ground Rules and Social Maps for Women', in S. Ardener (ed.), *Women and Space: Ground Rules and Social Maps* (Oxford: Berg, 1983), pp. 11–32.

Arnold, J., 'The Materiality of Unbelief in Late Medieval England', in S. Page (ed.), *The Unorthodox in Late Medieval Britain* (Manchester: Manchester University Press, 2010), pp. 65–95.

Baggs, A. P., Jurica, A. R. J., and Sheils, W. J., 'Bisley: Economic History', in N. M. Herbert and R. B. Pugh (eds), *A History of the County of Gloucester, Vol. 11: Bisley and Longtree Hundreds* (Victoria County History, 1976), pp. 20–30.

Bailey, J., *Unquiet Lives: Marriage and Marriage Breakdown in England, 1660–1800* (Cambridge: Cambridge University Press, 2003).

Bailey, M., *The Decline of Serfdom in Late Medieval England: From Bondage to Freedom* (Woodbridge: Boydell, 2014).

Barry, J., 'South-West', in P. Clark (ed.), *The Cambridge Urban History of Britain* (Cambridge: Cambridge University Press, 2008), pp. 67–92.

Bartlett, F. C., *Remembering: A Study in Experimental and Social Psychology* (Cambridge: Cambridge University Press, 1932).

Beattie, C., *Medieval Single Women: The Politics of Social Classification in Late Medieval England* (Oxford: Oxford University Press, 2007).

Ben-Amos, I. K., *Adolescence and Youth in Early Modern England* (New Haven: Yale University Press, 1994).

Bennett, J.M., 'Compulsory Service in Late Medieval England', *P&P* 209 (2010), 7–51.

Bennett, J. M., 'Wretched Girls, Wretched Boys and the European Marriage Pattern in England (*c.*1250–1350)', *Continuity and Change* 34 (2019), 315–47.

Blacker, R. B. H., 'Alderman John Jones, of Gloucester', *Gloucestershire Notes and Queries: Part XVI* (W. Kent & Co, 1882), pp. 143–5.

Botelho, L., 'Old Age and Menopause in Rural Women of Early Modern Suffolk', in L. Botelho and P. Thane (eds), *Women and Ageing in British Society since 1500* (Abingdon: Routledge, 2001), pp. 43–65.

Bowen, J., 'A "countrie" consisting wholly of woodland, "bredd of Oxen and Dairies"? Agricultural Regions and Rural Communities in Lowland Pastoral Shropshire during the Early Modern Period', in C. Dyer and R. Jones (eds), *Farmers, Consumers, Innovators: The World of Joan Thirsk* (Hatfield: University of Hertfordshire Press, 2016), pp. 49–62.

Bowen, L., 'News Networks in Early Modern Wales', *History* 102 (2017), 24–44.

Boyer, G. R., *An Economic History of the English Poor Law, 1750–1850* (Cambridge: Cambridge University Press, 1990).

Broadberry, S., Campbell, B. M. S., Klein, A., Overton, M., and Leeuwen, B. v., *British Economic Growth, 1270–1870* (Cambridge: Cambridge University Press, 2015).

Brodsky Elliot, V., 'Single Women in the London Marriage Market: Age, Status and Mobility, 1598–1619', in R. B. Outhwaite (ed.), *Marriage and Society: Studies in the Social History of Marriage* (Europa, 1981), pp. 81–100.

Burke, P., 'History as Social Memory', in T. Butler (ed.), *Memory: History, Culture and the Mind* (Oxford: Blackwell, 1989), pp. 97–113.

Butler, J., *Giving an Account of Oneself* (New York: Fordham University Press, 2005).

Capp, B., *When Gossips Meet: Women, Family, and Neighbourhood in Early Modern England* (Oxford: Oxford University Press, 2003).

Carus, A. W., and Ogilvie, S., 'Turning Qualitative into Quantitative Evidence: A Well-Used Method Made Explicit', *EcHR* 62 (2009), 893–925.

Cavill, P., 'Mortuary Dues in Early Sixteenth-Century England', *Continuity and Change* 36 (2021), 285–308.

Chakravarty, U., *Fictions of Consent: Slavery, Servitude, and Free Service in Early Modern England* (Philadelphia: University of Pennsylvania Press, 2022).

Chalklin, C. W., 'South-East', in P. Clark (ed.), *The Cambridge Urban History of Britain* (Cambridge: Cambridge University Press, 2008), pp. 49–66.

Chaytor, M., 'Husband(ry): Narratives of Rape in the Seventeenth Century', *Gender & History* 7 (1995), 378–407.

Churches, C., 'Women and Property in Early Modern England: A Case-Study', *Social History* 23 (1998), 165–80.

Clark, A., *Working Life of Women in the Seventeenth Century* (Routledge & Kegan Paul, 1982 [1919]).

Clark, P., 'The Migrant in Kentish Towns, 1580–1640', in P. Clark and D. Souden (eds), *Crisis and Order in English Towns, 1500–1700* (Routledge, 1972), pp. 117–63.

Clark, P., 'Migration in England during the Late Seventeenth and Early Eighteenth Centuries', *P&P* 83 (1979), 57–90.

Clark, P., and Hosking, J., *Population Estimates of English Small Towns, 1550–1851* (Leicester: University of Leicester Press, 1993).

Cockayne, E., *Hubbub: Filth, Noise & Stench in England 1600–1770* (New Haven: Yale University Press, 2007).

Cockburn, J. S., 'Early-Modern Assize Records as Historical Evidence', *Journal of the Society of Archivists* 5 (1975), 215–31.

Collinson, J., and Rack, E., *The History and Antiquities of the County of Somerset* (Bath: R. Cruttwell, 1791).

Connerton, P., *How Societies Remember* (Cambridge: Cambridge University Press, 1989).

Crawford, P., *Parents of Poor Children in England 1580–1800* (Oxford: Oxford University Press, 2010).

Creighton, C., *A History of Epidemics in Britain from A.D. 664 to the Extinction of Plague* (Cambridge: Cambridge University Press, 1891).

Cressy, D., 'Occupations, Migration and Literacy in East London, 1580–1640', *Local Population Studies* 5 (1970), 53–60.

Cressy, D., *Literacy and Social Order: Reading and Writing in Tudor and Stuart England* (Cambridge: Cambridge University Press, 1980).

Crowley, J. E., *The Invention of Comfort: Sensibilities and Design in Early Modern Britain and Early America* (Baltimore, MD: Johns Hopkins University Press, 2000).

Cust, R., 'News and Politics in Early Seventeenth-Century England', *P&P* 112 (1986), 60–90.

Davidoff, L., and Hall, C., *Family Fortunes: Men and Women of the English Middle Class 1780–1850* (Hutchinson Education, 1987).

Davis, N. Z., *Fiction in the Archives: Pardon Tales and Their Tellers in Sixteenth-Century France* (Cambridge: Polity Press, 1987).

Delap, L., *Knowing Their Place: Domestic Service in Twentieth-Century Britain* (Oxford: Oxford University Press, 2011).

De Moor, T., and Van Zanden, J. L., 'Girl Power: The European Marriage Pattern and Labour Markets in the North Sea Region in the Late Medieval and Early Modern Period', *EcHR* 63 (2010), 1–33.

Dobson, R. B., *The Peasants' Revolt of 1381* (Macmillan, 1970).

Dolan, F. E., *True Relations: Reading, Literature, and Evidence in Seventeenth-Century England* (Philadelphia: University of Pennsylvania Press, 2013).

Duffy, E., *The Voices of Morebath: Reformation and Rebellion in an English Village* (New Haven and London: Yale University Press, 2001).

Dunlop, O. J., and Denman, R. D., *English Apprenticeship and Child Labour: A History* (T. Fisher Unwin, 1912).

Dyer, C., 'Were Late Medieval English Villages "Self-Contained"?', in C. Dyer (ed.), *The Self-Contained Village? The Social History of Rural Communities, 1250–1900* (Hatfield: University of Hertfordshire Press, 2007), pp. 6–27.

Earle, P., *The Making of the English Middle Class: Business, Society, and Family Life in London, 1660–1750* (Berkeley: University of California Press, 1989).

Earle, P., *A City Full of People: Men and Women of London 1650–1750* (Methuen, 1994).

Eisner, R., 'Measure It to Make It Count', *Feminist Economics* 2 (1996), 143–4.

Emmison, F. G., *Elizabethan Life: Morals and the Church Courts* (Chelmsford: Essex Record Office, 1973).

Erickson, A. L., *Women and Property in Early Modern England* (Routledge, 1993).

Erickson, A. L., 'Coverture and Capitalism', *History Workshop Journal* 59 (2005), 1–16.

Erickson, A. L., 'Married Women's Occupations in Eighteenth-Century London', *Continuity and Change* 23 (2008), 267–307.

Erickson, A. L., 'Mistresses and Marriage: Or, a Short History of the Mrs', *History Workshop Journal* 78 (2014), 39–57.

Ewan, E., 'Mistresses of Themselves? Female Domestic Servants and By-Employments in Sixteenth-Century Scottish Towns', in A. Fauve-Chamoux (ed.), *Domestic Service and the Formation of European Identity* (Bern: Peter Lang, 2004), pp. 411–33.

Fentress, J., and Wickham, C., *Social Memory* (Oxford: Blackwell, 1992).

Fiebranz, R., Lindberg, E., Lindström, J., and Ågren, M., 'Making Verbs Count: The Research Project "Gender and Work" and Its Methodology', *Scandinavian Economic History Review* 59 (2011), 273–93.

Field, J., 'Domestic Service, Gender, and Wages in England, *c*.1700–1860', *EcHR* 66 (2013), 249–72.

Finlay, R., *Population and Metropolis: The Demography of London, 1580–1650* (Cambridge: Cambridge University Press, 1981).

Flather, A., *Gender and Space in Early Modern England* (Woodbridge: Boydell, 2007).

Foley, W., *A Child in the Forest* (London: British Broadcasting Company, 1974).

Fox, A., 'Rumour, News and Popular Political Opinion in Elizabethan and Early Stuart England', *The Historical Journal* 40 (1997), 597–620.

Fox, A., 'Remembering the Past in Early Modern England: Oral and Written Tradition', *TRHS* 9 (1999), 233–56.

Fox, A., *Oral and Literate Culture in England, 1500–1700* (Oxford: Oxford University Press, 2002).

Fox, H., 'Medieval Farming and Rural Settlement', in R. Kain, W. Ravenhill, and H. Jones (eds), *Historical Atlas of South-West England* (Exeter: University of Exeter Press, 1999), pp. 273–80.

Foyster, E., 'Silent Witnesses? Children and the Breakdown of Domestic and Social Order in Early Modern England', in A. Fletcher and S. Hussey (eds), *Childhood in Question: Children, Parents and the State* (Manchester: Manchester University Press, 1999), pp. 57–73.

Foyster, E., *Marital Violence: An English Family History, 1660–1857* (Cambridge: Cambridge University Press, 2005).

French, H. R., *The Middle Sort of People in Provincial England, 1600–1750* (Oxford: Oxford University Press, 2008).

Frisch, A., *The Invention of the Eyewitness: Witnessing and Testimony in Early Modern France* (Chapel Hill: University of North Carolina Press, 2004).

Froide, A. M., *Never Married: Singlewomen in Early Modern England* (Oxford: Oxford University Press, 2005).

Fussell, G. E., *The English Dairy Farmer 1500–1900* (Routledge, 1966).

Fussell, G. E., and Fussell, K. R., *The English Countrywoman: A Farmhouse Social History: The Internal Aspect of Rural Life AD 1500–1900* (Andrew Melrose, 1953).

Gaskill, M., *Crime and Mentalities in Early Modern England* (Cambridge: Cambridge University Press, 2000).

Gaskill, M., 'Little Commonwealths II: Communities', in K. Wrightson (ed.), *A Social History of England 1500–1750* (Cambridge: Cambridge University Press, 2017), pp. 84–104.

Gerrard, S., 'The Tin Industry in Sixteenth- and Seventeenth-Century Cornwall', in R. Kain, W. Ravenhill, and H. Jones (eds), *Historical Atlas of South-West England* (Exeter: University of Exeter Press, 1999), pp. 330–7.

Girouard, M., *Life in the English Country House: A Social and Architectural History* (New Haven and London: Yale University Press, 1980).

Given-Wilson, C., 'Service, Serfdom and English Labour Legislation, 1350–1500', in A. Curry and E. Matthew (eds), *Concepts and Patterns of Service in the Later Middle Ages* (Woodbridge: Boydell, 2000), pp. 21–37.

Glaisyer, N., *The Culture of Commerce in England, 1660–1720* (Woodbridge: Boydell, 2006).

Glaisyer, N., and Pennell, S., 'Introduction', in N. Glaisyer and S. Pennell (eds), *Didactic Literature in England 1500–1800: Expertise Constructed* (London: Routledge, 2016), pp. 1–18.

Goldberg, P. J. P., *Women, Work and Life Cycle in a Medieval Economy: Women in York and Yorkshire c.1300–1520* (Oxford: Oxford University Press, 1992).

Goldberg, P. J. P., 'What Was a Servant?', in A. Curry and E. Matthew (eds), *Concepts and Patterns of Service in the Later Middle Ages* (Woodbridge: Boydell, 2000), pp. 1–20.

Goldgar, A., and Frost, R. I., 'Introduction', in A. Goldgar and R. I. Frost (eds), *Institutional Culture in Early Modern Society* (Leiden: Brill, 2004), pp. xi–xxii.

Gowing, L., 'Language, Power and the Law: Women's Slander Litigation in Early Modern London', in J. Kermode and G. Walker (eds), *Women, Crime and the Courts in Early Modern England* (Chapel Hill: University of North Carolina Press, 1994), pp. 26–47.

Gowing, L., *Domestic Dangers: Women, Words and Sex in Early Modern London* (Oxford: Oxford University Press, 1996).

Gowing, L., 'Secret Births and Infanticide in Seventeenth-Century England', *P&P* 156 (1997), 87–115.

Gowing, L., '"The Freedom of the Streets": Women and Social Space, 1560–1640', in P. Griffiths and M. S. R. Jenner (eds), *Londinopolis: Essays in the Cultural and Social History of Early Modern London c.1500–c.1750* (Manchester: Manchester University Press, 2000), pp. 130–53.

Gowing, L., 'The Haunting of Susan Lay: Servants and Mistresses in Seventeenth-Century England', *Gender & History* 14 (2002), 183–201.

Gowing, L., *Common Bodies: Women, Sex, and Reproduction in Seventeenth Century England* (New Haven: Yale University Press, 2003).

Gowing, L., 'The Politics of Women's Friendship in Early Modern England', in L. Gowing, M. Hunter, and M. Rubin (eds), *Love, Friendship and Faith in Europe, 1300–1800* (Palgrave Macmillan, 2005), pp. 131–49.

Gowing, L., 'The Twinkling of a Bedstaff', *Home Cultures* 11 (2014), 275–304.

Gray, I., 'The Iconography of Archives, IV: The Monument of John Jones at Gloucester', *Journal of the Society of Archivists* 3 (1969), 488–9.

Griffin, E., *England's Revelry: A History of Popular Sports and Pastimes, 1660–1830* (Oxford: Oxford University Press, 2005).

Griffiths, P., *Youth and Authority: Formative Experiences in England, 1560–1640* (Oxford: Oxford University Press, 1996).

Griffiths, P., 'Meanings of Nightwalking in Early Modern England', *Seventeenth-Century Journal* 13 (1998), 212–38.

Griffiths, P., 'Tudor Troubles: Problems of Youth in Elizabethan England', in S. Doran and N. L. Jones (eds), *The Elizabethan World* (Abingdon: Routledge, 2010), pp. 316–34.

Haigh, C., 'Slander and the Church Courts in the Sixteenth Century', *Transactions of the Lancashire and Cheshire Antiquarian Society* 78 (1975), 1–13.

Haigh, C., 'Anticlericalism and the English Reformation', in C. Haigh (ed.), *The English Reformation Revised* (Cambridge: Cambridge University Press, 1987), pp. 56–74.

Hailwood, M., 'Time and Work in Rural England, 1500–1700', *P&P* 248 (2020), 87–121.

Hailwood, M., 'Rethinking Literacy in Rural England, 1550–1700', *P&P* 260 (2023), 38–70.

Hajnal, J., 'European Marriage Patterns in Perspective', in D. V. Glass and D. E. C. Eversley (eds), *Population in History: Essays in Historical Demography* (London: Edward Arnold, 1965), pp. 101–47.

Hajnal, J., 'Two Kinds of Preindustrial Household Formation System', *Population and Development Review* 8 (1982), 449–94.

Hamling, T., and Richardson, C., *A Day at Home in Early Modern England: Material Culture and Domestic Life, 1500–1700* (New Haven: Yale University Press, 2017).

Handley, S., *Sleep in Early Modern England* (Yale University Press, 2016).

Hassan Jansson, J., Fiebranz, R., and Östman, A., 'Constitutive Tasks: Performances of Hierarchy and Identity', in M. Ågren (ed.), *Making a Living, Making a Difference: Gender and Work in Early Modern European Society* (Oxford: Oxford University Press, 2017), pp. 127–58.

Hardwick, J., *Family Business: Litigation and the Political Economies of Daily Life in Early Modern France* (Oxford: Oxford University Press, 2009).

Harris Sacks, D., and Lynch, M., 'Ports, 1540–1700', in P. Clark (ed.), *The Cambridge Urban History of Britain* (Cambridge: Cambridge University Press, 2008), pp. 377–424.

Hartman, S., *Scenes of Subjection: Terror, Slavery, and Self-Making in Nineteenth-Century America* (New York: Oxford University Press, 1997).

Hassan Jansson, J., Fiebranz, R., and Östman, A., 'Constitutive Tasks: Performances of Hierarchy and Identity', in M. Ågren (ed.), *Making a Living, Making a Difference: Gender and Work in Early Modern European Society* (Oxford: Oxford University Press, 2017), pp. 127–58.

Havinden, M. A., 'The Woollen, Lime, Tanning and Leather-Working and Paper-Making Industries *c.*1500–1800', in R. Kain, W. Ravenhill, and H. Jones (eds), *Historical Atlas of South-West England* (Exeter: University of Exeter Press, 1999), pp. 338–44.

Havinden, M. A., and Stanes, R., 'Agriculture and Rural Settlement, 1500–1800', in R. Kain, W. Ravenhill, and H. Jones (eds), *Historical Atlas of South-West England* (Exeter: University of Exeter Press, 1999), pp. 281–93.

Hecht, J. J., *The Domestic Servant Class in Eighteenth-Century England* (London: Routledge & Kegan Paul, 1956).

Herbert, A. E., *Female Alliances: Gender, Identity, and Friendship in Early Modern Britain* (New Haven: Yale University Press, 2014).

Hill, B., *Servants: English Domestics in the Eighteenth Century* (Oxford: Oxford University Press, 1996).

Hill, C., *Economic Problems of the Church from Archbishop Whitgift to the Long Parliament* (New York: Oxford University Press, 1956).

Hill, C., 'Pottage for Freeborn Englishmen: Attitudes to Wage Labour in the Sixteenth and Seventeenth Centuries', in C. H. Feinstein (ed.), *Socialism, Capitalism and Economic Growth: Essays Presented to Maurice Dobb* (Cambridge: Cambridge University Press, 1967), pp. 338–50.

Hill, C., *Society and Puritanism in Pre-Revolutionary England* (London: Penguin, 1991).

Hindle, S., 'The Shaming of Margaret Knowsley: Gossip, Gender and the Experience of Authority in Early Modern England', *Continuity and Change* 9 (1994), 391–419.

Hindle, S., *The State and Social Change in Early Modern England, c.1550–1640* (Palgrave, 2000).

Hindle, S., *On the Parish? The Micro-Politics of Poor Relief in Rural England c.1550–1750* (Oxford: Oxford University Press, 2004).

Hindle, S., 'Technologies of Identification Under the Old Poor Law', *The Local Historian* 36 (2006), 220–36.

Hockaday, F. S., 'The Consistory Court of the Diocese of Gloucester', *Transactions of the Bristol and Gloucestershire Archaeological Society* 46 (1924), 195–287.

Hodges, M., 'Widows of the "Middling Sort" and Their Assets in Two Seventeenth-Century Towns', in T. Arkell, N. Evans, and N. Goose (eds), *When Death Do Us Part: Understanding and Interpreting the Probate Records of Early Modern England* (Oxford: Leopard's Head Press, 2000), pp. 306–24.

Hoskins, W. G., 'Harvest Fluctuations and English Economic History, 1480–1619', *Agricultural History Review* 12 (1964), 28–46.

Houlbrooke, R. A., *Church Courts and the People during the English Reformation 1520–1570* (Oxford: Oxford University Press, 1979).

Hoyle, R. W., 'Shrewsbury, Dearth, and Extreme Weather at the End of the Sixteenth Century', *Agricultural History Review* 86 (2020), 22–36.

Hubbard, E., *City Women: Money, Sex, and the Social Order in Early Modern London* (Oxford: Oxford University Press, 2012).

Hubbard, E., 'Reading, Writing, and Initialing: Female Literacy in Early Modern London', *JBS* 54 (2015), 553–77.

Hufton, O., *The Poor of Eighteenth-Century France, 1750–1789* (Oxford: Clarendon Press, 1974).

Humphries, J., 'Household Economy', in P. Johnson and R. Floud (eds), *The Cambridge Economic History of Modern Britain, Vol. 1: Industrialisation, 1700–1860* (Cambridge: Cambridge University Press, 2004), pp. 238–67.

Humphries, J., 'Girls and their Families in an Era of Economic Change', *Continuity and Change* 35 (2020), 311–43.

Humphries, J., and Horrell, S., 'Women's Labour Force Participation and the Transition to the Male-Breadwinner Family, 1790–1865', *EcHR* 48 (1995), 89–117.

Humphries, J., and Weisdorf, J., 'The Wages of Women in England, 1260–1850', *Journal of Economic History* 75 (2015), 405–47.

Hurl-Eamon, J., 'The Fiction of Female Dependence and the Makeshift Economy of Soldiers, Sailors, and Their Wives in Eighteenth-Century London', *Labor History* 49 (2008), 481–501.

Hylland Eriksen, T., *Small Places, Large Issues: An Introduction to Social and Cultural Anthropology*, 4th edition (London: Pluto, 2015).

Ingram, M., 'Ridings, Rough Music and the "Reform of Popular Culture" in Early Modern England', *P&P* 105 (1984), 79–113.

Ingram, M., *Church Courts, Sex and Marriage in England, 1570–1640* (Cambridge: Cambridge University Press, 1988).

Ingram, M., 'Scolding Women Cucked or Washed: A Crisis in Gender Relations in Early Modern England?', in J. Kermode and G. Walker (eds), *Women, Crime and the Courts in Early Modern England* (Chapel Hill: University of North Carolina Press, 1994), pp. 48–80.

Ingram, M., *Carnal Knowledge: Regulating Sex in England, 1470–1600* (Cambridge: Cambridgd University Press, 2017).

Johnson, J. M., *Wicked Flesh: Black Women, Intimacy, and Freedom in the Atlantic World* (Philadelphia: University of Pennsylvania Press, 2020).

Johnson, M., *English Houses, 1300–1800: Vernacular Architecture, Social Life* (Harlow: Pearson Longman, 2010).

Kane, B., *Popular Memory and Gender in Medieval England: Men, Women and Testimony in the Church Courts, c.1200–1500* (Woodbridge: Boydell, 2019).

Kelsall, R. K., 'Wage Regulations under the Statute of Artificers', in W. E. Minchinton (ed.), *Wage Regulation in Pre-Industrial England* (Newton Abbot: David and Charles, 1972), pp. 93–197.

Kowaleski, M., *Local Markets and Regional Trade in Medieval Exeter* (Cambridge: Cambridge University Press, 1995).

Kussmaul, A., *Servants in Husbandry in Early Modern England* (Cambridge: Cambridge University Press, 1981).

Kussmaul, A., *A General View of the Rural Economy of England, 1538–1840* (Cambridge: Cambridge University Press, 1990).

Laslett, P., *Family Life and Illicit Love in Earlier Generations: Essays in Historical Sociology* (Cambridge: Cambridge University Press, 1977).

Laslett, P., 'The Bastardy Prone Sub-Society', in P. Laslett, K. Oosterveen, and R. Smith (eds), *Bastardy and Its Comparative History: Studies in the History of Illegitimacy and Nonconformism in Britain, France, Germany, Sweden, North America, Jamaica, and Japan* (Cambridge, MA: Harvard University Press, 1980), pp. 217–46.

Light, A., *Mrs Woolf and the Servants* (London: Fig Tree, 2007).

Lindström, D., Feibranz, R., Lindström, J., Mispelaere, J., and Rydén, G., 'Working Together', in M. Ågren (ed.), *Making a Living, Making a Difference: Gender and Work in Early Modern European Society* (Oxford: Oxford University Press, 2017), pp. 57–79.

Lindström, J., Feibranz, R., and Rydén, G., 'The Diversity of Work', in M. Ågren (ed.), *Making a Living, Making a Difference: Gender and Work in Early Modern European Society* (Oxford: Oxford University Press, 2017), pp. 24–56.

Ling, S., Hassan Jansson, K., Lennersand, M., Pihl, C., and Ågren, M., 'Marriage and Work: Intertwined Sources of Agency and Authority', in M. Ågren (ed.), *Making a Living, Making a Difference: Gender and Work in Early Modern European Society* (Oxford: Oxford University Press, 2017), pp. 80–102.

MacCulloch, D., 'Bondmen under the Tudors', in C. Cross, D. Loades, and J. J. Scarisbrick (eds), *Law and Government under the Tudors: Essays Presented to Sir Geoffrey Elton, Regius Professor of Modern History in the University of Cambridge, on the Occasion of His Retirement* (Cambridge: Cambridge University Press, 1988), pp. 91–110.

MacCulloch, D., and Fletcher, A., *Tudor Rebellions*, 7th edition (Abingdon: Routledge, 2020).

Macfarlane, A., *The Family Life of Ralph Josselin, a Seventeenth-Century Clergyman: An Essay in Historical Anthropology* (New York: Norton, 1977).

Macfarlane, A., 'History, Anthropology and the Study of Communities', *Social History* 2 (1977), 631–52.

Macfarlane, A., *The Origins of English Individualism: The Family, Property and Social Transition* (Oxford: Blackwell, 1978).

Macpherson, C. B., *The Political Theory of Possessive Individualism: Hobbes to Locke* (Oxford: Oxford University Press, 1962).

Mansell, C., 'Female Service and the Village Community in South-West England 1550–1650: The Labour Laws Reconsidered', in J. Whittle (ed.), *Servants in Rural Europe c.1400–1900* (Woodbridge: Boydell, 2017), pp. 77–94.

Mansell, C., 'The Variety of Women's Experiences as Servants in England (1548–1649): Evidence from Church Court Depositions', *Continuity and Change* 33 (2018), 315–38.

Mansell, C., 'Defining the Boundaries of Community? Experiences of Parochial Inclusion and Pregnancy Outside Wedlock in Early Modern England', in N. Pullin and K. Woods (eds), *Negotiating Exclusion in Early Modern England, 1550–1800* (Abingdon: Routledge, 2021), pp. 141–60.

Mansell, C., 'Objecting to Youth: Popular Attitudes to Service as a Form of Social and Economic Control in England, 1564–1641', in J. Whittle and T. Lambrecht (eds), *Labour Laws in Preindustrial Europe: The Coercion and Regulation of Wage Labour, c.1350–1850* (Woodbridge: Boydell, 2023), pp. 185–205.

Marshall, D., 'The Domestic Servants of the Eighteenth Century', *Economica* 9 (1929), 15–40.

Mason, R., 'Women, Marital Status, and Law: The Marital Spectrum in Seventeenth-Century Glasgow', *JBS* 58 (2019), 787–804.

Massey, D., 'A Global Sense of Place', *Marxism Today* (June 1991).

Mayhew, G., 'Life-Cycle Service and the Family Unit in Early Modern Rye', *Continuity and Change* 6 (1991), 201–26.

Maza, S. C., *Servants and Masters in Eighteenth-Century France: The Uses of Loyalty* (Princeton and Guildford: Princeton University Press, 1983).

McCarthy, H., *Double Lives: A History of Working Motherhood* (London: Bloomsbury, 2020).

McIntosh, M. K., 'Servants and the Household Unit in an Elizabethan English Community', *Journal of Family History* 9 (1984), 3–23.

McIntosh, M. K., *A Community Transformed: The Manor and Liberty of Havering, 1500–1620* (Cambridge: Cambridge University Press, 1991).

McIntosh, M. K., *Controlling Misbehavior in England, 1370–1600* (Cambridge: Cambridge University Press, 1998).

McIntosh, M. K., *Working Women in English Society, 1300–1620* (Cambridge: Cambridge University Press, 2005).

McIsaac Cooper, S., 'From Family Member to Employee: Aspects of Continuity and Discontinuity in English Domestic Service, 1600–2000', in A. Fauve-Chamoux (ed.), *Domestic Service and the Formation of European Identity: Understanding the Globalization of Domestic Work, 16th–21st Centuries* (Bern: Peter Lang, 2004), pp. 277–96.

McIsaac Cooper, S., 'Service to Servitude? The Decline and Demise of Life-Cycle Service in England', *The History of the Family* 10 (2005), 367–86.

McNabb, J., '"She Is But a Girl": Talk of Young Women as Daughters, Wives, and Mothers in the Records of the English Consistory Courts, 1550–1650', in E. S. Cohen and M. Reeves (eds), *The Youth of Early Modern Women* (Amsterdam: Amsterdam University Press, 2018), pp. 77–95.

Meldrum, T., *Domestic Service and Gender, 1660–1750: Life and Work in the London Household* (Harlow: Longman, 2000).

Merry, M., and Baker, P., '"For the House Her Self and One Servant": Family and Household in Late Seventeenth-century London', *The London Journal* 34 (2009), 205–32.

Michalove, S. D., 'Equal in Opportunity? The Education of Aristocratic Women 1450–1540', in B. Whitehead (ed.), *Women's Education in Early Modern Europe: A History, 1500–1800* (New York: Routledge, 1999), pp. 47–74.

Mitterauer, M., *A History of Youth* (Oxford: Blackwell, 1993).

Muldrew, C., 'The Culture of Reconciliation: Community and the Settlement of Economic Disputes in Early Modern England', *The Historical Journal* 39 (1996), 915–42.

Muldrew, C., *The Economy of Obligation: The Culture of Credit and Social Relations in Early Modern England* (Basingstoke: Palgrave Macmillan, 1998).

Muldrew, C., *Food, Energy and the Creation of Industriousness Work and Material Culture in Agrarian England, 1550–1780* (Cambridge: Cambridge University Press, 2011).

Muldrew, C., '"Th'ancient Distaff" and "Whirling Spindle": Measuring the Contribution of Spinning to Household Earnings and the National Economy in England, 1550–1770', *EcHR* 65 (2012), 498–526.

North, S., *Sweet and Clean? Bodies and Clothes in Early Modern England* (Oxford: Oxford University Press, 2020).

Ogilvie, S. C., *A Bitter Living: Women, Markets, and Social Capital in Early Modern Germany* (Oxford: Oxford University Press, 2003).

O'Hara, D., 'The Language of Tokens and the Making of Marriage', *Rural History* 3 (1992), 1–40.

O'Hara, D., *Courtship and Constraint: Rethinking the Making of Marriage in Tudor England* (Manchester: Manchester University Press, 2002).

Orlin, L. C., *Locating Privacy in Tudor London* (Oxford: Oxford University Press, 2007).

Ottaway, S. R., *The Decline of Life: Old Age in Eighteenth-Century England* (Cambridge: Cambridge University Press, 2004).

Outhwaite, R. B., *The Rise and Fall of the English Ecclesiastical Courts, 1500–1860* (Cambridge: Cambridge University Press, 2006).

Overton, M., Whittle, J., Dean, D., and Hann, A., *Production and Consumption in English Households, 1600–1750* (Abingdon: Routledge, 2004).

Paul, K. T., 'Credit, Reputation, and Masculinity in British Urban Commerce: Edinburgh, *c*.1710–70', *EcHR* 66 (2013), 226–48.

Paul, K. T., 'Accounting for Men's Work: Multiple Employments and Occupational Identities in Early Modern England', *History Workshop Journal* 85 (2018), 26–46.

Pelling, M., 'Old Age, Poverty, and Disability in Early Modern Norwich: Work, Remarriage, and Other Expedients', in M. Pelling and R. Smith (eds), *Life, Death and the Elderly: Historical Perspectives* (Routledge, 1991), pp. 74–101.

Penn, S., and Dyer, C., 'Wages and Earnings in Late Medieval England: Evidence from the Enforcement of the Labour Laws', *EcHR* 43 (1990), 356–76.

Pinchbeck, I., *Women Workers in the Industrial Revolution* (Abingdon: Routledge, 2005 [1930]).

Pollmann, J., *Memory in Early Modern Europe, 1500–1800* (Oxford: Oxford University Press, 2017).

Poos, L. R., *A Rural Society after the Black Death, Essex 1350–1525* (Cambridge: Cambridge University Press, 1991).

Price, F. D., 'The Administration of the Diocese of Gloucester, 1547–1579' (Unpublished thesis, University of Oxford, 1939).

Prytz, C., 'Life-Cycle Servant and Servant for Life: Work and Prospects in Rural Sweden, *c*.1670–1730', in J. Whittle (ed.), *Servants in Rural Europe, 1400–1900* (Woodbridge: Boydell, 2017), pp. 95–112.

Pullin, N., *Female Friends and the Making of Transatlantic Quakerism, 1650–1750* (Cambridge: Cambridge University Press, 2018).

Reid, M. G., *Economics of Household Production* (New York: J. Wiley & Sons, 1934).

Reinke-Williams, T., 'Women's Clothes and Female Honour in Early Modern London', *Continuity and Change* 26 (2011), 69–88.

Reinke-Williams, T., *Women, Work and Sociability in Early Modern London* (Basingstoke: Palgrave Macmillan, 2014).

Richardson, R., *Household Servants in Early Modern England* (Manchester: Manchester University Press, 2010).

Roberts, M., 'Sickles and Scythes: Women's Work and Men's Work at Harvest Time', *History Workshop Journal* 7 (1979), 3–28.

Roberts, M., '"Waiting upon Chance": English Hiring Fairs and Their Meanings from the Fourteenth to the Twentieth Century', *Journal of Historical Sociology* 1 (1988), 119–60.

Rogers, J. E. T., *A History of Agriculture and Prices in England* (Oxford: Clarendon Press, 1866).

Rollison, D., *The Local Origins of Modern Society: Gloucestershire 1500–1800* (Routledge, 1992).

Roper, L., *Oedipus and the Devil: Witchcraft, Religion and Sexuality in Early Modern Europe* (London: Routledge, 1994).

Ryrie, A., 'Sleeping, Waking and Dreaming in Protestant Piety', in J. Martin and A. Ryrie (eds), *Private and Domestic Devotion in Early Modern Britain* (Abingdon: Routledge, 2012), pp. 73–92.

Sarasua, C., 'Women's Work and Structural Change: Occupational Structure in Eighteenth-Century Spain', *EcHR* 72 (2019), 481–509.

Sarti, R., '"The Purgatory of Servants": (In)Subordination, Wages, Gender and Marital Status of Servant in England and Italy in the Seventeenth and Eighteenth Centuries', *Journal of Early Modern Studies* 4 (2015), 347–72.

Shahar, S., 'Who Were Old in the Middle Ages?', *Social History of Medicine* 6 (1993), 313–41.

Shapiro, B., 'Credibility and the Legal Process in Early Modern England: Part One', *Law and Humanities* 6 (2012), 145–78.

Shapiro, B., 'Credibility and the Legal Process in Early Modern England: Part Two', *Law and Humanities* 7 (2013), 19–54.

Sharpe, J., 'Domestic Homicide in Early Modern England', *The Historical Journal* 24 (1981), 29–48.

Sharpe, P., 'Poor Children as Apprentices in Colyton, 1598–1830', *Continuity and Change* 6 (1991), 253–70.

Shepard, A., *Meanings of Manhood in Early Modern England* (Oxford: Oxford University Press, 2003).

Shepard, A., 'Poverty, Labour and the Language of Social Description in Early Modern England', *P&P* 201 (2008), 51–95.

Shepard, A., 'Family and Household', in S. Doran and N. Jones (eds), *The Elizabethan World* (Abingdon: Routledge, 2011), pp. 352–71.

Shepard, A., *Accounting for Oneself: Worth, Status, and the Social Order in Early Modern England* (Oxford: Oxford University Press, 2015).

Shepard, A., 'Crediting Women in the Early Modern English Economy', *History Workshop Journal* (2015), 1–24.

Shepard, A., 'Worthless Witnesses? Marginal Voices and Women's Legal Agency in Early Modern England', *Journal of British Studies* 58 (2019), 717–34.

Shepard, A., and Spicksley, J., 'Worth, Age, and Social Status in Early Modern England', *EcHR* 64 (2010), 493–530.

Shepard, A., and Withington, P. J., 'Introduction: Communities in Early Modern England', in A. Shepard and P. J. Withington (eds), *Communities in Early Modern England: Networks, Place, Rhetoric* (Manchester: Manchester University Press, 2000), pp. 1–15.

Shoemaker, R., *Prosecution and Punishment: Petty Crime and the Law in London and Rural Middlesex, c.1660–1725* (Cambridge: Cambridge University Press 1991).

Slack, P., *The Impact of Plague in Tudor and Stuart England* (London: Routledge, 1985).

Slack, P., *The English Poor Law, 1531–1782* (Basingstoke: Macmillan, 1990).

Smith, R., '"Modernisation" and the Corporate Medieval Village Community in England: Some Sceptical Reflections', in A. R. H. Baker and D. Gregory (eds), *Explorations in Historical Geography: Interpretative Essays* (Cambridge: Cambridge University Press, 1984), pp. 140–80.

Snell, K. D. M., *Annals of the Labouring Poor: Social Change and Agrarian England 1660–1900* (Cambridge: Cambridge University Press, 1987).

Snell, K. D. M., 'The Culture of Local Xenophobia', *Social History* 28 (2010), 1–30.

Spicksley, J., '"Fly with a Duck in thy Mouth": Single Women as Sources of Credit in Seventeenth-Century England', *Social History* 32 (2007), 187–207.

Spicksley, J., 'Usury Legislation, Cash, and Credit: The Development of the Female Investor in the Late Tudor and Stuart Periods', *EcHR* 61 (2008), 277–301.

Steedman, C., *Labours Lost: Domestic Service and the Making of Modern England* (Cambridge: Cambridge University Press, 2009).

Steinfeld, R., *The Invention of Free Labour: The Employment Relation in English and American Law and Culture, 1350–1870* (Chapel Hill and London: University of North Carolina Press, 1991).

Stone, L., *The Family, Sex and Marriage in England 1500–1800* (Weidenfeld and Nicolson, 1977).

Stoyle, M., 'The Dissidence of Despair: Rebellion and Identity in Early Modern Cornwall', *JBS* 38 (1999), 423–44.

Stoyle, M., '"Fullye bente to fighte oute the matter": Reconsidering Cornwall's Role in the Western Rebellion of 1549', *English Historical Review* 129 (2014), 549–77.

Stretton, T., 'Women, Custom and Equity in the Court of Requests', in G. Walker and J. Kermode (eds), *Women, Crime and the Courts in Early Modern England* (Chapel Hill, University of North Carolina Press, 1994), pp. 170–90.

Stretton, T., 'Women, Legal Records, and the Problem of the Lawyer's Hand', *JBS* 58 (2019), 684–700.

Tadmor, N., 'The Concept of the Household-Family in Eighteenth-Century England', *P&P* 151 (1996), 111–40.

Tadmor, N., *Family and Friends in Eighteenth-Century England: Household, Kinship, and Patronage* (Cambridge: Cambridge University Press, 2001).

Tadmor, N., 'Early Modern English Kinship in the Long Run: Reflections on Continuity and Change', *Continuity and Change* 25 (2010), 15–48.

Tadmor, N., *The Social Universe of the English Bible: Scripture, Society and Culture in Early Modern England* (Cambridge: Cambridge University Press, 2010).

Tarver, A., 'The Due Tenth: Problems of the Leicestershire Tithing Process 1560–1640', *Transactions of the Leicestershire Archaeological and Historical Society* 78 (2004), 97–107.

Tawney, R. H., 'The Assessment of Wages in England by the Justices of the Peace. (Schluß)', *Vierteljahrschrift für Sozial- und Wirtschaftsgeschichte* 11 (1913), 533–64.

Taylor, H., 'The Price of the Poor's Words: Social Relations and the Economics of Deposing for One's "Betters" in Early Modern England', *EcHR* 72 (2019), 828–47.

Thirsk, J., *England's Agricultural Regions and Agrarian History, 1500–1750* (Basingstoke: Macmillan, 1987).

Thomas, K., 'Numeracy in Early Modern England', *TRHS* 37 (1987), 103–32.

Thomas, K., *Religion and the Decline of Magic: Studies in Popular Beliefs in Sixteenth- and Seventeenth-Century England* (Harmondsworth: Penguin, 1991).

Thomas, K., 'The Perception of the Past in Early Modern England (1989 Creighton Lecture)', in D. Bates, J. Wallis, and J. Winters (eds), *The Creighton Century, 1907–2007* (University of London Press, 2009), pp. 181–218.

Todd, S., 'Domestic Service and Class Relations in Britain 1900–1950', *P&P* 203 (2009), 181–204.

Tönnies, F., *Community and Association: Gemeinschaft und Gesellschaft* (Routledge & Kegan Paul, 1887).

Tycko, S., 'Bound and Filed: A Seventeenth-Century Service Indenture from a Scattered Archive', *Early American Studies: An Interdisciplinary Journal* 19 (2021), 166–90.

Underdown, D., *Revel, Riot and Rebellion: Popular Politics and Culture in England 1603–1660* (Oxford: Oxford University Press, 1985).

Underdown, D., 'The Taming of the Scold: The Enforcement of Patriarchal Authority in Early Modern England', in A. J. Fletcher (ed.), *Order and Disorder in Early Modern England* (Cambridge: Cambridge University Press, 1985), pp. 116–36.

Vage, J. A., 'The Records of the Bishop of Exeter's Consistory Court, c.1500–1660', *Transactions of the Devon Association* 114 (1982), 79–98.

Vage, J. A., 'The Diocese of Exeter 1519–1641' (Unpublished thesis, University of Cambridge, 1991).

Valenze, D., 'The Art of Women and the Business of Men: Women's Work and the Dairy Industry, c.1740–1840', *P&P* 130 (1991), 142–69.

Valenze, D., *Milk: A Local and Global History* (New Haven: Yale University Press, 2011).

Vickery, A., 'Golden Age to Separate Spheres? A Review of the Categories and Chronology of English Women's History', *The Historical Journal* 36 (1993), 383–414.

Vickery, A., *Behind Closed Doors: At Home in Georgian England* (New Haven: Yale University Press, 2009).

Vincent, S., 'From the Cradle to the Grave: Clothing the Early Modern Body', in S. Toulalan and K. Fisher (eds), *The Routledge History of Sex and the Body 1500 to the Present* (Abingdon: Routledge, 2013), pp. 163–78.

Voth, H.-J., 'Time and Work in Eighteenth-Century London', *The Journal of Economic History* 58 (1998), 29–58.

Waddell, B., 'Writing History from Below: Chronicling and Record-Keeping in Early Modern England', *History Workshop Journal* 85 (2018), 239–64.

Wales, T., '"Living at Their Own Hands": Policing Poor Households and the Young in Early Modern Rural England', *Agricultural History Review* 61 (2013), 19–39.

Walker, G., 'Women, Theft and the World of Stolen Goods', in J. Kermode and G. Walker (eds), *Women, Crime and the Courts in Early Modern England* (Chapel Hill: University of North Carolina Press, 1994), pp. 81–105.

Walker, G., 'Expanding the Boundaries of Female Honour in Early Modern England', *TRHS* 6 (1996), 235–46.

Walker, G., *Crime, Gender and Social Order in Early Modern England* (Cambridge: Cambridge University Press, 2003).

Walker, G., 'Rape, Acquittal and Culpability in Popular Crime Reports in England, *c*.1670–*c*.1750', *P&P* 220 (2013), 115–42.

Wall, R., 'The Age At Leaving Home', *Journal of Family History* 3 (1978), 181–202.

Wall, R., 'Economic Collaboration of Family Members within and Beyond Households in English Society, 1600–2000', *Continuity and Change* 25 (2010), 83–108.

Weir, D. R., 'Rather Never than Late: Celibacy and Age at Marriage in English Cohort Fertility', *Journal of Family History* 9 (1984), 340–54.

Whittle, J., *The Development of Agrarian Capitalism: Land and Labour in Norfolk, 1440–1580* (Oxford: Oxford University Press, 2000).

Whittle, J., 'Housewives and Servants in Rural England, 1440–1650: Evidence of Women's Work from Probate Documents', *TRHS* 15 (2005), 51–74.

Whittle, J., 'Servants in Rural England *c*.1450–1650: Hired Work as a Means of Accumulating Wealth and Skills Before Marriage', in M. Ågren and A. L. Erickson (eds), *The Marital Economy in Scandinavia and Britain, 1400–1900* (Aldershot: Ashgate, 2005), pp. 89–107.

Whittle, J., 'The House as a Place of Work in Early Modern Rural England', *Home Cultures* 8 (2011), 133–50.

Whittle, J., 'Enterprising Widows and Active Wives: Women's Unpaid Work in the Household Economy of Early Modern England', *The History of the Family* 19 (2014), 283–300.

Whittle, J., 'A Different Pattern of Employment: Servants in Rural England *c*.1500–1660', in J. Whittle (ed.), *Servants in Europe, c.1400–1900* (Woodbridge: Boydell, 2016), pp. 57–76.

Whittle, J., 'A Critique of Approaches to "Domestic Work": Women, Work and the Pre-Industrial Economy', *P&P* 243 (2019), 35–70.

Whittle, J., 'Attitudes to Wage Labour in English Legislation, 1349–1601', in J. Whittle and T. Lambrecht (eds), *Labour Laws in Preindustrial Europe: The Coercion and Regulation of Wage Labour, c.1350–1850* (Woodbridge: Boydell, 2023), 33–54.

Whittle, J., and Hailwood, M., 'The Gender Division of Labour in Early Modern England', *EcHR* 73 (2020), 3–32.

Whyte, N., 'Custodians of Memory: Women and Custom in Rural England *c*.1550–1700', *Cultural and Social History* 8 (2011), 153–73.

Williamson, F., *Social Relations and Urban Space: Norwich, 1600–1700* (Woodbridge: Boydell, 2014).

Wood, A., *The Politics of Social Conflict: The Peak Country, 1520–1770* (Cambridge: Cambridge University Press, 1999).

Wood, A., *The Memory of the People: Custom and Popular Senses of the Past in Early Modern England* (Cambridge: Cambridge University Press, 2013).

Wood, A., *Faith, Hope and Charity: English Neighbourhoods, 1500–1640* (Cambridge: Cambridge University Press, 2020).

Wood, D., 'Discipline and Diversity in the Medieval English Sunday', *Studies in Church History* 43 (2007), 202–11.

Wright, S., '"Churmaids, Huswyfes and Hucksters": The Employment of Women in Tudor and Stuart Salisbury', in L. Charles and L. Duffin (eds), *Women and Work in Pre-industrial England* (Croom Helm, 1985), pp. 100–21.

Wrightson, K., 'Infanticide in Earlier Seventeenth-Century England', *Local Population Studies* 15 (1975), 10–22.

Wrightson, K., *English Society, 1580–1680* (Routledge, 1993).

Wrightson, K., 'The Politics of the Parish in Early Modern England', in P. Griffiths, A. Fox, and S. Hindle (eds), *The Experience of Authority in Early Modern England* (Basingstoke: Palgrave Macmillan, 1996), pp. 10–46.

Wrightson, K., and Levine, D., *Poverty and Piety in an English Village: Terling, 1525–1700* (Oxford: Oxford University Press, 1979).

Wrigley, E. A., Davies, R. S., Oeppen, J. E., and Schofield, R. S., *English Population History from Family Reconstitution 1580–1837* (Cambridge: Cambridge University Press, 1997).

Wrigley, E. A., and Schofield, R. S., *The Population History of England 1541–1871: A Reconstruction* (Edward Arnold, 1981).

Wrigley, E. A., and Shaw-Taylor, L., 'Occupational Structure and Population Change', in R. Floud, J. Humphries, and P. Johnson (eds), *The Cambridge Economic History of Modern Britain, Vol. 1: 1700–1870* (Cambridge: Cambridge University Press, 2014), pp. 53–88.

Wunderli, R., *London Church Courts and Society on the Eve of the Reformation* (Cambridge, MA: Medieval Academy of America, 1981).

You, Xuesheng, 'Female Relatives and Domestic Service in Nineteenth-century England and Wales: Female Kin Servants Revisited', *EcHR* (2023), 1–28.

Youngs, Deborah, *Humphrey Newton (1466–1536): An Early Tudor Gentleman* (Woodbridge: Boydell, 2008).

Subject Index

Place Index

Person Index

Printed and bound by CPI Group (UK) Ltd, Croydon, CR0 4YY

28/09/2025

14742924-0001